DIVIDED CONSCIOUSNESS

> **WILEY SERIES IN BEHAVIOR**
> KENNETH MacCORQUODALE, Editor
> University of Minnesota

A Temperament Theory of Personality Development
ARNOLD H. BUSS AND ROBERT PLOMIN

Serial Learning and Paralearning
E. RAE HARCUM

Increasing Leadership Effectiveness
CHRIS ARGYRIS

Stability and Constancy in Visual Perception:
Mechanisms and Processes
WILLIAM EPSTEIN

Divided Consciousness: Multiple Controls
in Human Thought and Action
ERNEST R. HILGARD

DIVIDED CONSCIOUSNESS: MULTIPLE CONTROLS IN HUMAN THOUGHT AND ACTION

EXPANDED EDITION

ERNEST R. HILGARD

A WILEY-INTERSCIENCE PUBLICATION

JOHN WILEY & SONS, New York • Chichester • Brisbane • Toronto • Singapore

Copyrights and Acknowledgments appear on page xiii, which constitutes a continuation of the copyright page.

Copyright © 1977, 1986 by John Wiley & Sons, Inc.

All rights reserved. Published simultaneously in Canada.

Reproduction or translation of any part of this work beyond that permitted by Sections 107 or 108 of the 1976 United States Copyright Act without the permission of the copyright owner is unlawful. Requests for permission or further information should be addressed to the Permissions Department, John Wiley & Sons, Inc.

Library of Congress Cataloging in Publication Data

Hilgard, Ernest Ropiequet, 1904-
  Divided consciousness.

  "A Wiley-Interscience publication."
  Bibliography: p.
  Includes index.
    1. Dissociation (Psychology)   2. Hypnotism.
  3. Consciousness.   4. Psychology, Pathological.
  I. Title   [DNLM: 1. Consciousness.   2. Dissociative
  Disorders.   3. Hypnosis   WM 173.6 H644d]
  RC553.D5H54   1986   154   86-1578
  ISBN 0-471-80572-6

Printed in the United States of America

10 9 8 7 6 5 4 3 2

CONTENTS

Preface to the Expanded Edition vii
Preface ix
Copyrights and Acknowledgments xiii

CHAPTER

1 Divided Consciousness and the Concept of Dissociation 1
2 Possession States, Fugues, and Multiple Personalities 17
3 Hypnotic Age Regression 43
4 Amnesia and Repression 62
5 Dreams, Hallucinations, and Imagination 87
6 Voluntary and Involuntary Control of Muscular Movement 115
7 Automatic Writing and Divided Attention 131
8 The Hypnotizable Person and the Hypnotic Experience 155
9 Divided Consciousness in Hypnosis: The "Hidden Observer" 185
10 How the Hypnotized Person Perceives and Interprets the Hidden Observer 204
11 A Neodissociation Interpretation of Divided Consciousness 216
12 Neodissociation in a Wider Context 242

APPENDIX.
The Measurement of Hypnotic Responsiveness 257

REFERENCES AND BIBLIOGRAPHIC INDEX 267

ADDENDUM 293

INDEX 301

PREFACE
TO THE EXPANDED EDITION

Because some of the proposals in the original edition were both novel and controversial, it is appropriate to acknowledge what has happened in the decade since the book appeared. The *Addendum* indicates how the major themes have been developed since the original edition, chiefly by those at work in other laboratories than mine. The original chapters have been reproduced unchanged, except that the reference list has been corrected for those items then reported as "in press." It is a satisfaction to find how well others have gone beyond the findings that intrigued me.

Ernest R. Hilgard

Stanford, California
February 1986

PREFACE

The psychology of the normal personality has long been kept apart from that of the abnormal for reasons that lie within the social history of science rather than scientific logic. Obviously, if we know how the body works in disease, we can learn more about how it works in health. We would not have discovered the roles of vitamins without scurvy or pellagra; now vitamins take a positive role in health maintenance. The same applies to knowledge of mental activity. Modern theories of color vision owe a great deal to the discovery of color blindness; split brains have told us about the functioning of intact ones.

Why, then, do "general experimental psychologists" on the whole tend to ignore unusual states and set them aside for others to deal with? An experimenter prefers to have the maximum control over relevant variables. For many of his experiments the availability of subjects with "normal" vision, "normal" hearing, and "normal" muscular coordination simplifies the enlisting of subjects and permits others to verify his results more conveniently. Patients with diseased or injured brains may produce symptoms valuable for the understanding of brain processes, but such patients are infrequent and highly variable; also access to them is not easy and, for some investigators, not congenial. Hence many experimenters interested in brain processes are likely to produce the brain injuries that interest them by working on animals; their results then classify as normal experimental and physiological psychology. Abnormal psychology remains very largely a human psychology.

Hypnotic phenomena, because they were first investigated by clinical practitioners, tended to be assigned to abnormal psychology for historical reasons that are no longer pertinent. Both Charcot and Janet interpreted hypnosis as a hysterical manifestation, and hysteria, like other derangements, was abnormal. Ever since Liébeault and Bernheim this has no longer been an acceptable characterization of hypnotic susceptibility. A sensible effort was made by those responsible for *Psychological Abstracts* to list hypnosis and suggestion as rubrics under experimental psychology for a few years between 1965 and 1973. New editors changed the journal headings, however, and hypnosis lost this affiliation because experimental psychology also disappeared as a general heading. Very few experiments on hypnosis find their way into the general experimental journals. The primary outlet among the journals of the American Psychological Association is, by agreement of the editors, the *Journal of Abnormal Psychology*.

My own preference is to see hypnosis "domesticated" as a part of normal psychology, on the assumption that understanding of the normal human mind and behavior will be enhanced if hypnosis is taken seriously along with perception, learning, motivation, and the other accepted topics of general psychology. This preference extends also to other aspects of personality study that have been assigned to "abnormal" psychology, such as fugues and multiple personality. Hence I have reexamined dissociation theory—a theory that came out of abnormal psychology—and have attempted to develop a current form of it, to be taken seriously within general psychology.

The problems that this book addresses are age-old, and my interest in them antedated by many years my investigations of hypnosis. It was, in fact, because hypnosis provided a convenient entering wedge into exploring some of these relationships that I was led into hypnosis research rather late in my career. The record shows that these interests go back as far as my doctoral dissertation in which I considered the differences between conditioned responses and voluntary responses as two types of control over movement (Hilgard, 1931); the puzzling problems of the division of oneself in autosuggestion was the occasion for published research a few years later (Berreman and Hilgard, 1936). There appeared a series of papers with several collaborators on the interaction between voluntary processes and the more automatic consequences of selective reinforcement in a conditioned discrimination paradigm (for a summary, see Hilgard, 1938). I returned to some of these considerations in my presidential address before the American Psychological Association in 1949, entitled "Human motives and the concept of the self" (Hilgard, 1949).

Despite these earlier evidences of my interest in related problems, the instigation for the book is more recent, based on findings that have been accumulating at the present time in the research laboratory on hypnosis that I direct and through experimentation in which I actively participate. Some of the new data enlighten aspects of the problematical situations that earlier seemed most baffling.

This laboratory has been in active operation since 1957, with initial support from the Ford Foundation, and other support from the Robert C. Wheeler Foundation, the San Mateo County Heart Association, and the U.S. Air Force Office of Research (Contract AF 49/638/1436), and some private donors. The most continuous support has been from the National Institute of Mental Health of the Department of Health, Education and Welfare, Grant

MH-03859, from 1961 to the present time. My colleagues and I are deeply grateful to all of these.

Many persons have contributed to the writing of the book and its preparation for publication; I am deeply indebted to all. First are the members of the research teams in the laboratory, the names of whom appear as authors of the reports of our investigations, many cited in the reference list. The names are too many to mention individually, except for those longest associated with the work: my wife, Josephine R. Hilgard, Hugh Macdonald, and Arlene Morgan. In addition, Helen Joan Crawford has been a more recent collaborator in the pain and deafness experiments, and she has made helpful comments on the manuscript while it was in preparation. The greatest debt of all is to Josephine Hilgard, whose skilled interviewing has resulted in the reports of the experiences in hypnosis as perceived by the hypnotized person, given theoretical interpretation by her, and used extensively in the book. She has been at my side during the writing, offering both criticism and encouragement. The book would not have been completed without her patient help. The manuscript was read, in several of its stages, by Kenneth S. Bowers, Albert H. Hastorf, Irving L. Janis, and the series editor, Kenneth MacCorquodale. Their helpful suggestions have in every instance resulted in changes, although they have not had an opportunity to approve the changes, for which I must accept the responsibility. Harriet Besser typed the manuscript and performed faithfully many other tasks in connection with the reference lists, illustrations, and other aspects of preparing the final copy. Credit is due also to the encouragement and skilled help of the staff at Wiley, including particularly Peter W. Peirce and J. Frances Tindall.

Permission to make use of previously copyrighted material has been generously granted by a number of authors and publishers. Citation to the original source is given where the material appears.

ERNEST R. HILGARD

Stanford, California
June 1977

PIERRE JANET (1859–1947), noted French psychologist and psychotherapist, at the height of his career. Although a successor to Jean-Martin Charcot, he was too independent to be considered a disciple. He proposed the concept of dissociation in his dissertation of 1889. Photograph courtesy of Henri F. Ellenberger.

COPYRIGHTS AND ACKNOWLEDGMENTS

The author expresses appreciation for permission to reproduce material in the book's figures and tables:

Figure 2 By permission of the author and the R. M. Bucke Memorial Society.

Figures 4 and 5 From Ludwig, A. M., Brandsma, J. M., Wilbur, C. B., Bendfeldt, F., and Jameson, D. H. The objective study of a multiple personality. *Archives of General Psychiatry, 26*, 298–310. Copyright 1972 by the American Medical Association.

Figure 6 From *Hypnotic Susceptibility* by E. R. Hilgard, copyright © 1965 by Harcourt Brace Jovanovich, Inc. and reprinted with their permission.

Figure 7 By permission of Prentice-Hall, Inc.

Figure 8 Reprinted by permission from Erika Fromm and Ronald E. Shor: *Hypnosis* (Chicago: Aldine Publishing Company); copyright © 1972 by Erika Fromm and Ronald E. Shor.

Figure 9 By permission of Plenum Publishing Corporation.

Figure 12 From Stevenson, J. H. Effect of posthypnotic dissociation on the performance of interfering tasks. *Journal of Abnormal Psychology, 85*, 398–407. Copyright 1976 by the American Psychological Association. Reprinted by permission.

Figure 13 From Norman, D. A. *Memory and Attention*, 2nd ed. New York: Wiley, 1976.

Figure 14 From Hilgard, E. R., Weitzenhoffer, A. M., Landes, J., and Moore, R. K. The distribution of susceptibility to hypnosis in a student population: A study using the Stanford Hypnotic Susceptibility Scale. *Psychological Monographs, 75*, Whole Number 512. Copyright 1961 by the American Psychological Association. Reprinted by permission.

Figure 16 Reprinted by permission from Erika Fromm and Ronald E. Shor: *Hypnosis* (Chicago: Aldine Publishing Company); copyright © 1972 by Erika Fromm and Ronald E. Shor. In Tart, C. T. *States of consciousness*. New York: E. P. Dutton & Co., Inc., 1975.

Figure 17 By permission of *Acta Neurobiologiae Experimentalis*.

Figure 19 Reprinted from E. R. Hilgard and J. R. Hilgard, *Hypnosis in the Relief of Pain*. Copyright 1975 by William Kaufmann, Inc. Reprinted by permission.

Figure 21 From Hilgard, E. R. A neodissociation interpretation of pain reduction in hypnosis. *Psychological Review, 80*, 396–411. Copyright 1973 by the American Psychological Association. Reprinted by permission.

COPYRIGHTS AND ACKNOWLEDGMENTS

Tables 1 and 2 Modified from *Hypnotic Susceptibility* by E. R. Hilgard, copyright © 1965 by Harcourt Brace Jovanovich, Inc. and reprinted with their permission.

Table 3 From Tart, C. T. Types of hypnotic dreams and their relation to hypnotic depth. *Journal of Abnormal Psychology, 71,* 377–382. Copyright 1960 by the American Psychological Association. Reprinted by permission.

Table 4 Modified from Arkin, A. M., Hastey, J. M., and Reiser, M. F. Post-hypnotically stimulated sleep-talking. *Journal of Nervous and Mental Disease, 142,* 293–309. Copyright © 1966 Williams and Wilkins. By permission.

Table 5 Modified from Sutcliffe, J. P., Perry, C. W., and Sheehan, P. W. The relation of some aspects of imagery and fantasy to hypnotic susceptibility. *Journal of Abnormal Psychology, 76,* 279–287. Copyright 1970 by the American Psychological Association. Reprinted by permission.

Table 6 From J. R. Hilgard, *Personality and Hypnosis: A Study in Imaginative Involvement.* Copyright © 1970 by The University of Chicago Press, and reprinted with permission.

Table 9 From Blum, G. S., and Porter, M. L. The capacity for selective concentration on color versus form of consonants. *Cognitive Psychology, 5,* 47–50. Copyright 1973 by Academic Press, Inc., and used with permission.

Table 10 From Hilgard, E. R., Weitzenhoffer, A. M., Landes, J., and Moore, R. K. The distribution of susceptibility to hypnosis in a student population: A study using the Stanford Hypnotic Susceptibility Scale. *Psychological Monographs, 75,* Whole Number 512. Copyright 1961 by the American Psychological Association. Reprinted by permission.

Table 13 Reprinted from *Revised Stanford Profile Scales of Hypnotic Susceptibility, Forms I and II.* Palo Alto, Calif.: Consulting Psychologists Press. © 1967 by the Board of Trustees of Stanford University, and used by permission.

The author wishes to thank the following for permission to quote material in this book:

Hull, C. L. *Hypnosis and Suggestibility.* Copyright 1933, Irvington Publishers, Inc., 551 Fifth Avenue, New York, N.Y. 10017. Quoted by permission.

The Discovery of the Unconscious: The History and Evolution of Dynamic Psychiatry, by Henri F. Ellenberger, © 1970 by Henri F. Ellenberger, Basic Books Inc., Publishers, New York. Quoted by permission.

Dorcus, R. M. Recall under hypnosis of amnestic events. Quoted from the January 1960 *International Journal of Clinical and Experimental Hypnosis.* Copyrighted by The Society for Clinical and Experimental Hypnosis, January 1960. By permission.

Fromm, E. Age regression with unexpected reappearance of a repressed childhood language. Quoted from the April 1970 *International Journal of Clinical and Experimental Hypnosis.* Copyrighted by The Society for Clinical and Experimental Hypnosis, April 1970. By permission.

Gardner, M. *Fads and Fallacies in the Name of Science.* Copyright © 1957 by Martin Gardner; Dover Publications, Inc., New York. Quoted by permission.

Hilgard. E. R., and Bower, G. H. *Theories of Learning,* 4th ed. Copyright 1975, Prentice-Hall, Inc. Quoted by permission.

Milner, B. Amnesia following operation on the temporal lobes. In C. M. Whitty and O. L. Zangwill (Eds.), *Amnesia.* Copyright ©1966, Butterworth Publishers, Inc., Woburn, Mass. Quoted by permission.

French, T. M., and Fromm, E. *Dream Interpretation: A New Approach.* Copyright © 1964 by Thomas M. French and Erika Fromm, Basic Books Inc., Publishers, New York. Quoted by permission.

Dement, W. C. *Some Must Watch While Some Must Sleep.* Copyright 1972 by William C. Dement; published by the Stanford Alumni Association. Quoted by permission.

COPYRIGHTS AND ACKNOWLEDGMENTS

Orne, M. T. Hypnotically induced hallucinations. In L. J. West (Ed.), *Hallucinations.* Copyright © 1962 by Grune & Stratton, Inc. Quoted by permission.

Hilgard, J. R. *Personality and Hypnosis: A Study in Imaginative Involvement.* Copyright © 1970 by The University of Chicago Press, and quoted by permission.

Hilgard, E. R., and Marquis, D. G. *Conditioning and Learning.* Copyright 1940, Prentice-Hall, Inc., and quoted by permission.

Crasilneck, H. B., and Hall, J. A. *Clinical Hypnosis: Principles and Applications.* Copyright © 1975 by Grune & Stratton, Inc. Quoted by permission.

Stanford Hypnotic Susceptibility Scale, Forms A and B, by André M. Weitzenhoffer and Ernest R. Hilgard. Palo Alto, Calif.: Consulting Psychologists Press. © 1959 by the Board of Trustees of Stanford University, and quoted by permission.

Revised Stanford Profile Scales of Hypnotic Susceptibility, Forms I and II, by André M. Weitzenhoffer and Ernest R. Hilgard. Palo Alto, Calif.: Consulting Psychologists Press. © 1967 by the Board of Trustees of Stanford University, and quoted by permission.

DIVIDED CONSCIOUSNESS

CHAPTER 1

DIVIDED CONSCIOUSNESS AND THE CONCEPT OF DISSOCIATION

The unity of consciousness is illusory. Man does more than one thing at a time—all the time—and the conscious representation of these actions is never complete. His awareness can shift from one aspect of whatever is currently happening inside his body or impinging on him from without, or events that are remembered or imagined. Furthermore, as an active agent, he is always making decisions and formulating or implementing plans, and he likes to believe that he exerts control over what he is doing; often, however, he may be deceived about the causes of his behavior.

Because consciousness is recognized as partial we speak of paying attention, implying that some things going on in the present may not be attended to. We do not choose simply to attend to something while neglecting everything else, for our attention may be divided among two or more streams of thought or courses of action. Such divided attention is familiar in everyday experience and may be illustrated by what happens in a conversation between two people. They may appear to be taking turns, one talking while the other listens; a little reflection tells us that much more is taking place. Person A, while listening to Person B, is simultaneously planning his reply, and even while replying he may monitor how well he is doing by watching the facial expression of Person B, perhaps changing the direction of his argument if he appears to be unconvincing. At the same time he may be telling himself that the conversation has continued long enough, and some way should be found to end it. How can such divisions of consciousness and attention be accounted for? It may be that attention shifts about, like a spotlight in the dark, permitting one facet at a time to be examined and acted on. Or, alternatively, the several things may be going on in parallel, with sufficient attention given to listening to register what is being said, with enough surplus attentive effort remaining to allow for the simultaneous preparation of the intended reply. Even more intriguing and puzzling is the possibility that in some instances part of the attentive effort and planning may continue without any awareness of it at all. When that appears to be the case, the concealed part of the total ongoing thought and action may be described as *dissociated* from the conscious experience of the person.

Problems suggested by this example can be brought into focus by way of investigations employing hypnosis, because hypnosis may interfere with and divide the normal attentive processes and may alter the balance between voluntary and involuntary control. The phenomena are baffling and many obstacles have to be overcome to investigate them properly; enough has been learned already, however, to tell us a great deal about human functioning in settings not defined as hypnotic. The many references to hypnosis in the succeeding chapters imply that findings from hypnotic experiments can be instructive in providing answers to larger problems of human thought and action.

PSYCHOLOGY'S REVIVED INTEREST IN CONSCIOUSNESS

The mysteries of mind and personality have been receiving renewed attention by both psychologists and nonpsychologists. For a time, the advances in behavior theory and behavior control techniques under the influence of Pavlov and the American behaviorists from Watson to Skinner seemed to remove most of the mystery of consciousness by showing how behavior comes under stimulus control through the rewards ("reinforcements") that follow the behavior. In the 1960s a substantial fraction of people, particularly the young, fed up with technology and contemporary society, turned inward to discover the range of human potential in other ways. These other ways included experimentation with psychedelic drugs, meditation, Eastern religions, ESP, and occultism. Much of this searching lay outside the scientific establishment, but it did not leave the scientists unaffected. In psychology there came a growing interest in what was loosely called humanistic psychology, unified—

to the extent that any unity could be detected—around the theme that a responsible psychology must be concerned with human values and the deeper meaning of life.

When such stirrings occur in the larger community, they influence the laboratory scientists as well. For those familiar with the social history of science, it comes as no surprise that followers of Skinner turned to coverants, or hidden behaviors—whimsically called by Homme (1965) operants of the mind—and as a result one of the large issues became that of self-reinforcement. The social learning theorists, once self-reinforcement came to the fore, showed an interest in the planning function (e.g., Mischel, 1973). A few years before, some "subjective behaviorists" were already talking about plans and self-direction (Miller, Galanter, and Pribram, 1960). Social psychologists began to talk about attribution theory, which refers to the question of whether the person sees his behavior as self-initiated or responsive to external pressures (e.g., Bem, 1972; Jones and others, 1972.) Clinical psychologists have stated the same idea in somewhat different words, speaking of locus of control—again whether the person feels himself in charge, or as a pawn of others who push him around (e.g., Rotter, 1966). New substantive topics, or rather old and neglected ones, again became prominent, such as the study of sleep and dreams, drug states, hypnosis, imagination, and creativity. What began as an anti-intellectual movement in the counterculture gradually shifted the center of gravity within the academic and scientific culture as well. The scientists who preserved their identity with the scientific tradition did not give up their naturalistic interests, but they focused some of their attention on new problems.

This is not the first time that a major shift of interest has occurred among psychologists and psychiatrists because of happenings in the nonacademic community. In the latter half of the nineteenth century, spiritualism became a great fad. Mediums had not been common in civilized society until the Fox sisters, with their table rapping attributed to spirits of the deceased, caused excitement in the United States in the late 1840s; the wave of interest soon spread to England, Germany, France, and throughout the world, and was not stemmed when one of the Fox sisters confessed that it had all been a fraud. Spiritualism was a partial answer to man's loss of dignity as a consequence of Darwin's teaching, for if evidence could be found of the soul's survival of bodily death, man's unique place in nature would be firmly established. The essence of the spiritualist movement was not anti-Darwinism any more than the essence of the counterculture was antibehaviorism, but the parallels are instructive. The new science that has since come to be called parapsychology emerged as serious investigators such as F. W. H. Myers and Edmund Gurney in England began to investigate spiritualist claims from a sympathetic as well as a critical viewpoint, followed soon by their friend William James in the United States. The London Society for Psychical Research was founded in 1882, followed shortly thereafter by the American Society of Psychical Research.

At that time, a number of psychologists and psychiatrists became impressed by the dual controls operating in human functioning, a "subconscious mind" along with a "conscious mind." Borrowing from the psychic investigators such methods as automatic writing, they gathered their evidence not from mediums but largely from hysterical persons, who had lost to some degree their ordinary sensorimotor controls as shown by functional paralyses, blindness, anesthesias, and, in a few dramatic cases, multiple personalities. Pierre Janet became a leader in this group of serious scientists, particularly drawing attention to the new field by his book *Psychological Automatism* (1889). His French contemporary and friend Alfred Binet, later to become important in the history of intelligence measurement, wrote in English a book with the title *Double Consciousness* (1889–1900). Max Dessoir, a well-known German psychologist of the same period issued his book, *Das Doppel-Ich* (The Double Ego), in which he identified the two streams of mental acitivity as an "upper consciousness" and a "lower consciousness" (Dessoir, 1890).

Such divisions of consciousness were very much "in the air" when Freud began to write about the role of the unconscious in mental illness. The philosopher-psychologists of the early nineteenth century had prepared the way before the psychical researchers and hypnotists. Herbart, Kant's successor at Königsberg in 1809, had the concept that ideas could exist below the limen of consciousness in a state of inhibition as "tendencies," representing a kind of active unconscious. Later, in 1869, but in a more romantic vein, von Hartmann wrote his famous book *Philosophy of the Unconscious*. Freud did not "discover" the unconscious, though the brilliance of his clinical insights gave his views a special prominence.

The purpose in returning to an examination of the pre-Freudian material is to examine aspects of human cognitive functioning that were impressive then. At the same time, with the better methods now available, some of the earlier insights may be reformulated and extended to cover phenomena with which the early writers were unfamiliar.

DISSOCIATION THEORY AND ITS CRITICS

The problems of conflict, indecision, self-deception, on one hand, and persistence toward deliberately set goals, on the other, are important and baffling. Psychologists have proposed a number of ways of accounting for the manner in which an individual controls his behavior, especially when one kind of control is set against another, as in the voluntary–involuntary distinction, or the conscious–subconscious distinction. One of the early attempts to deal with some extreme manifestations of split controls was in terms of dissociation, a concept that was prominent for a time and then almost disappeared from the psychologist's vocabulary.

Janet and His Successors

The beginnings of the concept of dissociation are commonly attributed to Pierre Janet in 1889. Although his first term was *désagrégation* in French, the term *dissociation* became accepted in English, as by William James in his *Principles* (1890), and by Janet himself in his Harvard lectures, *The Major Symptoms of Hysteria*, in 1907. Janet's interpretation is that systems of ideas are split off from the major personality and exist as a subordinate personality, unconscious but capable of becoming represented in consciousness through hypnosis.

Janet was the first to introduce the term *subconscious* to refer to a level of cognitive functioning out of awareness that could on occasion become conscious. The term *unconscious* was very familiar before Freud, as traced by Whyte (1960). Janet, by introducing the term subconscious, hoped to avoid the romantic excesses that were already centered in the term unconscious. Later, Morton Prince introduced the term *coconscious* to emphasize the splitting of a normal consciousness into separate parts.

Janet's term dissociation derived from the prevalent doctrine of association. If memories were thought to be brought to consciousness by way of the association of ideas, then those memories that are not available to association must be disassociated. Janet offered a simple diagram to show how a system of ideas, coherent in itself, might be separated off from the primary personal consciousness (Figure 1). The diagram was used to illustrate the case of Irene, who, in her somnambulistic state, repeatedly rehearsed the death of her mother which she had experienced under trying circumstances. In her normal condition she not only forgot what she had dramatized in her somnambulism, but she forgot the events themselves. "I know very well my mother is dead," she is reported to have said, "since I have been told so several times, since I see her no more, and since I am in mourning; but I really feel astonished at it. When did she die? . . . "

The two American writers who did the most, for a time, to keep Janet's concept alive were Boris Sidis and Morton Prince. Boris Sidis edited a large book *Psychopathological Researches: Studies in Mental Dissociation* (1902). At the time, the concept of dissociation was apparently so familiar that it had become anonymous; that is, it was no longer identified as any one person's term. Janet's name appears only once in the book, in connection with a case

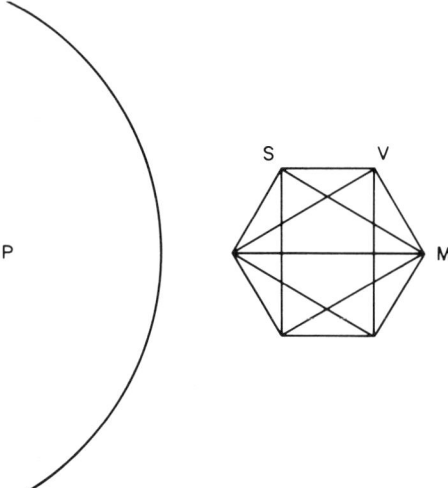

Figure 1 Janet's diagrammatic representation of the dissociation in the case of Irene. The polygon represents the ideas related to the death of her mother, separated from the main personality (P). S stands for the sight of the face of the dead mother, V for the sound of her voice, M for the feeling of movements in carrying her body, and so on. This isolated, yet integrated, set of ideas and memories is responsible for Irene's strange behavior in the somnambulistic state (Janet, 1907, p. 41).

study; there is nothing in the book to indicate that dissociation is at all puzzling as a concept, although the whole book is devoted to its empirical elucidation. The unacknowledged debt to Janet is clear in the interchangeable use of the terms *disaggregation* and *dissociation*, as in this quotation:

> The whole domain of the subconscious belongs to these stages of disaggregation in the course of the pathological process, such as the phenomena of hypnosis, of somnambulism, of motor and sensory automatisms, of the so-called "hysterical" sensori-motor disturbances of various organs, the functions of which are found on examination in regions of the subconscious over which the personal consciousness has lost control by reason of neuron disaggregation or dissociation (pp. x–xi).

Morton Prince continued to use the notion of dissociation, titling his book on the Beauchamp case (he always pronounced it *Beecham*) *The Dissociation of a Personality* (1906). Actually his support of the concept of dissociation was somewhat guarded. He preferred to describe the hidden aspect as *coconscious* rather than subconscious. The word coconscious made clear that the ideas of which the subject is unaware are still active, and that subconscious cerebration is going on concurrently, as revealed, say, in automatic writing. Prince did not demand a complete dissociation: "Certainly in many cases there is a halting flow of thought of the principal intelligence, indicating that the activity of the secondary intelligence tends to inhibit the untrammeled flow of the former" (1929, p. 411).

Early Attempts to Support Dissociation Through Experiments

Most early investigators were convinced of the reality of dissociation through their clinical studies; thus when they set out to do laboratory-type experiments, it was confirmation that they sought.

Janet performed some informal experiments with Lucie. The experimental design was to hypnotize her, then give her the suggestion that she would perform some simple automatic act at a signal when out of hypnosis. She was told that she would not be aware of what she was doing. The experimentation included posthypnotic automatic writing; for example, on one occasion Janet suggested that, awakening from hypnosis, she would write a letter. While carrying on a casual conversation her hand wrote:

Madam,
I shall not be able to come Sunday as I had intended. I pray you will forgive me. It would give me great pleasure to come to you but I cannot accept for that day.

Your friend,

Lucie

P.S. Best regards to the children, please.
(Quoted by Messerschmidt, 1927–1928.)

When Janet showed her the letter, she was unable to understand how it could have been written and believed that the doctor had copied her signature. On another occasion Lucie carried out the multiplication of 739 by 42 while continuing to talk about her day's activities.

Prince carried out similar experiments with a subject who also had a dual personality (Prince, 1909). She showed the classical picture of personality A having no awareness of personality B, but B having awareness of A. Only B was hypnotizable and, following hypnosis, was amnesic for what had happened during hypnosis. This was the clinical picture that Prince decided to test experimentally.

Assigning the label b to B when hypnotized, we have the three states to consider: A, B, and b. Prince set the task in the following manner. While A was engaged in a secondary task, b would add some figures that were to be presented only while A was present and busy. The task assigned to A was writing some familiar verses on a sheet of paper. The figures to be summed by b were written unobtrusively on the margins of the paper. The overt personality, with control of the speaking and writing mechanisms, is that of A. While *b* is coconscious, it is *b*'s task to add the figures and to be prepared to give the sum when *b* is made conscious. In one experiment the sum to be added was 53 and 61. As soon as A had completed the verses, there was a prompt shift of control to *b*, who promptly announced, almost shouted, "114," the correct number. Questioned in the dominant position, *b* could recall in detail where the numbers appeared on the paper, what A had been doing, and how the computations had been made. Other trials led to the same conclusions, which Prince put in this way:

> . . . that such perceptions, interpretations, calculations, and translations could have been made by *pure physiological processes without thought* is inconceivable and not substantiated by anything that we know of physiological processes.

This was, of course, his reply to those who were willing to concede that physiological brain processes might go on out of awareness, but denied that they were accompanied by intelligible cognitive activity. He thought his experiments gave positive support to his concept of the coconscious.

The same kind of experiment was undertaken later with normal subjects who did not have the divided personalities of the cases studied by Janet and Prince. Such experiments, using hypnosis with three normal subjects, were reported by Burnett (1925) with the engaging title "Splitting the Mind." The subject, while hypnotized, was assigned a task to be done posthypnotically without awareness, while the conscious part of himself was to be engaged in some other task. For example, while reading a book out loud, he might be assigned the task of adding the number of taps the experimenter made with his pencil to the page number at which the book was open when the experimenter asked for it. The subjects were able to complete several such tasks accurately, without awareness of what they were doing. However, back in hypnosis, they were able to recall their instructions, and to remember how the task was carried out.

Burnett performed some control experiments with the simultaneous tasks both in awareness. The quantitative arrangements were not very satisfactory, but he concluded that there was less interference when one task was subconscious than when both were conscious. This rather faulty interpretation led others to accept noninterference as a criterion of dissociation, despite the earlier indications by both Janet and Prince that there might be genuine dissociation from awareness, though some interference could be detected.

In reviewing these studies later, Hull (1933) was in fact careful to accept the positive findings that simultaneous activities could be carried out with one of them not recalled, but he did not accept the noninterference interpretation. He was correct, as we shall see, in separating the two questions; first, can a subject remain ignorant of a task being performed simultaneously with another task of which the subject is aware? and second, do the tasks interfere? Of Burnett's experiment, he said:

> There seems to be little room for disagreement with the conclusion of the author on the first question, i.e., that post-hypnotic suggestion rather easily brings about a condition in which a person will perform fairly complex intellectual tasks and yet will deny all knowledge of the process at the very moment that it is taking place. Burnett's work is particularly convincing on this point. But in answer to the second question the experiments cited above are not nearly so conclusive (Hull, 1933, p. 176).

The only other experiment that tended to support functional independence of the dissociated processes was that of Barry, MacKinnon, and Murray (1931). They used a different approach, based on the hypothesis that there should be personality differences between hypnotizable and nonhypnotizable subjects that would show in reduced task interferences in simultaneous tasks, even when the subjects were not hypnotized. Although their results came out in the right direction, it turned out that their hypnotizable subjects were better at the isolated (noninterfered with) tasks as well; thus little could be made of their reduced task interferences.

Experiments Critical of Dissociation

Under Hull's direction, Messerschmidt (1927–1928) carried out a carefully designed experiment in which task interferences could be studied in both the waking condition, with both tasks conscious, and in the hypnotic condition, with one task subconscious. She found some indication of greater interference in the competition between a conscious and a subconscious task than between two conscious ones, a result clearly in contradiction to the noninterference theory. (See further details in Chapter 7.)

It is important to note that the main criticisms of dissociation theory depend on the importance assigned to noninterference between tasks. Hull, for example, had this to say as his final conclusion on the matter:

> We may now summarize the experimental results bearing on the dissociation hypothesis as applied to hypnosis. Post-hypnotic amnesia is a fact as well established as anything in hypnosis. Furthermore, there can scarcely be any doubt that complex intellectual processes such as continuous addition may go on and the subject orally deny all knowledge of the activity at the very time it is taking place. It is difficult to understand how these phenomena could exist without some very special suspension or interference of the normal association process. In this limited sense it would seem that the concept of dissociation has some reason for existence. In view of the clinical interests of Janet and Prince, together with the notions of the nature of mind prevalent at the time, it is not surprising that

this solid basis of fact should have led to the extension of the principle of dissociation to include something quite different, i.e., a functional independence of the processes dissociated . . . The results . . . suggest rather strongly that the whole concept of dissociation as functional independence is an error (Hull, 1933, p. 191).

The attack on dissociation as functional independence has permitted the primary conclusions to be largely overlooked. Those who originated the concept of dissociation did not require such total functional independence.

The overvaluing of the noninterference characterization was also shown in a study by Rosenberg (1959), announced as a refutation of dissociation. Rosenberg found that attitudes implanted in hypnosis, even though out of awareness, influenced attitudes in the waking state. These attitudes could still have been considered dissociated because they were not present in awareness, just as in one of Janet's cases, Lucie, who was afraid but knew not why. Her fears, like Rosenberg's attitudes, were influenced by what Janet would consider to be dissociated processes, even though they also had influences on consciousness.

THE DECLINE OF DISSOCIATION

Although experimental reports have appeared from time to time and the term dissociation is used descriptively on occasion, the fading of dissociation theory was very rapid after the first decades of this century. A count of the references to dissociation in the first ten volumes of *Psychological Abstracts*, from 1927 through 1936, showed 20 abstracts indexed; the next ten volumes indexed 8; the next ten, 2, and the next ten, 3. Although this is a somewhat crude measure, the failure to find the word dissociation in the titles of papers and books is some indication of the decline in prominence of the topic.

What happened? It was not negative findings of interference experiments such as Messerschmidt's that would have caused the decline. It is more likely that several trends in the social and intellectual climate were responsible.

The upsurge of interest in psychoanalysis during these years may have been one factor, because psychoanalysis presented an alternative conception of unconscious processes, substituted repression for dissociation, and was on the whole negative toward hypnosis and the concepts related to it after Freud had rejected them.

The growth of behaviorism in America probably played a part in the decline of the dissociation concept. The lack of interest in consciousness would be reflected also in a lack of interest in subconsciousness. Hence, when the behaviorists became interested in psychopathology, they were more likely to turn to neo-Pavlovian concepts than to Janet and Prince, or to translate psychoanalytic concepts into stimulus-response (S–R) terms. However, such generalizations must always be tempered. Hull was a prominent behaviorist, and his studies of hypnosis and dissociation did not violate his behaviorist commitment. Another of Hull's collaborators, Robert Sears, wrote an important theoretical paper in 1936, reviewing functional abnormalities of memory. He attempted to explain certain aspects of repression and amnesia in S–R terms, similar to those used by Hull in his learning theories. He concluded, coherent with his own efforts at an S–R theory, that "If the theory of dissociation were completely restated in the stimulus-response idiom . . . there seems good reason for considering it a valuable hypothesis coordinate with the repression hypothesis as an explanation for amnesias of reproduction" (Sears, 1936. p. 269).

Although both Hull and Sears indicated the desirability of further experimentation on dissociation, little more was done at the time. After dissociation had all but disappeared from contemporary discussion, White and Shevach (1942) wrote a kind of epitaph for the concept, giving a clear and sympathetic account of Janet's use of it, reviewing experimental attempts to study it, citing some new data of their own, and reaching a clear conclusion: "Whatever the nature of the hypnotic state, it does not seem to be adequately characterized by dissociation" (p. 327).

However, if the evidence of White and Shevach is reviewed in detail, it is found to contradict only that extreme form of dissociation theory that implies complete noninterference. Much of their evidence can be interpreted as supporting phenomena indicative of dissociated activities. "There is no doubt that hypnotic suggestion can bring about a separation of activities in a way that could not be duplicated by ordinary volition" (p. 326). Their own experiment, although failing to yield results that were impressive statistically, nevertheless pointed in the direction of an exaggeration of dissociation through hypnosis. They chose the Kohnstamm phenomenon for study, calling it tensive perseveration. This was familiar to me in my childhood as a kind of game that many children played. If the arm, held stiffly at the side, is pressed against a wall, with the body weight carried by the shoulder because of space between the arm and the side of the body, removing the load by stepping away from the wall produces in many children—and adults—a tendency for the arm to rise involuntarily. This is so impressive that it appears to be "physiological," owing to some kind of aftereffect from tensed muscle; not all people do it, however, and the rise is probably correlated with hypnotic susceptibility, (e.g., Snyder and Scheerer, 1961). White and Shevach produced the effect by suspending a weight from the the outstretched arm and then removing the weight. They found that more highly susceptible subjects exaggeraged the response beyond its normal amount when they were inattentive to it by being preoccupied by reading aloud at the same time. White and

Shevach felt that some qualified form of dissociative interpretation might be appropriate, but they did not elaborate on this and instead turned to suggestion as more useful than dissociation in explaining hypnosis. Curiously enough, the return to suggestion moved toward the earlier interpretation favored by Bernheim (1888) which Binet (1889–1890), Janet (1889), Sidis (1898), and Prince (1909) had found so diffuse that they preferred to replace it with dissociation.

Dissociation theory went out of favor without effective criticism. Other topics in psychology have had their day, suffered periods of neglect, and then returned. Examples are readily at hand. Once prominent topics such as attention and reaction time virtually dropped out, only to come back vigorously in the last few years. Attitudes, once the basic substance of social psychology, have played a very minor part during the past decade. Tropisms, once prominent, seem no longer to interest comparative psychologists, except for an occasional study in behavioral genetics. These examples show that the decline of interest in a topic does not mean that it lacks substance or that phenomena associated with it have been proved false or nonexistent. New interests drain attention into new channels, and older topics are merely set aside.

The experimental "refutations" of dissociation have rested primarily on an all-or-nothing interpretation of the separateness or noninterference between dissociated activities. The originators of the concept held no such extreme positions. It is sensible, if dissociation is to be examined carefully, to accept the amount of interference between partially dissociated activities as an empirical problem, but how the answers come out is not critical in establishing the fact that dissociations occur.

A NEODISSOCIATION INTERPRETATION

It has been pointed out that the decline of interest that led to a neglect of dissociative phenomena may reflect social history more than scientific advance. From this standpoint it is desirable to examine the phenomena anew. Such an examination is made in the next chapters, including both case material and experimental data. Because most of the experimental data have been derived from research in which hypnosis has played a part, the later chapters examine hypnotic interactions more closely. I believe that the existence of a variety of phenomena bearing on a common problem will become convincing as the examples multiply, after which the need for a theoretical integration will become imperative. An attempt is made to satisfy this need at the end through a neodissociation interpretation. The name implies that what I propose is historically rooted in early dissociation theory, but that I am uncommitted to the early theories in any precise form. Instead, an effort is made to reformulate the theory in contemporary terms, using what psychologists have since learned about information processing, divided attention, and brain function.

Consciousness remains a baffling topic. American psychology is outgrowing the strictures of behaviorism by recognizing what Neisser (1967), in the context of the new cognitive psychology, has called the vicissitudes between stimulus and response that behaviorists tended to neglect. These vicissitudes can often be inferred from overt activity, but often they are reflected well in what the participating subject is able to tell the experimenter about what went on. To insist that consciousness is admissible only as verbal behavior—as behaviorists since Watson have been wont to do—is to deny that the words refer to anything of substantive interest. If a subject describes a flight of colors by giving their names, today we are interested in the fact that he has seen colors—not only that he is engaged in some sort of utterance in which color names appear. Words have their limitations in describing conscious experience, not only because people can lie, but also because they can be deceived while trying to tell the truth. This problem is not unique to words, however. People can "cheat" if they wish in an experiment in which only "objective" measures are taken, as in strength measured by squeezing a dynamometer; all that is required to correct for error is that the experimenter exercise sufficient ingenuity, as in the use of "false alarms" in signal detection experiments. There is no reason to avoid introspective accounts because they sometimes go wrong; acceptable risk is characteristic of all experimentation, and in psychology we learn to account for background noise as well as for the significant signals in our data.

It is useful to assign two modes to consciousness, a receptive mode and an active mode (Deikman, 1971). The receptive mode is reflected in the relatively passive registration of events as they impinge on the sense organs, made familiar in the study of sense perception. Of course, such registration is not merely passive, for stimulation may be sought after and valued. For those who seek enriched conscious experiences, such experiences are savored for their special meanings, affective, esthetic, or religious, as in meditation, Eastern religions, mystical experiences, and ecstasy. Many trends in the contemporary culture—the drug culture, the cultivation of experiences of the miraculous through various forms of mind expansion— place emphasis on passive receptivity, once the appropriate conditions have been established. The broad range of receptive and sensitive experiences defines the first mode of consciousness.

The second mode of consciousness is the active, planning one. Voluntary activity has long been accepted as closely affiliated with being conscious— knowing what you want, seeking to reach your goals through decisive action and deliberate effort. Without consciousness of plans and purposes, of means–end relationships, nothing very inventive and self-originated would happen.

The problems of divided consciousness reflect both these modes. On one hand, memories may be split apart, so that reflection on experiences registered in the first mode may be disrupted; on the other hand, the voluntary and involuntary controls systems may be reversed through dissociation, so that an activity that is usually voluntary may be impossible, whereas an activity that is normally involuntary may be brought under voluntary control; compulsive activity is carried out automatically and involuntarily, even if it is a kind of behavior usually under voluntary control. The concept of divided control becomes very important, and this will be increasingly evident as the phenomena of dissociation are examined. Conceiving the two modes of consciousness in this way produces a simplification that will prove useful, although any such simplification is partial only because there are always interactions between any two modes of functioning.

This then is the background for the survey of the phenomena that pose the problems for a neodissociation interpretation.

NOTES

Much of the material in this chapter is based on my earlier accounts of dissociation (Hilgard, 1973a, 1973b, 1974, 1976). Although the material has been reorganized and edited, some reflection of earlier statements is inevitable. The historical material owes much to Ellenberger (1970).

Psychology's Revived Interest In Consciousness

The trends in the sociology of psychology that lead to new emphases related to the broader culture are too complex to summarize succinctly. With the turning inward, it is not too surprising to find the operant behaviorists accepting self-reinforcement (e.g. Kanfer and Marston, 1963). This is quite distinct from the humanistic psychologists, spurred on by Abraham Maslow (1954), who had introduced the appealing concept of peak experiences. This led to the founding of a society and the *Journal of Humanistic Psychology* under the editorship of Anthony Sutich in 1961, enlisting in its support, in addition to Maslow, Charlotte Bühler, Hadley Cantril, Kurt Goldstein, S. I. Hayakawa, Aldous Huxley, Rollo May, Lewis Mumford, David Riesman, Carl Rogers, and others. They early described themselves as a "third force," of which the other two were "behaviorism," in which they included practically all of experimental psychology, and "psychoanalysis," which in all its forms they rejected as holding too pessimistic a view of human nature and being too occupied with pathology. The academic community could not help but be aware of humanistic psychology, even though its visible influence at the center of psychology has not been great.

Strands in contemporary psychology, other than those described in the chapter, might equally well have been pointed to as illustrating the influence of the *Zeitgeist* from the larger culture. For example, cognitive psychology, now overwhelming behaviorism, can be traced, at least in part, to developments outside psychology itself, including the high-speed computer, advances in linguisitics, and the sociopolitical consequences of the shock produced by the Russian launching of the satellite Sputnik in 1957. Ten years later, the new viewpoint was well enough advanced for psychology to be ready for a book such as that of Neisser (1967).

Consciousness now appears in the titles of numerous books covering many topics other than those dealt with here. Some examples are the books of Globus, Maxwell, and Savodnik (1976), Jaynes (1977), Ornstein (1972) (1973), Schwartz and Shapiro (1967), and Tart (1969) (1975).

Two dichotomies that recur in different forms may prove to be related to dissociation. The *bimodal consciousness* of Deikman (1971) begins with the distinction made in the chapter between an "action" mode and a "receptive" mode, with the two ultimately leading to two rather distinct life styles, very much in the spirit of Ornstein's (1972) distinction between the psychologies of East and West. My own position is that every experience or act has both aspects, and that those who become enamored by consciousness expansion and mystical experience are making one-sided value judgements that may be as distorted as those who believe that overt action is all that is of interest.

The *bicameral mind* posited by Jaynes (1977) represents a different position, that consciousness as we know it is a product of later civilizations, whereas early man (up to the time of Homer's Iliad) trusted the gods to provide hallucinated guidance, substituting for an individual consciousness. The family resemblance to Deikman's position appears because the residues of the earlier bicameral mind are said to be found in the hallucinatory visions or voices even today often associated with religious or mystical experiences.

Janet and His Successors

Pierre Janet has received an overdue recognition in a lengthy chapter by Ellenberger (1970, pp. 331–417).

Morton Prince's scattered studies were collected and reissued with notes by A. A. Roback in Prince (1939); additional studies were assembled and published with an introductory essay by N. G. Hale, Jr., in Prince (1975).

Prince had his own terminology. He preferred to use *subconscious* as a generic term to include the *unconscious* and the *coconscious*. He limited the unconscious to neural dispositions and processes, whereas his coconscious referred to subconscious ideas (in Janet's sense) that do not enter the content of conscious awareness (Prince, 1914, p. 253).

Boris Sidis wrote his *Psychology of Suggestion* in 1898, with an introduction by William James. The reference in the text is to a later book, replete with experimental studies (Sidis, 1902). Sidis is of interest for a secondary reason; his studies of automatic writing, in which Gertrude Stein acquired the skill, may have influenced her later writing style (Skinner, 1934).

Experimental Dissociation and the Decline of Interest

The experimental literature on dissociation is reviewed in somewhat greater detail by Hull (1933, p. 162–192). See also Sears (1936) and White and Shevach (1942). The decline of interest as related to psychoanalysis had been noted by Hart (1929) and McDougall (1938).

CHAPTER 2

POSSESSION STATES, FUGUES, AND MULTIPLE PERSONALITIES

In the ordinary experience of living, the sense of wholeness and continuity is maintained through the continuity of memories: I am the same person who traveled to Europe last summer, and I am the same person who watched the game being played yesterday. This does not mean that I always behave the same, for I am various people at various times, according to the roles that I play as husband, father, grandfather, teacher, researcher, voter, or loafer. Within these variations I know that I am only one, however, for I carry my memories around with me when I move from one scene to another and adopt one role or another.

The existence of the various roles nevertheless implies subordinate control systems brought into play when the role is foremost, whether the role is a domestic one, a professional one, or the exercise of some special skill, such as playing the violin. What we propose to examine are those instances when these subordinate systems, appropriate to varying roles, lose communication with each other. In such cases it is appropriate to refer to the bifurcated roles as *dissociated*. In this chapter and the next one we examine some instances of these dissociations that set the stage for the later interpretations.

The main criteria of dissociated behavior are as follows:

1. The dissociated systems can be identified as relatively coherent patterns of behavior with sufficient complexity to represent some degree of internal organization. In the case of a fugue, as we shall see, the behavior does not have to be present repeatedly in order to qualify. If, however, it is repeated, as in the cases of multiple personality to be described, each of the subordinate systems will have identifying characteristics, such as preferences, skills, and memories.

2. There is commonly some amnesic barrier that prevents integration of the dissociated systems, at least during the time that the dissociation persists. This is the primary mark that distinguishes between alternating normal roles and alternating personalities as found in psychopathology. Sometimes system A may be aware of system B, without system B being aware of system A. A one-directional amnesia is enough.

3. The experience of being "possessed" by an alien personality represents a dissociation of a somewhat different kind, in which the mutual amnesias are not essential because the two "personalities" in some sense conduct a battle for control of the one body. The first criterion holds, of identifiable characteristics of the two split-off personality systems; thus each is recognizable, and both are different.

4. There are minor dissociations occurring in ordinary experience and in hypnosis that are so much less dramatic than fugues, multiple personalities, or possession states that they are more difficult to delimit precisely, for as in the case of possession states, they are determined more by modification of controls than by identifiable amnesias. Among these are automatisms, such as compulsive behavior or obsessive thoughts, or the conversion reactions in hysteria. It may be inferred that there is some kind of concealed motivation for the behavior, commonly assigned to unconscious processes. When comparable behavior is produced by hypnosis, however, and is readily reversed, it is appropriate to include the loss or modification of voluntary control as illustrative of dissociation.

The relationships as they are found to exist in "experiments of nature" occurring in the real world are so complex that it is necessary to use case descriptions to make the domain familiar. Some warnings are in order. The stories of multiple personalities are so dramatic that there is a tendency for the case histories to be overdramatized; they do, in fact, make good material for novels and motion pictures and have been so used. Robert Louis Stevenson's *The Strange Case of Dr. Jekyll and Mr. Hyde* (1886) is probably the best-known fiction case, and *The Three Faces of Eve* the best-known movie based on an actual case (Thigpen and Cleckley, 1957). In addition to the overdramatization of the material itself, sufficient caution has not always been exercised by the psychotherapist to distinguish between what he discovered and what he produced. Very early in the history of medical reports of such cases, Janet noted that when a secondary personality is identified and named, it tends to take on a more distinct existence. Hence, in giving the accounts of actual cases, an effort is made to note what was known prior to the intrusions by the therapist, particularly if he used hypnotic techniques.

POSSESSION STATES

The idea of spirit possession is age old. There is the familiar Biblical story of Jesus casting out the devils from the disturbed Gadarene. The devils ("My name is Legion") requested thay they be sent into the herd of swine, and the possessed herd rushed down the bank and perished in the sea. The fact that, presumably, both the demoniac host and the demons spoke to Jesus suggests the possibility of something like multiple personality. The idea of demoniac possession has persisted, in some circles, to the present time. The motion picture, *The Exorcist*, brought the matter to light in the 1970s, somewhat to the embarrassment of the Catholic Church, whose rituals for exorcism still exist, although their use is largely frowned on.

Hypnosis and exorcism had a confrontation two hundred years ago at a time when Father Johann Joseph Gassner (1717–1799) was curing many of his parishioners, and others from afar after his fame spread, by using the Church's rituals of exorcism. He had cured himself by getting rid of "the Evil One" while he was a Catholic priest in a small village in Switzerland. There was much opposition to Gassner, because this was the Age of Enlightenment, and many wished to be rid of practices that they considered magical and irrational. The Prince-Elector Max Joseph of Bavaria appointed a commission of inquiry in 1775 and invited Franz Anton Mesmer (1734–1815), then an Austrian physician, to show that the results of exorcism could be obtained as well by his "naturalistic" method of animal magnetism, the precursor of hypnosis. Mesmer was able to produce the same effects that Gassner had produced—causing convulsions to occur and then curing them. Mesmer won the day, and Gassner was sent off as a priest to a small community. Pope Pius VI ordered his own investigation, from which he concluded that exorcism was to be performed only with discretion.

Forms of possession are still in common use by the healers in cultures that cling to old traditions. I had the opportunity in 1974 of visiting several such healers and personal advisers in Singapore, under the guidance of Dr. Chong Ton Mun, an expert in hypnosis who has made it a point to familiarize himself with these practices (Chong, 1975). In a favorite ceremony practiced in the Chinese community, the practitioner or medium goes into a kind of trance, at which time he becomes possessed by the Monkey God. The evidence for possession as I witnessed it included jumping on the chair in a squatting position resembling a monkey's actions and shouting as a monkey might. After the medium calms down, the client's questions can be answered, sometimes directly, sometimes through an interpreter, for the Monkey God may talk in a language unintelligible except to an initiate who serves as the interpreter. This practice is reminiscent of "speaking in tongues" (glossolalia) that goes back at least to Biblical times and occurs in some Christian churches today. In the Malaysian community of Singapore a similiar practice is carried out by the "Bomoh," one of whom was willing to demonstrate his trance for me. He had a choice of spirits to call on. The spirit would possess him and then answer questions, particularly making recommendations for the cure of illness, including the special curative powers of a charmed glass of water. Among the spirits were some princesses living on a mountain top, whom he treated with deference and courtesy, and later a warrior who showed through violent aggressive movements that he was in possession.

These trance states appear to have very much in common with self-hypnosis. The Chinese medium who called on the Monkey God had photographs of himself with his cheeks pierced with sharpened sticks and other sticks thrust into his chest or back, apparently without pain. The lore is that no scars are left by the sticks, but there were indeed visible scars on his face, if one looked carefully.

In an attempt to classify these states, Bourguignon (1968) found it convenient to distinguish between trance states with their associated beliefs and possession states with their associated beliefs, even if the two categories often overlap. The classification derived from a study of 700 cultural groups all over the world. The classification of trance and possession behavior and beliefs is diagrammed in Figure 2.

There are, of course, any number of variations on these common themes. A trance is usually defined as a temporary change in the person when he seems to be very different from his usual self, familiar before the episode and found again when the trance is ended. Both naturalistic and supernaturalistic explanations can be found in cultures remote from modern civilization, but both persist in more modern cultures as well. In Figure 2 the naturalistic explanations are translated into terms that are familiar, although these are not the categories used by the people themselves.

The supernaturalistic explanations fall into the two groups of nonpossession and possession beliefs. The nonpossession beliefs differ not so much in their consequences as in the causal agents assigned. If one can become ill naturalistically from a poisoned arrow, he can also become ill supernaturally if a witch pierces his image with an arrow.

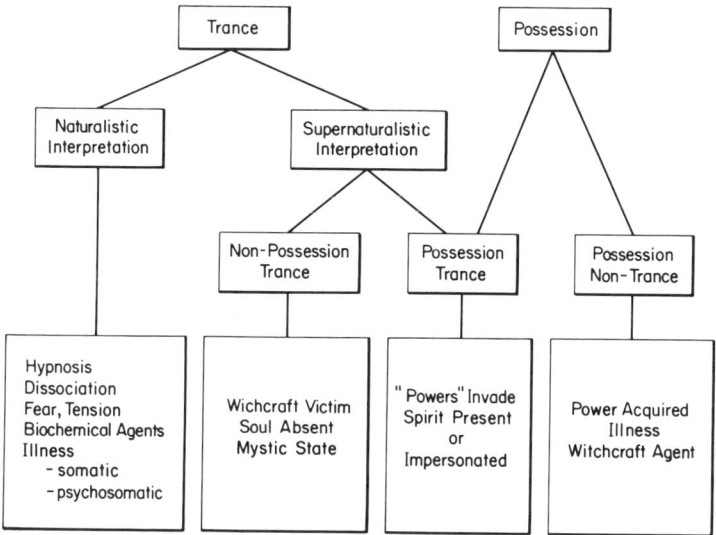

Figure 2   Trance and possession states and associated beliefs. Abbreviated, with modifications, from Bourguignon (1968), Tables I and II.

In possession trance, as different from nonpossession trance, the person is believed to be invaded by a spirit or a new sense of power for good or ill. If the possession spirit is good, manipulations such as the healing of others can take place; if the possessing spirit is evil, rites of exorcism may have to be attempted. Possession may occur without trance behavior. The person may remain essentially himself, although he may become ill because invading spirits eat at his soul. On the positive side, the transfered spirit may give him some permanent power.

These aspects of trance and possession are found in all parts of the world. Both positive and negative features of the trance are expected; occasionally, negative experiences may be transformed into positive ones. Two forms of trance, such as the possession form and the nonpossession form, may be found in the same society.

Although we may think of the beliefs of societies undeveloped by our standards as "primitive," such beliefs have not died out in Western societies. Christians use the terminology of possession when they speak of being possessed by the Holy Spirit, and demonic possession continues to be occasionally believed. The motion picture, the *Exorcist*, previously mentioned, represented a twentieth century form of this belief. The belief in special powers remains part of the ritual of canonization of a saint.

The persistence of these beliefs means that they meet some deep human need for coming to grips with the uncertainties of human existence, and the earlier motives have not been displaced by the advance of science. Their persistence is not a persuasive argument that the beliefs are true, for many beliefs that are known to be false have a way of persisting when the will to believe is strong enough.

It was only with the decline of the widespread belief in possession that personality disturbances came into the realm of medical science; hence fugues and multiple personalities as we know them are largely a post-Mesmer set of phenomena.

FUGUES

A fugue is defined in modern psychiatry as a dissociation characterized by amnesia in which the person runs away from his conflicts or problems by seeking a new environment, or in some other manner demonstrates his flight from reality. During the episode of the fugue, he may behave quite normally in the new environment, but very differently from his usual behavior. When he returns to his usual condition he picks up where he left off and does not remember the events of the fugue. The fugue may be short or long, and it may be a single episode that is not repeated.

The best-known case is that of Reverend Ansel Bourne, studied and reported on in detail by William James (1890, Vol. 1, p. 391–393). Because the details of the case are impressive, I take the liberty of giving James' account in the form in which he presented it.

> The Rev. Ansel Bourne, of Greene, R.I., was brought up to the trade of a carpenter; but, in consequence of a sudden temporary loss of sight and hearing under very peculiar circumstances, he became converted from Atheism to Christianity just before his thirtieth year, and has since that time for the most part lived the life of an itinerant preacher. He has been subject to headaches and temporary fits of depression of spirits during most of his life, and has had a few fits of unconsciousness lasting an hour or less. He also has a region of somewhat diminished cutaneous sensibility on the left thigh. Otherwise his health is good, and his muscular strength and endurance excellent. He is of a firm and self-reliant disposition, a man whose yea is yea and his nay, nay; and his character for uprightness is such in the community that no person who knows him will for a moment admit the possibility of his case not being perfectly genuine.
>
> On January 17, 1887, he drew 551 dollars from a bank in Providence with which to pay for a certain lot of land in Greene, paid certain bills, and got into a Pawtucket horse-car. This is the last incident which he remembers. He did not return home that day, and nothing was heard of him for two months. He was published in the papers as missing, and foul play being suspected, the police sought in vain his whereabouts. On the morning of March 14th, however, at Norristown, Pennsylvania, a man calling himself A. J. Brown, who had rented a

small shop six weeks previously, stocked it with stationery, confectionery, fruit and small articles, and carried on his quiet trade without seeming to any one unnatural or eccentric, woke up in a fright and called in the people of the house to tell him where he was. He said that his name was Ansel Bourne, that he was entirely ignorant of Norristown, that he knew nothing of shop-keeping, and that the last thing he remembered—it seemed only yesterday—was drawing the money from the bank, etc. in Providence. He would not believe that two months had elapsed. The people of the house thought him insane; and so, at first, did Dr. Louis H. Read, whom they called in to see him. But on telegraphing to Providence, confirmatory messages came, and presently his nephew, Mr. Andrew Harris, arrived upon the scene, made everything straight, and took him home. He was very weak, having lost apparently over twenty pounds of flesh during his escapade, and had such a horror of the idea of the candy-store that he refused to set foot in it again.

The first two weeks of the period remained unaccounted for, as he had no memory, after he had once resumed his normal personality, of any part of the time, and no one who knew him seems to have seen him after he left home. The remarkable part of the change is, of course, the peculiar occupation which the so-called Brown indulged in. Mr. Bourne has never in his life had the slightest contact with trade. 'Brown' was described by the neighbors as taciturn, orderly in his habits, and in no way queer. He went to Philadelphia several times; replenished his stock; cooked for himself in the back shop, where he also slept; went regularly to church; and once at a prayer-meeting made what was considered by the hearers a good address, in the course of which he related an incident which he had witnessed in his natural state of Bourne.

This was all that was known of the case up to June 1890, when I induced Mr. Bourne to submit to hypnotism, so as to see whether, in the hypnotic trance, his 'Brown' memory would not come back. It did so with surprising readiness; so much so indeed that it proved quite impossible to make him whilst in the hypnosis remember any of the facts of his normal life. He had heard of Ansel Bourne, but "didn't know as he had ever met the man." When confronted with Mrs. Bourne he said that he had "never seen the woman before," etc. On the other hand, he told of his peregrinations during the lost fortnight,* and gave all sorts of details about the Norristown episode. The whole thing was prosaic enough; and the Brown-personality seems to be nothing but a rather shrunken, dejected, and amnesic extract of Mr. Bourne himself. He gives no motive for the wandering except that there was 'trouble back there' and he 'wanted rest.' During the trance he looks old, the corners of his mouth are drawn down, his voice is slow

---

*He had spent an afternoon in Boston, a night in New York, an afternoon in Newark, and ten days or more in Philadelphia, first in a certain hotel and next in a certain boarding-house, making no acquaintances, 'resting,' reading, and 'looking around.' I have unfortunately been unable to get independent corroboration of these details, as the hotel registers are destroyed, and the boarding-house named by him has been pulled down. He forgets the name of the two ladies who kept it. (Footnote in original source)

and weak, and he sits screening his eyes and trying vainly to remember what lay before and after the two months of the Brown experience. "I'm all hedged in," he says: "I can't get out at either end. I don't know what set me down in the Pawtucket horse-car, and I don't know how I ever left that store, or what became of it." His eyes are practically normal, and all his sensibilities (save for tardier response) about the same in hypnosis as in waking. I had hoped by suggestion, etc., to run the two personalities into one, and make the memories continuous, but no artifice would avail to accomplish this, and Mr. Bourne's skull to-day still covers two distinct personal selves.

The case (whether it contain an epileptic element or not) should apparently be classed as one of spontaneous hypnotic trance, persisting for two months. The peculiarity of it is that nothing else like it ever occurred in the man's life, and that no eccentricity of character came out. In most similiar cases, the attacks recur, and the sensibilities and conduct markedly change.*

James assumed that the fugue of Bourne was that of a spontaneous hypnotic trance of two months duration. This explanation does not appear valid. That the memories could be recovered through hypnosis means only that hypnosis could break the amnesic barrier; it does not mean that hypnosis had produced the amnesia in the first place. For our purposes, at this point, the case is useful as a dramatic instance of a prolonged dissociation that exhibits the phenomena in dramatic form, whatever their interpretation.

ALTERNATING PERSONALITIES

As already noted, the early dissociation theorists derived their beliefs in dissociation largely from multiple personalities that came to their attention in the course of clinical practice. Overt multiple personalities of the kinds they studied appear to be rather rare experiments of nature, but they continue to appear from time to time, and it is pertinent to try to form a contemporary estimate of their scientific status.

Common criticisms of the concept of multiple personality make the assumption that this is a so-called iatrogenic disease—that is, a disease created by the physician treating the person. The criticism has often been made, early voiced as a danger by Janet, and by William James, who was worried about one of Prince's earliest cases. After hearing a lecture by Prince, James said:

---

*The details of the case, it will be seen, are all *compatible* with simulation. I can only say of that, that no one who has examined Mr. Bourne (including Dr. Read, Dr. Weir Mitchell, Dr. Guy Hinsdale, and Mr. R. Hodgson) practically doubts his ingrained honesty, nor, so far as I can discover, do any of his personal acquaintances indulge in a sceptical view. (Footnote in original source)

It is very easy in the ordinary hypnotic subject to suggest during a trance the appearance of a secondary personage with a certain temperament, and that secondary personage will usually give itself a name. One has, therefore, to be on one's guard in this matter against confounding naturally double persons and persons who are simply temporarily endowed with the belief that they must play the role of being double (Discussion of Prince, 1890; reproduced in Prince 1975, p. 55).

Actually, a number of cases can be cited in which the patient exhibited the multiple personalities before being treated by anyone who suspected their existence and certainly before any hypnotic procedures were used in calling them forth. Fortunately, there have been a number of able reviews of the cases from the past. The most detailed of these was made by Taylor and Martin (1944), and a careful summary and interpretation has been provided by Ellenberger (1970). There have been a number of new cases reported since Ellenberger's review, indicating either something in the unsettled value systems of our times that leads to these divisions of personality or that psychotherapists are becoming more alert to them.

Ellenberger offered a classification of the cases to give some order to these complex manifestations. His classes, with some of his illustrations in brief, are as follows:

1. Simultaneous Dual Personalities. In this most uncommon condition there are two personalities manifesting themselves at once, not just two separate "streams of consciousness," but two personalities, each with its feeling of identity; this is similar to some forms of "possession states."

Hélène Smith, a medium studied by Flournoy (1900), reports a protector, Leopold. Having a spirit intermediary of this kind is not uncommon in the spiritualist tradition, but what brings her case in the dual personality category is that she sometimes *became* Leopold; in the transient state both she and Leopold existed as one was turning into the other. Her case has a somewhat contemporary sound, because it included a visit to the planet Mars.

I find the specification of this category rather unsatisfactory; in any case the coexistence of both personalities is not an enduring matter, and presently one of them is dominant, even though the other may be dimly in the background, just as the dreamer sometimes knows that he is dreaming.

2. Successive Dual Personalities, Mutually Cognizant. The first category, just described, readily merges into the second. Because both personalities know each other, the usual discontinuity of memories is not conspicuous, and the few cases of this kind appear to correspond to excessive mood shifts, with corresponding role behavior. A case reported by Cory (1920) is illustrative.

The alternating personalities in a 29-year-old woman were designated A and B. Personality A was the normal, habitual personality, that of a bright and cultured woman of good background. She was rather shy and inhibited. Although she played piano, she sang poorly. Personality B seemed older and bolder, but remained dignified and serious looking. She claimed to be the reincarnation of a Spanish singer. She sang well (in contrast with A). When speaking English (her native tongue) she added a strong Spanish accent. At times she spoke "Spanish," but it was made up of broken Spanish and Spanish-sounding words in a crude imitation of Spanish. Although A was sexually inhibited, B pretended to be a voluptuous, fascinating beauty and claimed to have been a dancer, a courtesan, and the mistress of a nobleman.

Although the two personalities knew each other and were on friendly terms, each was able to hold back a little information from the other, as two friends might.

Some additional information about the relationships between the personalities was obtained under hypnosis. Cory was able to hypnotize A and B separately. When A was hypnotized, she remembered some things of which she was not aware in her waking state; some of them B had already told Cory in her normal state, not hypnotized. Hence some discontinuity in memories, common in multiple personality, was present here also.

Whenever hypnosis has been used in a case of this kind, it is important to inquire whether the hypnotic procedures were required to identify the split; if so, the suspicion remains that hypnosis may have been responsible for the findings. In Cory's case the secondary personality had emerged at the time of the father's suicide, had persisted for three years before coming to Cory's attention, and hence cannot be attributed to hypnosis. The sexual repression-expression conflict is in evidence in the contrasts between A and B; the Spanish content may reflect some experiences she had with Spanish-speaking children in a convent school and some attraction to a Spanish man shortly after her father's death. The spirit-possession aspect may have been reinforced by the reward B received in a circle of believers in spiritualism.

3. Successive Dual Personalities, Mutually Amnesic. As Ellenberger has noted, the phenomena of possession throughout history have had some of the features of multiple personality, but as long as possession states were interpreted supernaturalistically they did not become identified as alternating personalities. Hence it was only with the decline in belief in possession that multiple personalities became part of the medical literature. An early case, reported by Gmelin in 1791, was identified as an "exchanged personality" and fits the pattern of mutually amnesic states.

A young German woman, impressed by the aristocratic refugees arriving in Stuttgart at the time of the French revolution, suddenly exchanged her personality for the manners of a French lady, speaking French perfectly and

German with something of an accent. In the French personality, the young woman remembered all that she had said and done in her previous French states, but in her German condition she knew nothing of the French state.

4. Successive Dual Personalities, One-way Amnesic. This is probably the most frequent type of multiple personality, in which personality A has its own memories but not those of personality B, while personality B has the memories of A as well as of B.

An early case of this kind was published by Azam (1887) after many years of observation and has since been referred to frequently as a kind of prototype of dual personality. His patient, Felida X, earned her living as a seamstress in her normal personality. She was described as sullen and taciturn, with many headaches and neuralgias that would today be described as psychosomatic. After a crisis, however, she would awaken as a different person, gay, vivacious, and free of symptoms. This secondary person, more "healthful" than the "normal" one, knew all about the symptoms of the primary personality, but the primary person had no awareness of the secondary one, except as she was told about it by others.

It is important to note that the secondary or hidden personality can sometimes be more "normal," better adjusted, healthier than the primary personality. Typically, the secondary personality has the whole set of memories, and therapy is directed to bringing about an integration based on it rather than on the typical personality that at first presents itself as the primary one. This conclusion was reached some time ago by Mitchell (1925), who noted the two points: (1) that it is the secondary personality B that has the memories of both A and B, whereas the primary personality A is cut off from B's memories, and (2) the secondary personality B is often healthier according to common social or mental health criteria.

MULTIPLE PERSONALITIES: THREE OR MORE

The case of Charles Poultney reported by Franz (1933) is the first of those mentioned here in which there is a third personality. In this case the personalities are defined almost entirely according to the continuities and discontinuities of memories. In terms of social behavior or general characterization there was not much change, except as required by the circumstances engendered by lost memories. The two main parts into which his life was cut by memory discontinuity were the memories of Charles Poultney (his correct name) from birth in 1887 to age 27 in 1914, and Charles Poulting, an assumed name, February 1915 to March 1930, ages 28–43. A gap between September 1914 and February 1915 may have been filled by a third personality, but little is know about this personality. In 1930 he came to Franz's attention. Franz unraveled his story by reintegrative techniques, such as the use of a map to restore his memory of wartime experiences taking place in Africa; hypnosis was not used.

As the story was pieced together, it was found that he had first been picked up in Los Angeles in 1919 in a dazed condition, wandering the streets. Although he had identification papers made out to Charles Poulting of Florida and had British and French war medals with him, he did not know who he was. He spoke with an Irish accent, thought he might be a Canadian, and Michigan seemed to have had some importance to him. He was tattooed with Buffalo Bill and an American flag. He had traveled widely since World War I, trying to find himself, for he had lost all memories prior to February 1915. In a curious interlude, a woman thought he was her long-lost son and took him into her home, but everything, including the Seventh-Day Adventist religion, was so foreign to him that he refused to accept this solution and continued to wander in search of his identity.

The police again found him wandering in a dazed condition in March 1930, now having regained the memories and identity of Charles Poultney from birth to 1914, but having lost all recent memories. He now thought he was back to 1914 and looked on newspapers with the 1930 dates as some strange "futuristic" sheets because they gave no war news. He missed his uniform and, when seeking to return things to a pocket, automatically fumbled for the breast pocket of his uniform, where there was no pocket in his civilian clothes.

In this second state, as Charles Poulting, it was possible to "introduce him" to the memories of the first state, as Charles Poultney, by way of the biography that he had written while in that state. This did not help much until, with the map of Africa before him, the two personal memories were integrated in a flood of emotion. The place name of Voi proved to be the trigger. The dynamics of repression appeared to be operative with respect to his interim in Africa because of the recall of two tragic events. About one he felt no guilt, but the other burdened his conscience. Out in the forest with another soldier in leopard country, his companion refused to climb a tree and tie himself there to spend the night. During the night he was attacked and eaten by leopards. This did not bother Poultney; he had seen many battle deaths, and this was his companion's fault for not taking the precaution that he had recommended and himself taken. However, the other event was different. He had a monkey with him when nightfall occurred in the same territory. He tied the monkey to the base of the tree, while he found his own secure place up in the tree. During the night the monkey was attacked and eaten; had Poultney not tied him at the bottom of the tree he could have escaped. By contrast with the death of his human companion, the death of the monkey—his fault—was an intolerable burden to think about, and he became amnesic for the event and for other events surrounding it. Although dramatic with respect to this particular incident, this is not the whole story, for there were earlier fugues before the monkey came along, although all of them were preceded by physical or emotional traumas. Once the monkey episode came to light, all the subsequent memories of Poulting and Poultney became fused, and the man felt essentially cured, even though there were still some memory gaps.

He now knew the date and place of his birth, his address in Dublin, the names of his parental family and of his own wife and two children to whom he had not returned after his military service. He had come to the United States in 1913 and had indeed lived in Michigan. That Michigan had some prominence in the alternate personality in which he was amnesic for these events indicates that the amnesia barrier was somewhat permeable.

The case illustrates very well the role of amnesia in disrupting the continuity of self-identity.

Complex cases like that of Franz, including those of Pierre Janet's, had appeared from time to time. One of the women Janet studied, Léonie, began with a dual personality, but soon a third one emerged which, he noted, had also been discovered many years earlier (Janet, 1889).

Léonie was Janet's first reported and most thoroughly experimented case. She came to Janet's attention early in his career, when he appears to have been more interested in experimenting on her than in attempting to resolve her problems. She had apparently had natural attacks of somnambulism since the age of 3 and had been repeatedly hypnotized by all sorts of people from the age of 16 on; she was 45 when Janet studied her. Her childhood had been spent in peasant surroundings, but the rest of her life had been spent in "drawing rooms and doctors' offices," as Janet put it. In her normal state she was serious, timid, mild, and a little sad; when hypnotized she became vivacious and noisy, with a tendency to irony and jesting toward the strangers who had come to witness her hypnotic behavior. Janet at first performed some dramatic but poorly controlled studies of hypnotic influence at a distance, but he repudiated parapsychological influences and attempted to give a purely naturalistic account of what he observed. Léonie eventually turned up with three personalities uncovered with the aid of hypnosis, on occasion called Léonie I, II, and III, sometimes given the names by which the first two referred to themselves: Léonie and Léontine and, for the third, Léonore, a name given by the "magnetizer" who had first discovered the third personality. Léontine appeared when hypnotized by Janet, as she had for other hypnotists before him. Later on, when Léontine was herself hypnotized, a third personality, Léonore, made her appearance. It was only after studying Léonie for some time that Janet found out that she had been treated hypnotically years before by some of the magnetizers of that period and that the "new" personality had been elicited and christened 20 years earlier.

In a much-studied and hypnotized case of this kind, doubts arise as to the role of the hypnotist in consolidating personalities out of amnesic material; Janet, as noted earlier, was aware of the problem. He recognized the role that naming played in defining the secondary personality: "Once baptized, the unconscious personality is clearer and more definite; it shows the psychological traits more clearly" (Janet, 1889, p. 318). The three personalities of Léonie showed signs of their origins. The first was appropriate to her upbringing as a simple country girl and housewife who was now placed in a sophisticated urban setting. She had had her first child while hypnotized and spontaneously fell into the hypnotic state when her other children were born; it is not too surprising that the hypnotized personality (Léonie II) claimed the children as her own, while assigning the husband to Léonie I, who accepted both the husband and the children. Léonore (Léonie III), doubtless a product of the hypnotic manipulations, might have been made use of to reintegrate the personality, for she was quite aware of the others, although she judged Léonie I to be stupid and Léonie II to be disturbed. The amnesic barriers that persisted made Léonie I know only herself; Léonie II knew Léonie I as well as herself; Léonie III knew them all.

Dual personality is probably a more common manifestation than divisions into three or more personalities: we know that more are possible, having met the three personalities of Charles Poulting (if the amnesic period prior to restoration can be called a personality) and of Janet's Léonie.

The best known of these multiple cases was described in Morton Prince's history of Miss Beauchamp (Prince 1906). In her case the four ultimate personalities all arose after she had been in hypnotic treatment for some weeks; thus William James' questions were well raised. Miss Beauchamps' eventual personalities were as follows:

B I, the primary personality of Miss Beauchamp.
B II, a secondary personality, an intensified version of B I.
B III, Sally, who showed scorn and contempt for B I.
B IV, the Idiot, a regressed personality.

Prince eventually succeeded in integrating them all.

The memory overlaps are illustrated for the three main personalities in Figure 3, in which the direction of the arrow indicates access to knowledge of the other personality. (B IV may be ignored.) Only the primary personality, B I, is without knowledge of the other two. B II knows B I, but not B III. B III has full access to the other two.

This completes the categorization of types of dual or multiple personalities that have been reported.

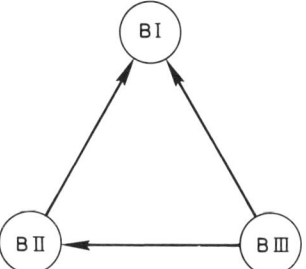

Figure 3 The component personalities of Miss Beauchamp, with direction of awareness of one personality for another. The arrowhead points in the direction in which one personality knows another. After Prince (1906).

RECENT CASES

During recent years a number of reports of multiple personalities have appeared, and others, unreported, have come to my attention. Whether this is a genuine increase in their presence is a mute question because the numbers are too few to permit a statistical or demographic demonstration. As noted earlier, I am inclined to believe that the intellectual atmosphere, in which matters of consciousness are of high interest, may be responsible for a greater alertness to the presence of these phenomena. There is a paucity of references to dual or multiple personalities in the psychoanalytic literature, possibly through the selection of cases for treatment, or as a consequence of aspects of the psychoanalytic methods. With a wider representation of other types of therapy today there may be a greater openness to the manifestations of these personalities. It may also be that the conflicting value systems of our times throw people into the kinds of conflict that generate multiple personalities. This would be coherent with a position expressed earlier by Gardner Murphy (1947): "Most cases of multiple personality appear essentially to represent the organism's effort to live, at different times, in terms of different systems of values."

We may examine several recent cases with some of these questions before us. These cases have all come to my attention since the review by Ellenberger (1970).

Sibyl

The case of Sibyl has thus far been published only in the form of a fictionalized account, although the main details are assented to both by the patient who is the subject of the account and by the psychiatrist who treated her (Schreiber, 1973). The total of 16 personalities that emerged, of both sexes, suggests multiple role enactments, once the process got started. At the end, in a kind of "group therapy," the most important subpersonalities had to agree as to which would survive and which would disappear, and, in order to fuse, they all had to grow up to the same age, even though at least one had enjoyed *not* growing up.

Some features of the case are quite convincing. In the early discovery by the therapist that she was dealing with more than one "personality," what came to her attention was such evidence as the patient opening her purse to show her a letter in it, only to report her surprise that "someone" had torn it up without her knowing it. This "someone" might be the person to whom the therapist found herself talking on the next visit. One of the features of the history—common to many cases of multiple personality—is a severely brutal period in childhood, making appropriate identifications impossible to integrate and, in turn, producing difficulty in achieving a personal identity.

Jonah

This case has been carefully studied from a psychological point of view (Ludwig and others, 1972; Brandsma and Ludwig, 1974). The same psychiatrist who treated the Sibyl case is represented among the authors giving the account of Jonah, a 27-year-old man who came to a hospital with complaints of severe headaches that were often followed by memory loss. Hospital attendants noticed striking changes in his personality on different days, and the psychiatrist in charge detected three distinct secondary personalities prior to any attempt to explore the patient's problems with the help of hypnosis. Hypnosis was then used in the effort to fuse the personalities, and the patient was discharged from the hospital. However, the result was unsuccessful, and on the patient's return the hospital staff was prepared to do a more thorough study of the personalities before attempting to fuse them again.

The relatively stable personality structures that emerged are diagramed in Figure 4. The four personalities may be characterized briefly:

JONAH. The primary personality. Shy, retiring, polite, passive, and highly conventional, he is designated "the square." Sometimes frightened and confused during interviews, Jonah is unaware of the other personalities.

SAMMY. He has the most intact memories. He can coexist with Jonah or set Jonah aside and take over. He claims to be ready when Jonah needs legal advice or is in trouble. He is designated "the mediator." Sammy remembers emerging at age 6, when Jonah's mother stabbed his stepfather, and Sammy persuaded the parents never to fight again in front of the children.

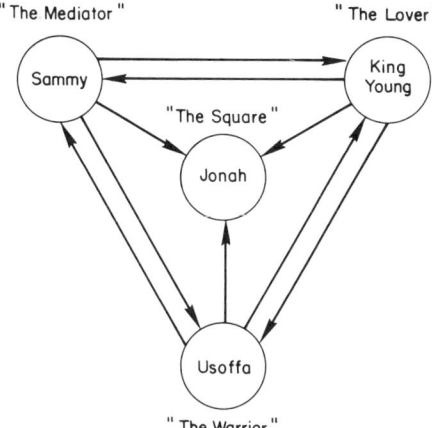

Figure 4 The four component personalities, with their degrees of awareness of each other. The three personalities on the periphery have superficial knowledge of each other but are intimately familiar with Jonah, who is totally lacking in knowledge of them. Another temporarily emerging personality, De Nova, is not shown. From Ludwig and others (1972).

KING YOUNG. He emerged when Jonah was 6 or 7 to straighten out his sexual identity after Jonah's mother occasionally dressed him in girls' clothing at home, and Jonah became confused about boys' and girls' names at school. King Young has looked after Jonah's sexual interests ever since; hence he is designated "the lover." He is aware of the other personalities rather dimly, but takes over when Jonah needs assistance in seeking sexual gratification with a woman.

USOFFA ABDULLA. A cold, belligerent, and angry person, Usoffa is capable of ignoring pain. It is his sworn duty to watch over and protect Jonah; hence he is designated "the warrior." He emerged at about age 9 or 10, when a gang of white boys beat up Jonah, who is black, without provocation. Jonah was helpless, but when Usoffa emerged, he fought viciously and vehemently against the attackers. He is only dimly aware of the other personalities. The fact that the personalities see themselves in these roles is evident from their self-portraits made during the course of the study (Figure 5). The psychological study showed that the four personalities tested very differently on all measures having to do with emotionally laden topics, but scored essentially alike on tests relatively free of emotion or interpersonal conflict, such as intelligence or vocabulary tests.

The outcome of the treatment, in which the four personalities were to be fused into one, has not been reported, although some early indications were

Figure 5   Self-portraits of the separate personalities of Jonah. From Ludwig and others (1972).

that Jonah seemed "sicker" with all the strands of the personality out in the open than when the secondary personalities were in abeyance except when needed. The authors conjectured that, for him, four heads were perhaps better than one.

Again we note, in the quarrels between mother and stepfather and in the mother's failure to provide a clear sex-typed role for Jonah, that the identification figures of childhood do not permit clear identifications and hence do not lead to a satisfactorily integrated personality.

Katherine—Kathy

This unpublished case, furnished to me by Dr. Monroe S. Arlen, the psychiatrist who treated Katherine, reveals some of the childhood difficulties so common in these instances of divided personalities.

Katherine, the 29-year-old mother of a 15-month-old daughter, had become depressed, tense, and irritable and rejected the sexual advances of her husband after the birth of the daughter, a first child. In the previous three years of marriage she had, by his account, been relaxed and an enjoyable sex partner. She was treated briefly by a psychotherapist who used progressive relaxation and hypnosis in the attempt to make sex enjoyable to her once more; this was within three months of the infant's birth. Her husband reported that this had ended in failure, and now, a year later, "She acts like a child, says sex is bad and dumb and wants to die. She responds only to the name Kathy and seems to be in a trance."

Unfortunately the details of the first psychotherapeutic sessions are lacking, but the inference is that the birth of a daughter served as a trigger to bring out postpartum symptoms related to her earlier life. Her husband arranged to have her treated by Dr. Arlen, and the first interview was with the husband. He felt that, in observing his wife, he could detect two secondary personalities, one a suckling infant and the other a sensuous teenager who admitted that sex was bad but enjoyable. He also observed that, during the trance-like states, she would mis-identify him as her mother. It later appeared that Kathy was the only important secondary personality and could appear in behavior as anything from an infant to a teenager. When she wished to prevent sex, she would force Katherine into a fetal position that appeared totally regressed.

Her secondary personality—called Kathy—was immature, varying in age between 7 and 17, and sometimes "wishing to be a baby." Katherine knows about Kathy, and they talk together: hence in some respects it is like a case of possession, in which Kathy will not let Katherine do what Kathy does not wish her to do. Their memories are not entirely in common; for example, Kathy knows about a sexual assault on Katherine by an older brother when she was 7, which Katherine does not recall, although Kathy has told her about it.

Katherine's personal history of sexual traumas was enough to cause concern over sex. There may have been some fantasy overlays, because many of the details came out only in hypnotic age regression within which some distortions are possible. She reported an attempt by a young brother to have sex with her at the age of 5, at the urging of an older sister, but he was unsuccessful and she did not know what it was all about. The important incident occurred at the age of 7, when an older brother forced both oral and anal sex on her in a corn field near their home. This was a painful and frightening experience for her. She could not explain why she was late for dinner, and when her father punished her severely for being late, she accepted this as punishment also for her sexual transgression. Katherine, who does not recall the incident, remembers a frightening dream a year later, "A wolf came out of a corn field, I ran inside to lock the windows, but the wolf jumped in." The split in personality is dated from this event. One part of her, Katherine, became shy and inhibited and blocked out the whole experience. The other part, Kathy, refused to grow up to adulthood; she retained the experience and began to exert a subtle influence over Katherine's general behavior and attitudes, especially in the sexual sphere.

The unfortunate experiences with sex did not stop with this incident. At the age of 10 she saw her 12-year-old sister raped by several boys; at the age of 17 she was raped by three boys, and on another occasion her father, while drunk, made sexual advances to her, but Kathy emerged to stop him, calling him "dumb and stupid." Somehow Katherine fended off these memories, but Kathy retained them and sought to restrict Katherine's adult sex life.

Therapy now consisted in subordinating Kathy's control over Katherine and in dealing with the general problems of guilt over sex. The sexual relations between Katherine and her husband improved; she was able to experience orgasm, and the therapy was terminated, although Kathy had not completely disappeared and occasionally reappeared for a brief outburst.

One is tempted to interpret why the birth of Katherine's daughter was followed by the symptoms in a form not previously shown. The probability is that the appearance of the baby meant a necessity to adopt a truly adult role as a mother, and the mother figure for Katherine was her own mother who had the feeling that sex was dirty and nasty. Combining this with that part of herself that had been traumatized by sex and preferred not to grow up, a conflict ensued. The conflict was difficult to resolve because sex was not wholeheartedly rejected; in fact, Katherine said at one point, while she was still fearing sex; "My top half is scared, but my bottom half wants it." Later, in therapy, as she had outgrown some of her inability to express emotion, she sized up her relation to Kathy: "She keeps the bad feelings and memories and keeps me away from sex. She's afraid of growing up, but I'm trying to talk with her and explain to her that sex is not naughty and it's not something you are going to get spanked for any more."

Martha-Harriet

Another recent case, reported by Frankel (1976), is that of a 36-year-old married woman, Martha, who was referred to him because she had puzzling physical symptoms that might be diagnosed as hysterical and was troubled by an angry voice that occasionally spoke out of her mouth. The voice offended those about her by its insults; she claimed that she had no knowledge of its source, and, because she was unable to control it, felt no responsibility for its utterances.

In the first interview, seated in a wheelchair with a scarf wound around her neck to oppose the emergence of the voice, she was persuaded to allow it to emerge. After some grimacing and jerking the concealed personality of Harriet emerged. She attributed Martha's illnesses to the pressure from her husband to behave properly on all occasions; Harriet, by contrast, was well, had no pain, and could walk perfectly, which she demonstrated by walking across the room before returning to the wheelchair.

Harriet claimed to have been a childhood friend of Martha's who had died and then had become a part of Martha, somewhere between the ages of 4 and 6. It was not possible to verify the historical fact of a Harriet in Martha's childhood, and the possibility exists that Harriet may have been an imaginary companion. In any case, according to Harriet, Martha does not know of Harriet's origins and is aware of Harriet's actions only from time to time, as in the vocal utterances; Harriet is always aware of Martha's thoughts and actions. The picture is partly that of "possession" and partly that of double-personality with a better integrated part beneath a disturbed surface personality. Harriet withdrew from the scene and Martha returned, unaware of Harriet's appearance, before the first interview was terminated. No formal hypnosis had been used in the first interview, and hypnosis could not have been responsible for the personality division because the symptoms had been in evidence for years.

Martha proved highly responsive to hypnosis, and in seven subsequent interviews hypnosis was used to explore the life history and to reintegrate the two fractions of the personality, with the relief of all her symptoms.

The Three Faces of Evelyn

A recent case of multiple personality is of special interest because of its resemblance to (and difference from) the three faces of Eve case earlier reported (Osgood and others, 1976). In both these cases, the subpersonalities were studied through a blind analysis of their semantic differentials, with results quite coherent with the clinical material. The semantic differential is derived from ratings by the subject to determine the connotative meanings associated with selected concepts, such as my mother, my father, hatred, love, fraud, as well as specifically named people known to the subject. The dimensions on which the concepts are rated include valuable-worthless, strong-weak, deep-shallow, relaxed-tense, and other bipolar adjectives. By using the same concepts and the same scales, similarities and differences among the personalities could be judged without access to the clinical information.

The patient, Gina, the open "face" of Evelyn, who presented herself to the psychiatrist, Dr. Jeans, was a single woman, aged 31, ordinarily a businesslike, efficient, and productive person, earning a good salary as a writer for an educational publishing firm. She was the youngest of nine siblings in a family of Italian-Protestant extraction. She came for treatment at the advice of friends because of somnambulisms, episodic amnesia, and some behavior out of keeping with her usual personality.

The three major personalities that emerged after some weeks of treatment were Gina, the one who presented herself for treatment, Mary, opposite to Gina in several respects, and Evelyn, the last to emerge, who served to integrate all three.

Although at one state hypnosis had been attempted, it proved ineffective, and the remaining therapy was carried on without it. In contrast to those cases in which the different personalities make their appearances in turn, most of the information came from "inner conversations" in which Gina would be talking with her other named selves. It was while attempting such a conversation with Mary that she found herself talking to Evelyn, who seemed to her a much more sensible person than Mary. Evelyn said that she was "coming out" once a day to get used to the world, and would come out to see the therapist when she got stronger. Several other personalities appeared in these conversations, but the account largely disregards them in favor of the main three. Gina began using a borrowed tape recorder to keep track of what was happening to her during the amnesic episodes that took place at night. For example, although she and her roommate both disliked chocolate, she commonly found a cup that had contained hot chocolate in the sink in the morning. This was a sign that some other personality fraction had been in control during the night.

Evelyn gradually accumulated information from Gina and Mary, and the integration moved forward as Evelyn displaced the two by fusing them all into one, as she set aside their defenses and adopted more mature ways of behaving. It was while Evelyn was attempting to get matters straight that it was possible to obtain the semantic differentials by calling on each of the three personalities in turn.

It was possible to show, for example, that Mary and Evelyn were closer to each other in their relation to their mother than Gina and Mary were, whereas no two were very close to each other in relation to the father. The three personalities revealed themselves as quite unlike, and the inferences that the blind raters made were largely supported by the clinical data.

The major traumatic events in childhood that appeared related to the emerging personalities were centered around the ages of 2 and 12. Up to the age of 2, the patient had been well cared for by an older sister, Marilyn, who, as a substitute mother, provided an identification model; perhaps this had something to do with the choice of Mary as the name for one of the personalities. The first major traumatic event came at the age of two when Marilyn left to get married after heated arguments with the domineering mother, leaving the little patient bereft and in the care of a mother with whom she could not identify. Lonesome without Marilyn, she cried a lot; the otherwise rather passive father, slapped her in exasperation. In seeking an identification model, she apparently turned to a neighbor, Bill B., and took on some masculine characteristics, still noted in Gina. It is a matter of conjecture as to how much splitting occurred at this time between the more feminine nature still identified with Marilyn and the more masculine one identified with Bill.

At the age of 12 at least two traumatic events occurred, and the first memories of sleepwalking date from this time. There was a good deal of pathology among the siblings, but the most normal of them, by common consent, was the sister Elaine. The patient was 12 when Elaine left the home to marry, a blow to the child who was having difficulty enough with her intrafamily relationships. The name of Evelyn perhaps derives from this favorite normal sister. At about the same time (the exact chronology is unclear), Gina's next older sister by six years, Jenny, told her mother that she wanted to get married. According to Gina, her mother beat up Jenny every night for two weeks. She reported hearing her mother going upstairs intent on killing Jenny and ran up to save her.

These events provided the background for such dissociations as persisted during the years intervening between age 12 and age 31, when she sought treatment. Gina's masculine identification and her good work habits permitted her to do well, earn a master's degree, and hold a good job despite her sleepwalking and amnesic episodes. She had difficulties in relating to men, and a conflictual affair with a married man was part of the picture when she sought therapy.

The case is particularly puzzling because the amnesic episodes are not accounted for (as in the case of Eve White and Eve Black) by the dominance of the other personality. For example, we do not find Mary admitting that she is the one who liked the hot chocolate; for all the reader knows, it may have been Evelyn. Similarly, there were scenes for which Gina was amnesic, vaguely reported as having occurred in bars, but with no account of who was responsible. These difficulties may be a matter of exposition rather than the nature of the amnesias or perhaps the failure to be able to use hypnotic techniques that occasionally uncover such material.

A follow-up eight years after termination of treatment showed that Evelyn (the name assigned to the integrated person) was happily married to a physician and there had been no recurrence of symptoms.

CONCLUDING NOTE ON MULTIPLE PERSONALITIES

That multiple personalities represent in some sense an effort at coping with a very difficult childhood appears to be the most common feature of these cases. The evidence does not favor cultural causes in the larger sense, but rather a disintegration of values at the heart of the family, with violent and excessive punishment, overt sexual assaults in childhood, unbalanced parental roles, one parent occasionally sadistic, the other rather passive and aloof. In resolving the conflicts over identification and guilt, and in trying to cope in a context in which a unified strategy cannot work, the person divides; sometimes, as in the case of Jonah, the strategy is moderately successful. The solution, however, carries within it so many problems, that at least the restoration of communication among the divided memories is called for; role divisions are acceptable if they are mutually understood and do not cause intolerable confusion.

In summarizing cases of multiple personality it is clear that sometimes the concealed personality is more normal than the presenting one, and sometimes the secondary personality is less acceptable than the primary one. Each is dissociated from the other and accessible at different times. The fact that the concealed part may be more rational and socially acceptable than the presenting part may mean that it will prove particularly useful in the integration of the personality. What has been noted, but not elaborated, is that the cause of the dissociations in these clinical cases lies in motivational conflicts that are often deeply unconscious. Having open access to the dissociated personalities does not in itself account for their origins.

NOTES

Possession States

A useful summary is provided by Raymond Prince (1968) in the book he edited covering a great deal of anthropological literature in addition to miscellaneous topics bearing on trance and possession. The contemporary manifestations in American religious movements are documented by Zaretsky and Leone (1974). On speaking in tongues (glossolalia), see Samarin (1972). The history of the confrontation between Father Gassner and Mesmer is given in detail in Ellenberger (1970, p. 53–57). Chong (1975) has described some of his Singapore experiences, with photographs. Accounts exist for many specific cultures; examples of these are, for Ethiopia, Giel, Gesahegn, and Van Luijk, 1968; for New Guinea, Salisbury, 1968. See also Kiev (1969) and Figge (1973).

Fugues

The category of fugues is not well delimited; thus almost any temporary amnesic episode may sometimes be classified as a fugue. For a review, see Kirshner (1973). Interesting cases have been described by Crasilneck and Hall (1975, pp. 234–235) and Frankel (1976,pp. 66–71).

Alternating and Multiple Personalities

Ellenberger (1970, 176, footnote 54) lists in chronological order 12 surveys of multiple personality between 1888 and 1947. Of these, the most complete one is by Taylor and Martin (1944). The discussion in the text depends very heavily on Ellenberger's account. A useful source, not cited by Ellenberger, is a critical review by Sutcliffe and Jones (1962), including an appendix of 16 brief case histories, of which ten are accepted as properly diagnosed cases of multiple personality.

A conceptual controversy has gone on within hypnosis for a number of years over the appropriateness of the concept of "trance" or "state," kept alive primarily by Barber (1969) and Sarbin and Coe (1972). As in the instinct controversy that has so long troubled psychologists, the issue is a conceptual one; people get hypnotized and show "trance" behavior, just as birds build nests appropriate to their species. At a phenomenal level there is little disagreement, although one may of course question any one illustration; a shaman who gets paid for his healing services may indeed be simulating trance behavior even when not appropriately "possessed." Furthermore, not all "trances" should be called hypnotic. Many of the conceptual debates appear to be somewhat futile, particularly when there are so many phenomena still requiring careful description and explanation (Hilgard, 1973c).

Recent Cases of Multiple Personality

A dozen or more published cases have appeared since the last case in Ellenberger's review, which was that of Thigpen and Cleckley (1957). Their case, the three faces of Eve, has come under subsequent discussion, for example, Lancaster (1958). More recently, the original Eve, tired of concealing her identity, gave a news release under her own name, Mrs. Chris Sizemore, with the story appearing in many papers throughout the country, for example, *The Washington Post*, September 14, 1975. She indicated that the three personalities that repeatedly emerged were the "Eve Black," and the "Eve White," and a "Real Eve" that persisted throughout.

The semantic differential method, used with both Eve and Evelyn, is given in detail in Osgood, Suci, and Tannenbaum (1957). As applied specifically to the personalities of Eve, the report is by Osgood and Luria (1954), and to those of Evelyn, by Osgood, Luria, Jeans, and Smith (1976).

I wish to express my gratitude to Dr. Monroe S. Arlen for permission to digest the report that he furnished me on the case of Katherine-Kathy. Identifying characteristics have been disguised in all the reported cases; care was taken not to modify the essential substance of the individual histories.

The many cases that have appeared since 1970 provide a justification for my belief that therapists are becoming more alert in detecting their appearance. Those not represented in the chapter include Allison (1974) (1975), Cutler and Reid (1975), Fast (1974), Gruenewald (1971), Kohlenberg (1973), and Wagner and Heise (1974). In the report with Osgood and others (1976), Jeans states that a half dozen cases other than Evelyn (his case) have come to his attention, and that multiple personality must not be so rare a phenomenon as the few reported cases have led us to believe.

Hypnosis and Multiple Personality

Hypnotic methods can produce behavior simulating multiple personality, but it must not be inferred that when hypnosis is used it is therefore responsible for the appearance of such personalities. Leavitt (1947) produced multiple personalities in his subject by hypnosis; he noted that the resulting personalities were consistent with personality trends already present. Bowers and Brecher (1955) interpreted their findings as showing that the personalities that emerged in hypnosis had been latent in the subject. This issue has been well discussed by Sutcliffe and Jones (1962), who recognized that multiple personalities may flourish within hypnosis, but need not have been produced by hypnosis in the first place. They pointed out that there were more multiple personalities when they were in style, but their argument can be used the other way: when not in style, multiple personalities may go unrecognized.

Bowers and others (1971), in discussing methods of therapy for multiple personality, give a number of cautions in the use of hypnosis.

CHAPTER 3

HYPNOTIC AGE REGRESSION

No matter how one dips into the recesses of the mind, one stumbles on the same problems—the storage and retrieval of information, some true, some false; imaginative and creative reconstruction; circumstances that inhibit and circumstances that facilitate. The major reason for approaching the examples of dissociation topic by topic is that each topic in turn, such as age regression, assures that special aspects of the phenomena of dissociation will not be overlooked.

Regression has many meanings; all imply a backward movement in time. The kinds of regressive experiences that we need to examine are those in which an older person returns in some sense to an earlier period in his life. In a psychoanalytic context, this commonly implies a return to the more primitive thought processes of an earlier period of development—primary-process thinking—without necessarily any content that refers to that earlier period. Hence, when Gill and Brenman (1959) define hypnosis as a regressive experience, they mean it in this sense. There may, of course, be some representation of the earlier period, as when in regressive-transference the psychoanalyst symbolically substitutes for the child's parent and, through interpreting the transference, explains some residues from the past. The content of the past is present by symbolization rather than through direct reinstatement, although the content itself may be recovered through association. If specific content is unimportant, the regression is a kind of *primitivation*.

The studies of age regression in hypnosis move directly to the earlier experience; instead of primitivation, a genuine *retrogression* is implied, in which there is a return, through memory, fantasy, and hallucination, to something actually experienced at an earlier time in the person's life. Once the retrogression has occurred, there may be a substantial *revivification;* thus the experience is relived as if it were taking place in the present.

CHARACTERISTIC BEHAVIORS AND EXPERIENCES

The phenomena of hypnosis are derived from two sources: the psychotherapeutic interaction and the laboratory experiment, with the laboratory a late comer.

Janet (1889), in his case of Marie, at first had little success in treating the troubling symptoms that consisted of terror, delirium, and vomiting of blood at the time of her menstrual periods. After some months he resorted to age regression to her first menstruation, which she had arrested by plunging herself into a large bucket of cold water, with the consequence that she became ill and had several days of delirium. She did not menstruate again for five years, but when she did the presenting symptoms emerged at the time of each menstrual period. Janet described his therapy thus:

> I was able to succeed only thanks to a singular means. It was necessary to bring her back into the initial circumstances of the delirium, convince her that the menstruation had lasted for three days and was not interrupted through any regrettable incident. Now, once this was done, the following menstruation came at the due point, lasted for three days, without any pain or delirium. (Janet, translation by Ellenberger, 1970, p. 363)

The difficulty with Janet's statements is one that plagues many studies of age regression: How true to fact are the remembered experiences? In this case Janet, who had already learned the true story under hypnotic questioning, produced a false account, to be experienced as true in the regression, for therapeutic purposes. In other words, he suggested that the actual traumatic incident had not happened and confirmed his suggestion by having the subject recall, in age regression, a normal menstruation at the time she had actually interrupted it. It is evident that a hypnotist can manipulate the veridicality of an event experienced during age regression so that such memories cannot be trusted unless validated in other ways.

Janet, in exploring another of Marie's symptoms used age regression both to obtain the truth and later to produce a distortion, again for therapeutic purposes. The hysterical symptom that Marie did not at first wish to have explored was a blindness in one eye, which she insisted was present from birth. However, when regressed to the age of 5 years, she was able to see with both eyes, and by moving to the age of 6, Janet was able to find the incident that had led to the blindness. It had started when she had been forced to sleep with a child who had impetigo covering the left side of her face; Marie developed impetigo also, and when cured of it, had anesthesia of the left side of her face, accompanied by the blindness in the left eye that had persisted. Using somewhat the same misleading method of having her sleep at the age of 5 with the child who now does *not* have impetigo, the blindness was cured, just as the menstrual difficulty was.

Although this is a kind of cathartic cure, it is significant to note that it is not abreaction, in the familiar psychoanalytic sense of reliving the emotion, hence getting it out of the system. Instead, the early experience was falsified to make its emotional residue inappropriate.

Because age regression can be supplemented by suggestion, as in Janet's case of Marie, care must be exercised to determine what belongs to the regression and what to the suggestions made, once the regression has occurred. The fact that the experience may be altered provides, of course, a therapeutic opportunity. This was examined in a study from our laboratory by Suzanne Horowitz (1970). Theorizing that a snake phobia might be best overcome by recalling the earliest recollections associated with it, along with a corrective emotional experience, she compared the results under three main conditions: first, a hypnotic recall with a reliving of the original emotion; second, a recall in which the early events were recalled *without* the emotion, on the grounds that the emotion belonged to the past and was inappropriate in the present; third, a control in which there was a discussion of the phobia, but no treatment until a retest at the interval over which the others were tested. She found that the regressive recall *without* the emotion was more effective than the recall *with* the emotion, hence essentially substantiating Janet's findings without actually denying the original event as he did. The separation of the cognition of the event from the emotion accompanying it may be considered another illustration of dissociation.

The enhancement of recall associated with the hypnotic regression to an earlier time is occasionally used in assisting a witness to recall the events of a crime.

Dorcus (1960) gave an account of the recovery of memories of four crime-related events. Three of the four yielded information of help to the police, although the actual information recovered was very fragmentary. One of the cases he described thus:

> This case involved a witness of a tavern holdup. She was a young woman in her late twenties who worked as a waitress in the tavern. The circumstances that she

could recall for the police were as follows. While she was working one evening a man entered and demanded money from the barkeep, threatening to shoot if the barkeep refused. She recognized the holdup man as a person who had been in the tavern several weeks earlier and who had "struck up" a conversation with her. He had on the previous occasion shown her a union card which gave certain information about him. The waitress was able to describe him but could not remember very pertinent information which she had previously seen on the card. Under hypnotic recall she was able to add some additional information which was very helpful to the police. For legal reasons the additional information cannot be supplied in detail here. (Dorcus, 1960, pp. 58–59).

Age regression may be accompanied by an increase in the material that can be recalled from the past; sometimes that supplementary information is rather convincing. I once demonstrated the nature of age regression before a group of psychiatric residents with the help of a college student whose previous hypnotic experiences had shown that she was an unusually responsive subject. I first interrogated her about her third grade class in school, and she was so successful in naming a half dozen members of her class and knowing her teacher's name and seemed so well oriented that I thought the demonstration would surely fail. However, under hypnosis I had her return to the class and asked her to name her classmates, and she gave a most remarkable performance. She reported that the class was seated in a circle at this time, so that she would go around the circle, looking at each child and telling me if she knew his or her name. She named 19 of 24 correctly, indicating the seating position of those she didn't know: "I'm sorry that I don't know the name of the boy sitting between Maybelle and Henry." Out of hypnosis, when I asked her why she had not found a position for herself in the circle, she said: "I forgot to tell you I was the blackboard monitor and was sitting up in front; that's why I could see everything so well." She was astounded at the clarity with which everything had been recreated.

Sometimes the report in regression is given as if the person is again a child, speaking as a child, in the present tense; sometimes, even though the events are seen and experienced vividly, they are told as if memories are being described. In fact, one method of studying age regression is to ask the person to see the event on a motion picture or television screen, when, as an adult watcher, he "sees" the party going on at his sixth birthday. Regardless of how the report is made, there are commonly two aspects of the person involved: the experiencing part, involved in the hypnotic events as though they were reality, and an adult observing part that can reflect on the experience. This "observing ego" is not always present, but when present it need not interfere with the vividness of the regressed experience.

One interesting case was that of a boy raised in China, who, while age regressed, handled the pencil given him to write his name as though it were a brush and wrote his name in Chinese characters. He was quite surprised when, out of hypnosis, he found that his name, written more nearly to fit a perfect square (as he had been taught as a child) did not have the slant with which he wrote his name in Chinese characters when he was a college student. He also made the observation that he was surprised, in the midst of the regression, that he was able to understand the English of the hypnotist, for he "did not know" that he could understand English.

Another illustration revealing the reality of the reliving under hypnotic regression was that of a boy from a Japanese-American family. Now a graduate student, he had been born in California five days before Pearl Harbor and spent his early years in a relocation center in which a great deal of Japanese was spoken. His own home, with American-born parents, was entirely English speaking, and no Japanese was spoken after they left the relocation center after the end of the war. In a first hypnotic regression, to age 7, Don failed to understand simple questions in Japanese and insisted, out of hypnosis that he knew only a few words, such as *arigato* ("thank you") that he had learned from his grandmother, who was bilingual in English and Japanese. His grandparents and parents had since died; thus he had no further contact with Japanese language. In a second regression he was first regressed to the age of 8, when he continued to talk and play games with the hypnotist, using only the English language. He was then regressed to the age of 3, to a day on which he felt happy and good. After a few moments of silence he broke into a stream of Japanese and talked on for 15 to 20 minutes. When progressed to the age of 7, he spontaneously reverted to English.

After a few weeks he was regressed again for therapeutic as well as experimental purposes. Now he had more childhood experiences available and talked excitedly in English as he was progressively relaxed to the age of 7, then 5, then 3— still speaking English. The hypnotist-experimenter did not wish to suggest that he speak Japanese, but found an indirect method of prompting Japanese by saying "Hi" to the regressed child. The word *hai*, meaning "yes" has the same sound in Japanese as the familiar *hi*, as a greeting in English. After hearing the word, he repeated it three times and then lapsed into excited Japanese. With a tape recorder now present, a record was kept that was later translated by one familiar with the Japanese language, who could verify the content and flow of the Japanese communication.

The subject had spontaneous amnesia for what had occurred, as indeed he had had following the earlier sessions, but now, encouraged to remember, he reported the dissociated nature of the experience, as the observing part of him had been aware of it:

> It was like my lips all of sudden would move into these funny shapes. And then I would want to say something and wouldn't know what I was really saying. The

words just came out and I wasn't sure whether they were real or not. The strangest thing is that my muscles without my my volition would just take over. It was really like my mind wasn't involved in it. (Fromm, 1970, p. 82)

He was unable to make much of what he had said when he later listened to the tape, but he remembered some of the thoughts and what the language might mean. He had chattered about a cute dog with big eyes, and the word he had used for eyes was baby talk, he said, *menme*, instead of the adult word *me*. The tape showed that his inference was correct; he had just received the present of a dog and was thanking his mother repeatedly for it. In the waking state, Don did not remember having a dog, and he thought dogs would have been forbidden in the relocation center ("concentration camp," as he called it).

In the course of therapy he could again use the Japanese language that he had learned as a child, indicating that some of the events of the troubled early years had caused a repression or amnesia that could be lifted.

The preservation of an observing part of a person within age regression is illustrated by the experience of one of my experimental subjects, a university student, in a study in which the effort was made to modify hypnotizability; some kinds of experiences within hypnosis were extended for a longer period than in the usual testing situation (Aas, Hilgard, and Weitzenhoffer, 1963).

The regression under hypnosis had taken place to a childhood experience in which the subject had accompanied her mother and grandmother on a shopping expedition and now found herself in a department store. She became separated from her adult companions and was quite frightened, but the hypnotist, in the role of a sympathetic stranger, comforted her and assured her that her mother would soon come. She saw her mother come to meet her and was happy again. Grandmother bought her a balloon; she held tightly to it because she saw a little boy lose his in the wind.

The reason for telling this little story was her account of it after she was aroused from hypnosis: "I felt so sorry for that little girl," she said, "because I knew all the time that her mother was going to find her, but *she didn't know it*." Here we have what resembles a multiple personality type of dissociation between the regressed part (that of the child) and the observing part (that of the adult), both belonging to the hypnotized person.

REGRESSION TO BIRTH OR TO AN EARLIER EXISTENCE OR PROGRESSION TO THE FUTURE

Extreme claims for hypnotic age regression have been made for many years, going back to the heyday of hypnosis in the 1880s and 1890s. One such claimant was a Colonel de Rochas (1911) who succeeded, according to his claims, in regressing his subjects to their infancy, birth, and fetal period, and then to their previous lives. He also introduced the possibility of a forward progression in time, in which his subjects lived what was going to happen in the future. Before these exaggerations are excused as the enthusiasm of someone becoming acquainted with hypnosis many years ago, a warning is in order that there are contemporary practitioners making similar claims. It is important to distinguish between those who perform an exercise to show how misleading the phenomena may be and those who are convinced of the truth of what they observe.

The Case of Bridey Murphy

Mr. Morey Bernstein, a businessman of Pueblo, Colorado, hypnotized Mrs. Virginia Tighe, a brown-haired housewife, in the year 1952. Under hypnosis, she began to talk in an Irish brogue, in the personality of a red-headed Irish girl, Bridey Murphy, who claimed to be her previous incarnation. The *Denver Post's* Sunday supplement, *Empire*, carried a serialized version of the story in September 1954, and the reader response indicated that a book would be welcome. The book, prepared with the assistance of an editor from the *Denver Post*, appeared under the authorship of Virginia's hypnotist with the title *The Search for Bridey Murphy* (Bernstein, 1956). The book was an immediate best seller and was translated into a number of languages.

In no time there were numerous articles and books in criticism and in support. One of my colleagues at Stanford, a professional in the Stanford University Library, himself born and raised in Ireland, wrote a devastating article. He argued that the unreality of the story was evident in many details, such as Virginia's answers to some leading questions about when she was being courted:

Brian came to your house?
Uh-huh.
When you were seventeen?
Uh-huh.

Ready comments: "Now there is many an answer that an Irish girl would give to a query about her young and burgeoning love, but by all the powers that be it would never be *Uh-huh*" (Ready, 1956).

There are always those who seek the miraculous, and the true believer is hard to discourage. Some experienced hypnotists came out with a book, *Scientific Report on "The Search for Bridey Murphy"* (Kline, 1956), in which they showed how easy it was to obtain material of this sort, but that did not convince the gullible.

In this particular instance, the ultimate facts became abundantly clear and should have disposed of the Bridey Murphy belief once and for all. A group of enterprising reporters in Chicago looked into Virginia's background, instead of sending delegations to Ireland to pick up evidence. The reporters' stories appeared in the *Chicago American* and were syndicated in the New York *Journal American* and other Hearst papers in June 1956. The essence of their reports has been summarized thus:

> With the help of Rev. Wally White, pastor of the Chicago Gospel Tabernacle where Virginia attended Sunday School, it did not take them long to locate Mrs. Anthony Corkell. Now a widow with seven children, she was living in the old frame house where she had lived when Virginia was in her teens. For five years Virginia lived in a basement apartment across the street. Mrs. Corkell's Irish background had fascinated the little girl. One of her friends recalled that Virginia even had a "mad crush" on John, one of the Corkell boys. Another Corkell boy was named Kevin, the name of one of the imaginary Bridey's friends. Note also the similarity of Corkell and Cork, the city where Bridey was supposed to have lived. And what was Mrs. Corkell's maiden name? Bridie (with an "ie") Murphy! (Gardner, 1957, p. 318).

The finding of Bridey was reported in *Time*, June 18, 1956, with the comment: "Yes, Virginia, there is a Bridey."

Other Fantastic Age Regressions

As an illustration of the extent to which a hypnotic subject will role play an extreme regression on demand, Kline (1953) had a subject regress beyond birth and down the evolutionary ladder that man has presumably climbed. When his subject was moving about the floor, apelike, she could not talk. According to a prearranged posthypnotic suggestion, she would communicate by sneezing involuntarily when an appropriate letter of the alphabet was presented; the letters she selected, when asked "What are you?" spelled out C-H-I-M-P-A-N-Z-E-E. Kline (1951) had earlier studied age progression in one subject, a young woman of 22 who was "progressed" to age 65. Although Kline felt that some of the changes in intelligence and masculinity-femininity scores were age appropriate, the findings are more interesting as unconscious role enactment than as a demonstration of the accuracy of a target age.

A somewhat more extensive demonstration of age progression was later attempted with medical students (Rubenstein and Newman, 1954). When progressed to a later stage of their careers as practicing physicians, they gave quite realistic performances, such as delivering a baby and starting its breathing and crying by holding it up and spanking it in a manner that they had witnessed in the delivery room of the hospital.

A number of practicing clinicians who employ hypnosis regularly use regression to the birth experience as part of their reconstruction of the case history. A patient of one of them told me that she first learned of her mother's rejection of her by recalling the experience of birth, and this was validated by her mother's admission to her, when confronted by the evidence, that she was in fact an unwanted child. Such testimony is, of course, worthless as evidence for the reality of the birth memory, but illustrates how readily a hypnotic patient may accept what is told her by her physician.

One story of a prior life came to our laboratory in this manner. A bright male college student had submitted to hypnosis in a social gathering and had found himself thoroughly at home in England in the mid-nineteenth century, speaking in contemporary terms about the Royal family, and knowing the names and ages of Victoria's children when they were young. He came to the laboratory convinced that this was a genuine reincarnation experience, but was willing to have it subjected to criticism. When carefully interviewed about events that might have provided memories that could have been evoked under hypnosis, it turned out that, many years earlier, he had made an intensive study of the British Royal family, although, with a subsequent change of interest from literary to scientific pursuits, he had forgotten all about it until the biographical search brought them to light. Although the evidence is against the reincarnation interpretation, it is interesting in its own right because it shows that memories may be recaptured without identification (as in source amnesia) and woven into a realistic story that is believed under hypnosis by the inventor of the story.

AGE REGRESSION AS AN ABILITY IN WHICH PEOPLE DIFFER

The scales used to test hypnotic responsiveness sample a great many different performances, and serve to give an idea of the manner in which these performances differ within a general population. Some kind of indicator is commonly chosen to make a quantitative rating of selected performance possible, although any one indicator is limited and fallible. In the construction of the Stanford Hypnotic Susceptibility Scale, Form C (Weitzenhoffer and Hilgard, 1962), we found that a handwriting change was associated often enough with regression to an early grade in school to serve conveniently as such an indicator. Examples of present and regressed handwriting are shown in Figure 6.

In the process of testing the regression we obtained other information that did not contribute to the total score, yet served to substantiate the use of the handwriting indicator of regression. Some results of such a comparison are presented in Table 1.

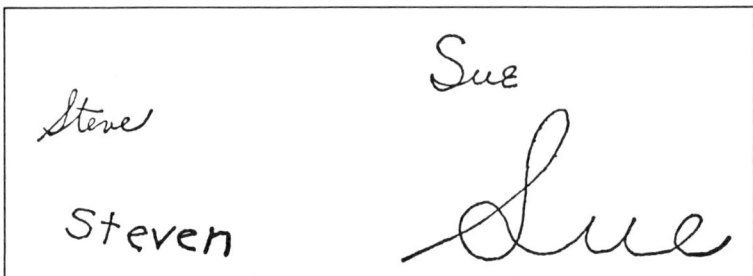

Figure 6 Normal and regressed handwriting. From Hilgard (1965, p. 170).

The data are given for the regression to the second grade; those from the fifth grade produced essentially the same relationships. Those who passed the handwriting change were predominantly judged to have illustrated good regression in other respects. As presented, the two estimates yield a correlation $r_t = .87$. The main point is that, by either criterion, less than half of the student population satisfactorily met the criterion of this rather simple age regression and therefore could be judged as able to regress satisfactorily under the conditions of testing.

An interesting aspect of the handwriting change, apart from a generally immature appearance of the writing at the supposed earlier grade levels, was a tendency to shift to printing from cursive script at the second-grade level. It has been a very widespread practice in American schools to teach children to print (to use "manuscript writing") before they are taught cursive writing. Hence the printed name would be characteristic of the second grade. The actual printing was often found to be somewhat too mature for the age, yet the compulsion to print was felt strongly by some of those who felt incompletely regressed. Among the 73 students in this sample who passed regression, 50 printed their names at the second-grade level, whereas the remaining 23 used cursive script.

The observing part of the hypnotized person was investigated by the hypnotist's question in the midst of the regression, "Do you know who I am?" This was done with the Stanford Profile Scale. The replies, from those for whom the question was asked, are summarized in Table 2. Of those judged not to have displayed regression, practically all identified the hypnotist correctly, as expected. Among those who were judged to be regressed, just under a third correctly identified the hypnotist, whereas the others mostly saw him as a stranger who had intruded into the regressed experience. One of my subjects, regressed to a birthday party in a park, saw me as the caretaker who was picking up paper on a pointed stick.

Those who saw the hypnotist as himself included some of the most hypnoti-

Table 1
HANDWRITING CHANGE AS AN INDICATOR OF AGE REGRESSION
(Modified from Hilgard, 1965, p. 199)

Regression as rated from change in handwriting (second grade)	Regression as judged by hypnotist from other evidence		Total (percent)
	Absent (percent)	Present (percent)	
Present	4	38	42
Absent	42	16	58
Total	46	54	100 ($N = 192$)

cally responsive by other criteria; thus the preservation of an observing part of the hypnotized person is compatible with a very rich hypnotic experience, including vivid regression. Some contact with the normal ego must remain for all subjects, or they would not be responsive to the suggestions to grow up again.

INTERPRETATIONS OF HYPNOTIC AGE REGRESSION

Because in hypnotic age regression the person commonly behaves as if a child again, just what is going on has invited speculation.

The Ablation Theory

The ablation theory interprets extreme hypnotic regression to mean that all habits and learning that took place after the age to which the person has been regressed are so extremely inhibited that they may be considered functionally ablated—functional only because they can be restored when the regression is terminated.

This extreme view scarcely requires refutation. It is not possible to reverse the growth of bones and muscles, even if the skills in using them are inhibited. An adult who takes the fetal posture in regression may *wish* to return to the womb, as in the case of Kathy (p. 34), but he cannot accurately make himself into a baby. Still, the claims of something of the sort are rather extreme, such as the reappearance of the Babinski reflex in a regressed adult (Gidro-Frank

Table 2

REPLIES TO QUESTION: "DO YOU KNOW WHO I AM?"
IN MIDST OF AGE REGRESSION
(Modified from Hilgard, 1965, p. 171)

Person hypnotist said to be	Judged regression	
	Absent (percent)	Present (percent)
1. Himself, the hypnotist	95	29
2. Someone else		
a. A stranger	–	52 ⎫
b. Friend of the family	5	16 ⎬ 71
c. Specified other	–	3 ⎭
Total	100	100
	(N = 20)	(N = 80)

and Bowersbuch, 1948), or the lack of the typical EEG in epilepsy when the subject was regressed to the time before the epilepsy developed (Kupfer, 1945), or the return of a visual disorder when regressed prior to the time of an operation that corrected it (Ford and Yeager, 1948). The evidence in all these studies is somewhat unreliable; the observations may be sound without the evidence pointing clearly to the nature of hypnotic regression. It may be recalled that Janet's Marie was also able to see when regressed prior to her blindness, but her blindness was obviously hysterical. In Ford and Yeager's case, if the surgery really cured the blindness, it is difficult to see how hypnosis could have reinstated it, unless, again, on the level of hallucination.

Age-Consistency Evidence

The age-consistency theory argues for the reality of age regression on the basis of the appropriateness of abilities associated with that age, not necessarily anything personally experienced by the subject. Hence age-specific abilities, such as intelligence-test responses or behavior appropriate to Piaget's stages of cognitive development, can be assessed to see how well age-specific regression suggestions hit their mark.

In the decade after World War II, a large number of these studies were performed including personality studies using the Rorschach test, when these tests were popular and hypnosis was finding renewed interest. They were well reviewed by Weitzenhoffer (1953) and are not reviewed here. In general, the studies found that there were indeed test scores appropriate to younger ages under regression, but they usually missed the target by scoring higher than they should have. Orne (1951) summarized the matter as he found it then by stating that the regressions were not, in fact, age accurate, but the subject creates a hallucinated environment appropriate to the suggestion, combines random memories from the period (and years before and after), and contributes a certain amount of confabulation.

The issue came to a head again with a serious investigation published in book form by Reiff and Scheerer (1959). The book included a theoretical discussion of memory and had many observations in a variety of contexts, but two features of the experiments have drawn the widest attention. The first is the reported heightened memory under hypnosis for early school experiences, such as names of teachers and fellow pupils, checked against contemporary records where possible. The second is the age-specific performances on Piaget-like tests. The authors used simulator controls to see what a nonhypnotic subject acting as if hypnotized would do in these test situations.

Consider, for example, the levels achieved on the Piaget hollow tube test. A green, a yellow, and a red bead were tied on a string, about four inches apart, in that order. A hollow tube 14 inches long and 1 inch in diameter permitted the beads to be placed inside it, out of sight, with the subject required to answer questions about the order of the beads. Having ascertained that the subject could name the beads by color, the experimenter said, "Now watch me carefully. I am going to put them through the tube like this." He then inserted the string of beads, the green one entering the tube first, and pulled the three beads through the tube to a point at which they were no longer visible. The experimenter then asked the subject, "Now, if I keep on pulling them through, which one will come out first, which one will be next, and which one will be next?" This is the first and easiest of six questions that the experimenter asks at each of the regressed ages. The most difficult question is to ask the subject to imagine that the experimenter had turned the tube through twenty 180-degree turns. Now in what order will the beads come out? The correct solution is to be able to state that, for even numbered turns, the original order will be preserved (hence holding for the 20 turns), whereas the reverse would be true for odd numbers. This is a superior performance, beyond age 10. The performance levels were defined by the six questions. The results as reported showed that the truly regressed averaged close to the expected developmental levels, usually slightly below; the simulators averaged above the levels, and they differed significantly from the regressed except at the youngest age.

The authors stated their conclusions from the age-specific findings thus:

1. The regressed subjects tended to function at a level consistent with the experimental age.

2. The regressed subjects functioned more consistently than the simulating subjects on the various tasks at each experimental age level.

3. When the regressed subjects deviated from the experimental age, they tended to function below that age level.

4. The simulating subjects tended to function above the experimental age level.

5. The lower the experimental age, the more the simulating subjects tended to function above that level.

Such results seemed to give rather dramatic support to the idea that highly hypnotizable subjects, when age regressed, behaved cognitively very much like children of that age, and the simulators, not hypnotized, were unable to match their performances.

These findings did not go unchallenged. A careful replication by O'Connell, Shor, and Orne (1970) serves as a useful illustration of how scientific knowledge progresses by experimental refinement of earlier investigations. These investigators followed the appropriate method of duplicating very closely the original study in its major respects, and their hypnotizable and regressed subjects behaved essentially the same as those in the Reiff and Scheerer study. They had modified the simulator control treatments, however, to conform more nearly to the practice that Orne had recommended too late for Reiff and Scheerer to have the benefit of his suggestions (Orne, 1959). Actually, Reiff and Scheerer had not treated their simulators symmetrically with the reals, having used one set of simulators for each age comparison and the same group of reals throughout. O'Connell, Shor, and Orne argued that practice in age regression might have improved the performance of the reals and might have improved the performances of the simulators also, had they had the opportunity. Hence in their replication, O'Connell, Shor, and Orne treated their nonhypnotizable simulators exactly as they did the reals, the experimenter not knowing which was which and unable to tell from their behavior as "regressed" subjects. The quantitative evidence bore this out: The differences between reals and simulators found by Reiff and Scheerer were not supported.

It should be noted that this negative bears on the special problems of *hypnotic* age regression, but it does not necessarily negate a *dissociative* component in the regressed behavior of the simulators. There appear to be residues from earlier styles of behavior that are recoverable in context, and what O'Connell, Shor, and Orne showed was that this recovery need not depend solely on hypnotic aptitude or a hypnotic state. This should not be altogether surprising when one thinks of sleep and dreaming. These may be influenced by hypnosis in the susceptible, but it does not require hypnotizability for a person to experience the dissociations of sleeping and dreaming. The results, although not crucial for dissociation theory, are important in that they caution against attributing too much to hypnosis. The question of memory facilitation associated with age regression is somewhat separable from that of the age consistency of performances of the cognitive ability type. Some memories are personal, dated in the past, and presumably revivable when the old context is recreated through the hallucinations of age regression. Reiff and Scheerer referred to such memories as *rememberances*, with an autobiographical index, and other memories as *memoria*, without such an index; this is a distinction that Tulving (1972) later made between episodic memory (memory for specific happenings) and semantic memory (memory for meanings, not autobiographical). In their study of contextual recall, Reiff and Scheerer first had the adults fill out a questionnaire regarding their residence and school experiences at age 4, then up through the fifth grade. The memories for the hypnotizable subjects were tested in hypnosis, without regression, and then with regression to the different ages. The results indicated better recall by the reals than by the simulators for ages 7 and 10.

Validation was attempted for four specific memories: (1) the school in which the subjects attended the second and fifth grades, (2) the name of the second-grade teacher, (3) the fifth-grade teacher's name, and (4) two fellow pupils in each of the classes. The investigators went to school records to check the names and dates and felt that their results validated the gain under age regression. In view of the other difficulties with the experimental design, O'Connell, Shor, and Orne were not convinced by these data.

The Role-Enactment Theory

At about the same time that the investigation was going on in Orne's laboratory, a doctoral dissertation in the same general area was being prepared in our laboratory by Suzanne Troffer. She was in touch with the workers in Orne's laboratory and knew of their work; thus no priority is involved because her dissertation bears an earlier date (Troffer, 1965). The experiment was done with the aid of an assistant who did not know the purpose of the experiment, but was given an appropriate rationale for what she was doing. Without the assistant's knowledge, each subject came from one of three groups: highly hypnotizable regressed subjects, highly hypnotizable subjects not hypnotized but simulating the role of regressed subjects, and nonhypnotizable subjects simulating the role. The assistant's purported duty was to test the subject with some of Reiff and Scheerer's tasks under two conditions; these were germane to the experiment, but the assistant was led to believe that they were the sole significant parameters and hence was not alerted to the detection of hypnosis in relation to role enactment. The two conditions consisted in different degrees of role support to regressed behavior. In the high role-support condition, the assistant behaved in a manner appropriate to an adult speaking to a child in a friendly and supportive manner as the subject was engaged in performing the requested tasks. Under the other condition, the assistant gave low support, interacting minimally with the subject, maintaining more of an observer role.

The results showed in general that the hypnotizable subjects were little benefited in their childlike behavior by being regressed rather than simulating regression. Both did somewhat better than the unhypnotizable role players, falling somewhat between the findings of Reiff and Scheerer and those of O'Connell, Shor, and Orne.

The most consistent finding of the experiment had to do with the effect of the high and low role-support conditions. For all three groups, the high role-support condition yielded more childlike performances than the low on all tasks. The support that the experimenter gave to the subject acting like a child is crucial in helping the subject, whether regressed or role playing, to maintain the illusion that he is indeed a child, and to behave accordingly.

The childlike behavior in regressed subjects may be subjectively convincing; the adult believes himself to be reliving the experiences of a child. This was amply attested to in the subjective reports from Troffer's subjects. In fact, some of the highly hypnotizable simulators became so involved in their simulation that they reported that they felt the reality of the return to childhood also, and it is possible that the role enactment acted for them as a form of self-hypnosis, despite instructions not to become hypnotized.

In conclusion, hypnotic age regression is not an ablation of everything later than the age of the regressed experience; it does not necessarily achieve accuracy in demonstrating age-specific abilities at the regressed age; it is not miraculous in uncovering experiences of birth or a prior life; but it is interesting in the subjectively convincing experience of reliving earlier experiences with hallucinatory intensity. The fact that many aspects of the regression can be achieved by nonhypnotizable subjects weakens the special role of hypnosis without denying the presence of dissociative features.

UTILITY OF AGE REGRESSION IN CLINICAL SETTINGS

These somewhat skeptical conclusions about the claims for hypnotic age regression in experimental settings need not detract from its usefulness in clinical settings. Memories for traumatic events may be concealed through repression or amnesia in a form that can be uncovered through hypnosis, as indicated in the case material quoted in the studies of multiple personality. Witnesses whose memories for traumatic events have been disrupted through aroused emotions may have their recall facilitated through reliving. The vividness of the regressed recall of more pleasant times has been used in therapy with cancer patients to turn aside from the present and to relive enjoyable experiences, resulting in pain reduction, improved appetite, and more comfortable sleep. These benefits are products of dissociation, and the dissociations are typically furthered by hypnotic procedures. Matters of dispute in theoretical discussion may not always be pertinent when the goal is a practical one, as in helping a suffering patient.

NOTES

Reviews of the earlier studies of age regression in hypnosis may be found in Barber (1969, p. 179–192; 1972, p. 143–146), Gebhard (1961), Reiff and Scheerer (1959, p. 64–81), and Weitzenhoffer (1953, p. 184–195).

Characteristic Behavior

The possible therapeutic role of separating the memory of the experience from its emotion at the time came to Horowitz's attention from an unpublished study by Clyde (1947). This has some resemblance to Janet's method, except that Janet brought it about by altering the cognition also. The catharsis in the protected environment of psychoanalytic therapy may not be so different, because the experienced emotion in that setting is likely to be much milder than the original panic that it relieves, and in psychoanalytic treatment a much longer time is devoted to relieving the problem.

Reiff and Scheerer pointed out that, under some circumstances, it may very well be possible to be more accurate in a waking cognitive recall of an event than in hypnotic age regression in which personal-emotional aspects play a larger part.

Regression to Birth and to Prior Existence

The account of Bridey Murphy owes a great deal to Gardner (1957). The fact that so many distortions of memory can be found in hypnotic age regression, including the creation of fantasies of birth and earlier life, shows that memories revived under hypnosis, no matter how convincing to the subject, cannot be trusted until verified by external criteria (e.g., Kelsey, 1953). The "will-to-believe" may be so strong in the hypnotist as well as the subject as to give the impression of validity. Committed belief is an old story that has sustained astrologers and fortune-tellers over the centuries.

Individual Differences in the Ability to Experience Age Regression

There has been very little in the way of a "census" of age regression abilities; hence the chapter relies on the results of the standardization samples from the Stanford

Hypnotic Susceptibility Scales, Form C, and the Stanford Profile Scales, Form II, in which age regression occurs.

Barber and Calverley (1966) tested a short regression, based on a classroom experiment to be recalled later either under hypnosis with regression suggestions or with regression suggestions without hypnosis. However, they used very superficial criteria of regression, evident because *all* those in the hypnotized group met their criteria, although they were unselected for hypnotic responsiveness, and 70% of the nonhypnotized succeeded. A somewhat comparable experiment was conducted in the Stanford laboratory in 1965 by Errol Schubot and Bruce Sanders (1966). Subjects were brought to the laboratory for the ostensible purpose of establishing norms on a number of simple tests to be used later in our experiments. They did this in small groups, in which some finished and some did not because of the time allowances, but all were thanked for helping to decide what time limits should be assigned to each item. Some weeks later all were brought back and tested individually in much the manner of the Barber and Calverley study, some with no hypnosis at all (and no suggestions of regression), others hypnotized with suggestions of regression. The unhypnotized subjects recalled as many of the tasks they had performed as the hypnotized ones, but the truly regressed often described vividly the reinstatement of the prior experience, including the emotions involved in their competition with others taking the test at the same time, and a hallucinated experience of being around the same table, with the test before them and a pencil in hand. When they looked down at the test sheet, however, it was blank. Even though those in the hypnotic portion of the experiment had been preselected on the basis of known hypnotic responsiveness, not all of them indicated satisfactory regression by the criteria used in our laboratory, thus contradicting the generality of regression described by Barber and Calverley.

Interpretations of Hypnotic Age Regression

The three interpretations of hypnotic age regression are designed to answer different questions and hence are not as contradictory as they seem.

The ablation interpretation attempts to account for a revivification of a previous event in the person's life—usually involving either specific or massive physiological manifestations. Because these manifestations are revived even though there has been subsequent surgery or therapy to correct them, the ablation interpretation is that the regression suggestions have temporarily obliterated these later events (Erickson, 1937; Erickson and Kubie, 1941; Spiegel, Shor, and Fishman, 1945). However, the possibility of reproducing an enactment of the earlier behavior through a contextually "conditioned" or "fantasied" revival brings the behavior within the orbit of response to implicit demands, albeit conformity to the demands need not be deliberate or conscious.

The age-consistency explanation goes beyond the matching of cognitive performances with age-specific norms to reinstating a total configuration of personality appropriate to the age. Puzzling questions of this kind are not settled by a few studies. In a recent investigation those of high hypnotic responsiveness were found to be better at reproducing age-consistent performances on Piaget tests than those less hypnotically responsive, even though none were hypnotized, and the instruction was simply to behave like a child of a stated age (Attard and Holden, 1976). The success was found to be related to a talent for hypnosis, rather than to hypnosis itself.

Walker, Garrett, and Wallace (1976) have opened up an interesting possibility for the recovery of a once-lost childhood talent. They found that older subjects through hypnotic age-regression could in some instances recover their very vivid imagery known as eidetic imagery, even though no longer capable of it, provided they had been able to demonstrate it as children.

Age Regression in Hypnotherapy

For a discussion of various ways in which age regression is useful in hypnotherapy, see Kline (1960). An illustrative case has been given by Fromm (1965).

CHAPTER

AMNESIA AND REPRESSION

Amnesia, as a temporary loss of memories that may later be recovered, is the key to the understanding of dissociation. Disruptions of the continuity of memories plays a central role in the interpretation of dissociative phenomena (Chapter 11).

Repression and amnesia are similar in that they imply intact memories that are in storage but are not retrievable except under appropriate circumstances. Amnesia is the more neutral term, for repression implies the theory that memories are excluded by the motivation to avoid troublesome consequences that would ensue were the memories recalled.

As we continue to examine the phenomena of dissociation, we must take a closer look at these processes. It will be recalled that amnesia was shown to be an important feature of fugues and multiple personalities; thus in this sense we are carrying further the exploration that we have already started.

THE NATURE OF MEMORY

If amnesia and repression are disorders of memory, we would do well to examine the normal processes of memorizing and of forgetting before turning to the distortions of memory. Fortunately, the study of memory has been a favorite among psychologists ever since psychology became experimental, and the knowledge of memory has been greatly enriched within the last decade. It all started with Hermann Ebbinghaus (1885), who performed very careful experiments on himself that set the general pattern of experimental studies of memory for the next 80 years. The general pattern was that of rote verbal learning, in which verbal materials—often nonsense syllables—were memorized under standard conditions, and retention was tested under other conditions. A very important literature developed, leading to a number of summarizing volumes along the way; a representative one is that of McGeoch and Irion (1952). Motor skills were studied according to the same general pattern, except that more attention was commonly given to the acquisition of skills than to their retention. This came about because, once acquired, skills are long retained, as anyone knows who learned to ride a bicycle in his youth, only to try it again many years later for exercise or to save fuel.

With the emergence of cognitive psychology, the whole emphasis changed, and since about 1965 the older type of experiment has all but disappeared. The new theorists (and experimenters) have been described as *memory theorists*, as contrasted with the earlier more empiricist students of verbal learning (Tulving and Madigan, 1970). The conceptual problems have become more complex, with greater attention to the organization of materials, coding, rehearsal strategies, and a distinction between short-term and long-term memory. As an example of this newer way of looking at memory, consider the block diagram presented as Figure 7.

The purpose of such a diagram is to show where the problems lie, rather than to offer a theoretical solution, although some theoretical styles of explanation are implied. The implied processes are only in part sequential. The stimulus input must be attended to, recognized, and coded. Although this is a "first step," it is evident that cognitive processes and previous memories are used in this very first step. They are implied by the arrow that leads to the first block from "control processes." The material to be memorized then is coded in a preliminary manner and enters into short-term memory. It usually must be rehearsed immediately, as shown by the arrow circling back to the short-term memory block. Some information may be lost from short-term memory through ordinary forgetting, but that which is retained is transferred to the long-term memory, where it is assimilated or organized into memory structures. These are some of the cognitive structures that we repeatedly meet. Modern memory experiments deal with the problems to which the block diagram calls attention and with others not represented on this diagram, such as techniques by which memories are retrieved from long-term memory.

Most problems that have been raised in this new perspective remain to be solved, although a large number of new facts and relationships have emerged.

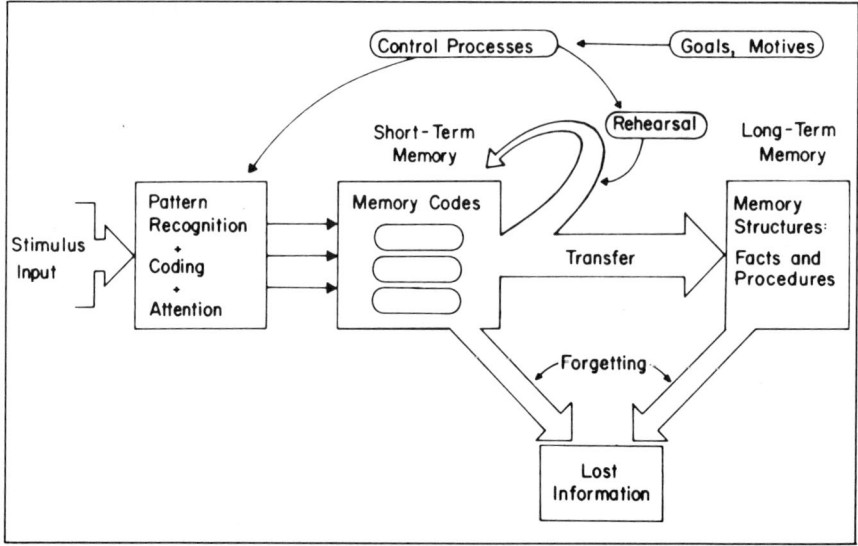

Figure 7 Diagram representing modern theories of memory. From Hilgard and Bower (1975, p. 578).

As an illustration of the cautions needed, Hilgard and Bower (1975, page 583f.) have listed six problems with the block diagram as presented:

1. Long-term memory is involved in pattern-perception and coding at the very beginning of the process, and this is not evident from the diagram.
2. The requirement of active rehearsal for short-term memory does not appear essential for nonverbal memory.
3. Rehearsal is not simply repetition, but is often a process of organizing the material for retrieval.
4. Possibly material may be entered into short-term and long-term memory at the same time through some sort of parallel processing rather than in sequential order from short to long term.
5. Often, new learning is imbedded in a context of familiar learning, and when storing in memory the learner makes a distinction between what he already knows and what is being newly acquired. This complex process is not represented.
6. The later retrieval of an item depends on "depth of processing" at the time of learning; thus if it is incorporated in one kind of organized structure it will be more readily retrieved than if in another.

These statements are intended to indicate the seriousness with which the present students of memory face the complexities of the information processing that goes on in memorizing and retrieving. The perplexities mean, however, that as we continue our effort to understand amnesia we do not have a generally accepted memory theory firm enough to require only one interpretation. It may be that the studies of amnesia will make their own contribution to the understanding of memory.

There are various demands made on memory, reflected in different kinds of remembering. Some memories are clearly autobiographical, and the memories are dated in the past. These are sometimes called *redintegrative* or *episodic* memories, because they reinstate particular events on the basis of appropriate cues. The word *souvenir* (originally meaning *to remember* in French) is illustrative. The faded pressed flower may be enough to reinstate the social occasion when it was in full bloom; it is a redintegrative cue. Recall of something previously learned—the stanza of a poem—represents another kind of memory performance (*semantic* memory, according to Tulving), and its success does not require recollecting when it was learned. We have a great deal of information that we can recall, such as a word in our vocabulary, without the slightest idea when it was first learned. *Recognition* is another kind of memory; all that the task implies is the ability to say that what is perceived has been met before. Many people say that it is easier to remember a face than a name, without noting that the face must only be recognized, whereas the name must be recalled—different memory tasks. Disruptions of memory may affect these several performances differently.

Three aspects of contemporary studies of memory may be mentioned as pertinent to later discussions in this chapter and in later chapters: directed forgetting, imagery as a facilitator of memory, and hierarchical organization of memories.

Directed Forgetting

Directed forgetting means deliberate forgetting of something that has been experimentally presented as part of a memory task. Bjork (1970) called this positive forgetting; Epstein (1972) attempted an explanation while naming it directed forgetting. An experiment can indicate how this shows up in the laboratory. The experimenter presents single words to the subject at regular intervals with the instruction to the subject that he will be asked to recall the whole list later. Even though, according to the primacy principle, the early items should be the best learned, if the experimenter at some point tells the subject that he can forget all the words up to that point but will be responsible only for the words to come, his recall shows that he has indeed forgotten them when unexpectedly he is later asked to try to recall them despite the instruction to forget. Such memory traces as persist from the earlier items did not appear to compete with the new items learned (Bruce and Papay, 1970).

It may be noted that directed forgetting is not in principle very different from a hypnotic suggestion to forget. To compare the processes, serious efforts would have to be made to determine if the "forgotten" items could be recovered by more subtle methods. If recovered, directed forgetting would be a model for suggested amnesia. In any case, as we shall see, directed forgetting is a *component* of the behavioral response in suggested amnesia, even though something else is inferred to be operative.

Imagery

Imagery as a factor in memory has come to the fore with experiments by Paivio (1971), and Bower (1972). They, and others at work in the area, have argued that mental imagery is one of the primary modes of representation of information in memory, and it differs from the verbal system in important respects.

> For example, the imagery system seems specialized for dealing with information presented simultaneously, in parallel, from sources distributed about in space, whereas the verbal system would appear specialized for dealing with information presented sequentially, in series, from sources distributed over time. (Hilgard and Bower, 1975, p. 588).

In many experiments with paired-associate learning, it is found that those who either spontaneously or by instruction use imaginary intermediaries to structure the pairs to be associated succeed far better than those who rely on verbal rehearsal alone. Of course, this has long been known by the "memory experts" who demonstrate their skills and then propose to teach a "system" that commonly involves exactly such imaginary intermediaries. The remarkable man studied by the eminent Russian psychologist Alexander Luria could remember a long list of objects by positioning them in imagination along a walk from Pushkin Square down Gorky Street. He could memorize lists of more than 100 items of various kinds and recall them a year or more later (Luria, 1968). It has taken laboratory psychologists a long time to return to the recommendation of mnemonic devices, after having previously dismissed them as excess baggage.

The tendency to tease about mnemonic devices as unnecessary crutches was illustrated in one of the leading textbooks of his time by Dashiell (1928, p. 383). Indicating that success depended on the resolve of the person to improve, he ended his discussion with the statement: "If a given course of mnemonics costing ten dollars profits a man, the same course bought for twenty dollars would profit him still more." To make the case clearer, he added a footnote quoting from the well-known humorist Stephen Leacock:

The best illustration . . . is the series of the names of the Presidents of the United States in order of office. . . . Take the first link in the chain. We want to remember that after Washington came Adams. . . . We connect with the name Washington anything that it suggests, and then something that that suggests, and so on until we happen to get to Adams—
Washington evidently suggests washing.
Washing evidently suggests laundry.
Laundry evidently suggests the Chinese.
The Chinese evidently suggest missionaries.
Missionaries evidently suggest the Bible.
The Bible begins with Adam.
How ridiculously simple!

Hierarchical Structure

This refers to the organizing of knowledge into relationships that are semantically meaningful so that retrieval processes are more orderly and efficient. For example, if the experimenter "preorganizes" the material to be learned to reveal the hierarchical relationships inherent in the material, the subject greatly benefits from this assistance (Bower and others, 1969). Internal relationships within cognitive structures are important, and the possibility exists that some of these are disrupted in memory interference.

This is sufficient background regarding the contemporary psychology of memory to permit an understanding of how the facts of amnesia and repression can fit into it.

FUNCTIONAL AND ORGANIC AMNESIA IN MAN

Transient memory losses are very common, and if we think of those instances in which we are at a loss to recall a familiar name, only to have it suddenly come to mind, some experience of amnesia is almost universal. However, there are amnesias that are far more severe. Some of these arise in the course of living, without any disease or concussion to cause the problem; these are the functional amnesias, often relieved by psychological methods. If the amnesia has been caused by a brain injury in an accident or by brain surgery undertaken to relieve some other problem or because of some kind of poisoning in chemical or disease processes, it is called organic.

Functional Amnesia

Every now and then the newspapers carry an account of someone found wandering around who does not know who he is or how he got there. Otherwise he appears quite normal. These experiences are not very different from the fugues described in the last chapter, except that when a fugue is over the person is his old self. If the fugue is a loss of identity only, with no new identity established, it would be described as a major instance of amnesia. The distinction between an amnesic episode and a fugue is not a very sharp one.

Some years ago a man was found wandering the streets of Eugene, Oregon, not knowing his name or where he had come from. The police, who were baffled by his inability to identify himself, called in Lester Beck (1936), a psychologist they knew to be familiar with hypnosis, to see if he could be of assistance. He found the man eager to cooperate and by means of hypnosis and other methods was able to reconstruct the man's history. Little detailed information came from the first hypnotic session, although he recalled his wife's first name, and with that as a cue to further associations, he was restored to his family and friends in another city.

Following domestic difficulties, the man had gone on a drunken spree completely out of keeping with his earlier social behavior, and he had subsequently suffered deep remorse. His amnesia was motivated in the first place by the desire to exclude from memory the mortifying experiences that had gone on during the guilt-producing episode. He succeeded in forgetting all the events before and after this behavior that might remind him of it. Hence the amnesia spread from the critical incident to events before and after it, and he completely lost his sense of personal identity.

When his memories returned, he could recall events before the drinking episode and subsequent happenings, but the deeper repression of the period of which he was most ashamed successfully protected him from recalling its disagreeable events. When he was rehypnotized and a search made for these still-hidden memories, he became so agitated that Beck decided to let well enough alone.

This man illustrates a very common feature of an amnesia of this sort, namely, the limiting of memory loss to personal memories. The man had no trouble recalling the ordinary vocabulary required to carry on a conversation; he could count and use his money and buy railway tickets to a selected destination.

In addition to a protracted amnesia of this kind, a shorter amnesia commonly occurs, especially among people in later life, called *transient global amnesia*. Although some cerebral vascular insufficiency is suspected, no evidence can be found by neurological examination, including the EEG. In the midst of the attack the sufferer may show no evident signs; he may have lunch, play golf, drive his car to the office. Once there, he may have forgotten where he was, fail to name the day and date correctly, and show other signs of memory loss. All may come back in an hour or so, as quickly as it was lost. The person usually has no further attacks.

Organic Amnesia

There is often some uncertainty between functional and organic causes of behavior. Cases similar to those of global transient amnesia just described may, in fact, be the result of a problem of cerebral circulation; even though the memory returns, there may later be a massive stroke that leaves the person paralyzed or even dead.

Concussion is a frequent source of amnesia. The game of football as played in America provides enough cases for the problem to have a slang name among the players: those mildly concussed have been "dinged." Of 18 mildly concussed college football players interviewed, four had short-term memory impairment without any marked disturbance of consciousness. They could not recall the physical or psychological examination given them immediately after it was completed; all these recovered their memories within an hour (Yarnell and Lynch, 1973). For six other players with concussions, the memories for events just before the injury remained intact for a few minutes, but recall was lost 3–20 minutes later, only to return subsequently (Lynch and Yarnell, 1973).

The role of parts of the brain in amnesia can be inferred from cases with severe concussions or wounds, but the precise centers of brain involvement remain a matter of interest and study. One portion of the brain that appears to be significantly involved is the hippocampus, an area in the temporal lobes bordering on the lateral ventricles. Its involvement was found in a case that came to autopsy and was felt to confirm the authors' belief that the hippocampus is a "key-of-access" to stored memories (Penfield and Mathieson, 1974).

Surgical removal of the temporal lobes in the hope of relieving severe epileptic seizures led to the most famous recent case of organic amnesia, that known as H. M. The case was originally recounted by W. B. Scoville and Brenda Milner (1957), and H. M. has been much studied since, including a 14-year follow-up (Milner, Corkin, and Teuber, 1968).

This brief account gives the essential history and the main features of the symptoms:

This young man (H. M.), a motor-winder by trade, had had no obvious memory disturbance before his operation, having, for example, passed his high school examinations without difficulty. His birth and early history had been uneventful, except for a minor head injury sustained when he fell off his bicycle at the age of seven. Minor attacks began one year later, and then, at the age of 16, he began to have generalized seizures which, despite heavy medication, increased in frequency and severity until, by the age of 27, he was no longer able to work. Both neurological and radiological findings at this time were said to be normal, and EEG studies indicated diffuse, rather than focal abnormality.

Nevertheless, his prospects were by then so desperate that, on September 1, 1953, the radical bilateral medial temporal lobe resection was performed. The patient was drowsy for the first few postoperative days but then, as he became more alert, a severe memory impairment was apparent. He could no longer recognize the hospital staff, apart from Dr. Scoville himself, whom he had known for many years; he did not remember and could not relearn the way to the bathroom, and he seemed to retain nothing of the day-to-day happenings in the hospital. At the same time, it was discovered that he had an extensive though patchy, retrograde amnesia, such that he did not remember the death of a favorite uncle three years before, nor anything of the period spent in the hospital before the operation, but did recall a few trivial incidents that had taken place just before his admission to the hospital. His early memories were seemingly vivid and intact, his speech was normal, and his social behavior and emotional responses were entirely appropriate (Milner, 1966, p. 112f.).

The major defect that H. M. shows is impairment of recent memory. He shows this in many ways. When his family moved, he could not learn the new address, even after they had lived at the new address for a year. If left to find his way home, he would go to the old house. He reads the same magazines over and over again without any sense that he has seen them before.

Amnesias are commonly classified as retrograde—forgetting of something learned before the amnesia set in—and anterograde, inability to remember something learned after the onset of amnesia. H. M.'s deficit is primarily of the anterograde type, and his retrograde amnesia has diminished somewhat over the years, although he remains somewhat confused over the order of events that preceded the operation.

An experiment with H. M. showed how fleeting his new acquisitions are. If given two stimuli easily discriminable, such as clicks of different loudness, tones, colors, or nonsense figures, he was able to state whether they were the same or different without difficulty when they followed each other without delay. Normal subjects can make this kind of comparison between the members of a pair readily over an interval of 60 seconds, but H. M. made numerous errors as the interval was increased from immediate succession to 60 seconds.

The case of H. M. reminds us of two pertinent facts of memory loss: first, the temporal lobes are importantly involved in memory acquisition; second, the temporal lobe is not the "seat" of long-term memory, or H. M. would not have had as little retrograde amnesia.

Memory losses associated with chemicals provide additional cases of amnesia. Alcoholic blackouts represent one type. In a study of 13 male alcoholics with a history of blackouts (momentary lapses of consciousness) Tamerin and others (1971) found that short-term memory was progressively impaired with higher levels of intoxication; impairment of 24-hour recall was related to the amount of alcohol ingested the preceding day. Blackouts occurred particularly among those with short-term memory loss; unfortunately, evidence was not given of the extent to which the memories were recoverable. There is some evidence from other studies that the problem may be, in part, one of retrieval rather than memory storage, because, when next under the influence of alcohol, the subject may recall what he had forgotten while sober. The evidence is somewhat skimpy, however, and in an experiment on successful retrieval the subjects were nonalcoholic young men given nonextreme doses of alcohol for the purposes of the experiment (Goodwin, 1971).

The amnesic effects of some of the drugs used as anesthetics are striking, especially because the patient is often in verbal contact with the surgeon and others during the operation. One of the barbiturates (thiopental, trade name Sodium Pentothal) is very striking in this respect. In one of our experiments the subject under intravenous thiopental intoxication was able to recognize people who were present, to carry on sensible conversation, and to perform laboratory-type memory tasks. Once the session was ended, however, and the subject slept off the effects of the drug, he was often amnesic for what happened during the session (Osborn and others, 1967). An effort to recover the lost memories through hypnosis was only partially successful. It is clinically reported that obstetric patients given thiopental may show signs of great anguish during the delivery, with verbal complaints as well, only to report after resting that the experience was pleasant and pleasurable throughout. There is some hint that only the anguish is unremembered (Editorial, Lancet, 1974).

Even the most widely used tranquilizer (diazepam, trade name Valium) produces a short amnesia when given by parenteral infusion, that is, by injection rather than by mouth. Both the level of sedation and the amount of amnesia vary from person to person with diazepam only; when amnesia occurred, it lasted an average of 24 minutes in one study (Flinn, Wineland, and Peterson, 1975).

The recovery of memory under general anesthesia has been the subject of study over recent years. Results suggest that more may be registered in the memory store than is normally reported after the anesthesia is removed.

In one of the more carefully controlled studies, Levinson (1967) arranged an experiment that could be carried out in the operating room. Anesthesia was induced by a combination of chemical agents, including pentothal, flaxidil, ether, nitrous oxide, and oxygen. The patient's EEG was monitored to indicate that the anesthesia was profound. At a signal, the anesthetist stopped everything, saying audibly that the patient's lips were too blue, and that he was going to give more oxygen. He then pumped the rebreathing bag and said that everything was now all right and that the operation should proceed.

Each of ten patients, known to be hypnotizable, had an operation in which the above scene was reenacted. When interviewed a month later, the patient remembered nothing in the normal state. He was then hypnotized and told to relive the operation. The kind of report obtained may be illustrated by a verbatim report from one of the patients. During the hypnotic recall session, the hypnotized subject was told to lift one finger when the operation was starting, and to signal later if anyone was talking. When talking was first indicated, this conversation occurred:

> Who is it, who's talking?
> Dr. Viljoen. He's saying my color is gray.
> Yes?
> He's going to give me some oxygen.
> What are his words?
> He said I will be all right now.
> Yes?
> They're going to start again now. I can feel him bending close to me.

The experiment was not uniformly successful, but four of the ten patients were able to repeat words spoken by the anesthetist. Four others became anxious about reliving the operation and woke from hypnosis. Two reported that they had heard nothing.

The relationship of anesthesia to amnesia is complex, because the events recovered through hypnosis were apparently not in awareness at all before they were recorded in memory, unless they were briefly registered and as promptly forgotten. We meet other situations later in which this problem arises.

AMNESIA IN LABORATORY ANIMALS

In an effort to throw light on the neural mechanisms of memory and forgetting, hundreds of experiments have been conducted with animals since the use of electroconvulsive shock (ECS) with psychiatric patients was shown to be accompanied by amnesia. The use of ECS was introduced by Cerletti and Bini in 1938, and the disorders of memory were immediately noted. The animal experiments did not begin immediately; the first of them was performed by Duncan in 1949. Since then, there has been a continuous flood, which it would be impossible to review in a short space.

Many parameters have been investigated, but for our purposes the most interesting experiments are those on the recovery of the retrograde amnesia produced by the shock. A method that has come to be known as "the reminder effect" has been widely used in these recovery functions. The reminder effect is based on the assumption that the memory defect is one of retrieval rather than consolidation. If that is the case, a few relearning trials ought to suffice to reinstate the cues; if the memory is actually stored, it should then show recovery. Most of these experiments have used aversive learning (often avoidance of foot shock), but the method has been generalized to appetitive responses (food seeking) as well (Miller, Ott, Berk, and Springe, 1974). The debate goes on over consolidation or retrieval, but there is enough recovery, even following complete amnesia, for the relationship to functional amnesia to be instructive (DeVietti and Hopfer, 1974).

Another method for reversing ECS amnesia is to inject activating drugs, such as amphetamine (Mah and Albert, 1975). Quartermain and Botwinick (1975) have shown reversal of the amnesia through the administration of biogenic amines. Strychnine may also serve to reduce the amnesia (Duncan and Hunt, 1972).

Amnesias can be produced in animals by a number of drugs; the experiments are not limited to ECS. A number of them have been done with purmycin, which is especially effective with mice (Flexner and Flexner, 1975, for references). Because these amnesias are also reversible, the possibilities of restorable memories that were previously not available appear to be well established.

HYPNOTIC AMNESIA

Although mention has been made of hypnosis from time to time in the exploration of the amnesias that occur spontaneously or as a result of organic conditions, nothing very specific to hypnosis has thus far been described.

The occurrence of posthypnotic amnesia was discovered by Puységur prior to 1784, when his book appeared. Because this state resembled sleepwalking, in which the events of the nocturnal wanderings are also forgotten, he named the condition "artificial somnambulism," and the highly hypnotizable person is even today referred to by clinical hypnotists as a somnambulist, or somnambule.

Recent studies of hypnotic amnesia have attempted to answer a number of questions, such as:

1. Is posthypnotic amnesia characteristic of the hypnotic condition, or is it the result of expectation, either suggested or implied?
2. Are there several varieties of hypnotic amnesia?
3. How widespread is the ability to have posthypnotic amnesia?
4. What relation has been demonstrated between posthypnotic amnesia and ordinary forgetting?
5. What do details of responses to the release signal tell about the nature of hypnotic amnesia as a psychological process?

Answers to these and other questions about amnesia are all relevant to the study of dissociation, because amnesia is a prime representative of dissociative processes. We may turn now to the evidence bearing on these questions.

The highly hypnotizable person readily experiences posthypnotic amnesia; thus it is difficult to separate spontaneous amnesia from suggested amnesia. In a study designed especially for this purpose, conducted on 91 students, we found far less spontaneous amnesia (about 7% of the subjects showed it), than suggested amnesia (35%) (Hilgard and Cooper, 1965). How much the metaphor of sleep provides an implied suggestion of amnesia is not clear. As shown by Evans and Thorn (1966), unless recovery from amnesia is studied, the results on spontaneous amnesia are ambiguous; nonhypnotized subjects will forget some items experienced without any need to attribute the forgetting to amnesia. It is much clearer to experiment with suggested amnesia and its reversal, because the matter of expectations is better controlled than in spontaneous amnesia.

There are several varieties of hypnotic amnesia, not all of which are posthypnotic. These include (1) posthypnotic recall amnesia, an amnesia for the events within the hypnotic session; (2) posthypnotic recall amnesia for material taught during the hypnotic session, hence a failure of memory for something intentionally learned; (3) posthypnotic source amnesia, a retention of material taught during the hypnotic session, with a forgetting of when and how the material was learned; (4) posthypnotic partial amnesia, an amnesia for only some of the material by subjects capable of more massive amnesia; and (5) amnesia for some within-trance learning while the subject remains hypnotized.

Source amnesia, as introduced originally by Thorn (1960) and Evans and Thorn (1966), usually consists in teaching some little-known information, such as the color that an amethyst turns on being heated, or the population of Singapore. If the subject, when no longer hypnotized, is able to give these answers readily but is confused about how he happens to know the answers, he illustrates source amnesia. He may search for a rationalization as to why he happens to possess the knowledge. In a class demonstration, I once taught a hypnotized subject the populations of some remote cities in the United States, and later, not hypnotized, he was quite surprised to be able to give detailed census answers. On further questioning, he decided that he must have learned these in the course of a television program he had heard on the sizes of cities that supported local television stations.

Although Evans and Thorn (1966) thought the distinction between recall amnesia and source amnesia was great enough that they should be considered independent phenomena, both Cooper (1966) and Gheorghiu (1969) found that the subjects capable of source amnesia tended to be the same ones capable of recall amnesia; thus the differences appear to be more a matter of actual or implied differences in the form of suggestion.

The distribution of amnesia susceptibility among a general population of college students is bimodal, as shown in Figure 8. It is coherent with the interpretation that the lower mode is the result of normal forgetting in an incidental learning situation of this kind and has little to do with hypnosis. The truly hypnotized subjects may then yield the upper mode, with an undistributed maximum because those with extreme scores could have shown more amnesia had the test permitted it. Cooper and Moore (1967) carried out the necessary analysis and performed an experimental test by studying the forgetting of items when these were performed without any hypnotic induction and no reference to hypnosis; only motor items of the hypnotic scales were used, and no amnesia was suggested. The result was a distribution of normal forgetting that was a close match to the hypothesized curve that would fit the lower mode of the data found in the hypnotic distribution. It is quite clear that the data obtained in the ordinary testing of posthypnotic amnesia are a mixture of ordinary forgetting and true amnesia. If we follow Cooper's analysis, the distribution of true amnesia begins with scores near the mean of the nonhypnotic forgetting curve, with some four of ten items forgotten; the mean items forgotten by the truly amnesic comes close to nine of the ten items forgotten. The genuinely amnesic subjects, by this method of judging, represent some 27% of the total college population.

A better measure of amnesia would rely not only on the items forgotten but

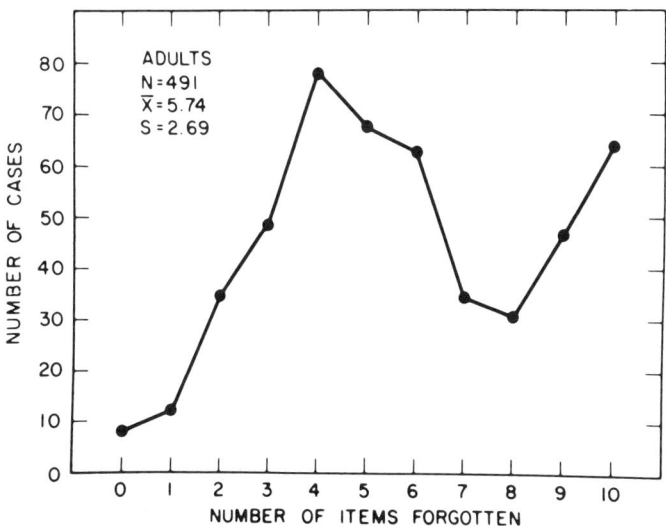

Figure 8 Distribution of posthypnotic amnesia in a college population. Cooper (1972, p. 232).

also on the items recovered, accepting the operational definition of amnesia as forgetting followed by recovery. This method has been proposed by Nace, Orne, and Hammer (1974). They found that the residual forgetting after amnesia was removed was alike for the high and the low hypnotizables, showing the difference between ordinary forgetting and reversible amnesia. The few items not recovered following the reversal of amnesia suggestions may represent true forgetting of items more deeply inhibited. Only further study will explain some of these finer details.

The relation of amnesia to ordinary forgetting has other facets. For example, are those with poorer memories under ordinary conditions more susceptible to amnesia? The evidence is against this; many of those highly hypnotizables who are most amnesic do in fact recover nearly all of the items, showing memory equal to the best. The independence of the two measures is indicated in one experiment in which, instead of amnesia suggestions, opposite suggestions were given to facilitate memory. For the highly responsive, both directions of suggestion appeared to have the appropriate effect (Saito, 1969).

What can be learned about the distinction between amnesia and ordinary forgetting by a more careful analysis of the responses? In a series of studies, Evans and Kihlstrom have explored the possibility that amnesia disrupts the ordinary retrieval process (Evans and Kihlstrom, 1973; Kihlstrom, 1975, 1977; Kihlstrom and Evans, 1976). They have shown this by the order in which items are recalled when amnesia is partial. If the partial retention is a result of ordinary forgetting, as by the less hypnotizable subjects, they found that items tend to be recalled in the chronological order in which they appeared. However, if the same number of items have been forgotten through hypnotic amnesia, the recall of the residual items appears to be in random order. When the amnesia is lifted, the recall of the rest of the items may be structured in the order that the items were learned (Kihlstrom, 1972). This means that the stored memory may have remained orderly and that the retrieval of the items was disrupted by the amnesia.

The studies of Evans and Kihlstrom help to explain a paradox that bears very clearly on problems of dissociation. Memory experiments can be arranged according to the standard retroactive inhibition paradigm, with items A learned and later recalled with intervening learning of items B. Recall of A items is interfered with by the intervening learning of B items, confirmed by appropriate control experiments. To adapt this as a test of the nature of hypnotic amnesia, the intervening items are inhibited by amnesia suggestions to see whether they will then no longer interfere (or will interfere less) with the recall of the earlier acquired A items. A number of experiments tell the same story: the interference is not reduced by the amnesia. If Evans and Kihlstrom are correct, the organized memories have not been disrupted by the amnesia, and it is this organized memory structure that is responsible for the retroactive inhibition.

How is Hypnotic Amnesia Produced?

Despite all that is known about hypnotic amnesia, its mechanisms are elusive. If it were better understood, many of the puzzles of hypnosis would be resolved.

1. The first and most impressive characteristic of the amnesic response is the *power of words* in producing and alleviating the amnesia. An effective verbal suggestion can be made directly in hypnosis ("When I ask you to recall what you have just learned, you will be unable to do so"), or the suggestion can be made that the amnesic response will occur posthypnotically ("After you have been aroused from hypnosis and I ask you to recall the things you have done while hypnotized, you will be unable to do so"). The posthypnotic form is the most familiar, but that is merely a convention deriving from the historically observed occurrence of spontaneous posthypnotic amnesia. A posthypnotic suggestion is not essential; amnesia to suggestions activated while the subject remains hypnotized can also be demonstrated. The power of words is again evident when the amnesia is reversed ("Now you can remember everything").

Some subjects report very little but surprise that the amnesia occurs and that the recovery is prompt. In one of our experiments, amnesia was tested within hypnosis for a short list of words that had just been learned to mastery. Matt described the experience: "I wasn't sure I was going to forget them after he told me to forget. I tried to remember or review them right after, and I couldn't. I would get only the first or the first two words and no farther. Later on I couldn't remember those. . . . You know it's there, you can *feel* it's there but it feels like a blank space. You can't get to it." When told that he could remember everything, Matt said: "It was not like a revelation hit me. I still had to try to remember. This time, I could remember."

The power of words may be related to ordinary self-control by way of self-talk. What may happen in hypnosis is that this self-talk is turned over to the hypnotist, as proposed by Miller, Galanter, and Pribram (1960). Or, what is essentially equivalent, some subjects report that they actually repeat the hypnotist's suggestion to themselves, converting it to autosuggestion. The automaticity with which the subject responds to the hypnotist's words varies from subject to subject.

2. Sometimes the subject indicates *selective inattention* to the material to be forgotten by the exercise of voluntary effort. Ann said that she accomplished amnesia for the word list by clearing her mind, forgetting everything, wiping the slate clean. "All was a blank." When told that she could remember, she said: "All kinds of things popped into my mind, the intonation of his voice, the order of the words, the way the room smelled." She in fact reinstated the total setting as well as the words to be recalled.

This voluntary inattentive behavior corresponds to the kind of self-instruction a person uses when, after retiring, he decides to stop thinking about his problems and is able to "turn his mind off" so that he can go to sleep.

The degree of voluntariness may vary. Many hypnotizable subjects are aware that some part of them is participating actively in producing the amnesia, even though they do not feel responsible for providing the initiative. Marie reported that a wall or screen had appeared between her and the words. "Suddenly it was as though a shade was drawn between the words and myself . . . it feels strange because you know something happened, but you feel stupid because you can't say it, yet you know he said you will not remember his words. . . . No matter how much effort you put into it, you couldn't do it . . . maybe in a couple of hours, but I wasn't given that much time." After being told that she could remember everything, "The screen rolled up sort of slowly. The words came back, one at a time."

3. *Imagery* may play an important role in producing the amnesia. Sometimes the imagery arises spontaneously. Lucille reported: "When told to forget, my head fills up with something soft and all ideas are squashed against the side of my head, against the bones, like styrofoam that can be squashed with a weight. When the weight is removed, the ideas or words bounce back."

Sometimes the imagery is carefully selected by the subject to produce the desired effect, and in other cases the hypnotist may suggest the appropriate imagery. Gerald Blum has sometimes advised the subject to imagine that the events to be forgotten have been stored in a trunk. The subject (in imagination) locks the trunk and throws away the key. The method appears to be successful in enhancing amnesia.

4. There may be aspects of the amnesic processes related to the personal history of the individual being studied, justifying an interpretation based on the dynamics of *repression*. In such instances, aspects of the person's early experiences, his personal style, his defensive systems, may be operative in selecting the manner in which amnesia is achieved. Amnesia and repression may interact in achieving the demonstrated forgetting; however, this does not mean that the one process can be completely described in terms of the other. The issues involved are discussed later in this chapter.

The foregoing account of the influences of direct verbal suggestion ("the power of words"), voluntary inattention, imagery, and repressive processes indicates some of the ways in which amnesia is achieved. All these are influences on memory retrieval; the memories as stored are not disrupted, and the inhibitory processes that result in amnesia can be reversed.

There are many transitional cases in which the suggested amnesia is incomplete. It is often difficult to know just where the difficulty in retrieval lies. There may be enough items recalled to indicate that the remaining items are not severely inhibited.

Instances of the familiar tip-of-the-tongue phenomenon (Brown and Mc-

Neill, 1966) show that partial amnesias are common in everyday experience, as well as in hypnosis. As one subject put it: "In amnesia for the word list, the words were *almost* on the tip of my tongue, but I couldn't get hold of what was happening. I knew something was happening, but I couldn't recall what. . . . When she told me I could recall, it's like all of a sudden, boom, it hit you. It's almost like you're embarrassed, it's so simple; it's right there, it's not difficult."

Occasionally a subject reports imaging the items to be recalled without being able to name them. In an extreme illustration of this, a subject was unable to speak at all when hypnosis was terminated with the suggestion that amnesia would follow. Much to the surprise of the hypnotist, Joe came out of a routine test of hypnotic susceptibility with a motor asphasia, a total inability to articulate words. When he was rehypnotized, with strong suggestions that he would remember everything that had happened and would have no difficulty talking, his normal behavior was readily restored. Ten years later, a number of subjects were located at random in their home communities for purposes of retesting their hypnotic responsiveness. Joe happened to be among those retested. Because the experimenters doing the follow-ups had not been permitted to review the earlier records for technical reasons, the new experimenter had no reason to expect any unusual behavior. However, the same reaction occurred, and Joe was again aphasic when the hypnosis was terminated and again responded to the corrective suggestions. Because his responses were so unusual, he was invited to return to the laboratory so that the nature of his amnesia could be studied more carefully.

The ten-year retest had been made in his residential community at some distance from the laboratory. In my further retesting in the laboratory, the same behavior occurred again. This time, however, instead of clearing up the motor aphasia immediately, I used a method of automatic writing to determine what he could recall. While he was still unable to speak, his hand, out of awareness, was able to write automatically the names of a number of the items that he had been able to picture but not speak about. The items were limited in number; this indicated that, had he been able to speak, he would have reported a partial amnesia. "I felt sure that I had pictured everything in my mind, but was unable to talk about what I could picture; now I know that I actually remembered only a few of the things; I wrote down for you all that I had pictured."

Hypnotic amnesia is a genuine experience for the subject, but its manifestations are varied, and its explanation remains incomplete. Of obvious importance are central control processes, similar to those involved in the "working memory," now recognized as an important supplement to short-term and long-term memory. The idea behind "working memory" is that active rehearsal is required to store memories—a "central" process—and other evidences of central processes are also found. One example is the interpreting (and retaining) of the meanings of sentences according to their contexts, even when the grammatical form is ambiguous (Bower, 1975).

AMNESIA AND THE CONCEPT OF REPRESSION

The psychoanalytic concept of repression is very similar to that of amnesia because repressed memories that were once available are no longer available for retrieval in the usual way. They are recoverable, however, as amnesic memories are, when appropriate methods, such as free association, are used. Repression also implies repressive forces to produce and maintain the inhibition against recall, and some of the related ideas lie at the very core of psychoanalytic theory.

A question may well be raised: If psychoanalysis has been successful in elaborating a well-worked-out theory of repression over the years, is there any need for another theory of amnesia? This question is an appropriate one. Certainly the losses of personal memories in cases of spontaneous amnesia, with the maintaining of impersonal ones, indicate that something similar to motivated repression is operating. Even those who are critical of psychoanalytic therapy commonly find it convenient to talk about defenses, often without reference to their psychoanalytic origin. Defenses, closely examined, have in them some reality distortion through repression, for example, in the substitution of an ego-acceptable reason for the real one. Posthypnotic amnesia, however, can have almost any kind of target, with little, if anything, to do with the personal motivational system of the hypnotized person. Source amnesia, for example, with respect to objective facts of any kind, does not seem to involve the personality dynamics of the subject. Of course, one can argue that acceptance of the hypnotic contract is itself drive related, and the hypnotist is assigned authority as a substitute parent. However, such an elaborate explanation does not appear to be necessary to account for what is seen in hypnosis.

Because, in a dissociation interpretation, the barrier between the separated activities is essentially an amnesic barrier, preventing the interchange of memories, whereas, in psychoanalysis, the barrier is based primarily on repression of unacceptable impulses, I have somewhat oversimplified the relationship. I have considered the Freudian barrier a horizontal one (carrying the metaphor of the unconscious being "deeper") and the dissociative barrier a vertical one; thus the split-off parts may have equal status in their cognitive aspects (Figure 9).

The two interpretations began to diverge as early as in the days of Freud's collaboration with Breuer (Breuer and Freud, 1895).

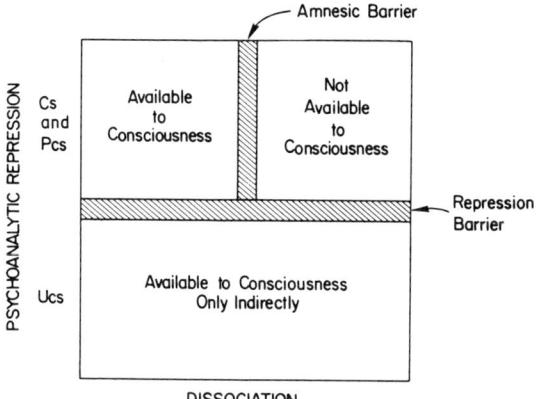

Figure 9 A distinction between the divisions of consciousness in dissociation and in psychoanalytic theory. In psychoanalytic theory (simplified for this purpose) the available memories lie in the conscious (Cs) and the preconscious (Pcs), whereas the hidden ones are concealed under a repression barrier and lie in the unconscious (Ucs). The unavailable ideas are largely those bound up with affect and impulse, and they enter consciousness only indirectly. In a dissociation through amnesia the split is among the usually available memories, and the unavailable memories need have no special affective or impulsive significance. From Hilgard (1976, p. 143).

Breuer gave his own account of the splitting of the mind in hysterics. According to him, the dissociation may result from a habitual duplication of consciousness in hypnoidal states. His case of Anna O. illustrated this, because, although entirely normal, she had habitually engaged in vivid daydreaming as she carried on her ordinary occupations. When profound anxiety entered her reveries, the hypnoidal state became enhanced and was accompanied by amnesia. Once such a split has occurred the mind is divided into a part whose ideational complexes never enter consciousness, and a part whose ideas are conscious. The total splitting of the mind that occurs depends on a readiness created by a kind of autohypnosis. Hence Breuer's position supports a dissociative interpretation of this aspect of hysteria.

By the time their book was completed, Freud had moved beyond the cathartic method of treatment that he had learned from Breuer and had begun to develop his psychoanalytic method as a substitute for hypnosis. His interpretation of the splitting of consciousness rested on the idea of defense, of active repression, and he embarked on a search for methods to overcome the resistances that prevented the warded-off ideas from becoming conscious. Breuer acknowledged that there might be some place for defense, but he felt that Freud's theory was insufficient. The differences between Breuer and Freud call attention to alternative possibilities of interpretation with a family resemblance to those of Figure 9.

The issue is not which of the two interpretations is true; both of them may be true. The diagram suggests, however, that it is a mistake to try to equate amnesia with repression, regardless of the possibility that, in some instances, they may have similar consequences.

In an early experiment from our laboratory, Clemes (1964) designed an experiment to test a relationship between amnesia and repression by constructing lists of words to be memorized that would reflect some of the personality dynamics of the individual being studied. He gave his hypnotizable subjects a Kent-Rosanoff word association test. In this test, the subject is asked to reply with the first word that comes to mind, and his replies are compared to norms that are available on hundreds of college students. When a response is very idiosyncratic, it is interpreted as a "complex indicator," possibly showing some emotional problem in connection with the word or what it stands for. Many of the words in the list of 100 are thought to be clinically relevant—words such as mother or sex. In addition to the chosen associate, another factor used as a sign of emotional involvement is a delay in response, either because of some inhibition against responding or perhaps a desire to "edit" a response thought to be inappropriate. Using this method, Clemes selected a number of words that were troublesome for a subject and a number that were apparently emotionally neutral. He then tailored lists of words to be memorized for each individual, choosing half neutral and half emotionally troublesome words. It was found that the emotional words caused no trouble in list memorization because each word had to be associated with the one that followed it, and these artificial associations were impersonal. The hypothesis was that, if such a list was learned while hypnotized and the subject then received the suggestion to forget half the list, the troublesome words should be the favored targets for forgetting. The hypothesis rests on the assumption that amnesia and repression have something in common. To avoid a technical difficulty that might arise if the subject were to have trouble in memorizing the conflict-laden word in the first place, only words were retained in the final comparisons that were recovered when the amnesia was lifted. That is, all words had been well enough learned to be retained throughout the experiment; thus when amnesia reversal was required, all items met this criterion of amnesia. The results turned out according to the hypothesis: when partial amnesia was suggested, the emotionally loaded words were the targets for the amnesia, as one would expect from repression theory.

An ingenious experiment by Williamsen, Johnson, and Eriksen (1965) showed that hypnotic amnesia and repression had in common the fact that association methods can gain access to the concealed memories. Their subjects in each of three groups learned six familiar words and then "forgot" them under different conditions. The *amnesic* group of highly hypnotizable subjects learned the words while hypnotized, were given suggestions for posthypnotic amnesia, and then had their memory tested. A *simulator* group of insusceptible subjects were instructed to behave *as if* hypnotized and received exactly the same experimental treatment, learning followed by suggested post-hypnotic amnesia. As is so often found in such experiments, the simulator group, accepting the fact that hypnotic subjects are expected to be responsive to posthypnotic amnesia suggestions, overreacted and recalled fewer of the words than the truly hypnotized. A *control* group, although hypnotizable, carried out the learning and memory tests in the normal condition, with no suggestions of amnesia. Subjects in the control group recalled more words than either of the others. The investigators went on to show that the amnesic material could be recovered through word association tests, without any formal release of the amnesia. In the word association tests the three groups (amnesic, simulator and control) gave essentially identical responses, indicating the influence of the words stored in memory regardless of the amnesia preventing their recall or recognition.

These illustrations show that amnesia and repression doubtless have much in common, and such issues as exist are subject to resolution by study rather than by debate. Although I believe evidence for repression to be sound, for the present it is not necessary to choose between amnesia or repression as explanations but to emphasize the dissociative features of the phenomena observed experimentally (and clinically) in the study of amnesia.

One reason for preserving the distinction between dissociation and repression is to call attention to an important finding noted in the cases of multiple personality—that the concealed (or dissociated) personality is sometimes more normal or mentally healthy than the openly displayed one. This accords better with the idea of a split in the normal consciousness (a justification for Prince's term coconscious) rather than with the idea of a primitive unconscious regulated largely by primary process thinking. Another way of stating it is that the dissociative split is not a regressive one, whereas repression commonly implies some regression.

NOTES

The Nature of Memory

The study of human memory according to the distinction between short-term and long-term memory, and between problems of consolidation and retrieval, has been an area of very active research over the last two decades; the introduction to the literature here is necessarily very selective. A much fuller account, in the context of information processing, can be found in Hilgard and Bower (1975, pp. 577–605). For one who wishes to dig deeper, there are reviews such as the book edited by Norman (1970) and the books by Anderson and Bower (1973), and by Baddeley (1976).

The "rediscovery" of mnemonic devices illustrates a limitation on the perspective of experimental psychologists. The experimental scientist, tied to a popular tradition of apparatus, method, and theoretical model, often fails to return to naturalistic observation for a fresh look; it is to the credit of those who do. Of course, folk wisdom, imbedded in common sense, is always imprecise and may be false or dangerous, but it is sometimes refreshing. Mnemonics have an ancient history, and most of us used them occasionally even when they were scientifically disreputable. ("Thirty days hath September. . . . ") For popularizations of memory systems, see Furst (1958) or Young and Gibson (1966).

Functional and Organic Amnesia in Man

A review of the status of knowledge on amnesia has been edited by Whitty and Zangwill (1966); it is somewhat more thorough on organic amnesias than on functional ones. The book by Talland (1965) is also a useful general source.

The temporary amnesias of daily life often go unnoticed because they are transient, and once the memory is recovered the episode is passed over. Freud (1898) gave a very detailed account of an instance in which he attempted unsuccessfully to recall the name of the artist who had painted some frescoes in a church that he was recommending to a friend as worth visiting. He could readily conjure up a self-portrait of the artist, in line with an observation of his that when a memory has been repressed something related to the repressed memory often emerges as an unusually vivid image. He proceeded to give a very complex account of how the associations to the forgotten name got deflected by the repressed conflicts they aroused. The episode appeared later in his *Psychopathology of Everyday Life* (1901), in which many other instances of motivated forgetting are presented. To the extent that these "forgettings" are later spontaneously recalled, they illustrate functional amnesia as well as repression.

Spontaneously occurring amnesias without evident neurological explanations are usually described as functional or psychogenic, although the psychological causal factors may be as unknown as the organic ones. Much of the literature is about transient global amnesia, as described in the chapter. Illustrative recent references are those of Gilbert and Benson (1972), Greene and Bennett (1974), who found an EEG abnormality, and Patten (1971).

The habit of reporting individual cases of amnesia, such as appear from time to time in the newspapers, has been largely discontinued in the scientific journals; thus many cases, such as that of Beck reported in the chapter, are older ones.

Organic amnesias are more frequently discussed in the scientific literature than functional amnesias because the cases occur more often as a result of their many causes. Many concussions are caused by accidental injury, other cases are caused by brain tumors, some may result from brain surgery undertaken for other purposes (as for the relief of epilepsy). The types of neurological cases have been reviewed by Warrington (1971), who has been actively experimenting on amnesic patients. Baddeley (1975) has summarized a number of theories.

The amnesic effects of convulsive therapy in man are neglected in this chapter. However, some effects, such as those on older memories, are better studied in man than in animals (e.g., Squire, 1974). The volume edited by Fink, Kety, McGaugh, and Williams (1974) covers the whole field, human and animal.

The recall of events under general anesthesia, as indicated by the Levinson study, has been a matter of repeated interest and study by David Cheek (e.g., Cheek, 1959, 1964, 1966). His case material is impressive. For a later review, by one who assisted in the original Levinson study, see Mostert (1975). In a somewhat different context, because chemical anesthesia was not involved, Chertok, Michaux, and Droin (1977) performed two surgical operations under hypnotic analgesia, with the patients reporting complete insensitivity and unawarness of the surgical procedures. Inquiry under subsequent hypnosis uncovered awareness of what had transpired during the operation, with a minimum of reported distress, even though some pain was acknowledged. Trustman, Dubovsky, and Titley (1977) have reviewed auditory perception during anesthesia, failing to note that all the successful studies have used hypnosis in recovering the memories.

The role of imagery in hypnosis and memory is a recurrent theme in this book. Even in organic amnesias, pictures may be recognized when verbal recognition fails (Piercy and Hupper, 1972), and imagery may provide a mnemonic aid in such cases (Jones, 1974).

Amnesias in Laboratory Animals

For a short but critical introduction to this vast literature, see Hilgard and Bower (1975, pp. 511–516). More extensive reviews are those by Deutsch (1973), McGaugh and Herz (1972), and Mah and Albert (1973).

The reversibility of the memory loss leaves room for a dissociation hypothesis. Much of the recent literature supplements the earlier emphasis on the disruption of the consolidation process by searching for methods by which lost memories can be recovered, hence attributing at least some of the disruption to retrieval rather than consolidation. Interpretations favoring retrieval rather than consolidation as the source of failure include those of Miller and Springer (1973, 1974), although not all agree, for example, Gold and King (1974).

Hypnotic Amnesia

The most thorough review of laboratory studies of hypnotic amnesia is that by Leslie Cooper (1972), on whose chapter I have relied very heavily in the preparation of this chapter. Nace, Orne, and Hammer (1974) reviewed a number of studies, particularly in reference to the reversibility of amnesia. Erickson and Rossi (1974) contributed an account of their experiences with a variety of amnesic phenomena in hypnosis, and they describe their techniques for producing them.

The studies on differences between posthypnotic amnesia and ordinary forgetting initiated by Evans and Kihlstrom are continuing; the most recent accounts are those of Kihlstrom (1975, 1977), and Kihlstrom and Evans (1976).

The studies of Orne (1966) and Graham and Patton (1968) are representative of those which have found the effectiveness of retroactive inhibition to persist despite suggested amnesia for the intervening learning.

Control processes, found to be so important in amnesia, have become increasingly important in the experimental study of memory as indicated earlier in the chapter (e.g., Figure 7, page 64). Their importance has led to a conception of "working memory" as an intermediate between short-term and long-term memory, as an essential in rehearsal, and in maintaining context, which is so important in the understanding of language (Atkinson and Shiffrin, 1971; Bower, 1975). It is coherent with this emphasis that "working memory" can be paralleled by "working forgetting."

Amnesia and Repression

The overlap between amnesia and repression is evident, and in emphasizing their differences I may be overstressing one aspect of the psychoanalytic theory, that is, its emphasis on the intrapsychic, drive-related nature of repression. Modern ego psychology within psychoanalysis has distinguished between those processes that are drive-related and those that are not. According to Hartmann (1939), there are many adaptive processes that belong to the "conflict-free ego sphere." I am proposing that some divisions of consciousness fall in the area in which drive conflicts are unimportant, whether or not they are present. Perhaps the concept of adaptive regression ("regression in the service of the ego") lies in this direction, although the concept still includes the distinction between primary process (impulsive, irrational) and secondary process (reality oriented, rational). This distinction is somewhat blurred in hypnosis (Hilgard, 1962a). Gruenewald, Fromm, and Oberlander (1972) express doubts about always considering as regressive the ideational factors subsumed under "primary process."

CHAPTER

DREAMS, HALLUCINATIONS, AND IMAGINATION

Some illustrations of dissociation are more convincing than others. Amnesias, fugues, multiple personalities, and age regressions at a conceptual level readily classify as dissociations; the transformed and split-off aspects of consciousness and personality they represent differ markedly from the retained normal conditions. In our survey of dissociative experiences we turn now to a category of cognitive activities differing in quality from those previously considered, but they too represent dissociations.

Dreams and hallucinations are products of imagination in which memories or fantasies are temporarily confused with external reality. The dreams and hallucinations have autonomy, and their courses of action are plotted independently of the usual conscious controls. In that sense they are conscious products that qualify as dissociated, even though they are available to consciousness.

Ordinary imagery and imagination are in a different category because they have less autonomy than dreams and hallucinations. The difference may be merely one of degree, for a person deeply involved in a fantasy experience, perhaps while absorbed in reading a book, may show signs of dissociation, such as failing to respond when called. In addition, initiated fantasy may serve as a deliberate agent of dissociation by deflecting attention from some aspect of reality that a person wishes to ignore, such as a source of pain. It is appropriate to examine certain instances of imagination in the same context as dreams and hallucinations.

Psychologists are more at home in the discussion of attention, perception, and memory than they are in the discussion of imagination and hallucination, not because these topics are less "psychological," but because objective studies are more difficult. Veridicality is easily demonstrated by the correspondence between something presented to the senses and a person's report of what he believes it to be, or something taught him that he is later asked to reproduce from memory. Imagination, by its very nature, must depart from correspondence with external reality. One way to put it is that perception is of things present, memory is of things past, and imagination is of things novel. Of course, imagination includes more than novelty, for ambiguous perceptual stimuli may be supplemented by imagination to make perceptual sense of them, and veridical memory may be enhanced by evoking imagery. In its own varied ways, imagination is more pervasive than veridical perception and veridical memory, but it is more elusive and more subject to neglect by experimental psychologists. Hallucinations represent an extreme of imagery, interpreted by the hallucinator as perceptions; a convenient way of describing them is believed-in imagination. Hallucinations fare even less well than imagination in psychology textbooks because they are readily assigned to the "abnormal," and those experimenting with normal psychology have a convenient tendency to neglect phenomena labeled abnormal. Much of this neglect is fortunately being corrected. Imagery has come to play an important role in the study of memory, and the study of dreams has been advanced by new techniques of psychophysiology. The drug culture of the 1960s brought hallucinations back into prominence. Hypnosis is a convenient method by which to approach these topics, and recent experimentation in hypnosis should help elucidate some of the issues.

DREAMS

Dreams are the hallucinations of the normal. Freud recognized this when he distinguished between primary and secondary processes in thought. Primary processes are said to be impulsive, irrational; when gratification of an impulse does not come quickly, primary processes stir up hallucinations of that which could satisfy the drives. He thought that hallucinations began in childhood before more rational secondary process was established, and the dream, in adults, represented this primitive tendency to hallucinate. Hence the dream was, as he said, "the royal road to the unconscious." Whether Freud was altogether right, he was certainly right in part. The dream is a cognitive product, and, when remembered, it qualifies as hallucination; furthermore, it has a spontaneous or nonvoluntary quality about it that distinguishes it from ordered rational thinking. In that sense it can be placed among dissociated experiences.

In another sense dreams do not belong among dissociations because the dream is more closely related to repressed experiences in the unconscious. That the hidden control processes that regulate dreaming are not directly recoverable and are known only by their derivatives indicates that they should be assigned to a deeper unconscious rather than to the more readily recoverable dissociations. When the manipulations are open to investigation, as in the hypnotic control of dreams and hallucinations, the dissociative aspects are more evident.

The psychoanalytic theory of dreams has been criticized from within psychoanalysis as well as by those unsympathetic to psychoanalysis. The concept of the dream as wish fulfilling was somewhat of a metaphor and has tended to be softened by now calling the dream drive related. The purpose of the dream as protecting the sleeper from his own disturbing thoughts also was somewhat extreme, and Freud, too, recognized that the dream, if this was its purpose, often failed, as in distressing nightmares.

An alternative dream interpretation, within a psychoanalytic context, was provided by French and Fromm (1964). While accepting much of Freud's theory, they objected to the incidental, completely unessential role that Freud assigned to problem solving in the dream work, because the dream was said by him to be dominated by the need to achieve hallucinatory fulfillment of an infantile wish. Although they accepted the role of such unfulfilled infantile wishes, they were interested in the motives of the dreamer, as an adult, to repress and act in opposition to infantile drives, and they emphasized that an adult's dreams, especially a series of them, represent his efforts to solve his problems. They did not accept a distinction as sharp as that which Freud made between primary and secondary process thinking. They preferred to distinguish between the verbal thinking that is used in ordinary communication and a more practical type of thinking, more Gestalt-like rather than associational, that has some of the qualities of primary process but is at the same time empathic and intellectually competent.

> When we begin to study practical thinking, we discover that the functional units in this living process are problems, not wishes or fantasies. Wishes are the dynamic stimuli that activate problems. Wish-fulfilling fantasies are attempts—often fleeting attempts—to solve problems. Both wishes and wish-fulling fanta-

sies are only parts or phases of a more comprehensive problem-solving effort. (French and Fromm, 1964, p. 94f.)

The problems of a patient who comes for psychoanalysis are those of someone who is troubled; thus the problems arise either out of his intrapsychic or his interpersonal conflicts or both. May not dreams also solve some of the practical problems that remain unsolved? There are, of course, some dramatic cases, such as that of Kekule, who dreamt of a snake composed of atoms, taking his tail in his mouth. This led to Kekule's solution of how carbon and hydrogen atoms could be arranged in a circle that became his discovery of the benzene ring. Another famous case was that of Hilprecht, the archeologist, who solved a Babylonian inscription in a dream.

Dreams have fascinated men throughout history, because, if they are meaningful, the sources of the meanings they convey are mysterious. Hence dreams may be interpreted as supernatural visitations, or they may be thought of as prophetic, as Pharaoh's dreams were interpreted by Joseph. The modern scientific study of dreams has moved away from interpretation, as we shall see, to study other problems, but it is to be hoped that the study of the dream as a cognitive product will continue supplementing the study of the dreams of patients coming for treatment.

There are occasional dreams that appear to uncover lost memories in thinly disguised form. This case is illustrative:

> Richard C., a skilled worker 40 years old, came to a mental hospital with serious depression and haunting ideas about death. As a child he had lost his mother under traumatic circumstances. About the actual death he could remember only being awakened from sleep in order to be taken to the hospital some distance away. When he and his sisters arrived there, his mother was dead. The mother's death was very disturbing to him, and it was evident to the psychiatrist who treated him that some of his present symptoms dated from it.
>
> In order to help him recall specific events of that period, the psychiatrist asked, among other questions, whether he recalled the time of night in which the memories happened. He could not remember. That these memories were repressed is suggested by the information that came in a dream the night following this interview.
>
> In the dream the patient saw two clocks. One was running and the other had stopped. The one that was running said twenty minutes to three, and the one that had stopped said twenty minutes to five.
>
> Because of the possibility that the clocks represented the repressed childhood memories, the man's older sister was located and asked about the circumstances of the mother's death. She had not heard of the dream. She said that they had been roused from their farmhouse about 2:30 A.M., and had driven to the distant hospital. When they arrived there about 4:30, their mother had just died. (Case courtesy of Josephine R. Hilgard.)

The Psychophysiology of Sleep and Dreams

Modern dream study took a new direction with the discovery by Aserinsky and Kleitman (1953) that rapid eye movements tend to occur when a sleeping person begins to dream. This was soon followed by many studies in which people were awakened from sleep in the dream laboratory when they were in EEG stage 1 sleep, and eye movements showed that they would most likely report a dream (Dement and Kleitman, 1957). If eye movements were absent, they would not be as likely to report a dream, although they might report "thoughts." In the two decades since, there has developed an enormous literature on sleep and dreams and an active society (Association for the Psychophysiological Study of Sleep) with an international membership that meets regularly.

It is now accepted that the three main states of consciousness that succeed each other each day are waking, NREM sleep (non-rapid-eye-movement sleep), and REM sleep (rapid-eye-movement sleep). There may, of course, be several longer or shorter cycles of each within a 24-hour period, and the distribution of these periods is one of the matters investigated by research workers.

Our interest centers on what has been learned from these studies about conscious (or subconscious) responsiveness during the various kinds of sleep. The period of NREM sleep has defined stages of depth of its own; thus the states have additional aspects to be specified.

Lets us ask and answer a few questions.

1. *Do externally imposed stimuli become incorporated into the dream?* This does happen, although not with universal regularity. Dement and Wolpert (1958) sprayed cold water on dreaming subjects from a hypodermic syringe after the subject had been in REM sleep for several minutes. He was then allowed to sleep for a few minutes before being awakened and asked for his dream recall. The investigators were able to find ten instances in which the cold water was incorporated into the dream in a recognizable fashion without waking the subject. This answers our question affirmatively. Dement and Wolpert had another purpose in mind, however, having to do with the duration of the dream. Having kept an accurate account of the time between the water spray and the awakening, they asked the subject to give the content of the dream. When the reported dream action was repeated in waking pantomime, it took about as long as it would have taken in the waking state; thus the idea of the "instantaneous" nature of the dream is contradicted.

As an illustration of the incorporation of the water spray into the dream, Dement (1972) gives this account:

I was walking behind the leading lady when she suddenly collapsed and water was dripping on her. I ran over to her and water was dripping on my back and head. The roof was leaking. I was very puzzled why she fell down and decided some plaster must have fallen on her. I looked up and there was a hole in the roof. I dragged her over to the side of the stage and began pulling the curtains. Just then I woke up.(p. 47)

2. *Do the eye movements in the dream correspond to action that the dreamer is watching?* They may, but the correspondence is very rare. One case was reported by Dement (1967) in which the back-and-forth eye movements corresponded closely to the report by the subject of watching a ping pong game from the side, in the midst of a lengthy volley.

3. *Is there any evidence that dreaming protects the sleeper from becoming aroused?* The finding was early established that it took a louder sound to waken the sleeper from stage 1 REM sleep than from stage 1 NREM sleep (Williams, Agnew, and Webb, 1964). Ordinarily it is more difficult to arouse the person from stages 2 or 3, but not during REM in stage 1. This would seem to correspond to the Freudian theory, but the exceptions are many; if personal remarks are made, for example, the person is more readily aroused. The prevalence of REM sleep in animals and infants also tells against this adaptive role.

Hypnotic Influences on Dreaming

Hypnosis enters the study of dreams and dreamings in at least three ways. First, a hypnotized person can be told that a dream will come, and he can immediately have a dream that he can remember. Second, he can be told that he will dream about a particular topic at night, when he is sleeping in his own bed as usual, and he may report in the morning that his dream was indeed influenced by the suggestion. Third, under special circumstances he can be given the suggestion that he will talk out loud about a night dream while it is happening, so that, essentially for the first time, there is such a contemporary account of what the dreamer experiences. None of these methods has been exhaustively studied, but a few examples show the possibilities. To the extent that a dream is a dissociated product, subject to manipulations similar to other behaviors in hypnosis, the relevance of dreams to the theme of this book is evident.

The question has often been raised whether the directly suggested and immediately experienced hypnotic dream is really like a night dream. The answer is "no," but with the cautionary statement that many night dreams are not "typical" dreams either. I have pointed out elsewhere that the hypnotic dream will differ from a night dream because it is not spontaneous, the topic is assigned by the hypnotist, it is produced without sleep as a background, and it lacks privacy because the hypnotized subject knows that he will be asked to report it (Hilgard, 1965, p. 150ff.). Such difficulties are relative only, and Tart (1966) has shown that many hypnotized subjects rate their hypnotic dreams as very similar to night dreams (Table 3). The 39 subjects whose data are presented in the table represent the approximately 45% of the subjects who, in a college sample, report some kind of dream after a standard hypnotic induction and a suggestion to dream. Of those nine subjects who reported their suggested dreams as corresponding to night dreams, only one fell in the lower third of hypnotic susceptibility, whereas five fell in the upper third.

In a subsequent study on a larger sample, of those in the upper one-fourth of hypnotizability (scores of 8 and above on SHSS-C), 109 of 172 who reported dreams, or 63%, said their dreams were like real night dreams (Hilgard and Nowlis, 1972). In any case, there are enough subjects who have experiences that they interpret as genuinely dreamlike for the method to be useful. A comparison of these hypnotically suggested dreams with night dreams from other sources gathered by the dream diary method (Hall and Van de Castle, 1966) showed some differences, as expected. One striking difference was that the subject himself was the only person in the dream far more often in the

Table 3

QUALITY OF HYPNOTICALLY SUGGESTED DREAM
AS RELATED TO HYPNOTIC SUSCEPTIBILITY AMONG THOSE
WHO REPORT DREAM EXPERIENCES
(Data from Hilgard and Tart, 1966, as Analyzed by Tart, 1966)

Dream quality	Susceptibility to hypnosis (SHSS-C)				
	Lower One-third	Middle One-third	Upper One-third	Total	Percent
Like a real dream	1	3	5	9	23
Like watching a movie, with visual imagery	4	3	7	14	36
Just thinking and daydreaming	5	8	1	14	36
Not ratable	1	—	1	2	5
Total	11	14	14	39	100

hypnotic dream than in the night dream—about 30% of the time, compared to 5% for the night dream sample.

Using a method for studying dream distortion developed by Perry (1964), we found that our hypnotic subjects produced more distortions than those who reported dreams in his sleep laboratory, although the samples are not directly comparable. We found that 42% of the sample showed transformations that were unusual (whether of the self, the surrounding scene, or other objects or events), and another 12% showed distortions contradicting usual reality (floating, falling, size changes). We have noticed the Alice-in-Wonderland types of distortion in many of these hypnotic dreams. We concluded from the study that the interpretation of hypnotically induced dreams should probably be that they lie on a continuum somewhere between TAT stories and night dreams.

The question of influencing night dreams by way of hypnotic suggestions has been most thoroughly investigated by Tart (1965a, 1965b). In some cases the influence is evident, but success is by no means universal.

The persistence of tendencies to process information even during REM sleep has been demonstrated by the effectiveness of posthypnotic suggestions to a prearranged signal that is presented to the subject while he is in the REM stage. It was arranged that, at a verbal signal, the subject would either touch his nose or readjust his pillow, depending on the instruction that was given. It was found that, while asleep, he could respond to such signals with the appropriate movements (Evans, Gustafson, O'Connell, Orne, and Shor, 1969).

Through posthypnotic suggestions implanted in the waking state, it proves possible in some instances to have the subject talk about his dream *while it is occurring*. Of course, the subject must be a natural sleeptalker, so that his talking does not waken him, and he must be highly susceptible to hypnosis; the method is therefore not widely applicable. One carefully selected subject was enough to show the possibilities (Arkin, Hastey, and Reiser, 1966). Among several methods tried with him, two can serve as illustrations. He was hypnotized and given this posthypnotic suggestion one hour before retiring: "Tonight you will sleep normally and naturally, and dream normally and naturally just as you do at home, but whenever you do have such a normal dream, you will *talk in your sleep without awakening and describe the dream in detail while the dream is going on.*"

This condition was repeated on several nights, with 60 episodes of recorded sleeptalking, of which 60% were associated with REM periods and 40% with non-REM periods. Of the few dreams recalled in the morning, only a little over one-fourth (28%) corresponded to the reports given during the REM-related talking during the night. The hypnotic method apparently produced some spontaneous amnesia, making it harder for the subject to remember his dreams in the morning. On other nights this difficulty was overcome by adding to the posthypnotic suggestion that, when awakened during the night, he was to relate all that had been passing through his mind for the previous 10 or 15 minutes. The procedure was then followed of waking him three to nine times during the night, either shortly after or remote from his sleeptalking. In this way, many more correspondences were found between this talking and the dreams reported when he was awakened. The percent of dreams reported adjacent to REM sleep that corresponded to the report prior to awakening now jumped from 28 to 88%. Correspondences are illustrated by the examples in Table 4, selected from a larger number in the published report.

The correspondences indicate that the reports during the dreams reflected the contents of the dreams as subsequently recalled; however, the sleeptalking tends to be so sparse as not to be very revealing. Hypnotic suggestion produced more talking during sleep on the part of the subject who already talked occasionally in his sleep. Both the sleeptalking and its enhancement through hypnosis bear on the presence of dissociated activity and the influence of hypnosis on it.

Sleeptalking and Sleepwalking in Relation to Dreaming

The foregoing account indicates that sleeptalking and dreaming are not incompatible in the experimental setting of posthypnotic instruction. Under ordinary circumstances of spontaneous sleeptalking, most of it goes on in NREM sleep. A total of 206 speeches recorded during the night from 13 subjects (averaging 3.9 speeches per subject per night) showed that 75–80% were from NREM sleep (stages 2, 3, and 4), and 20–25% were associated with REM sleep (Arkin, Toth, Baker, and Hastey, 1970).

Sleepwalking is also associated with NREM sleep; subjects usually are amnesic to the sleepwalking episodes, and the dreams they remember in the morning bear no resemblance to what they did while they were walking about (Jacobson and Kales, 1967).

Because sleeptalking, sleepwalking, and dreaming are all cognitive activities with internal organization and some measure of control, yet split off in some respects from the ordinary functioning of the cognitive system in waking, they provide further demonstrations of the ubiquity of dissociated activities and processes.

HALLUCINATIONS

Having noted that dreams are the hallucinations most frequently experienced in daily life, we turn now to other manifestations of hallucinations as cognitive products representing some degree of dissociation.

Table 4

SLEEP SPEECHES FROM REM PERIODS COMPARED
WITH SUBSEQUENT WAKING REPORTS
(From Arkin, Hastey, and Reiser, 1966)

Sleep speeches (REM associated)	Waking reports
"Now viewing a film of past experiences in gallery for small admission charge."	"Uh — (pause) — there's a theatre that you pay admission charge and they run films of your life — that's all I remember except that I was in one of those theatres a minute ago."
"Claudette Colbert is trying to seduce me into a dream and I think she's *horrible* but has a friend — a *beautiful* girl from the University of California."	"Mmb (pause) — Claudette Colbert — trying to put the make on me conversationally and she was so ugly — but she brought her daughter from U.C., and we were hitting it off and joking around. Claudette and we were getting in elevators and things and we would come out and there would be Claudette — and other kinds of illusions and elusive methods — going through tunnels — that's about all I can remember."
"Doctor Arkin will telephone a buddy of mine — and telegraph a cake — his birthday — it's on Good Friday — the buddy is Doctor Straw — and do this for birthday and All Saints Day."	"Uh — Doctor Arkin sent a gift to — a birthday gift to a buddy of mine on his birthday — he was very happy to receive it and it was a very timely gift — it was something he could use very much and he was overjoyed to get — there was something else — I can't think of it at the moment."

Hallucinations in Pathological Conditions

Hallucinations may be found in the delirium that accompanies disease, especially high fever, in psychiatric conditions, especially in some forms of schizophrenia, and as a consequence of the ingestion of drugs. These are sufficiently familiar not to require any detailed exposition, except to note one statistical property of these hallucinations. In a large proportion of the cases in which the hallucination is drug or disease produced, the hallucination is prominently visual; in functional psychosis it is often auditory: "the voices."

The transitional case appears to be alcoholic hallucinosis in which auditory hallucinations may be found, but some relation to schizophrenia in these symptoms may account for this. The cognitive systems in visual hallucinations may differ from those in the auditory ones in that the visual hallucinations are more patterned and less sequential in organization, whereas the verbal auditory hallucinations are characterized by sequential messages, often of abuse to the person who has them, even though they may resemble free association more than connected grammatical discourse.

The hallucinations experienced under drugs vary from those that are highly pleasurable ("good trips") to those that are frightening and disintegrative ("bad trips"). Hence, whatever their affect, they tend to be out of the control of the experiencing person, except to the extent, under some drugs, that they are influenced by the suggestions deriving from the social environment in which the drug is ingested. In a study of the effects of several drugs on suggestion, Sjoberg and Hollister (1965) found that mescaline and LSD increased suggestibility comparable to a short hypnotic induction, whereas psilocybin (a drug derived from the mushrooms that produce hallucinations) did not show this effect.

Hypnotically Produced Hallucinations

The hallucinations suggested by hypnosis are commonly classified as positive or negative. A positive hallucination is the experiencing of something as though it were perceptually present in the absence of the appropriate object to produce the perception. Seeing a bowl of flowers on a vacant table, hearing a voice over a nonexistent intercom device, or feeling a pencil as a hot element that must be dropped for fear of burning the hand are positive hallucinations that may involve any of the senses or several of them at once. A negative hallucination is one in which something is present that would normally evoke a perceptual response, but the response does not occur. Failing to see someone who is sitting in a chair, failing to hear a voice that is speaking loudly, or being unaware of a pinprick or an electric shock to the arm are negative hallucinations.

The distinction between positive and negative hallucinations is a convenient one for classificatory purposes, but the distinction is not sharp. To have a good positive visual hallucination of someone sitting in a chair, the back of the chair that is hidden by the person must be subject to negative hallucination; to have a negative hallucination so that a book on the table is not perceived, requires a positive hallucination to fill the space in which the book lies. Still, some people find it easier to produce negative hallucinations than positive ones. The relative difficulty of positive and negative hallucinations in hypnosis is of some interest, because negative hallucinations are very rare in the naturally occurring pathological hallucinations associated with mental problems, drugs, or injury (Zikmund, 1972).

It is difficult to arrange hallucinatory tasks in order of difficulty, except by the response to them; thus an independent measure of whether positive or negative hallucinations are easier is likely to be uncertain or imprecise. For example, in one form of the Stanford Profile Scales there is a positive hallucination of the smell of ammonia, in which distilled water is smelled as strong ammonia. In the standardization sample, 71 of 155, or 46%, reported some experience of smell identified as ammonia, either weak or strong; in the corresponding item of negative hallucination, 59 of 155, or 38%, were unable to smell ammonia at a concentration of 1:16 within hypnosis, although they had no trouble identifying it in the nonhypnotic condition. The difference between 46 and 38 does not reveal any important average difference in difficulty between positive and negative hallucinations. Another appropriate comparison might be that between a heat hallucination in which an unheated rod in the hand is interpreted as a heating element that becomes hot (positive hallucination), compared to the inability to detect a mild electric shock to the hand as a result of an analgesia suggestion (negative hallucination). In the same sample from which the previous data came, those for whom the rod became so hot that they had to drop it (positive) were 48 of 155, or 31%, whereas those who did not feel the highest shock presented as painful, and did not in fact identify it as shock at all, numbered 42, or 27%. Again there is no evidence that one form of hallucination, in the context of hypnosis, is strikingly more difficult than the other, although the slightly less prevalent negative hallucinations correspond to their lower frequency in pathology. Of course, this average result does not mean that for some individuals one kind of hallucination will not be more difficult than another; although the positive and negative hallucinations, when combined into scales, correlated .61 with each other, this allows for many discrepancies from one person to another.

The successes and actual experiences of the hypnotized subject in a negative hallucination experiment were studied by McKellar and Tonn(1967). Their basic problem was that of placing five objects before the subject (five stamps, or five playing cards, or five coins, some of them shiny, and then suggesting that two of them would be missing. With the negative hallucination established, could the positions of the cards be changed, and the hallucinations persist? Under some circumstances the position determined which cards would be negatively hallucinated; that is, if cards at the second and fourth position were not perceived following the negative hallucination suggestion, when the cards were rearranged, the cards newly in the second and fourth positions were not perceived. In other instances the tabooed cards remained unperceived, even when moved. With practice, one subject performed exceedingly well at the tasks; as might be expected, the subjects succeeded better when the negated objects were readily discriminable. The authors relied on the introspections of their subjects to clarify the subjective experiences and concluded that the results pointed up the importance of reexamining the dissociation hypothesis.

How can the experimenter know that the subject is actually hallucinating, and not simply reporting a product of his normal imagination? It is easy to role play that one is having a hallucination. If I wish to fool you, I can tell you that I see a monkey playing on the chair, and I can describe what he looks like and what antics he engages in. This does not mean that I have actually hallucinated the monkey, for when I report honestly I will tell you that I did not "see" the monkey as really there.

As a method of testing the veridicality of the hallucination, Martin Orne introduced the simulator-real control to which references have already been made. Simulators commonly differ from the reals. Here is the typical real:

> The subject is told that an observer is sitting in the chair opposite him, in the place where the observer actually had been sitting, but from where he has quietly moved during the trance induction. After the hallucination is induced and the subject is clearly reacting to it, he is told to turn around and identify the individual standing behind him, i.e., the observer who has moved behind the subject and well outside his range of vision.
>
> In this situation the truly hypnotized person is almost invariably startled, and will look back and forth between the observer and the chair where he has hallucinated the same individual. His behavior resembles what is colloquially known as a "double take." He will then identify both perceptions as Dr. _____, and may in a puzzled way ask why there are two of them. A highly intelligent subject who is acquainted with hypnotic phenomena may say, "I guess one of them is an hallucination." Such a subject when asked which of his perceptions is real, will study first one and then the other before deciding. In order to make the distinction some subjects have hit upon the ingenious idea of "thinking" that the observer should raise his hand, and reasoning that the image which did so was the hallucination. (Orne 1962, pp. 217–218.)

I have repeated comparable demonstrations on numerous occasions before my classes. The subjects are often quite clever in solving the problem, after first becoming baffled by making such tests as asking questions of both images and receiving answers that do not permit them to distinguish between the two. One had adopted the "thought transference" method of communicating with the observers, knowing that one was a product of his own mind; he reported cheerfully that he knew which was the hallucination because that one had just opened the door and left the classroom.

This experiment works, of course, only with very highly hypnotizable subjects who cannot tell the hallucinated person from the real person. These hypnotic virtuosos are very rare, and experimenters who try to refute this kind of experiment by a careless selection of subjects are bound to fail. Even a very hypnotizable person may proceed with the experiment to the point of seeing the two people, carrying on conversations with both, and describing both in the same terms. But when questioned about which is real, he may very well have no difficulty in deciding, because one of the persons is diaphanous, and the back of the chair is visible "through" him.

Some idea of the frequency of this general type of visual hallucination is provided by the test item on the Stanford Profile Scales that requires the hallucination of a second light on a small metal box that has one genuine light at one end. The parallel occurs because some subjects cannot tell which of the two lights is the real one. In a preliminary sample of 173 cases, 19, or 11%, reported seeing the two lights. Of these 19 subjects, ten were able to tell which light was real, because the hallucinated one was not lighted or was dim, failed to be reflected in the metal box, or floated above it. The remaining nine were unable to decide which was the hallucinated light; when asked to guess, seven were correct and two incorrect. Two of the nine inferred from the position at which the cord entered the box which light was real, but one of these was wrong; another who judged on the basis of which light was dimmer was wrong because the true light was judged as dimmer. Most of those who were correct in their guesses judged the hallucinated light to be the one that was dimmer or burned out.

These results correspond to those in Orne's experiment in that the distinction between the lights is hard for some subjects to make. The experiment differs in that the duplication of the same light is not logically inconsistent as is duplicating the same person, and the intelligent basis of resolving the issue through "thought transference" is missing. The occasional presence of a genuine hallucination that behaves irrationally (not casting a shadow; suspended above the box like a will-o'-the wisp) is comparable to the occasional diaphanous hallucination of a person.

IMAGINATION

The tie between imagination and hallucination is very close. Both depend on the memory store for the substance of the imagery that is used, because the image conjured up in both cases is made of fragments from the past, no matter how bizarre the combinations or distortions. If Columbus is pictured as flying in a spaceship, it is the Columbus of the bookplates in which he was pictured, and the spaceships are either adapted from actual launchings or as pictured on the covers of science fiction books or magazines. Novelty that is not sheer senseless confusion always has some ties to experiences from the past, and even the confusion, if pictorial, is in colors that have been seen. The difference between imagination and hallucination is one of belief, and even that distinction is not altogether sharp.

Imagery

To the extent that imagination is a matter of revived perception, it is often described according to sensory images, corresponding to the sensory modalities: visual, auditory, tactual, gustatory, olfactory, kinesthetic. Many years ago Sir Francis Galton began a kind of imagery census by asking many people to describe their imagery (Galton, 1883). A fairly elaborate study was conducted by Betts (1909), and his questionnaire has been relied on by investigators since then (Sheehan, 1967a, 1967b). Betts typically asked people to call up the image of something in which one or another of the senses was most prominent and then had them rate the vividness of the imagery that was evoked. One could imagine looking at a sunset for visual imagery, listening to a violin for the auditory imagery, or sensing the feeling in the muscles after running up a flight of stairs as kinesthetic imagery. With a number of opportunities in each modality, a "score" could be obtained both for one's general imagery ability and for the relative vividness of imagery corresponding to one or another of the sensory modalities.

In the reductive psychology of the time, when the simple elements out of which more complex experiences might be constructed were searched for, it was supposed that vividness of imagery was likely to be the basis for creative imagination. Consequently, such studies as there were tended to use the imagery scale and neglected other aspects of imagery. Gordon (1949, 1950) has been responsible for calling attention to the ability to control images as something to take into account beyond their vividness. Others have gone on to show that there is much more to imagination than imagery in either of these respects.

One possibility that has been explored, in the older vein, is the relation between vividness of imagery and hypnotizability. The hypothesis, a sensible one, is that the hallucinatory ability of the highly hypnotizable might rest on an underlying ability to form and recognize images. The results of the experimental studies have been tantalizing, because sometimes a significant correlation between imagery and hypnotizability is found, sometimes not; sometimes the correlation is significant for females and not for males, occasionally it is the other way around. One problem is that the correlations are commonly so low that, even though positive, they can fluctuate considerably with sample size or other aspects of experimentation. A common finding is that the relationship between hypnotizability and imagery is curvilinear, with the highly hypnotizable showing high imagery and the low hypnotizable little imagery, but imagery itself is not predictive of hypnotizability because many with high imagery are not hypnotizable; the role of imagination in hypnosis apparently requires some ability to make use of the images that are present in some special manner if imagery ability is to lead to hypnotizability. The relationship of hypnotizability to imagery is shown in the data of Table 5 (Sutcliffe, Perry, and Sheehan, 1970). For this purpose the subjects have been considered to have made "high" scores if they are in the upper fourths of their samples; it is clearly the case in hypnosis that a high cutoff point is needed for selecting those capable of the hallucinatory behavior that imagery is expected to predict. The choice of the same cutoff point for self-reported imagery permits the construction of a symmetrical table that is readily understood. It is clear that the cell that contains most subjects is that with low hypnotizability and high imagery; the nearly empty cell is that of high hypnotizability and low imagery. The other cells are symmetrical: high hypnotizability is associated with high imagery, low hypnotizability with low imagery.

The results shown in Table 5 were obtained in Australia; they were based on the total sample including both sexes. Essentially the same findings were reproduced in our Stanford laboratory (J. R. Hilgard, 1970). How good and poor hypnotic subjects contrast in their imagery scores in the Stanford

Table 5

IMAGERY AS MEASURED ON THE MODIFIED BETTS SCALE
(BETTS QMI) AS RELATED TO HYPNOTIZABILITY AS MEASURED
BY THE STANFORD HYPNOTIC SUSCEPTIBILITY SCALE, FORM A (SHSS-A)
(Data from Sutcliffe, Perry, and Sheehan, 1970)

	Imagery (Betts QMI)		
Hypnotizability (SHSS-A)	Low imagery (120+)	High imagery (59-119)	Total
High hypnotizability (8-12)	2	20	22
Low hypnotizability (0-7)	20	53	73
Total	22	73	95

sample is revealed in Table 6 (J. R. Hilgard, 1970). Self-reported imagery is always that productive of images on scales designed after Betts, and it is not surprising that such reported imagery is more highly related to items that require the production of a positive experience with imaginal or hallucinatory content. The items that call for inhibition of movement or experience are less closely related, and those with poorer imagery are nearer in their responsiveness to the high imagers than on the positive items.

A relative newcomer as a scale for measuring vividness of imagery is that of Marks (1973), which has shown some promise in relating visual imagery to hypnotizability. This scale, although also derived from that of Betts, differs from it because, in addition to a scale of vividness (which, unfortunately, gives the scale its name), there is some manipulation of the images involved, which moves it into the territory of creative imagination. For example, a storefront is pictured from across the street, and the items in the store window are viewed as though the viewer had moved in closer. Next some particular item is examined as though it were in full attention. By scoring vividness at

Table 6
REPORTED IMAGERY AS RELATED TO PASSING OF ITEMS ON THE STANFORD HYPNOTIC SUSCEPTIBILITY SCALE, FORM C, (SHSS-C) MOST LIKELY TO REFLECT THE USE OF IMAGERY
(10 Highest and 10 Lowest Imagery Reports among 45 Female Subjects)
(J. R. Hilgard, 1970, p. 97)

Item on SHSS-C	Number of passing scores	
	10 highest in imagery	10 lowest in imagery
Production of the Experience		
1. Taste hallucination	7	1
2. Dream	8	1
3. Age regression	8	0
4. Mosquito hallucination	9	2
Mean number of passing scores	8.0	1.0
Inhibition of the Experience or Movement		
1. Arm rigidity	7	3
2. Arm immobilization	5	4
3. Anosmia to ammonia	3	2
4. Posthypnotic amnesia	4	1
Mean number of passing scores	4.8	2.5

each of these points of manipulation, something is added to mere vividness of visual imagery as such. There is a kind of involvement in the creating of the image that becomes important in relation to full-flowered imagination and, in turn, hypnosis.

A positive relation between Marks' scale and hypnotizability has been found by McKenley and Gur (1975) and quite independently by 't Hoen (1977).

Imagination and Involvement

When one becomes absorbed or involved in imagination, the question of imagery takes second place to the setting aside of the constraints of ordinary reality. In other words, the involved imagination experience is itself a form of dissociated activity.

In her interview study of subjects who were about to participate in their first experience of hypnosis, Josephine Hilgard (1965, 1970) found that the trait above all others that characterized hypnotic susceptibility was the capacity for such imaginative involvement. Typical areas of involvement were reading, especially fiction, including science fiction; the dramatic arts, acting, watching, and informal dramatization; religion of personal commitment; affective arousal through sensory stimulation; adventuresomeness, as in "physical" spatial experiences such as mountain climbing, cave exploring, or skin diving, or a "mental" adventuresomeness in experimenting with drugs, parapsychology, or oriental beliefs. Subjects were also interviewed after their hypnotic experience to determine whether they were able to see any connection between hypnosis and these habitual imaginative involvements (J. R. Hilgard, 1974).

The relationships proved to be significant, both positive and negative. That is, those who enjoyed these experiences were found prominently among the high hypnotizables, and the experiences were rare among those with little responsiveness to hypnosis.

The following comments are representative of the remarks regarding reading involvement and hypnosis:

Question. *"Are there some experiences in everyday life in which you would become absorbed to about the same extent, or watchful to the same extent, as in hypnosis?"*

WINIFRED. "When I'm reading literature. There I'm watching for the responses of the characters the way I looked for my own in hypnosis, and I'd be tied up in an esthetic emotion the same way."

BARBARA. "When I'm reading fiction or looking at a movie and really interested. I put myself in the story and can relate it to myself."

MARTIN. "I can become involved while reading and occasionally while listening to a very dramatic lecturer."

LILLIAN. "Yes, perhaps in reading a book or even listening in class." (J. R. Hilgard, 1970, p. 34.)

Shor (1970) has reported similar findings in his study of the book-reading fantasy.

The adventurers of the out-of-doors proved to be a very interesting group, well able to describe the exhilaration of their experiences. The case of Sidney gives something of this flavor:

He said about his adventurous streak, "I call it adventurous. My parents would say foolhardy." Asked about his skin diving, he said, "It's *free* competition, like an adventure. It's exhilarating." The appeal of motor cycling was the "power," the feeling of the wind "whistling by" and the "freedom of which is like flying." He was asked about his mention of flying. "I've always wanted to fly and snow ski but I've had no opportunity. I would like to learn to do stunts in flying. My father was a fine pilot." (J. R. Hilgard, 1970, p. 129.)

In making a few generalizations about the reports of the adventurers and the relationship to hypnosis, Josephine Hilgard noted five characteristics of these subjects indicating a possible link to hypnosis.

1. *Enjoyment of the feelings of the moment.* This feeling, common to the involved person, is often reported by the hypnotized subject: nothing else matters now.

2. *Escape from the world of reality.* While in the midst of the adventure, the world about is not the ordinary world. The world that surrounds the skin diver as he relaxes at the bottom of the sea is strange and wonderful, as is the world of the glider pilot who finds himself floating on the wind. Comparable experiences are reported in hypnosis so commonly that Shor (1959) was led to describe an important aspect of hypnosis as setting aside the generalized reality orientation of ordinary life.

3. *A time-limited experience.* These adventuresome people are not habitually living in a dream world. They are mostly highly motivated and successful students in a competitive university. The adventures that they report are episodes of limited duration. The airplane pilot or the skier returns to his classes and other responsibilities. The exhilarating experience is enjoyed, then set aside. Hypnosis is commonly accepted in the same way, as something to be enjoyed from time to time, but to be set aside in meeting the realistic demands of personal and social life.

4. *An active involvement.* A life of imagination for these people is not a passive, receptive experience. Instead it is an active, participative one. They are seekers and do not wait for the experiences to come to them. Their adventures often require preparation and hard work to achieve the satisfactions. Despite the stereotyped picture of the hypnotic subject as passive and dependent, that picture is false. The hypnotized subject, too, creates much that he experiences.

5. *Childlike enjoyment of excitement and power.* There are many attractive features of childhood that tend to be lost in adult life. Elsewhere I have made the distinction between childishness, which is petulant, immature, and regressive, and childlikeness that preserves some of the sense of wonder that characterizes the child (Hilgard, 1971). Josephine Hilgard has described these adventurers as being childlike in enjoying "a sense of triumph over nature, a sense of mastery of the world, of omnipotence and freedom from restraint. The experiences we have described add meaning and zest to their lives" (J. R. Hilgard, 1970, p. 135).

These experiences, too, can be reinstated in hypnosis. Hence what came out spontaneously in the remarks of the students in these interviews makes good sense in relation to the phenomenology of hypnosis.

The kinds of experiences recorded in the interviews and the related experience inventories that were earlier developed by Shor (1960), Aas (1963), and Lee-Teng (1965) have since been used to show why there has been so little success in relating hypnotizability to personality as measured by familiar inventories. The fault lies with the standard personality inventories for not including enough questions related to the types of experiences that are significant as a personality background for hypnosis. This was well demonstrated in a study by Tellegen and Atkinson (1974). They proceeded to construct three self-report scales, following the pattern of the MMPI. Each scale was factorially distinct, measuring the two major factors of the MMPI (variously named, but essentially introversion-extroversion and stability-instability), and a third scale, called "absorption," based on the imaginative involvements shown in Josephine Hilgard's interviews and represented in the experience inventories. Their study showed, first, that the MMPI items, with all their range, had failed to tap sufficiently this dimension of personal experience. Second, they showed that neither of the major factors of the MMPI correlated significantly with hypnotic susceptibility, as many other studies had shown, but the absorption scale was positively correlated. Although the positive correlation is not high enough to have much predictive significance for determining how hypnotizable any one person will be, it confirms the understanding of the hypnotic experience as related to the capacity for this type of imaginative involvement.

Imagination and Creativity

The expression "creative imagination" is in common use to describe the inspiration of the writer or artist, implying that the exercise of imagination is an a priori condition for creativity. The issue was first attacked by Galton (1883), whose questionnaire on imagery was addressed to many members of the Royal Society and others. He found, to his astonishment, that many of the distinguished scientists, whose creativity he could not doubt, were deficient in imagery, and he attributed this to their tendency to think in language. The final sentence in the passage makes a tantalizing reference to the lack of imagery even in distinguished artists:

> Men who declare themselves entirely deficient in the power of seeing mental pictures can nevertheless give life-like descriptions of what they have seen, and can otherwise express themselves as if they were gifted with a vivid visual imagination. They can also become painters of the rank of Royal Academicians (Galton, 1883, p. 88).

Apparently the correspondence between imagery and creativity is not one-to-one; thus it is necessary to inquire further. The most influential current theories of creativity refer to two types of processes. One is related to free and somewhat unstructured fantasy, inner-controlled, and perhaps in some sense unconsciously guided. The other is related to the reality-oriented manipulations that produce a socially acceptable or useful product through the reworking of the raw materials in some kind of synthesis with materials from the ordinary world. One form of this is the proposal of Ernst Kris (1934) that there is a "regression in the service of the ego," in which there is a partial regression in which primary process thinking is mobilized, and then a return to ego activity that uses secondary process thinking. It will be recalled that primary process is impulse controlled; secondary process is rational. This conception is widely influential. A tie to hypnosis is implied in the theory proposed by Gill and Brenman (1959) that hypnosis represents a partial regression corresponding to regression in the service of the ego.

There are, however, other ways of formulating the distinction between the two processes, one of which leads to illumination, the other to realization. A less orthodox psychoanalyst, Rollo May (1975) objects to the term regression in relation to creativity, because it appears to imply a neurotic process and the reduction of creativity to something else.

With this material as a background, Kenneth and Patricia Bowers (1972) reviewed studies relating hypnosis to imagination, including those they had conducted.

To simplify somewhat, three chief quantitative ways of investigating creativity have permitted laboratory measurements to be made. The first, based on accepting the premise that the creative person ought to have access to primary process thinking, in line with the prevailing psychoanalytic theory, makes use of a manual that Robert Holt developed for scoring primary process manifestations in the Rorschach (Holt, 1963; Pine and Holt, 1960). The second, using the conception that creativity requires the exercise of divergent thinking by contrast with convergent thinking, is based on the work of Guilford (1959), who prepared test materials in his factor-analytic studies. The third method, epitomized by the Barron-Welsh Art Scale (Welsh and Barron, 1963), uses esthetic preference for colored patterns as a way of estimating creativity. The three approaches are based on rather different hypotheses about creativity, but they are not mutually exclusive, and it is often instructive to have the several measures used on the same population.

The first of the Bowers' studies was concerned directly with the effect of the hypnotic state on creativity (P. Bowers, 1967). The main variable to test the hypothesis was the instruction to the subject, under hypnosis, to be "free" in his thinking, in the hope that defensiveness would be reduced and regressive material made available for creative problem solution. The control condition gave "cognitive set" instructions instead, that is, to try to be deliberately creative and flexible on the tasks. The hypnotized subjects were more creative by Guilford's consequences test, giving support to the initial hypothesis.

Because of the subtle nature of the hypnotic interaction and the kinds of behaviors legitimized in hypnosis, K. Bowers and van der Meulen (1970) used the real-simulator design to check these factors and found no treatment effects attributable to hypnosis, despite their use of a richer variety of tests. They concluded that they had not demonstrated anything unique in hypnosis to enhance creativity test performance.

This negative answer to the first question posed above led to an examination of their data in answer to a second question: Is there something about the hypnotizable person that produces the results? When Bowers and van der Meulen compared the high hypnotic susceptibles with the lows, the highs scored significantly above the lows on eight of the nine creativity tests. Hence the negative answer to the first question was followed by an affirmative answer to the effectiveness of high hypnotizability as related to creativity scores.

The investigation of the second question was carried further by K. Bowers (1971). The conclusions of the Bowers and van der Meulen study were supported, but a new variable emerged as important, that of sex differences. For women, the correlation between hypnotic susceptibility and a composite creativity score was .41 ($N = 36$); for men, with the same sample size, it was .08. In hypnotic experiments, moderate-sized samples are subject to considerable sampling fluctuation because of the occasional presence or absence of those I have classified as hypnotic virtuosos; thus some of the sex differences in this study may not be entirely generalizable. In any case, the study points to the desirability of studying the interaction between level of hypnotizability and sex in creativity studies.

An extensive study of creativity measures as related to hypnotic susceptibility was reported later by Perry, Wilder, and Appignanesi (1973). Among 19 creativity measures, six yielded significant positive correlations with SHSS-C: Barron-Welsh Art Scale ($r = .34$), Barron-Welsh Revised ($r = .31$), Guilford's Object Synthesis ($r = .27$), Torrance Verbal Fluency ($r = .40$), Torrance Flexibility ($r = .33$), and Torrance Originality ($r = .25$). Of these, the two Torrance tests appeared to be most useful in producing significant differences consistently in the right direction for the mean scores of high, medium, and low hypnotic subjects. The relationship proved higher for female subjects in this study, as in that of K. Bowers (1971). It may be noted that the differences found again associate creativity with hypnotic talent and not with the hypnotic state.

Questions of this kind are seldom answered once and for all. In a later study, Gur and Reyher (1976) found some evidence for enhanced creativity in hypnosis, attributed to the hypnotic condition rather than to hypnotic talent because the comparison groups included simulators as well as waking subjects who were as susceptible to hypnosis as those hypnotized. However, the instructions to the simulators and waking subjects were given by posthypnotic suggestion, which imposed an added subconscious burden, in the one case to remain unhypnotized but to act as if hypnotized, in the other case, to remain awake even though given a hypnotic induction to which they had previously responded by becoming hypnotized. One consequence appeared to be that the instructions *reduced* the creativity of waking and control subjects as tested by the Torrance Creativity Test administered under these conditions; thus it is not clear that hypnosis actually enhanced creativity above those who might not have been burdened with secondary tasks.

Imagination and the Right Hemisphere

Phenomenal experience may be enough to justify a concept of dissociation, but it is only natural to look for brain processes that might provide a substratum or correlate for divisions of consciousness. Laterality of function is, of course, a good candidate, brought to the fore recently by the studies of the differential functions of the two cerebral hemispheres.

This new interest began with the studies of Gazzaniga, Bogen, and Sperry (1962) on patients who had had the fiber bundles between the cerebral hemispheres (the corpus callosum) cut surgically to control severe epileptic attacks. The research on these patients after their recovery from the operation revealed that the two halves of the brain are essentially two brains, nearly identical in conformation, but differing in what they do. In right-handed people, the left hemisphere is primarily concerned with verbal behavior and analytical tasks, whereas the right hemisphere is concerned with more global and patterned tasks such as imagination, space perception, and music. Because imagination is included in this list, it is appropriate to give brief attention to these findings here, as they relate both to imagination and hypnosis. In more general terms, two analogies are appropriate. The left hemisphere acts like a digital computer and the right hemisphere like an analog computer; or, the left hemisphere acts like a stimulus-response brain and the right acts like a Gestalt brain. The relationships may be reversed in left-handed people.

If electrodes are placed appropriately on the two sides of the head to detect which hemisphere is being more actively used, people with perfectly normal brains can be shown to use their half-brains differentially, repeating the kinds of reports from the split-brain patients (e.g., Galin and Ornstein, 1972). If, for example, a right-handed person speaks the words to a song without singing them, it can be shown that he is using the left (verbal) hemisphere; if he hums the music without the words he uses the right (nonverbal, patterning) hemisphere; if he sings the song—words and music—both hemispheres are activated (Schwartz and others, 1973).

Other methods are also available for studying when the two hemispheres are activated preferentially. One of these makes use of the tendency to divert the eyes while solving mental problems, first noted by Day (1967), and first related to hypnosis by Bakan (1969), then at work in our laboratory. A questioner may sit behind a strongly right-handed subject, who is looking ahead while being questioned. If the questioner asks a question of analytic type, such as mental arithmetic, the person tends to divert his eyes to the right while figuring out the answer. This indicates that he is activating his left hemisphere, the analytic one. If the question involved imagination ("imagine a child swinging a rope swing out over a garden") the subject tends to move his eyes to the left, indicating that the right hemisphere has been activated (Kinsbourne, 1972). The degree to which eye movements correspond to the type of question indicates how "lateralized"—how completely right- or left-handed—the subject is.

Something else happens, however, when the questioner sits facing the subject. Now the subject's eye movements have other components not related specifically to the nature of the question (R. E. Gur, 1975). For reasons that are not simple to explain, people in this situation differ in their *preference* for looking to the right or left with the same set of questions. In the first case, with the questioner behind, the determining factor was how lateralized the person was. Now, however, something else has entered—a habitual preference for diverting the eyes one way or the other, or in terms of brain function, a *preference* for using the right or the left hemisphere. This preference correlates with measured hypnotizability: right-handed persons who show hemispheric preference by looking more often to the left and therefore activating the *right* hemisphere (the one related to imagination) are the more hypnotizable. At present the relationship has been established primarily for right-handed males, but it is so striking as to be a confirmed finding (Bakan, 1969; Gur and Gur 1974.)

The argument about imagination as a dissociative process related to hypnosis is by now very convincing. The results suggest a moderate overall relationship of imagery to hypnotizability, a stronger relationship between imaginative involvement and hypnotic responsiveness, some relationships to creativity, and a relation to right hemisphere functioning that also brings imagination and hypnosis together.

There is enough in common among dreams, hallucinations, and imagination to suggest that a search for their common properties will help us understand consciousness and its divisions.

NOTES

The recognition that imagery in its various forms is an important field of research, and that it was earlier neglected, is nicely expressed in the title of a paper by Robert Holt (1964), "Imagery: The return of the ostracized." The advances since then are well recognized in the book edited by Sheehan (1972b).

Dreams

Freud's *Interpretation of Dreams* (1900) initiated a new interest in dreams and led to a consideration of them as sensible products rather than as bizarre. Correctives to Freud's theory have been offered from inside psychoanalysis by Erikson (1954) as well as by French and Fromm (1964), and by the interested outsider (e.g., Hall, 1953). However, the interpretation of the dream as a meaningful cognitive product seems to be here to stay, and this is Freud's lasting contribution.

The psychophysiological studies, I believe, have paid too little attention to content, because the interest in content does not rest entirely on a correspondence between the characteristics of the eye movements and the visual perceptions in the dream, on the frequency of dreaming, or even on the difference between the "thoughts" revealed in NREM sleep and the distinctive content of REM dreams (e.g., Monroe and others, 1965; Dement, 1972). The method ought to be more useful than the usual dream diary method of collecting large dream samples, the method that had to be relied on by Hall and Van de Castle (1966). I do not know whether there are any large samples of dreams from laboratory studies of sleep.

The studies of hypnotic dreams have not been carried as far as they might. The book by Moss (1967) is an introduction and republishes some of the more important papers. Sacerdote (1967) has shown that induced dreams, not only spontaneous ones, can be useful in psychotherapy with the aid of hypnosis.

Nothing is said in the chapter about claims for dream telepathy (Ullman, Krippner, and Vaughan, 1973). As indicated earlier, a scientific critique of parapsychological studies always leaves the believer unmoved. It should be noted, however, that the book referred to, although it gives a statistical summary, presents the statistics in such a miscellaneous fashion that no serious analysis of the data is possible. Replication by the skeptic would most likely prove futile, because only positive results would be convincing and the likelihood of obtaining them is so low as to make the attempt a poor use of the investigator's time when so many other tasks remain to be done.

Hallucinations

The book edited by West (1962), with 42 contributors from various disciplines, provides a good summary of knowledge as of its date. Siegel and West (1975) have edited a new symposium. At the earlier time, the hallucinations produced by sensory deprivation were a popular topic of discourse; some of the evidence is still sound, but the excitement has gone out of the field as the extremes of reported hallucinatory effects have been softened by such findings as those of Orne and Schiebe (1961) that expectations could greatly influence the phenomena of sensory deprivation without the actual deprivation. The interest in drug-induced hallucinations has led to many books, including the republication of the classical study of mescaline by Klüver (1966).

Orne's (1959) proposal of the double-person hallucination as a test of what he called "trance logic" was most seriously questioned in a doctoral dissertation by Johnson, published in collaboration with his Ph.D. supervisors, (Johnson, Maher, and Barber, 1972). Because the study was not designed adequately as a test of Orne's conjectures and was misleading in the data reported and omitted, I was led to write a corrective (Hilgard, 1972) that the original author in his rebuttal made no serious attempt to understand (Johnson, 1972). Orne (1959) no doubt overstated the case when he indicated that *no* simulator would act like a truly hypnotized subject, for simulators have various degrees of sophistication and expectations (Sheehan, Obstoj, and McConkey, 1976). The overstatement can be ignored, however, when the basic findings are so easily and convincingly demonstrated. Another replication of Orne's work has been done by McDonald and Smith (1975), with results more consonant with Orne's. Orne's concept of trance logic is not altogether unambiguous in view of the highly logical basis on which the subjects commonly resolved their dilemmas to find which of their perceptions represented a real person. Do they perhaps operate at two logical levels at once?

Imagination

Some linguistic problems are involved in distinguishing between imaging, imagining, and hallucinating, but, in context, these are not very troublesome. The problem does not reside in the words that are used in labeling, because the ambiguity of the phenomena themselves cannot be cleared up by an exercise in definition.

Imagery, which commonly refers to the revival of experiences similar to those provoked at other times by the stimulation of sense organs, has been reviewed in the context of hypnosis by Sheehan (1972a), with some references to the richer aspects of imagination. Sheehan addressed the question of sex differences in imagery as related to hypnotic susceptibility, because sex may be a moderating variable here, as it is in so many instances in which attention is paid to individual differences in performance. However, the evidence in relation to hypnosis is very weak. Sutcliffe, Perry, and Sheehan (1970) had found men to yield a significantly higher correlation between imagery and hypnosis than the women in their sample, but J. R. Hilgard (1970) found a nonsignificant difference between the sexes, with a numerically higher correlation for the women. Perry (1973), in an effort at replication, failed to find a significant relation for either sex, a result also found in a supplementary study from our laboratory (Morgan and Lam, 1969). Despite Perry's failure to find an overall correlation, he did report the same findings for the extremes: high imagery among the highly hypnotizable and low imagery among the low hypnotizables. Diamond and Taft (1975) found significant correlations between imagery and hypnosis for both sexes.

The Marks (1973) questionnaire, as an alternative to the original by Betts or its revision by Sheehan (1967a, 1967b), shows some advantages, but it could be improved. It has been validated as a measure of imagery affecting performance not only in the original report of Marks, but also in a study along somewhat different lines by Gur and Hilgard (1975). It has been related to hypnosis in studies by others, as indicated in the body of the chapter.

The role of imaginative involvement as shown in the work of Josephine Hilgard, Shor, and Tellegen and Atkinson, and confirmed by Spanos and McPeake (1975) has been validated again from a scale prepared by Swanson (1977) in another connection. Independently of the work of Tellegen and Atkinson, he developed a scale for measuring what would be called absorbing or involving experiences, using somewhat the same models. In a recent study, Finke and Macdonald (1977), using Swanson's scale along with that of Tellegen and Atkinson, found the relationship of both scales to each other and to hypnotic susceptibility scores. The scales correlated .65 with each other, and both correlated significantly (.27-.40) with hypnotic susceptibility as measured by a group scale. A failure of relationship by Spanos, McPeake, and Churchill (1976) is attributed by them to their use of the Barber suggestibility scale as their criterion measure.

The personality factors in the background of creativity continue to be baffling, as Bowers' review showed. The adaptive regression interpretation has been objected to by Schachtel (1959) as well as by May (1975). Kubie (1958) had also warned against the interpretation of creativity as a sign of neuroticism.

The mobilization of problem-solving insights or achieving organization through a kind of rumination, some at the unconscious level, is not necessarily the equivalent of regression. The famous story of the mathematician Poincaré, for whom the solution of a difficult problem came in a flash as he mounted the steps of a bus, does not require that he regressed to keep turning the problem over in his mind, even with low attention to it.

CH. 5 DREAMS, HALLUCINATIONS, AND IMAGINATION

The preferences for colored diagrams that are the bases for the Barron-Welsh creativity test require a preference for complexity rather than for simple order and balance. It is hard to see how this can be called regressive, except by a tendentious argument. The preference for complexity in musical forms was made the basis of a theory of esthetics many years ago by Moore (1914), who pointed out that, in the history of those who appreciated music, they gradually began to classify more and more difficult intervals as consonant. After a while, the easy intervals of children's songs are no longer as pleasing as the difficult intervals of modern music—a difficulty in synthesizing that Moore felt was part of the evolution of pleasing consonance. Guilford's divergent thinking characterizes invention quite as much as art, and different dimensions may be involved. From some dissatisfaction with these analytical (or "reductive") treatments, someone like May moves on to a greater sympathy for existentialism, which is much harder to integrate into general experimental psychology.

The chapter by the Bowers (1972) remains the best review of the relationship of hypnosis and creativity.

The split-brain studies have been well summarized in several books: Gazzaniga (1970), Dimond and Beaumont (1974), and Kinsbourne and Smith (1974). At the time of writing they had not caught up with the hypnotic studies described in the text.

CHAPTER

VOLUNTARY AND INVOLUNTARY CONTROL OF MUSCULAR MOVEMENT

One of the most striking features of hypnosis is the loss of control over actions normally voluntary and the occasional gaining of control over actions usually involuntary. Once it has been recognized that controls can be dissociated as well as the conscious contents of memories and thoughts, problems in the explanation of voluntary and involuntary action naturally arise. The chapters thus far have dealt primarily with cognitive processes, in which the alterations have been of self-perception, memories, or alterations of sensory-like experiences. This chapter focuses on muscular movements, emphasizing alterations in the voluntary-involuntary dimension in their control. These alterations in control reflect dissociations at the level of the executive function that carries responsibility for volitional activity.

THE PROBLEM OF VOLITION

Problems of voluntary control lie at the heart of personality theory. Because the "will" was so long a taboo concept in psychology, adequate discussions have been rare since 1900. William James' chapter (1890, II, Chapter 27) is still worth reading as one of the few serious efforts to struggle with the concept. More recently, the emphases on cognition, information processing, and decision theory have brought new attention to the planning function (a modern form of willing). Credit is due to Miller, Galanter, and Pribram (1960) for overcoming the constraints of the earlier behaviorism and again considering the problems raised by acts of will.

In a larger context, the problem of willing raises the question of the unity of the personality. Is strength of will a pervasive quality that endures through time and gives some unity to the characterization of the individual, or is it something fragmented and influenced by the constraints of the immediate situation? A general answer can be given: personality is much less unified than we would like to believe, and volition is subject to dissociations just as are perceptual processes.

Whatever their excesses in denying the significance of subjective processes in man, the behaviorists were right in emphasizing the importance of muscular performances, including speech, in accounting for much that is distinctively human. Man is a past master at the art of motion. We admire the litheness of the leopard, the soaring skill of the eagle, the wing movements of the humming bird, but in the range and precision of movements no organism comes near to man. Consider any other animal trying to imitate a concert pianist, violinist, or operatic soprano. The trained animals in a circus are impressive because they can enlarge their repertory of movement skills, but their tricks fade in comparison with what the human acrobats can do. Of course, an animal may be specialized for some skill that man cannot attain— a frog can beat a man in catching flies with his tongue—but man's tongue is the only one that can master the subtleties of speech sounds. Talking birds become very poor seconds. Hence the control of movements, voluntary or involuntary, tells us much about mind and behavior.

Words taken from the common vocabulary to describe scientific phenomena have the advantage of familiarity of reference and connotation, but the difficulty of imprecision. The words "voluntary" and "involuntary" represent a pair of such words. We know that operating a typewriter is a voluntary act, whereas sneezing from pepper in the nose is involuntary. But we also know that the skilled typist is carrying out much of the activity quite automatically, and that, if necessary, the person can withhold his sneeze. Even in our clearest examples, we have some confusion between what is voluntary and what involuntary.

The distinction between voluntary and involuntary parallels the distinction between conscious and subconscious (or unconscious), but the correspondence is inexact. That is, when a choice is made deliberately and the selected act carried out purposefully, we have an experience of conscious action. Voluntary action and conscious control then seem nearly synonymous. At the other extreme, homeostatic processes going on within our bodies, such as the secretion of hormones to maintain an appropriate chemical balance, represent processes that are unconscious and involuntary, and the terms again seem synonymous. That they are not completely synonymous is evident when we become aware of something over which we have no control, such as a toothache, when the consciousness is genuine, but there is no voluntariness about it. The concepts fall apart at the other end of the scale when an act, normally conscious, is performed without awareness, such as habitual movements or gestures, of which, when called to the person's attention, he says: "I didn't know I did that." There is sufficient overlap between consciousness and volition that they need to be examined together when divisions of consciousness are being studied.

Having raised questions about volition, it is illuminating to examine how controls over movement can be modified. Illustrations involving hysteria, hypnosis, and some related techniques follow.

HYSTERICAL PARALYSIS: LOSS OF VOLUNTARY CONTROL

When hysterical symptoms were more widely prevalent, it is no wonder that hysterical and hypnotic behaviors were recognized as much alike. The hysterical person exhibited paralyses and anesthesias that clearly had no basis in underlying nerve damage. A glove anesthesia in hysteria, for example, may have a line of demarcation at any point on an arm or leg, indicating the length of the glove. Such a line of demarcation does not correspond to the pattern of distribution of sensory nerves; the name glove anesthesia derives from this characteristic pattern for the functional disturbance. Such glove anesthesias are readily produced through hypnotic suggestion and are widely used in the treatment of pain. The hysterical person may also have a paralyzed body member, so that he cannot move it; the two symptoms are often found together, as though the arm or leg are subjectively interpreted as "dead." The hysterical paralysis is not so different from the movement inhibitions produced by hypnosis. In functional or suggested paralyses, hysteria and hypnosis may indeed involve similar or overlapping mechanisms, although the differences lie in the origins of the symptoms and in their persistence.

The influence of psychoanalytic thinking led to an interpretation of hysterical symptoms as *conversions,* that is, as defense mechanisms that avoided anxiety by giving intrapsychic conflicts expression through somatic symptoms. This interpretation became so dominant that the word hysteria was dropped for a time from the official glossary of the American Psychiatric Association, and conversion reaction was substituted. More recently, however, hysterical neurosis has again been recognized in the two forms of the *conversion type*, characterized by disorders of the voluntary nervous system, such as anesthesia and paralysis, and the *dissociative type*, including amnesias, fugues, and multiple personalities (Frazier and others, 1975).

The following case, which I studied in collaboration with Stanley H. Lindley, illustrates how conversion symptoms may arise, endure, and be relieved.

> Miss H., an unmarried school teacher, aged 32, had been in a motor car accident six years before coming for treatment. During these six years her left arm had been entirely useless to her, being totally paralyzed and anesthetic. Neurological examination showed the anesthesia to be of the glove type, with a line of demarcation at the shoulder. The symptoms were thus shown to be functional. The arm and hand showed considerable atrophy from disuse. Attempts by a psychiatrist to give the patient insight into the functional nature of the abnormality met with great resistance, although the fact that the patient had returned to the hospital voluntarily in the hope of a cure was considered a hopeful sign. The psychiatrist arranged to have the patient treated by conditioning methods in the psychological laboratory that adjoined the psychiatric unit.
>
> A finger withdrawal experiment was arranged. Two electrodes were used, one for each hand. The first series of experiments consisted in presenting a shock to the anesthetic hand as the conditioned stimulus, a shock to the normal hand as the unconditioned stimulus. This was designed to give evidence of sensitivity in the anesthetic hand, since a shock to it served as the signal for withdrawal of the normal hand. While little conditioning occurred, the desired effect was produced, and sensitivity gradually returned in the anesthetic arm and hand. Experiments were repeated daily, and the improvement was gradual. After recovery of sensitivity, the conditioning procedure was reversed for purposes of developing voluntary control. The normal hand was given a light shock which served as the conditioned stimulus. For the unconditioned stimulus, the paralyzed hand was given a more severe shock, to which it was now fully sensitive. Presently movement began to occur in the paralyzed hand at the signal given to the normal hand. This was the beginning of control, and voluntary movement was gradually restored. At this stage, the patient was given physiotherapy to strengthen the muscles that had been so long unused. The symptoms had not returned two years later, nor were any additional symptoms reported (Hilgard and Marquis, 1940, p. 297–298).

Although this appears to be a cure by a method that years later would have been called behavior modification, the basis of cure was probably little related to the specific conditioning methods used. The full understanding of the case involved a great deal more, even though these other factors did not enter directly into the treatment. There were secondary gains from her symptoms. She was excused from the housekeeping chores she had previously performed at the insistence of the demanding mother with whom she lived; it is not surprising that her return to the hospital to be cured came after her mother had died. She had been able to carry on satisfactorily as a school teacher with her left hand affected. That she no longer needed the symptom at home did not automatically relieve her of the symptom. Subconsciously she welcomed a face-saving therapy that would attribute the change to something done to her rather than to a change of heart on her part. She believed our machine to be making her well; in fact, she was so pleased by our contrivance that she sought to purchase it for home use.

That the dynamics of defense and conversion seem appropriate to this and other cases of hysteria does not mean that the same dynamics explain the similar symptoms in hypnosis. To be responsive to hypnosis, one need not have a hysterical personality, as the results of personality tests in relation to hypnotizability have shown (Hilgard, 1965). What may be common between them is a capacity for the disruption of normal control mechanisms. These disruptions make observations of both hysterics and hypnotized persons relevant to the concept of dissociation.

LOSS OF VOLUNTARY CONTROL IN HYPNOSIS

In hypnosis, the voluntary-involuntary distinction is sharpened, particularly in "challenge" items, when the subject is told that his arm has become stiff (presumably through an involuntary process engendered within hypnosis by the hypnotist's suggestions) so that he cannot bend it even if he tries, or he cannot speak his name. Voluntary and involuntary controls are now in conflict. That there is conflict is evident enough by watching the subject's behavior, but the nature of the conflict is not clear. It does not suffice to say that the conflict is between voluntary and involuntary processes, because some voluntary acquiescence was involved in making the arm stiff, and in losing the ability to say something familiar.

Confronted with the stiff-arm task many subjects say to the hypnotist, "I could have bent my arm if I had wanted to." Further inquiry will show that some of those who answer in this way felt that they had not wanted to try, or it did not seem worth the effort, or when they tried, the antagonist muscles tightened through some sort of compulsion to prevent the arm from bending.

An experiment was performed a few years ago to test the subjects' impression of their ability to resist such a suggestion (Hilgard, 1963). Previous experiments by Young (1927) and Wells (1940) had led to contradictory results; all of Young's subjects were able to resist, but most of Wells' subjects were not able to do so. Clearly it was necessary to undertake a more careful control of conditions. Because there was no point in testing the matter with subjects who did not give the usual response to begin with, subjects were selected who had "passed" challenge items in routine tests of hypnotizability; that is, they had been unable to overcome the suggested paralysis in the ordinary context of the hypnotic experience. The implication is, of course, that they are acting like hypnotically responsive persons if they are unable to contradict the suggestion, and the question remains, what happens if, instead, it is part of the contract that they try especially hard to do what the hypnotist has said they cannot do, or to resist doing what he says they will do. To test this, they were rehypnotized on another occasion and requested to become hypnotized as before. They knew in advance that they were going to be given six different test items of the kind that had been successful before, but the specific tasks were not indicated, and they were not told the order in which they would occur. A signaling arrangement was prepared so that they could indicate by means of a telegraph key concealed from the view of the hypnotist which of the next suggestions they would try especially hard to resist. The hypnotized subject is able to take initiative within hypnosis, and he has no trouble in following this instruction. Subjects were told to behave as they had in earlier hypnotic sessions on four of the six tests, but to select two of the six—at any point in the series—as the ones to resist. The telegraphic report was monitored in another room by someone assisting the hypnotist-experimenter; thus a record was available of those suggestions that were to be resisted, but in the conduct of the experiment the hypnotist did not know which ones were chosen and therefore gave all instructions in a uniform manner.

The results may be summarized thus:

1. The attempted resistance on two items, whether or not successful, did not reduce the responsiveness to the remaining items.
2. The suggestion to resist was not interpreted as a cancellation of the original suggestion (of stiffness, of hands locked together, etc.), but of the ability to cancel the suggestion once it was accepted. This may have been implied in the use of the term "resist," and is coherent with the belief commonly expressed in the normal testing situation: "It was stiff, all right, but I think I could have bent it if I had tried."
3. By marshalling effort, most subjects had some success in countering the inhibition. The degree of success varied, as shown in Table 7.

In general, among these moderately hypnotizable subjects, in a relatively permissive situation, difficulties in resisting were greater than the subjects expected them to be. Subsequent questioning revealed what techniques the

Table 7
DEGREE OF SUCCESS IN COUNTERACTING INHIBITORY SUGGESTIONS
("CHALLENGE ITEMS")
(After Hilgard, 1963)

Success	Number of subjects
Both selected items successfully resisted	6
One of the two selected items successfully resisted	5
Neither item successfully resisted	1
	12

subjects had used in trying to resist. These fell into four chief categories. First, two subjects reported that it required sheer effort and determination, that there was much to overcome, but they did it by making enough effort. Second, three subjects said that they gained confidence when they reflected that a cooperative subject was supposed to be capable of making effort even though hypnotized. Third, deliberate inattention to the hypnotist's suggestions weakened their effect for two subjects. Fourth, three subjects used autosuggestion to counter the hypnotist's suggestions. These categories, each represented by at least two subjects, accounted for 10 of the 12 subjects. Of the other two, the one unable to resist at all said: ". . . it takes a lot of effort . . . it seems you don't really want to . . . I was angry at myself for being unable to resist." The final subject had little to offer: "I was not surprised to be able to resist." There was uniform relief that the high degree of effort was no longer called for after resistance was no longer required. There were many evidences of behavioral conflict during attempted resistance: hands alternately being pulled apart and brought back together in resisting, fingerlock broken but clonic movements in the forearms after the hands were separated, and violent expression of anger or disappointment. It is not surprising that under some circumstances the subject preferred not to resist at all.

This experiment illustrates the difficulty of the voluntary-involuntary distinction in a conflict situation in which all movements are those normally under voluntary control. There is no damage in the peripheral neuromuscular apparatus, but the hypnotic procedures have interfered with normal control processes. These divided processes are relevant to the concept of dissociation; what is divided is access to the control of movement even though consciousness of what the hands are doing has not been altered.

The relevance to dissociation is that alternate modes of control conflict for ascendance. The hypnotist's suggestions subordinate some control systems to others, thereby producing a dissociated experience.

IDEOMOTOR CONTROL OF ACTION

Much of the control that a hypnotist exerts over the behavior of his subject, with that person's cooperation, depends on an old principle called *ideomotor action*, the principle that thinking about a movement tends to lead to that movement. William James did much to bring the idea to the attention of a broader audience:

> We may then lay it down for certain that *every representation of a movement awakens in some degree the actual movement which is its object; and awakens it in a maximum degree whenever it is not kept from so doing by an antagonistic representation present simultaneously to the mind* (James, 1890, II, p. 526).

Sensory discriminations must be made whenever skilled acts are performed; thus the concept of sensorimotor action is familiar. Ideomotor action is a different kind of concept because it assumes that the idea is the direct *instigator* of the action. Familiar illustrations outside hypnosis include "body English," in which a spectator, for example, helps out the athlete he is watching by making incipient motions to improve the performance. A closely related form is unconscious mimicry. Hull (1933, p. 41–46) had his assistant reach for the wall at some distance while a subject was unknowingly attached by a thread to a postural movement recorder. Soon the unsuspecting subject had leaned toward the wall some inch and a half beyond the range of his usual oscillations while standing quietly. Imagining a movement forward or backward also produced marked deviations in posture, even though the subject insisted that he had inhibited any tendency to make the movements imagined.

Here we may take a leaf from the behaviorist's notebook and propose that words and ideas are intimately related. If the hypnotized person can be placed in such a relaxed and sleeplike state that his self-talk is reduced, or perhaps confused so that he does not clearly integrate the verbal messages that he hears, he is ready for clear statements from the hypnotist, such as "Your outstretched hands are slowly moving together, moving, moving . . ." An interpretation of direct suggestion was proposed along these lines by Miller, Galanter, and Pribram (1960), who stated that the person's self-talk was replaced by that of the hypnotist. That is, the hypnotist takes over the planning function, and the subject carries out the plan as if it were his own. Anna Freud (1936) conceptualized it as though the subject relinquishes his ego to the hypnotist. What we see is a modification of control, in which a normally voluntary movement is made involuntarily in conformity to the words of the hypnotist.

The role of the words can be given quantitative study in simplified contexts. For example, if the arm is outstretched and the subject told that it is presently going to move down involuntarily—by itself—it can be shown that the rate at which it drops is a function of the rate at which the hypnotist reasserts his contol by saying "Now," "Now," "Now" at different rates. The motion then corresponds to the rate at which he says "Now" (Figure 10). Careful tests showed that the amount of movement, expressed in degrees, was not significantly different for arm levitation or arm lowering, or for the right or left arms. These results imply that the task is indeed a cognitive one, under the conditions of the experiment, and not dependent on strength or fatigue for its rate.

The power of control of the hypnotist's words may be very evident. For example, after some experience of hypnosis, the subject may enter hypnosis at a signal given by a single cue word previously accepted by him. The hypnosis

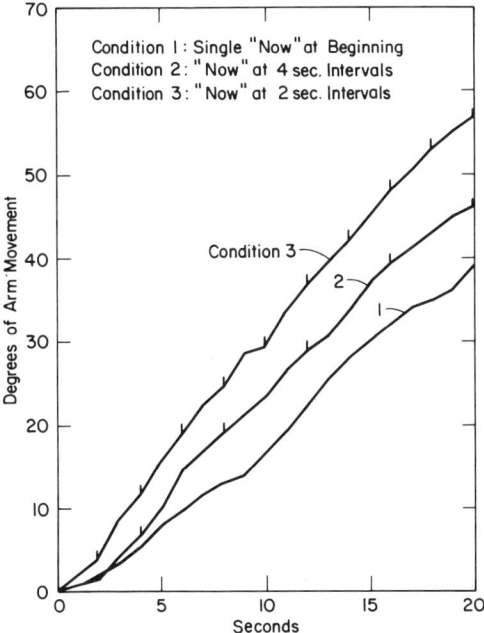

Figure 10 Cumulative arm movement in degrees under three suggestion conditions. Mean results for 12 subjects are plotted, each subject having previously scored 9 or more on SHSS-A. After the subject had been hypnotized and the arm positioned on a hinged board arranged for automatic recording, the following suggestion was given: "I want you to pay close attention to this arm because something very interesting will happen when I say 'Now.' Your arm is lowering (rising). Now . . . Now . . . ." McCleave, (1968).

appears to be reinstated immediately, as evidenced by the closed eyes and relaxed posture, but it is usually found, on questioning, that the subject is not actually very deeply hypnotized and welcomes either time or special procedures to become more deeply involved in hypnosis. How long the readjustment takes depends both on personal differences between subjects and on the amount of practice in using this method. In any case, the preliminary induction has been greatly shortened by the magic of a single word.

Ideation can be carried by images as well as words, and many subjects find that picturing a relaxed scene in imagery is a useful method of deepening hypnosis, once hypnosis has been undertaken. The effect in either case is to set ordinary reality aside and to accept the involvement in the hypnotic experience as the immediate reality.

VOLUNTARY CONTROL OF NORMALLY INVOLUNTARY PROCESSES

Students of conditioning have for many years been interested in the learned modification of autonomic processes, not surprisingly, in view of Pavlov's preoccupation with conditioned salivation. The study of the acquisition of voluntary control over these processes was a natural extension of this work, and it was carried on for many years before the current interest in voluntary control through methods now known as biofeedback. Much of the Russian work, dating from as far back as 1928, was summarized by Bykov (1957), who was one of the early investigators. Late in life, Pavlov came to the conclusion that in man the evidence for voluntary control always involved the use of words—his "second signal system"—to control the autonomic behavior.

The American work also goes back many years, with experiments on voluntary control of the pupil size (Hudgins, 1933) and vasomotor responses (Menzies, 1937).

Many muscular responses are semivoluntary; thus there is complex interaction between automatic or involuntary activity and deliberate or voluntary activity. Respiration provides the most familiar example, because a person can breathe fast or slowly, or he can hold his breath; at the same time, breathing continues whether he is awake or asleep. Many conditioned responses, such as the eyeblink, are also of this type. My collaborators and I examined the interaction between the relatively automatic conditioned responses of the eyelid and its voluntary control in experiments on conditioned discrimination by first setting up a conditioned discrimination through appropriate reinforcement and extinction (one light flash followed either by an air-puff to the cornea, or a different light flash not followed by an air-puff). Verbal instructions could be added to facilitate or inhibit the discriminatory response. A simple algebraic analysis showed that modifications could be produced in either direction, although facilitation was easier than inhibition, probably because a positive voluntary response may occlude the involuntary one, whereas a voluntary inhibitory tendency acts directly on the automatic responses without so readily displacing it (Hilgard, 1938).

The new interest in the control of involuntary responses that became an emphasis on biofeedback was initiated in part by the experiments of DiCara and Miller (1968) on the instrumental conditioning of vasomotor responses in rats and by Kamiya's work on learning to control EEG-alpha through hearing signals when alpha was "on" or "off" (Kamiya, 1969). This has now been extended to various other normally involuntary responses, such as skin temperature, heart rate, and blood pressure. The basic pattern is that the response the subject is learning to make is amplified through an electronic device and converted to a signal that the subject can watch or hear. That is, when the desired response is present he knows it, and when it is absent he also knows that. There may also be finer details, so that he knows if his blood pressure or skin temperature is rising or falling and by how much. That is the "feedback" feature. With such feedback, he can gain control by doing whatever modified the response. Through trial and error he eventually gains voluntary control of the response in question. He may not always be able to put into words how he does it. Once he has learned, he has established control in a form that was not present before.

To what extent can hypnosis parallel the results of biofeedback? For many years there have been claims that hypnosis could modify autonomic processes, hence achieving results comparable to biofeedback in the differential control of skin temperatures of right and left hands, in achieving relaxation of muscles, or in control of blood flow, perhaps even controlling allergic responses. Many of the positive results are impressive, but they are challenged by negative results of others; the exact conditions under which favorable results can be obtained remain elusive. The fact that results can be achieved by any methods (hypnotic or not) is all that is necessary for our present purposes, which is to indicate that cognitive controls can be altered, further confusing the voluntary-involuntary distinction.

Biofeedback and hypnosis may be supplementary. Their methods are, in fact, rather different. In biofeedback the subject is confronted with the realities of what goes in his body: his actual heart rate or skin temperature are amplified for him. In hypnosis the subject is commonly asked to set reality aside, to believe that there is no pain, rather than to find out how his body is reacting to aversive stimulation. The hypnotic dissociation is the very opposite of amplified reality. It may very well be that some highly hypnotizable persons are very poor candidates for biofeedback because they too readily hallucinate what they expect. Conversely, some persons firmly rooted in reality might be poor candidates for hypnosis but the best candidates for biofeedback. An investigation bearing on this problem compared differential temperature control through biofeedback for a group of highly hypnotizable subjects with a group low in hypnotizability and found the two groups equally responsive to biofeedback (Roberts and others, 1975). The results showed that less hypnotizable subjects were as responsive as the more hypnotizable. Hypnosis was not involved in the effort to control skin temperature. Thus more study is necessary; the possible success of hypnosis in this area was shown by Maslach, Marshall, and Zimbardo (1972). Highly hypnotizable subjects may, under some circumstances, be less successful at biofeedback than the less hypnotizable, as shown in an EEG-alpha experiment (Dumas, 1976). Learning to control alpha was significantly greater among the low hypnotizables. As in the experiments of Roberts and others, hypnotic suggestions were not involved.

THE TRANSCENDENCE OF NORMAL CAPACITY

The many claims for supernormal muscular performance under hypnosis are not justified by the results of laboratory studies. Stage performances, such as supporting the stiffened body between two chairs while a second person is supported by the outstretched body, are dramatic but not significant: the performance can be done as well with the subject not hypnotized.

Studies of supernormal capacity are plagued by the uncertain maximum performances of which people are capable when motivated and when conditions are optimal. The gradual increases in the records of track athletes reflect such uncertainties. Some of them, such as pole vault records, have to do with newer kinds of poles used today, and the high jump records are made with new styles of jumping; however, the 4-minute mile is probably a matter of motivation and not a function of new styles of running. It is necessary to use various methods of exhortation and motivation for comparison with hypnosis; when such methods are used, it is difficult to show that hypnosis yields performances above those which can be achieved in other ways.

The technical problems of producing an adequate experiment are great, particularly that of defining an upper limit or asymptote of performance that a subject can achieve outside hypnosis. Orne (1959) first had his subjects hold a kilogram weight at arm's length while hypnotized until the subject could no longer support the weight despite the suggestions that the arm would feel neither fatigue nor pain. Then, one-half hour later, he repeated the experiment in the waking state but with special motivation instructions. Now the subjects did even better than when hypnotized, so any advantage of hypnosis remained in doubt.

Obviously what is needed is *both* favorable motivation conditions *and* hypnosis to see if hypnosis adds an increment when it interacts with the most favorable nonhypnotic condition. Such an experiment was performed by Slotnick, Liebert, and Hilgard (1965). Subjects in two groups were first matched on their weight-supporting endurance following hypnosis with exhortation to do their best. On the following day additional motivation was provided by "involving" instructions that proved effective beyond the "exhortations" of the previous day. Both groups improved, one performing in the waking condition, one in hypnosis. The waking group duplicated Orne's findings that an appropriate waking condition might exceed hypnotic performance. However, the other group, hypnotized in addition to having the identical involvement instructions, increased significantly *more* than the waking group. This is the kind of test of hypnotic effectiveness that is needed on a larger scale, that is, with hypnosis tested under circumstances in which, without hypnosis, performance is near its asymptote.

One possibility is that, under favorable conditions, pains owing to muscular fatigue or strain can be reduced by hypnosis; thus these inhibitory signals are not experienced, and the performance therefore continues longer. This is somewhat like the second wind that is noted by some distance runners, who, after a time, seem not to notice their legs at all. A case of this kind was described by Miller, Galanter, and Pribram (1960, p. 109–110). A soldier in training was required to keep on running after he thought he could go no further, only to find that after he began running again he lost all consciousness of voluntary control. He looked down and saw some legs pumping away under him and was mildly surprised to notice that they were attached to his own body. Although no formal hypnosis was involved, this is similar to what may happen in hypnosis. In an active form of hypnosis, induced while the subject pedaled a laboratory bicycle (bicycle ergometer), the more hypnotizable pedaled faster as they became hypnotized, and seemed to suffer no feelings of fatigue, even though signs of effort were evidenced by the perspiration on their foreheads (Banyai and Hilgard, 1976). The alterations of control readily classify as dissociative.

THE BEARING ON DISSOCIATION

The examination of voluntary and involuntary processes and how the same process can sometimes be relatively automatic and involuntary and at another time deliberate and involuntary leads to two important conclusions about dissociated activities: first, that they do indeed occur; second, that controls can shift and activities once dissociated can become better integrated with the total personality. Both features are important, for if dissociations were fixed and unchangeable there would be little to do but catalog processes, some being automatic (reflex-like, without voluntary control), others being subject to voluntary decision processes. In a sense the old division of events as controlled by the autonomic nervous system or the central nervous system provided a kind of typology for what to expect. Now we know that none of these divisions is fixed, and that is a gain.

That modifiable dissociations occur is evident from the clinical cases of hysteria, in which anesthesias and paralyses may endure for years and still be subject to later remediation. These results are paralleled readily in the hypnotic experiments in which movements are inhibited or enhanced within hypnosis by the hypnotist's suggestions, with the subject (at least in some instances) relatively automatic in his responses once the hypnotic contract has been accepted. The restoration of function is then made quickly as the hypnotist cancels his suggestions.

The achievement of voluntary control over normally involuntary processes, as illustrated in the biofeedback experiments and in the hypnotic ones, when successful, represents an integration between voluntary and involuntary controls that are normally separated.

NOTES

The Voluntary-involuntary Distinction

Although we were writing in the context of conditioned responses to which self-initiation of action seemed at the time somewhat alien, Marquis and I included a chapter on voluntary action in our 1940 book, assembling such evidence as we could on the modifiability of conditioned responses through instructions to the subject (Hilgard and Marquis, 1940, Chapter 11).

The philosophical problems of freedom and determinism are at a different conceptual level.

Hysterical Paralyses

The best historical account of hysteria is that of Veith (1965). Hysteria, especially in its dramatic forms, was once more common than it is today. Perhaps higher educational levels, cultural expectations, modified methods of child rearing, and increased medical knowledge may all have led to a change in symptoms. The "conversion symptoms" that are found now less often take the form of central nervous functions such as anesthesias and paralyses, and more often show disturbance in vegetative functions, such as disturbances of digestion and elimination, or allergic reactions, which as a group receive the diagnosis of psychosomatic disorder rather than hysteria.

The empirical relationships between hysteria and hypnosis are still somewhat problematical. Gill and Brenman (1959) concluded that normal people were more hypnotizable than neurotics, but hysterics were the most hypnotizable among the neurotics.

Frankel and Orne (1976) have found that phobic patients are particularly high in their responsiveness to hypnosis.

Loss of Voluntary Control in Hypnosis

The "challenge" tests, in which the hypnotist produces by suggestion a paralysis of movement and then "challenges" the subject to try to make the movement, is but one among a number of evidences of shifts in voluntary control within hypnosis. Further data on the facilitation and inhibition of muscular responses within hypnosis were given in Hilgard (1965, Chapter 5).

An ethical issue has concerned investigators since the late nineteenth century. That issue is whether the hypnotist can gain enough control over the voluntary activity of the hypnotized subject to cause the subject to commit crimes or carry out other antisocial acts. The consensus is that such control is not possible, but there are bound to be borderline cases. For example, many people are led into lives of crime by their associates; if perchance one of them, who would have gone along without hypnosis, happened to have been hypnotized, hypnosis might be blamed even though hypnotic suggestion was an inconsequential causal factor. The experimental literature has been summarized by Barber (1961) and by Orne (1965). The issue is still alive (Coe, 1977; Levitt, 1977).

Ideomotor Action

Although William James receives the credit for naming ideomotor action, he built the conception on Alexander Bain's "Law of Diffusion," which stated that every sensory or emotional feeling has its movement consequences (Bain, 1859) and on Féré's conception of "dynamogenesis," that muscular action is increased by sensory stimulation (Féré, 1887). Thorndike (1913) devoted his presidential address before the American Psychological Association to a refutation of ideomotor action. In this address he was expressing his commitment to a direct control of responses by stimuli without the need for mediating ideas, showing how prior preferences affect the interpretation of additional data.

The "power of words" referred to in this and earlier chapters may be considered a natural extension of the ideomotor principle.

Voluntary Control of Normally Involuntary Processes

The biofeedback literature, primarily concerned with the gaining of voluntary control over autonomic responses, is now voluminous. The major papers have been collected annually in books since 1971, the first edited by Barber and others (1971).

Many of the claims for the control achieved have been exaggerated, especially in the popular books that have appeared. The reader is warned to temper his expectations through the exercise of critical judgment.

The evidence from hypnosis is also unsatisfactory, with claims, such as demonstrating the precise control of bleeding, much more common in the clinical literature than substantiated by careful experimental studies.

The Transcendence of Normal Capacity

Earlier experiments on motor response were reviewed by Hull (1933, Chapter 9) with the conclusion that little, if any, enhancement of strength or resistance to fatigue could be produced by hypnosis. Weitzenhoffer (1953, Chapter 16) reviewed the evidence 20 years later and attributed some improvement to hypnosis, especially for easier tasks. Nothing dramatic was claimed.

CHAPTER

AUTOMATIC WRITING AND DIVIDED ATTENTION

Automatisms have an uncertain relationship to awareness and hence to dissociation. The "pure case" is an activity carried out with no awareness whatever that it is going on. An activity may be carried out in awareness, however, without any sense of control over it; compulsive acts or obsessive thoughts may be of this kind. Sometimes the processes are only mildly dissociated, such as the "doodling" that occurs while one is talking on the telephone or listening to a lecture. All these instances are automatic to some extent. In the context of this chapter, most automatic writing is either totally out of awareness, while the writer is preoccupied with something else, or, if he is aware of it, he does not feel that he is its author. This latter case is rather like that of dreams, in which a remembered dream is a conscious product, but the authorship of the dream is obscure. It is *your* dream, just as it is *your* writing, even though you did not "will" it.

THE BACKGROUND IN SPIRITUALISM

As noted in Chapter 1, stirrings in the culture outside of established science have led in part to the recent interest in consciousness expansion and the development of a more cognitive psychology. The larger cultural setting provides what Boring (following James) liked to refer to as the *Zeitgeist;* what scientists do is influenced by what goes on around them, whether they go along with the popular movement or seek to correct its exaggerations. This happened in the nineteenth century as a consequence of a popular wave of spiritualism, with a residue in naturalistic psychological science of a renewed interest in hypnotism, with automatic writing as one of its methods.

The Fox Sisters

A wave of spiritualism began on March 31, 1848 in Hydesville, Wayne County, New York, when two sisters, Margaret Fox, 12 years old, and Kate Fox, then 9, reported strange rappings attributed to an invisible spirit. They reported that during the previous year they heard these rappings occur in their presence; on this date the rappings were the response to their request to a spirit, Mr. Splitfoot, to answer their questions after they went to bed. A much older sister, Leah, soon found that she, too, was able to communicate with spirits.

The Fox sisters were examined in 1849, with the conclusion that the sounds were made by voluntary effort, probably in their joints. This did not deter believers; as excitement mounted, they were frequently examined and often (though not always) exposed. In 1857 a newspaper, the Boston Courier, offered a prize of $500 to anyone able to produce authentic spiritualistic phenomena; Harvard professors Benjamin Peirce, Louis Agassiz, Eben Horsford, and a Cambridge astronomer, Benjamin A. Gould, served as judges. Kate Fox and her sister Leah competed, along with others. The jury did not award the prize to them or to anyone else, for they found nothing. All that resulted was more business for the mediums. The most important lesson to be learned from the case of the Fox sisters is the helplessness of science against committed belief, a helplessness that is shown even today after the exposure of one fraud after another.

Despite repeated evidences of deception, the experiences of the Fox sisters helped to inaugurate a wave of spiritualistic and mediumistic phenomena that spread around the world. Not all scientists were negative. As late as 1871, 23 years after the original rappings, sister Kate fooled Sir William Crookes, known for the Crookes tube that played a part in the development of vacuum tube technology, the radiometer, and other contributions to chemistry and physics. Impressed by her performance, he wrote:

> With a full knowledge of the numerous theories which have been started, chiefly in America, to explain these sounds, I have tested them in every way that I could devise, until there has been no escape from the conviction that they were true objective occurrences not produced by trickery or mechanical means (Crookes, 1874, p. 88).

The truth came out a few years later, in 1888, when the sisters confessed that it had all been a matter of trickery and fraud. The fullest confession was made by Margaret in a public meeting at the New York Academy of Music on Sunday evening, October 21, 1888.

Her comments appeared in the *New York World* the following day. She told of her hatred for the older sister Leah, who had forced them into commercializing their tricks, and explained in detail how they made the sounds with the joints of the big toe and fingers. Sister Kate had stated in print two weeks earlier: "Spiritualism is a humbug from beginning to end. It is the greatest humbug of the century" (Christopher, 1975, p. 9). Leah disappeared from sight.

Once their fame spread, the girls were called on for other spiritual services. They enter our account because of the voluminous "automatic writing" done by Kate at the behest of a serious doctor and his wife, Dr. and Mrs. George H. Taylor. Mrs. Taylor preserved a careful transcript of all that went on in repeated sessions between 1869 and 1892 (even after the confessions!), to be published many years later in a large book under her name by W. G. L. Taylor, her son, (Taylor, 1932). The last message is one reputed to have come from Benjamin Franklin, who served as a guiding spirit throughout, telling them each time when to meet again. The meetings were held in the old Madison Avenue Hotel, at the corner of Madison Avenue and 58th Street, New York. The book ends with the sad story that Kate had died of drink three weeks after the last session.

An interesting feature of the "communications" was that they were done throughout in mirror writing, which, unless it comes spontaneously, as it very well may, takes considerable practice to acquire. Kate was able to write in the ordinary manner, because one of the published letters from Benjamin Franklin is written in ordinary script from left to right; it is said to have been the only one done this way. The "automatic writing" is of no scientific importance except as a warning against gullibility. Yet the interest in communication with departed spirits by way of automatic writing has not ceased among the believers in spiritualism. For example, the automatic writing of Mrs. Verrall, reflecting communication with many departed persons, has recently been examined in great detail, with such conclusions as that the dead person can communicate directly only for about seven years after death (Lambert, 1971).

The Planchette

A book that appeared in 1869 celebrated the victory of spiritualism over science with the title: *Planchette; or, The despair of science* (Sargent, 1869). Sargent pointed out that the choice of title was dictated by the vogue of the planchette, which had appeared in great numbers in the booksellers' shops in the United States the previous year. It had been common in France for 12 or 15 years. A report from New York in 1868 showed that one manufacturer, a Mr. Kirby, had sold over 200,000 planchettes.

The planchette is a little heart-shaped table, usually about seven inches long and five inches wide. It stands on three legs, one of which is a sharpened lead pencil slipped into a rubber socket at the tip; the other two legs are mounted on casters so that the whole can move freely in any direction over the paper on which it writes.

Sargent pointed out how the planchette descended from the table rapping of the Fox sisters. Communications were at first received by the tedious process of calling out the alphabet and noting down the letters at which the rap was given. Through a series of improvements, in which a pencil was at first mounted on the leg of the table, the planchette described above developed.

Although entirely friendly to its use in spirit communication, Sargent noted that failures were very numerous.

> Probably not more than ten out of a hundred persons in a mixed assemblage could be found, through whom the phenomena would take place, and in the hundred there might possibly be one who would prove a good medium. Such a one will soon discard the planchette as of no use in the production of phenomena more extraordinary than any got by its aid (Sargent, 1869, p. 3).

The planchette is described here as a late nineteenth century invention, although something similar had probably been used occasionally from ancient times. Sargent notes that a Dr. Macgowan, writing in the *North China Herald,* reported a device similar to a planchette that he saw widely used in China in 1843, before the Fox sisters got started. A table was sprinkled with bran, flour, dust, or other powder. A hemispheric basket, turned upside down, was the equivalent of the planchette. The writing instrument could be any kind of stylus, such as a reed or a chopstick, thrust through the interstices of the woven basket. The edges of the basket rested on the hands of the "mediums" who sought a message. These operators claimed to be unconscious of the intelligence they communicated.

The use of the planchette in nonmediumistic settings was taken seriously by F. W. H. Myers and Edmund Gurney, the founders of the London Society for Psychical Research, and they collected numerous anecdotes on its use, often referring to its productions as something from the subconscious mind, rather than anything received telepathically or from spirits (although they also entertained these possibilities).

Many illustrations were assembled, of which a typical account is that by F. C. S. Schiller, at the time a Fellow of Corpus Christi College, Oxford. He was experimenting during a Long Vacation with his brother F. and sister L.

. . . Both F. and L. were at first entirely ignorant of what planchette was writing, and F. remained so to the end, nor did the occupations of his conscious self appear in the least to affect the progress of the writing. I have seen planchette write in the same slow and deliberate way both while he was telling an amusing anecdote in an animated way and while he was absorbed in an interesting novel; and frequently whole series of questions would be asked and answered without his knowing what had been written or thinking that anything else than unmeaning scrawls had been produced.

In L's case it is true that after some time she came to know what letters were being formed and was able to interpret the movements of her hand. This, of course, made it difficult to avoid, at times, a certain half-conscious influence on the writing, and makes it necessary to allow for the personal equation. . . .

An interesting experiment was tried of writing with two planchettes, F. having one hand on each. I suggested this in order to elucidate the connection between left-handed writing and "mirror-writing," and fully expected that the two hands would write the same communications. To my astonishment, however, the communications, though written simultaneously, were different and proceeded from different "spirits." . . . Whenever F. wrote with two planchettes, the left hand wrote mirror-writing, which was often very hard to decipher. (Myers, 1887, pp. 216–217).

These fragments suffice to show how the planchette, descended as it was from the table rapping of the Fox sisters, opened up possibilities for study in other settings, even though many of the early investigators continued to entertain the spiritualistic hypothesis along with the naturalistic interpretation of subconscious influence.

The Ouija Board

The ouija board (oui-ja = yes-yes in French and German) appears to have been a later invention than the planchette, but it has served similar purposes both as a kind of parlor game and as a means of communicating with departed spirits. Still in production and available for purchase at American toy stores, it differs from the planchette chiefly in that the moving table does not write but comes to rest on letters of the alphabet or numerals and in that way builds up its message.

As with the planchette, it was soon discovered that the hand might indeed produce sensible messages, often to the genuine surprise of the operator as well as the observers. From a naturalistic standpoint, this means that it is occasionally possible to tap levels of memory and imagination, cognitively comprehensible, that are not in the ordinary waking consciousness of the person whose cognitions are being displayed.

A few extreme cases came to light, of which one of the most striking was that of "Patience Worth." Mrs. Curran, a St. Louis housewife, began playing with the ouija board. She had not graduated from high school and she showed no evidence of literary capabilities or pretensions. After Patience Worth introduced herself to Mrs. Curran on the ouija board and took over guidance of her hand, Mrs. Curran soon became a successful author with the help of this unseen spirit. Five novels were published under the authorship of Patience Worth between 1917 and 1928; although they were not great, they had some literary merit and received favorable reviews at the time. Gradually the ouija board was displaced, and Patience Worth began dictating directly to Mrs. Curran. There were a number of poems in addition to the novels. The case is of sufficient interest to have been given a recent thorough review (Litvag, 1972).

It was noted by Sargent over a century ago that once a person was successful with the planchette he could abandon it, and Mrs. Curran demonstrated the same thing when she gave up the ouija board for direct dictation. Automatic writing by pen alone was commonly reported by Myers (1903).

AUTOMATIC WRITING IN PSYCHOTHERAPY

The work of Myers and Gurney in the 1880s may be thought of as transitional between the more purely mediumistic use of automatic writing and more modern clinical and experimental uses. Automatic writing was used in the late nineteenth century by Janet and Binet in France and William James in the United States. Without reviewing the history in any detail, some early twentieth century practices may prove illuminating.

Morton Prince's bell tower case (Prince, 1914, p. 389ff) illustrates the way in which automatic writing was used in psychotherapy. The history of the case, as later reconstructed, was that a young woman was praying in a hospital room for the successful outcome of an operation being performed on her mother in the room below. Outside the window she looked on a church spire in which a bell was tolling. In her distressed condition she was greatly annoyed by the bells, particularly because they symbolized death. Her mother died in the operating room. She later developed a phobia of bell towers that made her avoid the streets on which churches were located. She had forgotten the source of her fear. It was Prince's task to try to discover what lay behind her symptom, and he eventually resorted to automatic writing. Here he learned for the first time of the hospital episode and the connection of the bell phobia with the death of her mother.

The detailed methods are often skipped over in this and other clinical reports. Sometimes hypnosis was used, sometimes not; in any case the arrangement was always such that a strong element of suggestion was present.

A detailed account of her nonhypnotic practice was given in a book on automatic writing by Anita Mühl (1930). She placed the forearm of the writing person in a sling made of an adjustable bandage suspended from a rod above the writing table. With everything in readiness the suspended arm cleared the table by about an inch, allowing unhindered movement.

The experiment begins by distracting the subject, commonly by having the subject read aloud from a book. Once engrossed in reading a pencil is slipped in position for writing on the paper. Both experimenter and subject then wait to see what happens.

Mühl found that often little happened in the first session except for a few scrolls or wavy lines. That was acceptable and could be built on in later sessions. For example, in the next session Mühl begins whispering questions that can be answered by "yes" or "no." If the questions are not answered, the hand is raised from the paper by the wrist whenever a question is asked then lowered again until an answer is given. Once this stage has been reached, the main hurdle has been overcome. It is evident that the hand raising is a nonverbal suggestion that something more is expected.

Mühl's book is well illustrated with the products of automatic writing in the form of pictures as well as verbal communications. She proposes that automatic writing taps the personal unconscious, although acknowledges some one-way emergences from deeper levels. In introducing the book, William Alanson White, who observed her work at St. Elizabeth's hospital, noted that the prominence of psychoanalysis had led to a subsiding of interest in hypnosis and automatic writing. He regretted this because automatic handwriting had proved to be a valuable means of inquiry "into the submerged portions of the psyche."

Automatic writing appears today to be recommended primarily by those who make use of hypnosis in psychotherapy. Cheek and Le Cron (1968) have proposed related methods of inquiry directed to hidden aspects of experience, such as questioning by ideomotor methods that do not require the writing of sentences, using instead "yes" and "no" responses to questions. One method that can be used without hypnosis is to assign meaning to particular directions of the swinging of a Chevreul pendulum in reply to questions. Such a pendulum consists of something such as a lucite ball suspended from a cord held by the uppraised hand of the subject and responsive to unconscious motor movements engendered by the subject's thoughts. Like the planchette and ouija board, it is also an inheritance from the spiritualists. Another method, used primarily within hypnosis, is the method of signalling with the fingers of one hand. For example, the forefinger may be used to signify "yes," the middle finger "no," the little finger doubt, and the thumb a refusal to answer the question. Because this is merely an alternative for coding in words, it may well be asked why there is any advantage in the use of fingers. The complete answer is doubtless elusive, but it may be noted that these movements require very little energy, compared with arousing and organizing the breathing and vocal apparatus for speech in a deeply relaxed condition. Hence an "automatic" reply is, in the first place, easier to make. Second, there is a certain plausibility that is communicated to the suggestible person that he is less responsible for what the fingers report than for what he says in words. In this respect it is comparable to the psychoanalytic patient's reporting a dream that tells more about himself than he is prepared to state openly.

AUTOMATIC WRITING IN THE LABORATORY

The relative neglect of automatic writing in psychiatric practice during mid-century was reflected by its neglect in the laboratory. Although the phenomena were known, they were not congenial to the prevailing temper, and, when the interest turned to clinical appraisal of personality, related methods for revealing "hidden" aspects, such as the Rorschach inkblot test or the storytelling Thematic Apperception Test (TAT), served to produce equivalent imaginative productions that were to some degree automatic. That imaginative productions and automatic writing might have something in common was recognized before the Rorschach or TAT came along. For example, Lillien J. Martin began studies of the relation of spontaneous visual images to the unconscious in 1907 and published a paper ten years later comparing the production of such images to automatic writing (Martin, 1907, 1917). She preferred the method of spontaneous imagery because it was more widely applicable; she found that of 19 normal subjects only two produced satisfactory automatic writing. This ratio of one in ten, it may be noted, is about what Sargent had estimated to be the fraction of success 50 years earlier.

Harriman (1942) made use of automatic writing in a laboratory investigation that simulated clinical practice. He used the method of hypnotically induced conflicts with amnesia to create the setting and then tried by automatic writing to find evidence for the subconscious expression of the conflict. With ten subjects, five men and five women, all skilled in automatic writing, he found evidence that satisfied him that the automatic writing reflected their induced conflicts without their being aware of either the implantation of the conflicts or the writing.

Experiments of Messerschmidt and Cass

Although incidental reports were made from time to time, mostly in the clinical setting, the most careful early study was performed by Ramona Messerschmidt, working with Clark Hull as he began his hypnotic studies at the

University of Wisconsin before he moved his hypnosis laboratory to Yale. She designed her investigation to test the hypothesis that, when automatic writing is carried on simultaneously with a conscious task, the dissociation between the subconscious and the conscious tasks ought to reduce the normal interference between them (Messerschmidt, 1927–1928). She studied two combined tasks. One was the oral reading of Edman's *Human traits* (conscious), combined with serial addition of 7, 8, and 9 by automatic writing (subconscious). The other pair of tasks was oral serial addition of 6, 7, and 8 (conscious) simultaneously with the serial addition of 7, 8, and 9 by automatic writing (subconscious). The second pair of tasks, because they made use of very similar cognitive systems, might be expected to show more interference with each other. Controls consisted of doing each of the tasks singly so that the degree of interference could be estimated; unfortunately, an intended control in which the pairs of tasks were both fully conscious was performed on only one of the subjects.

The automatic writing suggestions were given while the subject was in the hypnotic trance, to be activated posthypnotically. The subject was told that, after she was wakened from hypnosis and heard the signal "Ready," she would cumulatively add to a two-place number to be given at the time (say, 37) the digit 7, then 8, then 9, then 7, then 8, then 9, and so on, in recurring cycles until the signal "Stop" was given. The totals arrived at following each of the additions were to be written quite unconsciously. The score was the number of correct additions performed in five minutes. For reading, the score was the number of words pronounced during the same period.

Three young college women participated in the experiment. All had shown perfect posthypnotic amnesia and a strong positive response to posthypnotic suggestion. Each subject repeated the five-minute tests 11 times under each condition.

Less interference was to be expected between the conscious reading and the subconscious written serial additions, but a substantial mutual conflict was found between the tasks. The number of words read suffered a loss of 41% and the additions a loss of 70%, compared to the single, uncombined tasks performed consciously.

The two very similar tasks, both serial addition, one conscious and the other subconscious, showed greater mutual interference, as might have been expected except for the hypothesis of complete dissociation between conscious and subconscious. Oral addition suffered a loss of 61% and the subconscious written addition a loss of 86%. The greatest interference was shown with the subconscious task in all instances, whatever the average interference. Although the results as they stand do not permit a comparison of interference when both tasks are conscious with interference when one of them is subconscious, it appears that, in the subconscious condition, there may be more interference than if the second task were also conscious. The results of the control experiment with the single subject showed that, when one of the interfering tasks was subconscious, there was more interference than when both were conscious.

The experiments were convincing enough that few attempts were made to repeat or extend them. Fifteen years later, William Cass at the University of Oregon performed a somewhat comparable experiment as a master's thesis, but he published only an abstract of his results (Cass, 1942). He combined a conscious oral color-naming task with a subconscious written arithmetic task in an arrangement similar to that of Messerschmidt, also with three subjects. For one of his subjects he found some advantage for the subconscious condition; although it appeared that further experimentation would be desirable, he did not follow up this initial work.

Automatic Writing in the Stanford Profile Scales

After our hypnosis laboratory began operation in 1958, we had an opportunity to become familiar with a wide range of hypnotic phenomena by incorporating them within the scales we developed for the measurement of hypnotic responsiveness, or hypnotic susceptibility, as we then named it. A simple posthypnotic automatic writing item was included in one of the scales, Form II of the Stanford Profile Scales of Hypnotic Susceptibility (Weitzenhoffer and Hilgard, 1963, 1967; Hilgard, Lauer, and Morgan, 1963).

The detailed instructions to the hypnotized subject were stated as follows:

> I am going to give you a pad of paper and a pencil to write with. Just keep your eyes closed . . . Do you write with your right or left hand? . . .
>
> *(Place pad in subject's lap, steadied by the nondominant hand; place the pencil in the dominant hand.)*
>
> I want you to keep this pad on your lap . . . and to hold this pencil ready to write. . . . That's fine. . . . Now write your name . . . and the date. . . . That's fine. . . . Now I want you to forget about your hand and the pencil and the pad. In a moment when I tell you to do so, you will cease to be hypnotized. You will open your eyes and you will be fully alert, and feel fully alert, just as you were before I hypnotized you. . . . Until I begin counting remain deeply hypnotized. . . . I will remove the hypnosis by counting backward from 10 to 1. As I count you will gradually become less hypnotized, and at one, not sooner, you will open your eyes and you will no longer be hypnotized. After you open your eyes you will remember nothing about the pad and pencil I gave you a few moments ago, and you will not be aware of them. Even though you are no longer hypnotized, you will not be aware of the fact that there is a pad on your lap and a pencil in your hand. However, I will ask you some questions to which

you will answer "yes" and "no," and every time you answer "yes," your _____(name which) hand will write "no." Every time you answer "no," your hand will write "yes," always the opposite of what you answer. But you will not be aware that your hand is writing or even moving, and you will not be aware of the pencil or the pad. You will have no idea that they are there, or of what you have written. Your hand will write in this manner until I take the pad and pencil away. When I do this there will be no further need for your hand to write anything more in this manner. Is this clear? . . . Now continue to be hypnotized and go deeper until I begin to count. . . .

(Allow 20 seconds to pass before counting then start counting backwards from 10.)

10, 9, 8 . . . you are becoming less and less hypnotized . . . 7, 6, 5 . . . less and less hypnotized . . . 4, 3, 2 . . . at the next count you will no longer be hypnotized. . . . One.

(Allow a few moments to pass after arousing the subject, then ask)

Are you awake?
Is your name (give a false name)?
Is today (give a false day)?
Is tomorrow (give correct day)?
Are you writing anything?

(If subject notes that he has been writing, record remarks and go to b. If he denies writing, whether or not he has been writing, go to a.)

a. Subject denies writing. *(Note if subject looks at pad or pencil)* Look down toward your lap. . . . Do you see anything on it? . . . What is in your hand? . . . What did I say you would do? . . . *(Note replies; go to b.)*

b. For all subjects. I shall now remove the pad and pencil . . . *(Remove them)* . . . Now close your eyes. As I count five you will be hypnotized again. . . . One . . . two . . . three . . . four . . . five. . . . In a few moments I am going to ask you to take a deep breath and open your eyes. . . . You will then be wide awake, no longer hypnotized. . . . You will remember all of your experiences, including what you just did with the pad and pencil, and you will feel fine, and there will be no after-effects. . . . Now take a deep breath . . . open your eyes. . . . Wide awake!

Inquiry. Did you feel any compulsion to write a few minutes ago? Please tell me about it in your own words. *(Record reply)* We are now through with hypnosis for this period but I would like to ask you a few more questions about your experience.

In scoring the responses, replies were grouped according to the number of replies in which the automatic writing followed the suggestions, with the highest score obtained by answering all five questions in writing, consistently reversing "yes" and "no" from the verbal answer. Table 8 shows the results for the standardization sample of 112 students selected by eliminating the 30% of the more general sample who scored 0–3 on the 12-point SHSS-A. Under the circumstances of the experiment, with its strong demands for compliance, a few responses were given by 45% of the selected sample, or the equivalent of 31% in the general student population. However, if we adopt the more severe criterion of continuing to write for all the five questions, the ultimate figure is 9%, which is about that estimated by Sargent and also by Martin. Obviously, a general figure of this sort is meaningless unless the difficulty of the task is specified.

An interesting feature of Table 8 is that there were more subjects who wrote four or five automatic answers than subjects who stopped with one or two. It appears that once they were into the performance there was some tendency to continue, although many fell off along the way. The tendency to continue may be evidence that the performance is indeed out of awareness, because, when a posthypnotic compulsion is performed with the awareness that it is being performed (even though the suggestion to perform it is forgotten), the feedback from the unusual behavior tends to inhibit its continuation. Evidence for this statement comes from another item of the Stanford

Table 8

RESPONSES ON AUTOMATIC WRITING ITEM, STANFORD PROFILE SCALE
(Previously unpublished data, Stanford Laboratory)

Number of automatic responses	Number yielding	Percent of sample	
		Standardization	Estimated unselected[a]
0	62	55	69
1	2	2	1
2	9	8	6
3	10 } 50	9 } 45	6 } 31
4	15	13	9
5	14	13	9
Total	112	100 $N = 112$	100 $N = 160$

[a]48 Subjects scoring 0-3 on SHSS-A were eliminated as unsuitable for Profile Scale testing. The assumption was that they would have yielded no automatic writing.

Profile Scales in which the subject receives the suggestion to say "February" by posthypnotic compulsion whenever the number "three" is symbolized in any form (the figure 3 or III, three objects pictured, etc.). The subject is able to hear himself responding "February" completely out of context; it is not surprising that the rate of falling off on successive trials differs from than in automatic writing. Responses to the two tasks are plotted in Figure 11. The date from automatic writing are shown in Table 8; the data for the posthypnotic compulsion are from the same population sample. The high values for one and two responses to the "February" suggestion of automatic compulsion mean than they drop off rapidly when the subjects hear what they are saying; fewer of those who respond to automatic writing drop off early, presumably because they have no conscious feedback on what they are doing.

How the Subject Experiences Automatic Writing

In a subsequent experimental setting, automatic writing of the type studied in the Profile Scales was used for the purpose of subject selection for more difficult dissociative tasks. The suggestion was made that in answer to each question the subject would verbally answer correctly with "yes" or "no" while

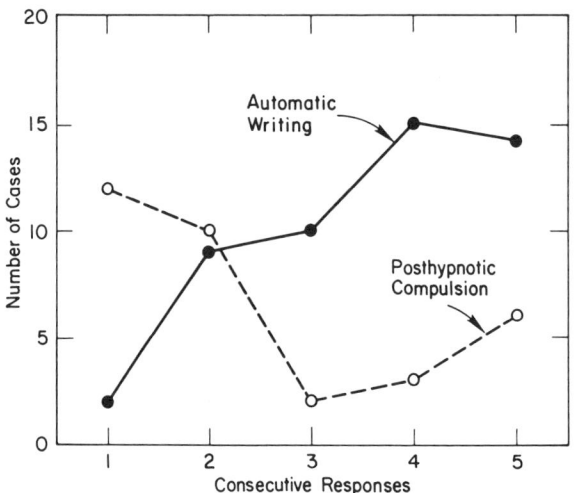

Figure 11 Consecutive responses to suggested automatic writing compared with responses given as a posthypnotic compulsion. The numbers whose maximum responses are 1,2,3,4, or 5 in succession show a more rapid dropping off for posthypnotic compulsion than for automatic writing, both items on the Stanford Profile Scales. Responses are from the same population of 112 subjects used in standardization. Previously unpublished data from the Stanford Laboratory.

the hand, automatically and subconsciously, would write the opposite. Those who participated were interviewed afterwards to find out how they experienced the automatic writing.

The responses of writing were commonly reported to be quite automatic and not consciously experienced. Matt, for example, remembered having the pencil sitting between his fingers, but he did not know that it had moved at all. According to Marie: "I didn't know what was going on. I didn't realize my hand was writing. It was as if my hand were not part of my body, as though it were acting on its own brain." Or, for Peter, "In the writing there was no sensation that my arm was moving. I didn't notice writing answers. I didn't think I had done it at all." Ann said simply: "The writing just happened. I don't know why or how."

In interpreting dissociative experiences it is often necessary to distinguish between the control of movement (executive functions) and the consciousness of what is going on (observing or monitoring functions). This distinction was made by some of those who carried out the automatic writing compulsively yet knew that something was happening. Lucille said: "Something was happening, but I couldn't control it. I knew my hand was writing, but 'yes' and 'no' suddenly meant the same thing. The part that knew I was writing was like a detached observer." Cornelia's hand had written the opposite of her verbal replies consistent with the suggestions. "It was really automatic writing, but I was not amnesic. . . . I found myself in a contradiction. How can I be thinking and verbalizing something and doing precisely the opposite with my hand? . . . I felt I had set up a conflict in observing this." This conflict was disturbing enough to her that after hypnosis she telephoned her husband for reassurance that she was well integrated again.

There was no doubt on the part of the interviewer about the genuineness of the experience of automatic writing.

Recent Experiments on Automatic Writing in Interfering Tasks

With this experience of the reality of automatic writing, it appeared desirable to find out more about the nature of the dissociation involved and to extend the type of experiment that Messerschmidt and Cass had performed. Two published studies have since come from our laboratory.

The first of these was a doctoral dissertation by James Stevenson (1972, 1976). He essentially repeated the Messerschmidt experiment, using Cass's materials, with the controls for single task and waking conditions that were incomplete in the earlier experiments and with the addition of the simulator control advocated by Orne (1959, 1972).

He introduced two important features, in addition to using the simulator control. First, he tested performance on individual tasks unaccompanied by an interfering task both when the task was conscious and when subconscious to determine the difference made by the requirement of performing the single task without awareness. Second, he used two levels of difficulty in the tasks selected for subconscious testing to determine whether task difficulty might influence the ability to dissociate one task from another.

Whenever he presented two tasks simultaneously, one of them was conscious color naming, the subject naming verbally color patches presented on a wall display. As a secondary task, he required the subject to perform written arithmetic, sometimes conscious, sometimes subconscious. The easier arithmetic task was repeated counting, in writing, from 1 to 10 in successive cycles; the more difficult task was serial addition, in writing, in the form that had been used by Messerschmidt.

When the arithmetic tasks were performed singly, conscious and subconscious, the subconscious performance suffered by comparison with the conscious one. Apparently some cognitive effort was required to prevent the arithmetical activity from becoming conscious, making the arithmetic more difficult to perform. The effect was much more pronounced with the more difficult serial addition task than with the easier counting one.

Interferences between color naming and arithmetic were greater when the two tasks were attempted simultaneously, whether the secondary task was conscious or subconscious. When counting was the secondary task, the total interference was not significantly affected by its being subconscious. With serial addition, however, there was a significant further interference when the task was subconscious. Had a task still easier than counting been used, it is possible that an advantage for the subconscious condition might have been found, but no such advantage was demonstrated in the experiment; added interference through subconsciousness was the rule.

The results with the simulators were unexpected but instructive. They showed *less* interference than the real hypnotic subjects while simulating hypnosis (Figure 12). The results validate the performances of the genuine hypnotic subjects in doing worse under the subconscious conditions, for if they were trying to please the hypnotist by responding to the demands of a dissociation experiment they would have done more nearly what the simulators did.

Stevenson interpreted his data as showing, at least for the more difficult addition, that the task decrement could be assigned to two components, the first of which depended on the effort required to keep a task subconscious (not actually required of the simulators), and the second related to attempting two tasks at once (required of both simulators and reals). He presented a preliminary model by which these two effects would be influenced by task difficulty.

A second experiment performed later although published earlier, by Knox,

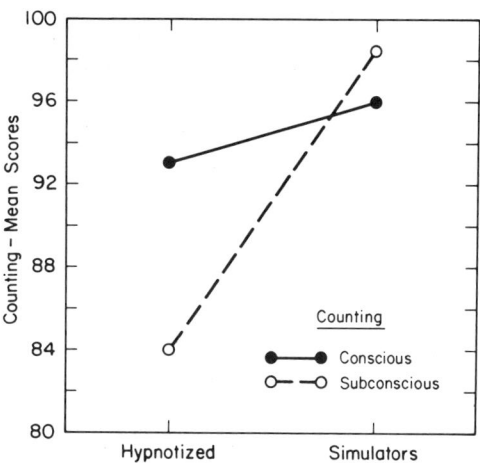

Figure 12 Performances of those simulating hypnosis compared with the genuinely hypnotized. Counting scores are plotted, averaged over trials in which counting was done alone and in which counting was done jointly with conscious color naming. Keeping the task subconscious interfered with performance for the truly hypnotized. From Stevenson (1976).

Crutchfield, and Hilgard (1975), was designed similarly to Stevenson's experiment, except that the subconscious task was selected to permit a better analysis of the strategies used in doing two tasks at once and to show the effect of the instructions for automaticity on these strategies. The conscious color-naming task was the same as that used by Stevenson. A key-pressing task was substituted for the arithmetic tasks as the one to be used simultaneously with conscious color naming in either the conscious or subconscious condition. It consisted of pressing each of two keys mounted in a box out of the subject's line of vision in the order three times left key pressing followed by three times right key pressing, with the cycle then repeated for the minute that the trial lasted. The keys were connected to the same polygraph on which a voice key recorded the oral naming of the colors, permitting an analysis of the relationship of individual key pressing to the naming of individual color patches. For purposes of tabulating the overall results, key pressings were counted as units, one unit being two triplets of key pressing, correctly 3L-3R. A unit was in error if there was an extra or an omitted press, for example, 2L-3R or 3L-4R.

The overall results confirmed Stevenson's findings of two interfering factors, one due to the hypnotic instructions for doing the key pressing subconsciously, the other due to interfering simultaneous tasks. Simulator controls were not necessary, because in Stevenson's experiment differences had already been demonstrated between those subjects simulating hypnosis and the reals. The key-pressing task proved to be of a difficulty roughly equal to that of the counting task used by Stevenson, although, with 15 real subjects instead of eight, the interference between conscious and subconscious single performance now proved to be significant even with this rather easy task. The interference showed in the errors made rather than in the number of key pressings attempted.

The experiment went beyond Stevenson's because it permitted a study of the strategies employed. Six strategies were identified, all involving an integration between the key pressing and the color naming. One strategy was used most commonly and rather successfully by eight of the 15 subjects. Because some decision time is involved in naming colors, each subject apparently selected the color name and held it in readiness to announce simultaneously with key pressing, for the record showed that he pressed a key once, then announced the color and pressed the remaining two of the triplet, for example, 3L pressed as L-color-LL. Apparently deciding on the next color while permitting the relatively automatic act to continue, he turned to the first press of the next triplet, 3R, pressing once, announcing the color name, and then continuing the two additional presses. If this integration was performed consistently, the result was that two colors would be named for each full set of six key presses, a ratio that was often found. The next most often used strategy, used by three of the 15 subjects, alternated color naming and key pressing; for one unit of six key presses there would be six colors named. The consequence was a slower rate of key pressing when tasks were simultaneous than when key pressing was done alone. The other strategies were used by only one subject each: naming the color between triplets rather than simultaneously with pressing, naming the color after pressing the keys twice, and naming a color at each key press rather than between them. When both tasks were conscious, subjects tended to use a preferred strategy 85% of the time. When the key pressing was subconscious, the same strategy was used only 59% of the time, owing to some break in the integration between the tasks.

Two conclusions are justified by the results of these two experiments on the dissociation of simultaneous tasks, one conscious and one subconscious: first, the subjective ignoring of the subconscious automatic tasks while a conscious task is being performed is very real to some highly hypnotizable subjects; second, the interference is increased by the effort to maintain one task as subconscious, and this effort is a function of the difficulty of the task. Mutual interferences between conscious and subconscious tasks are found; the division between the tasks depends on the strategies available for their integration.

AUTOMATIC WRITING AND THE PROBLEM OF DIVIDED ATTENTION

Experiments on automatic writing deal with active exclusion from consciousness. Such active exclusion relates automatic writing to studies of selective attention as represented, for example, in the dichotic listening experiments, in which the two ears are considered to be two channels of information. When attention is directed to one of these, the information from the other is inhibited. Inattention that excludes one source of information represents only one facet of the problem common to automatic writing and attention; the other facet requires that sufficient attention of another kind, or at some other level, is preserved so that the excluded material can be recovered. In the attention literature there are many studies in which it is shown that some information is secondarily neglected because attention is directed primarily to another source or channel, but active exclusion is often overlooked in these studies; this neglect has been commented on by Blum and Porter (1972, 1973), who have studied active inattention hypnotically.

In the attention literature, what happens to the inhibited channel and the information received there has led to several models of the process. One model proposes that some information may never be processed at all, as though two objects are trying to enter one funnel and one of them is excluded. Broadbent's (1958) theory is of this type. Another possibility is that information from both channels enters into the cognitive processing systems, but the processing of one stops short of coming to perceptual consciousness. This is the position taken by the Deutsches (1963). Treisman's (1969) position is somewhat intermediary.

Norman (1968, 1976) elaborated the theory of the Deutsches in a manner reflecting some of Treisman's theory. He has presented the diagram of Figure 13 in explanation. Because the storage system, represented by the central box, contains processed information prior to its final selection and attention, it would not be difficult conceptually to interpret these stored cognitive structures as dissociated and perhaps available for retrieval by alternate methods of excitation. The expectations, linguistic system, and pertinence, represented by the boxes on the right, imply the importance of regulatory control processes that are emphasized later as part of a neodissociation interpretation (Chapter 11).

Although each of the attention theories has been criticized in some respects, and none has gained universal acceptance in the conventional literature of attention, the hypnotic experiments suggest rather strongly that processing of information may go on at some level while being deflected from consciousness through an inhibitory process.

An experiment by Corteen and Wood (1972) in a nonhypnotic context shows the possibilities. City names that appeared in a word list were followed by an electric shock. These city names were then included in a message that was sent to the rejected ear in a shadowing task; thus they were not identified. The shadowing task consisted of repeating a continuous verbal message that came to one ear. The task required close attention because the subject had to listen to what was being said while repeating what had just been said;

AUTOMATIC WRITING AND THE PROBLEM OF DIVIDED ATTENTION 149

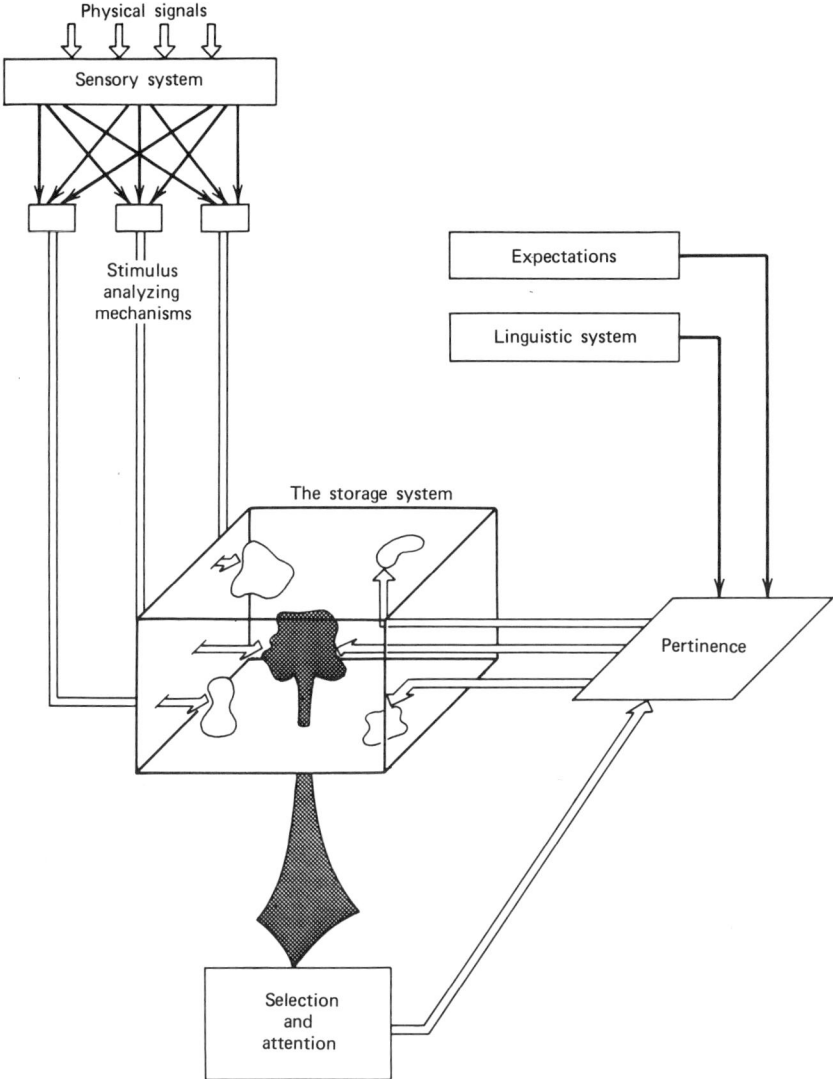

Figure 13   The selection process in attention. A variety of physical inputs are analyzed and represented in the storage system, shown here as unshaded figures. The darkly shaded one, owing to pertinence and other factors, receives the highest excitation and is selected for further attention (Norman, 1976, p. 31).

this concentration on the one ear deflects the awareness of messages coming to the other ear. The point of the experiment was that the city names, even though not "heard" by the subject, still produced galvanic skin responses. To the extent that the results of the experiment are valid, they show some kind of processing of the words from the rejected channel. The results of the study are still quite tentative, and the exact conditions for successful replication are elusive, with several failures to replicate. As a paradigm for obtaining the kind of data required by the Deutsches' theory, the experiment, even though uncertain in its results, serves a useful purpose.

An experiment by Bowers and Brenneman (1976), making use of the hypnotic dissociation paradigm, gives support to some of the implications of the Corteen and Wood experiment. The hypnotized subject was taught to make a simple motor response to a verbal signal embedded amid other items; the response consisted of touching his nose briefly with a finger. He was then given the posthypnotic instruction that whenever he heard this signal he would carry out this act, but he would not be aware of the fact that he was doing it or that he had been told to do it. Then, in the waking condition, he participated in a shadowing experiment similar to that of Corteen and Wood. While listening and repeating ("shadowing") a prose passage to the right ear, single letters of the alphabet were presented as part of the rejected message to the other ear. For the successful subjects, when the cue (a number from 1 to 12 in the midst of the letters) appeared, the finger went briefly to the nose, indicating that the number was selectively effective. The control experiment consisted in attempting to respond to the number simultaneously with shadowing when the posthypnotic suggestion had not been implanted. As in other experiments of this kind within hypnosis, individual differences are very important, and not all subjects were able to conform to the instructions. For the successful ones, however, the subconscious performance was carried out smoothly. It interfered very little with the shadowing, far less than when waking attention was required to be alert for the signal from the normally rejected message. The lack of interference contrasts with the automatic writing experiments from our laboratory and may well be a consequence of the lesser cognitive demand in producing the simple movement than that made by even such an easy task as counting. In any conflict situation the balance of forces operating can be shifted in many ways. In the Bowers and Brenneman experiment the inhibition of the message to the rejected ear probably did not take the same degree of effort that is involved in keeping a writing hand out of awareness; the shadowing task provides a distraction that may reduce the need for added effort. What the posthypnotic suggestion does in the experiment is primarily to facilitate attention to the posthypnotic signal sufficient for it to trigger the response.

Results differed strikingly between one group of four subjects and another group of eight subjects, all treated alike; thus generalizations are hazardous. Four of the subjects were virtually paralyzed by the shadowing task, and when hypnosis was added, their errors increased substantially. Their results parallel those in the experiments of Stevenson and Knox, Morgan, and Hilgard, as previously reported, in which fulfilling the posthypnotic response out of awareness merely added one more task. The other eight subjects, however, benefitted by the condition in which they responded posthypnotically to the signals in the unattended channel. They substantially reduced their errors in shadowing over the errors made while trying to respond consciously to the signals of the unattended channel. If the findings can be substantiated, they will prove to be of great significance to theories of divided attention and hypnotic dissociation. This is the only experimental support alluded to for the noninterference interpretation of the dissociation of one of two simultaneous tasks; it shows that a range of tasks must be explored before generalizations can be stated confidently.

Somewhat different but related approaches have been taken by Gerald Blum in a long series of experiments in which he has made very detailed analyses of shifts in attentive consciousness, using hypnosis as a means of controlling the degree of alertness of concentration, sometimes divided between aspects of a single presented stimulus. For example, in the experiment of Blum and Porter (1973), attention was directed selectively either to the form or the color of a number of consonants that were tachistoscopically presented one at a time. Form perception meant naming the consonant; color perception meant naming its color. They showed that under appropriate posthypnotic instructions the form perception could be greatly disturbed while the color perception remained intact, or the reverse could be done. Control experiments showed that the results could not be obtained in the normal waking condition without the hypnotic preparation of the subjects. Although they were concerned with such matters as the amount of priming time needed to maximize the effect and the influence of stimulus strength as represented by the duration of the exposure of the letters, one additional aspect of the experiments is particularly cogent in relation to the present discussion.

In one cycle of the experiment, when the names of the consonants were being given with a high frequency of error, an additional response was required, called second guessing. This bears on the question of whether something may have registered beyond the material in awareness. For two of the three subjects the results were striking: the second guess showed that at some level the consonants had been perceived more accurately than the subject had been able to report under the standard conditions of the experiment (Table 9). The third subject (F2) had discordant results, but these were explained on the basis of a particular "set" she adopted when required to give two guesses, preventing her from yielding results similar to the others.

Table 9

CONSONANTS IDENTIFIED TACHISTOSCOPICALLY
UNDER THREE INSTRUCTIONS
(After Blum and Porter, 1973)

Posthypnotic instruction	Percent successful identification		
	Subject M	Subject F_1	Subject F_2
High concentration	98	97	100
Low concentration			
Primary guess	16	19	43
Secondary guess	56	78	8

Concluding Remarks on Automatic Writing

Automatic writing provides a good testing ground for the study of hypnotic dissociation, particularly in the paradigm of task interference. The experiments reported have merely scratched the surface, with many possibilities open for parametric studies in which comparisons can be made along dimensions of difficulty of both tasks, conscious and subconscious, of practice in automatization, and of qualitative distinctiveness of tasks. If properly designed, these experiments should bear importantly on the task interference problem in general and particularly on the problems of parallel processing. The experiments to date show that direct hypnotic suggestions and posthypnotic suggestions can modify the subjective aspects of the simultaneous tasks. Some processing of information and task performance goes on out of awareness, but the evidence indicates that, as dissociated activities, they are in most cases less efficient than simultaneous conscious activities.

NOTES

The Background in Spiritualism

The two-volume work of F. W. H. Myers (1903) is a rich source on efforts to separate evidence for spirits from evidence for the subconscious in the nineteenth century. The shortened version edited by Susy Smith (Myers, 1961) places the voluminous notes back into the text; the book is more readable, but some of the rich detail is necessarily lost. Myers' felicitous style and his struggle for dispassionate inquiry make it easy to understand why he and William James were close friends. James sat outside his hospital room when Myers was dying in the hope of catching a message when Myers' spiritual self departed his earthly body, but James was disappointed (and Myers too?) when the message did not come through (Munthe, 1929). Ellenberger (1970, p. 83–85) has noted the impact of spiritualism on the development of a dynamic psychiatry.

The history of the Fox sisters is drawn largely from Christopher (1975) and some from Hansel (1966). The quotation from Crookes was given by Hansel (p. 208). There is little formal literature on the planchette or the ouija board. The currently available version of the ouija is marketed by Parker Brothers. A warning was sounded about uncritical use of it by someone who thought it was not a harmless toy (Gründer, 1920).

Automatic Writing in Psychotherapy

Apart from Anita Mühl's (1930) book and a later chapter by her (Mühl, 1952), there has been little formal assessment of automatic writing in psychotherapy. For those who have used it in connection with hypnosis, it has been largely taken for granted as a useful adjunct (e.g., Lindner, 1944; Wolberg, 1945). It classifies as an uncovering technique in the search for hidden memories that may prove of significance in therapy. Whether as a projective technique it brings out significant aspects of the personality unknown at a conscious level, including creative abilities, has not been demonstrated, although some of Harriman's (1942) subjects wrote emotion-filled poems while under the influence of his experimentally induced conflicts. The Chevreul pendulum is named for an early investigator who believed that many "psychic" effects could be explained by unconscious movements (Chevreul, 1833, 1854).

One case of unfortunate consequences stemming from self-taught automatic writing by a woman who took seriously the messages that appeared and became a psychiatric problem has been reported (Earle and Theye, 1968).

Automatic Writing in the Laboratory

The experiments of Ramona Messerschmidt were part of the program that Clark Hull initiated to establish an objective account of hypnotic phenomena. It was to his credit that as a committed behaviorist he felt that cognitive processes should be brought under the behaviorist tent and that nothing of psychological interest should be excluded. He found the experimentation on hypnosis rather distasteful, and after the book was completed (Hull, 1933) paid no further attention to it, although, as he wrote in his private notebook, he felt it was a good book and had been worth doing (Hull, 1962, p. 852).

The automatic writing experiments were reviewed by Hull according to the dissociation hypothesis, and he discussed in some detail the experiments of Janet (1889), Prince (1909), Burnett (1925), and Barry, MacKinnon, and Murray (1931), pointing to their inadequacies as proofs of the dissociation hypothesis.

Automatic Writing and the Problem of Divided Attention

The attention literature is by now voluminous, with several useful summary volumes, such as that of Broadbent (1958), who did much to bring the topic back into the forefront of psychological experimentation, Moray (1969a) (1969b), Kahneman (1973), and Norman (1976).

The dichotic listening experiments and the shadowing method were introduced by Cherry (1953) and Cherry and Taylor (1954). For a summary of attempts to replicate the Corteen and Wood (1972) results, see Neisser (1976 p. 107). The study by von Wright, Anderson, and Stenman (1975) appears to have given the most concordant results.

Gerald Blum's theory of selective inattention extended his earlier models of cognitive processes (Blum 1961; Blum, Geiwitz and Stewart, 1967; Blum and Porter, 1973).

CHAPTER

THE HYPNOTIZABLE PERSON
AND
THE HYPNOTIC EXPERIENCE

In assembling the evidence for a variety of dissociative manifestations in life both outside and inside the laboratory, many illustrations have been drawn in the earlier chapters from studies of hypnosis. Because of the centrality of the hypnotically based data, the remaining chapters lean almost exclusively on information derived from experimentation on hypnotic phenomena, including the careful interviewing of the hypnotized person to determine how he views his experiences in the context of hypnosis.

Three aspects of the data from hypnotic experiments are particularly pertinent: first, the nature of the hypnotic talent that makes some people more hypnotizable than others, resulting in a small fraction at the top who may be thought of as hypnotic virtuosos; second, the nature of the established hypnotic condition commonly referred to as the hypnotic trance or the hypnotic state, permitting the subject to recognize his own depth of hypnotic involvement; and third, what happens as the hypnotic subjects respond to specific suggestions while hypnotized. Each aspect bears on dissociation as a capacity for an experience of some kind of division of the self and provides a background for the discussions in the subsequent chapters.

THE HYPNOTIZABLE PERSON

The preferred method of measuring hypnotic response in the laboratory is to give the subject an opportunity to behave as a hypnotized person typically does and then to find some way to compare what he does with what others do, particularly those who have the most pronounced experiences of alteration when they are hypnotized. In the literature of industrial psychology this kind of test would be called a "work sample." This is a test of ability that takes specimens of what the worker can do now to predict how well he will do when his job makes similar demands on him.

Apart from procedural details, such an assessment of hypnotic responsiveness involves three steps with each subject, alone or in a group: first, an induction of hypnosis (or some alternative to it) is attempted; second, following the opportunity to become hypnotized, selected suggestions are given with behavioral signs scored as indications of the success or failure of the appropriate responses; and third, some sort of inquiry is conducted after the termination of hypnosis to find out the subjective experiences associated with the observed behavior. A number of possibilities exist within this framework, but the behavior of the hypnotized person is found to be so much the same today as it was 100 years ago that the sampling of items tested covers about the same domain as it would have then, had such a test been devised.*

Much of the evidence on specific aspects of hypnotic performances is presented in the preceding chapters. The various areas such as psychomotor responses to direct suggestions, challenge items when the subject is invited to try to overcome a contracture produced by suggestion, positive and negative hallucinations, dreams, age regression, amnesia, and posthypnotic suggestion, may be assumed to be familiar.

Most psychological measures, when plotted to illustrate the distribution of individual differences, yield a unimodal distribution, roughly that of a normal probability curve, with most subjects in the middle range, tapering off to a few at either extreme. Although hypnotic tests conform roughly to the usual pattern of a very few who are totally unresponsive to hypnotic induction and hypnotic suggestions and a few unusually responsive, with others falling in the middle range, a peculiarity in the distribution commonly noted is that there is often bimodality such as already met in the distribution of amnesia scores (Chapter 4, Figure 7). The bimodality of amnesia was accounted for by the distinction between ordinary forgetting and the recoverable memories lost through suggested amnesia. The same explanation does not necessarily apply to the bimodality that is found in the scores that resulted in the standardiza-

---

*For those unfamiliar with hypnotic practices, a typical hypnotic induction and further details on hypnotic responsiveness tests are given in the Appendix.

tion samples of the Stanford Hypnotic Susceptibility Scales, Forms A and B (Figure 14). There appears to be no simple way to account for the appearance of what may be two overlapping distributions, as indicated by the fitted curves, except perhaps that something like waking suggestion accounts for the lower mode and "true" hypnosis for the upper mode. If that is the case, the bimodality will have an explanation not very different from that of amnesia.

The possibility that there is a distinction between the very highly hypnotizable and those falling in the lower ranges of the distribution is related to the nature of the dissociations found in hypnosis. The familiar performance alterations in hypnosis, such as movement responses to suggestion, are changes primarily in *control* processes and do not produce very great changes in the subject's consciousness. Even though he demonstrates involuntary responses and inhibits voluntary ones, he is often not sure whether he has been hypnotized because he feels so little different. In fact, he may not have been hypnotized in the conventional sense, because such responses to suggestion can be produced readily without a prior induction of hypnosis. These responses are

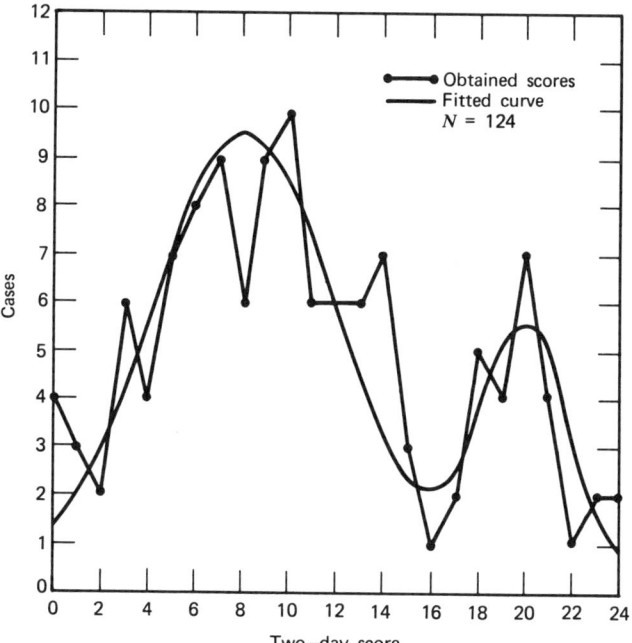

Figure 14 Bimodality in hypnotic susceptibility scores. The scores are summed from Form A on one day and from Form B on another. The solid curve is fitted on the assumption of overlapping normal curves. From Hilgard and others (1961, p. 13).

indicative of minor dissociations, however, because the normal control systems have been altered when what is normally voluntary becomes involuntary and what is normally under voluntary control can no longer be performed. When an easier cognitive performance, such as an age regression in which the person imagines himself again as a child is suggested, there are degrees of reality to the experience, and the less hypnotizable tend to see the child's experience as in the past, viewed by them as adults, rather than fully reliving the experience. The division may feel genuine in that there may seem to be a greater reality to the child's experience than usual, including perhaps a compulsion to write or speak as a child. As long as the changes are matters of degree, all we can say is that the person who is more highly responsive does what the less responsive does, only more so. Bimodality may mean, however, that there is some sort of qualitative change, and a clue to such a change will be found in the next and succeeding chapters. That change rests on the discovery that, for the highly hypnotizable, the very processes that provide for high susceptibility to amnesia permit a deeper dissociation, with some experiences registered and the information processed, without their ever having been conscious. Consideration of these deeper dissociations is reserved for the later chapters; the familiar less pronounced ones are considered here. Because of the range of abilities and the possibility of bimodality reflecting in part the existence of a special group of highly hypnotizable persons, more must be said about the highly hypnotizable.

Experienced hypnotists commonly discover a few very highly hypnotizable subjects, that is, those who experience practically everything that is suggested, no matter how bizarre, and who initiate some variations on their own. The name that has long been assigned to high responders as a group is *somnambulist* (or *somnambule*), a term that literally means sleepwalker. It originally referred to the complete spontaneous amnesia of some hypnotic subjects, paralleling the sleepwalker's commonly reported amnesia for what he did while moving about when he should have been in bed. The term has now lost this original meaning and refers to a highly responsive group including those appropriately termed hypnotic virtuosos.

How large a fraction of the population do these represent? At present the number of these exceptionally hypnotizable depends on an educated guess, the order being probably under 5% and perhaps as low as 1% of an unselected population of college students, less than those in the upper mode of Figure 14.

The scales most widely used for the selection of subjects for experiments on hypnosis are relatively simple and convenient ones. When it is desired to study subjects who are highly responsive, experimenters often select the upper 30% or so according to scores on these scales, scoring in the area of 8–12 on the Stanford Hypnotic Susceptibility Scale, Form A (SHSS-A). Although the hypnotic virtuosos will be found among those selected, many who are designated as high on these scales will be far below the possible in hypnotic performance. For an estimation of how many should be called virtuosos, it is necessary to use scales that are more discriminating. The Stanford Profile Scales of Hypnotic Susceptibility, Forms I and II, are available for such a purpose. These scales cover a wider range of topics than the simpler scales, and many of the items are quite difficult. The differences in scoring between subjects who are in the upper ranges of scores on the easy SHSS-A scale and those who do well on the Profile Scales is illustrated in Figure 15. The results are based on earned scores of 8–12 on SHSS-A for subjects who were later tested on the Profile Scales in the course of the standardization of the scales. Total scores on the two forms of the Profile Scales have a maximum of 54; only 10% of the student population unselected for hypnotic responsiveness scored at 40 or above on these combined scales. Hence 40 has been chosen as a cutoff point in distinguishing between the very high and the moderately high subjects who are included when selected by scores of 8–12 on SHSS-A. It can be seen from Figure 15 that even of those who score at the very top of SHSS-A, only a little over half (five of eight) made scores as high as 40 on the Profile Scales. None of those who scored as low as 8 on SHSS-A made Profile Scores that high. The true hypnotic virtuoso must lie closer to the top of the Profile Scale; he is likely to be found among the less than 1% of subjects who make top scores on the scales or in the 2% who score within 5 points of the top.

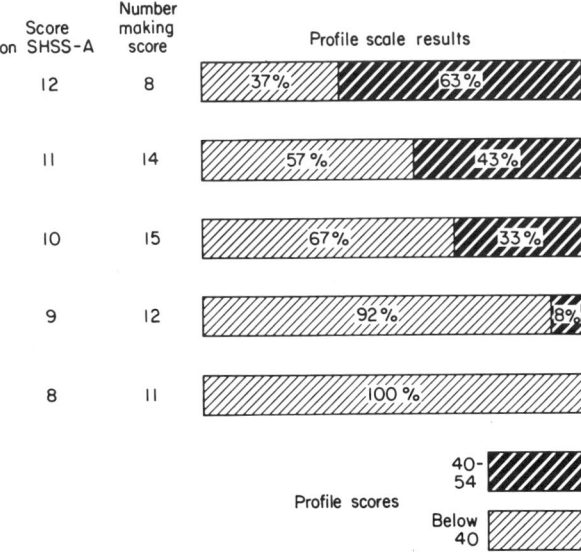

Figure 15 High scorers on SHSS-A classified according to higher and lower scores on the profile scales. Unpublished data, Stanford Laboratory.

What can we say about the very highly hypnotizable? Of course, the test scores show that they do what others do, only more successfully and over a wider range of phenomena. When they age regress, they believe they are actually children again; they describe what happens in the present tense and do not identify the hypnotist as such. When they hallucinate, they have difficulty in distinguishing the real from the hallucinated, even when told that one of the percepts is hallucinated. They can readily add content to the suggestions of the hypnotist, as in elaborating a fantasy or describing the scenes in a hallucinated motion picture. They can perform automatic writing, composing messages or solving problems without awareness of what the dissociated hand is doing. They can carry out posthypnotic suggestions, even rather bizarre ones, without being ill at ease over what is happening. The difficulty in distinguishing between these subjects and other high hypnotizables is that there is no one threshold to be crossed for inclusion in the category of hypnotic virtuoso unless it can be shown that some additional quality associated with a deeper dissociation has entered.

We now know a great deal about the hypnotizable person, on the basis of hundreds of interviews conducted before and after the experience of hypnosis (J. R. Hilgard, 1965, 1970) plus supporting data from questionnaire and experimental studies. A primary emphasis that emerged from the interviews was the significance of *imaginative involvements,* usually developed in childhood and often acquired from parents who shared such involvements. These have been more fully described in Chapter 5, when imagination was discussed.

These involvements take various forms, as in reading, dramatic viewing or acting, music listening or performance, enjoyment of nature, and adventure. The person who becomes temporarily involved sets ordinary reality aside as he becomes totally absorbed in the imaginative experience. The departure from reality is temporary only, and the person is able to return promptly to his normal coping with external reality. Those who habitually had such experiences proved to be among the most hypnotizable, whereas those who could report none of them were among the least hypnotizable. These findings have now been supported by a number of converging lines of evidence, showing relationships between imagery and hypnosis and preferences for right-hemisphere functioning in the more highly hypnotizable, as related to imagery (Chapter 5).

In a later study Josephine Hilgard interviewed extensively a contrasting group of highly susceptible subjects and a group of low susceptibles, showing again how significantly these involvements are related to hypnotizability (J. R. Hilgard, 1974). The 42 highly susceptibles had scored either 9 or 10 on a modified form of the Harvard Group Scale (HGSHS-A) with a maximum of 10, or an average of 10.9 of a possible 12 on an individual Form C of the Stanford Scale (SHSS-C). The comparison group of lows all passed less than

2 items on the 12-point Form C scale. Her findings confirmed the earlier studies by showing that 93 percent of the highs (39 of 42) expressed a marked interest in the savoring of sensory experiences, such as an esthetic interest in nature, and, of these, all showed deep involvement either in reading or drama or both. By contrast, among the lows, only 20 percent (3 of 15) could be rated as high in the savoring of sensory experiences, and their involvements in reading and drama were equally infrequent.

The deep nature of these involvements was evident in many of the comments from those scoring high. One young woman who had read the book *Island* during the summer had been unable to answer a question her roommate asked her until a full 10 minutes had elapsed. She said of her reading:

> I don't especially identify with any person. If there's a hero, I hope he'll win. If a bad guy, I hate him. I'm emotionally involved as a bystander. I'm somebody who's there. (Invisible?) Yes, they don't know I'm there, but I'm in the middle of the action. *Sometimes* I identify with the character, and then will dream I'm that character for 2 or 3 nights. I continue with the story rather than having it end. . . . In some ways I know I'm myself, I have my own identity, but on many levels I'm that other person—thinking like that person and acting the way that person would act (J. R. Hilgard, 1974, p. 141).

It is easy to see how experiences of this kind prepare the person for the experience of hypnosis. However, there may actually be counter trends in the personality that are strongly at variance with giving free play to the imagination, even when the capacity for imaginative involvement is present. The consequence is that there may be conflicts between the trends, interfering with hypnosis. This must be recognized, because the prediction of hypnotic performance from imaginary involvements is at best imperfect. Some of those who show these conflicts continue to score as highly hypnotizable, but they give evidence of the conflict in their reactions to hypnosis through temporary symptom formation. The following cases are illustrative

Owen was a highly highly hypnotizable college student who had earned a score of 11 of 12 on SHSS-C. The experimenter suggested that he come for a special interview because he had indicated that he had been nauseated throughout the testing session.

> The nausea started as soon as I began to feel hypnotized, about 5 minutes into it . . . waves of nausea, hurting in my stomach as though I would throw up . . . I had to sit very still. I did the tests, I could still hear directions, didn't hear much else she said. Each test added a little more discomfort.

Owen indicated in the interview that he always took the role of leader, whether in social affairs, athletics, or student organizations in school. He wanted very much to experience hypnosis but had doubted that it would happen because of his leadership tendencies. To be a leader, he said, it is necessary to experience everything that others have experienced, hence his desire to be hypnotized.

The interviewer uncovered other events in his background that had led to nausea, for example, when learning to fly an airplane with an instructor at the controls. His nausea in flying had disappeared as soon as he began to fly solo, when he was completely in charge. After it was explained to him that self-hypnosis might be similar to flying the airplane himself, he agreed to try it. He learned readily to hypnotize himself, going deeply into hypnosis, with no trace of nausea. Subsequently he used self-hypnosis daily to help him to study longer, with greater concentration, while feeling relaxed. The interpretation of his nausea symptoms in hypnosis was that part of him wanted to be hypnotized, whereas part of him resisted control by the hypnotist, with nausea a consequence of the conflict.

Ardell, another high scorer, was observed to be unusually nervous and tense, especially during the session in which she was being tested by the more advanced Stanford Profile Scales. Because such symptoms are rare among the highly hypnotizable, the hypnotist-experimenter arranged for her to have a supplementary interview. She responded:

> Some of the things were really frustrating. I like to be able to handle things. After the suggestion about the scissors, I felt bad. I couldn't use them then, and I didn't know how. I felt very nervous.

She commented that she had had the same feeling about the arithmetic impairment, another item on the Stanford Profile Scales. In hypnosis when it was suggested that she was a person who would be confused by the arithmetic problems, or perhaps find the answers impossible, she had found herself unable to solve the problems that should have been easy.

> I'm good at math, but I couldn't do it. It made me feel inadequate. . . . I have to make sure that I can work things out, know exactly what's going on. I spend more time than others making sure I understand something completely. It was frustrating to feel inadequate in something I can do.

She gave evidence of a conflict between the ego-alien hypnotic requirement of a poor performance on her part, after she has schooled herself so consistently to excellent performance. She could not refrain from trying to meet the hypnotic demands, consistent with her fulfilling of accepted obligations, but the resulting conflict meant frustration and nervousness. The symptoms disappeared entirely when the hypnotic session ended.

THE HYPNOTIC STATE

After a subject has agreed to participate in hypnosis and has been hypnotized according to any of the several methods, he perceives that some changes have taken place, partly as a response to the suggestions that have been given in the induction, such as relaxation of his muscles, drowsiness and other subtle changes that are part of the total experience for him. If asked to do so, he finds it easy to assign a numerical value to indicate his degree of hypnotic depth or involvement. This feeling of being hypnotized, being in some kind of changed condition or state, makes him ready to accept the suggestions of the hypnotist to produce the specific responses that are called for, such as muscular movements or inhibitions, hallucinations, and so on. Hence the first task is to examine some of the alterations that are associated with the hypnotic state before turning to the manner in which the subject responds to specific suggestions.

The subject who has experienced the relaxing suggestions of a standard induction will report many of the experiences given in Table 10; the higher his susceptibility score, the more experiences he tends to report. As we shall see later, when alert hypnosis is under discussion some of the responses in Table 10 are those which have been suggested, such as the similarity to sleep or the general immobility associated with deep relaxation; it is not surprising that many of the relatively insusceptible also note some general relaxation. Such changes cannot be taken as essential to the hypnotic state, but their influence on the self-awareness of hypnosis may still be genuine. A subject who, after hypnotic induction, feels himself more relaxed than he has ever felt before has a right to attribute this to hypnosis. If he has other feelings such as a special sense of detachment from the environment, these have become part of his description of the hypnotic state.

The hypnotist also observes a number of consequences of successful hypnotic induction in addition to noting the success with which the subject follows his suggestions.

The following have been noted among the kinds of behavior giving rise to a conception of hypnosis as an altered state:

1. *Increased suggestibility.* This characteristic of hypnosis has been so much emphasized that, since Bernheim (1888), many have defined hypnosis according to the changes in suggestibility that it produces. Although these changes can be demonstrated, alone they provide a very limited characterization of the total alterations that hypnosis produces.

2. *Enhanced imagery and imagination, including the availability of visual memories from the past.* The prominence of imagery, spontaneous as well as instructed, and its correlations with hypnotic susceptibility give it a high place in de-

Table 10

SUBJECTIVE REPORTS BASED ON AN INQUIRY
FOLLOWING ATTEMPTED HYPNOSIS
(Modified from Hilgard, 1965, p. 12)

	Affirmative replies to inquiry as related to hypnotic susceptibility (percent)[a]			
Inquiry	High ($N = 48$)	Medium ($N = 49$)	Low ($N = 45$)	Slightly susceptible ($N = 17$)
Where you able to tell when you were hypnotized?	65	60	47	31
Any similarity to sleep?	80	77	68	50
Disinclination to act:				
to speak?	89	79	68	31
to move?	87	77	64	50
to think?	55	48	32	12
Feeling of compulsion?	48	52	20	6
Changes in size or appearance of parts of your body?	46	40	26	0
Other feelings of changes:				
of floating?	43	42	25	12
of blacking out?	28	19	7	6
of dizziness?	19	31	14	0
of spinning?	7	17	0	6
of one or more of the prior four feelings?	60	60	39	25

[a] Based on an inquiry following the taking of one of the two forms of the Stanford Profile Scales of Hypnotic Susceptibility, after having scored at least 4 on SHSS-A; the insusceptible are not included.

scribing what happens in hypnosis. Visual images from the past, including those from childhood, are familiar in age regression. Imagination and memory are necessarily closely related, for the elements of something imagined must be something previously experienced in some form and retained in memory.

3. *Subsidence of the planning function.* The hypnotized subject loses initiative and lacks the desire to make and carry out plans of his own; he appears to have turned over much of this to the hypnotist. The change from the normal controls is relative only, for the hypnotic subject retains the *ability* to initiate or terminate action, or, within a task assigned by the hypnotist he can exer-

cise initiative. For example, if told to deliver a political speech he can improvise one of his own choosing; what is impressive is that without encouragement he has little desire to do so. The avoidance of initiative is illustrated by statements such as this from one of our subjects: "Once I was going to swallow, but decided it wasn't worth the effort. At one point I was trying to decide if my legs were crossed, but I couldn't tell, and didn't quite have the initiative to move to find out."

4. *Reduction in reality testing.* Reality distortions of all kinds, including acceptance of falsified memories, changes in one's own personality, modification of the rate at which time seems to pass, doubling of a person seated at the table, absence of heads or feet of people observed to be walking around the room, inappropriate naming—these and many other distortions of reality that would normally be readily detected and corrected can be accepted without criticism in the hypnotic state. This fact has led Orne (1959) to speak of *trance logic,* denoting this peculiar acceptance of what would normally be found incompatible.

Other aspects might be mentioned, such as the prominence of amnesia and some alterations in the attentive functions, but those mentioned suffice to indicate how the subject has enough evidence to convince himself that he is hypnotized and how the experimenter-hypnotist can recognize that he is.

Alert Hypnosis and the Problem of a Single Hypnotic State

The subject knows when he is hypnotized because of changes that he perceives in himself, but some of these changes are produced by the specific suggestions that he received in the induction, and the state might have been different if other suggestions had been given. This possibility of more than one state raises a problem for those who may wish to define hypnosis as a unique kind of state, with appropriate physiological correlates. It is known that hypnotic states can be produced without any suggestions of relaxation; thus to characterize hypnosis as a deeply relaxed state is to limit it unnecessarily. It did not take laboratory experiments to discover this, for the trance states of the whirling dervishes or the dancing Balinese are just as real as the states of those who achieve trance states by quiet meditation, and all may resemble hypnosis.

An active-alert hypnosis can be produced in the laboratory without any suggestions of relaxation or sleep. Even if induction has been of the relaxation-sleep type, the state itself can readily be converted to an active one. There are, then, these two chief ways of producing the active state; to begin with the more usual relaxation method and convert it, or to begin directly with an active-alert induction.

In the first method the usual induction stressing relaxation and employing the metaphor of sleep may lead the person into the familiar kind of hypnotic condition. Then, at the suggestion of the hypnotist, the subject can alert himself without destroying his sense of being hypnotized. The stage hypnotists have made such a procedure widely familiar. They usually induce hypnosis in conventional ways but soon have their subjects dancing about or crowing like roosters. Strenuous activity is not incompatible with conventional hypnosis as studied in the experimental laboratory. Hypnotized subjects who are given suggestions to perform at their maximum in learning tasks or strength tasks are more successful if the subject, while hypnotized, is first alerted and then given added suggestions that he is strong or able (e.g., Liebert, Rubin, and Hilgard, 1965; Slotnick, Liebert, and Hilgard, 1965).

The second method of inducing alert hypnosis is to begin immediately with an alert induction. It is not necessary to detach the subject from his usual reality orientation to the environment by reducing proprioceptive or visual feedback. Essentially the same results can be accomplished by telling him that he feels more alert, that he is less fatigued by exertion, that the surroundings seem brighter. In an experiment along these lines Ludwig and Lyle (1964) produced a hyperalert state in their hypnotized subjects, driving them to a kind of frenzy that they found unpleasant. In a later experiment in our laboratory Eva Banyai demonstrated that an active induction, carried out without going to extremes, led to responses to scaled items on the Stanford Hypnotic Susceptibility Scales essentially similar to those following the more usual relaxed or passive induction (Banyai and Hilgard, 1976). The method was to seat the subject on a stationary laboratory bicycle (a bicycle ergometer, in laboratory parlance) and to have the subject pedal continuously against a load that felt like actual rapid riding. The subject's eyes were open, and the riding led to increased breathing and perspiration, as expected. However, the subject received suggestions that the pedaling would not seem difficult and would be without discomfort, that the room would seem bright, and that alertness would be increased as the pedaling went on. The induction was, in fact, modeled after that used in the usual test, but where drowsiness had ordinarily been suggested, alertness was substituted, and where relaxation had been suggested, increased effort was substituted. Although there were naturally some different descriptions of such a trance and the usual one, the fact of an altered condition was reported by the same subjects who reported a change in the relaxed induction. Control experiments showed that the active induction increased hypnotic responsiveness over the waking condition; thus more was involved than waking suggestion while on the bicycle.

Once it is recognized that the usual relaxed hypnotic state can be converted to strenuous participative activity by suggestion or that the more strenuous state can be produced directly, the contrast between the two is between induction procedures rather than between unique hypnotic states. Both types of induction produce enough changes for the subject to identify that some massive changes have taken place (if he is hypnotically responsive), and these changes have a common influence on responsiveness to suggestions. The alternative inductions will modify the aspects of the hypnotic state according to which the subject defines his involvement and will doubtless alter the accompanying physiological changes; the modifications of control systems that result have enough in common to define the effects of either induction as hypnosis.

Deep Hypnosis and Its Characteristics

Hypnotic responsiveness and hypnotic depth are related in that the more hypnotizable person can experience greater depth of hypnosis. Responsiveness and depth are not the same thing, however, because a responsive person can experience hypnosis at greater or lesser degrees of depth and has no difficulty in assigning numerical values to the depth as he perceives it. To obtain a more complete picture of the massive dissociations possible in hypnosis, it is essential to work with the highly responsive persons as described here and to permit them to experience hypnosis at depths beyond those usually attained.

The concept of depth of hypnosis, like depth of sleep, is a convenient metaphor. The metaphor is an ancient one and is carried also by the word profound, with the root meaning of near the bottom (Latin, *pro fundus*). The psychologies deriving from Freud are often called depth psychologies. The notion of exploring the depths of personality goes back at least to a fragment from Heraclitus (ca. 500 B.C.):

> You could not discover the depths of the psyche, even if you traveled every road to do so; such is the depth of its meaning.

The metaphor of depth is very compelling, but it is only a metaphor; care must be taken not to embody it with our own values. In hypnosis it means only the pervasiveness of the changes from the normal condition and can as well be described as degree of involvement or immersion in the hypnotic experience.

Depth cannot be described solely by the responsiveness to suggestions as these are scored in tests of hypnosis; at greater depths, responses to suggestion, instead of being enhanced, may disappear entirely. When deep hypnosis is involved, the best measures are numerical estimates made by the subject on his own scale. This is equivalent to magnitude estimation as used in psychophysics and is very satisfactory. As in psychophysical experiments, very little practice is required for the subject to learn to assign self-consistent numbers for his subjectively experienced depth. If he uses a number between 5 and 10 to define his depth when he is capable of meeting the usual demands made on a hypnotized subject, he may assign numbers as high as 50 or 100 or even higher as he goes still deeper.

To achieve great depth it is necessary to select a responsive subject and permit him to increase his depth over time, either by repeated and prolonged suggestions by the hypnotist or by extensive self-hypnosis.

Charles Tart (1970, 1972) had experimented for some time with self-report scales of hypnotic depth before conducting his experiment on great depth. His case of William represents the deep hypnosis experiences of a subject who scored within a point of the maximum of the Profile Scales, hence in the upper 1 or 2% of hypnotic responsiveness. He had been hypnotized 18 times previously for various purposes, often with an emphasis on depth. Although extreme depth had not been stressed, on his scale William usually gave reports of 40 or 50, with amnesia experienced at 30. He had never gone beyond 60.

A session was undertaken in which he agreed to attempt to go much deeper than he had gone before. He was instructed that at each 10-point interval on a depth continuum he should remain at that depth as the experimenter had him describe what he was experiencing. Tart has presented a somewhat complex summary of his reports associated with depth, a few of which have been selected for reproduction in Figure 16.

His reports of changes at the depths more commonly studied in the laboratory repeat the familiar: an early relaxation, a fairly normal awareness of the experimenter, although he may become a little distant, an increase in peacefulness, a gradual withdrawal from the environment. Beginning at a level of about 50 on this scale, however, distortions of consciousness occur that have some similarity to the reports of mystical experiences. The experimenter's voice becomes impersonal, the passage of time becomes meaningless, the body seems to be left behind, a new sense of infinite potentiality emerges, ultimately reaching the sense of oneness with the universe. These reports from this single subject are intriguing enough to indicate that the full potential of hypnosis may not be explored in most of the experiments or in clinical applications that rely on demonstrable changes in behavior brought about by the hypnotic interaction.

One feature of William's account that is interesting in relation to dissociation is the intrusion, in the earlier stages of the now deeper hypnosis, of the experience that some part of him is amused by his participation in these consciousness-alerting activities. This sudden intrusion of a critical observing part amused by the turn of events began about 50, was first reported clearly at 70, and then dropped out at 90 and was no longer mentioned. A hint of a

THE HYPNOTIC STATE   169

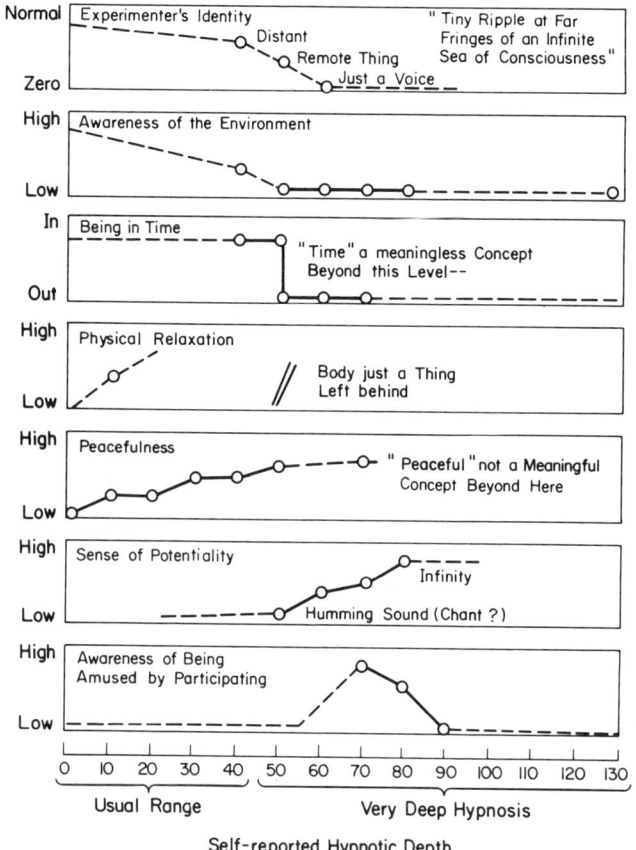

Figure 16 Self-reported hypnotic experiences at various depths by one selected subject. Modified from Tart (1972).

hidden observer is implied.

In our studies of deep hypnosis in a few pilot subjects who were not as experienced in hypnosis as William, many similar experiences have been reported. Our method has been to select moderately high subjects (not necessarily those classified as virtuosos), to hypnotize them, and then to invite them to experience deeper hypnosis without repeated suggestions from the hypnotist. They are to report their depth on a numerical scale from time to time, but there is little questioning of the experience while it is occurring. A protective suggestion is given that, if a subject should happen to lose contact with the hypnotist's voice at a deeper stage, his depth can be lightened by the hypnotist's hand placed on the shoulder, and he will then be back in communication with the hypnotist. We recognize that there is an implied suggestion here that such a state may be reached, and we have not yet performed the necessary control experiments to determine the role of the subject's expectations and his interpretation of the experimenter's demands.

Our arbitrary scale starts somewhat lower than Tart's, for our subjects have assigned a depth of about 8 or 10, in most cases, to the established hypnotic state in which they experience analgesia and amnesia, can perform automatic writing, and so on. However, they go on to much deeper states by themselves. Those who have lost contact with the experimenter as evidenced by no longer replying to requests for a depth report have done so typically at a depth of about 50. They may then continue to depths they later report to have been 80 or 90. After the experimenter places his hand on the shoulder to reduce the depth and inquires about the current hypnotic depth, he asks what the deepest depth had been. This completes the deep hypnosis part of the experiment, and the subject is told that he will remember his experiences when aroused from hypnosis and will be able to talk about them. A thorough inquiry then follows.

Observations frequently include a loss of any connection with the body, a failure of time to have any meaning, the pleasantness of the experience, and some reports characteristic of mystical experiences—a sense of oneness, a feeling of having acquired some knowledge that is not communicable. What the subject reports is colored by his nonhypnotic experiences of meditation, perhaps of familiarity with Gestalt therapy, sometimes evident in the vocabularies used to describe the experiences, such as the nonlinearity of the experiences or their Gestalt qualities. The method is more like meditation than ordinary hypnosis in that the experimenter is so much less intrusive; in hypnosis the subject commonly waits for what the experimenter is going to ask him to do; in self-deepening, the deepening is his own affair, and the depth reports are quite automatic. Tart reports William as saying that the appropriate number to describe his state just popped into his mind. He had no idea how these numbers were generated, and it was reported that he did not "understand" them. Our subjects confirmed this nature of the numerical reports of depth.

The experiments just described have not gone into the question of prolonged hypnosis, and little evidence is available. Erickson (1952) gave his account of deep hypnosis, leading to what he described as a *plenary* trance, in which the subject becomes essentially inert or stuporous. His discussions are generally quite informal; therefore, comparison with the deep state produced in the laboratory studies is not possible. However, it may be noted that the primary symptom Erickson emphasized was losing contact with the body; restoration sometimes came as a shock, and he warned that care should be taken to restore the normal condition slowly as a precaution against this. Although responses to the hypnotist came more slowly in the deep trance, his subject, according to Erickson, did not in fact lose contact.

Because hypnosis is usually studied at much lighter levels of involvement, it is more often described according to the characteristic responses to the hypnotist's suggestions. The studies of deep hypnosis indicate that these specific responses may not occur in the context of massive dissociations characterizing the more involved hypnotic condition.

HOW THE SUBJECT RESPONDS TO SUGGESTIONS: HYPNOTIC ANALGESIA AND DEAFNESS

The objective results obtained from the items of the hypnotic responsiveness scales indicate how difficult the various suggestions are according to the number of subjects who pass and fail them following an attempted induction of hypnosis. The statistical findings, valuable as they are for many purposes, must be supplemented by careful interrogations if we are to understand how the hypnotist's suggestions are interpreted and acted on. For this purpose, the successful management of experiences that others find hard to achieve often yields the most pertinent information. Among such difficult experiences that we have studied extensively from a statistical standpoint and have at the same time followed up with careful interviews are those of pain reduction and suggested deafness.* Earlier interviews, as previously noted (page 160), had shown the important role of imaginative involvements and had provided other information as background for the present inquiries.

Hypnotic Analgesia

The experiences reported here are mostly from a highly selected group of subjects who could reduce the pain produced by placing a hand and forearm in circulating ice water and leaving it there for some 45 seconds. By that time, the pain ordinarily has mounted to a critical level at which the subject would very much wish to have the experience terminated. Only a few can eliminate the pain entirely and feel nothing following hypnotic analgesia suggestions, but a reduction of a third or more suffices to keep the pain at a tolerable level. Even that much pain reduction typically requires a high level of hypnotic responsiveness, as illustrated in Figure 17. Success depends on the degree of hypnotizability, but even in the highest group, as classified here, only two-thirds could reduce their pain by a third or more of the normally felt pain.

The most noteworthy finding in the interviews with the highly hypnotizable was the extent to which the subjects supplemented in their own ways the suggestions given by the hypnotist. The formal suggestions, adapted from

---

*The postexperimental interviews were conducted by Josephine R. Hilgard, who has been in charge of the laboratory's interviewing program for many years.

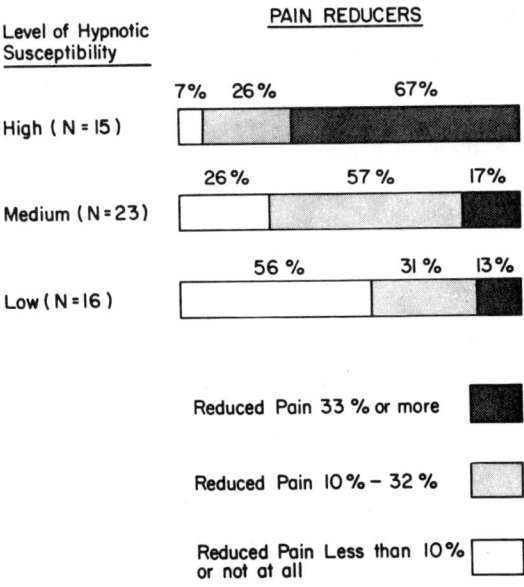

Figure 17 Reduction of pain through hypnotically suggested analgesia as related to susceptibility to hypnosis. The subjects were 54 university students whose prior experience of hypnosis was limited to the procedures for measuring hypnotic responsiveness. From Hilgard and Morgan (1976).

Spanos, Barber, and Lang (1974), were as follows, as presented by a tape recording:

> I want you to succeed in not being disturbed by the water by doing the following. Try to the best of your ability to imagine and think of your left hand and arm as numb and insensitive. Think of your left hand and arm as unable to sense any cold, pain, or discomfort. Please try to think of your hand and arm as numb and insensitive, as if just a piece of rubber, until I remove your hand from the water. Other students have been able to think of their hands and arms in this way and it isn't as hard as it seems. What I want you to do is to control your thoughts and think continuously that your left hand has no feeling. Keep thinking that it is unable to feel any cold, pain, or discomfort. Continue to think of your hand and arm as without cold, pain, discomfort, or feeling of any kind. Please try to the very best of your ability to think continuously and to imagine vividly that your hand is numb, insensitive, and like a piece of rubber until it is out of the water. Now keep thinking and vividly imagining that your left hand and arm are becoming more numb and insensitive....

The idea of a rubber, insensitive arm was, in fact, used by several of the subjects, but often with some additions, as noted by their comments.

"I pictured my arm as a rubber tire which had treads and everything. It was attached to my shoulder. I recall mentally seeing this strip of rubber in the water."

"My arm was not there. It turned into a rubber hose. There were no nerve endings in that the sensory parts would be there." This subject added, however: "In addition, I was on a hill watching butterflies."

The image of a rubber arm was not always successful:

"Imagining it as rubber was not helpful. . . . Initially my arm was tingling, but using the image of how numb my mouth had been at the dentist's, I had no sensation of my arm resting on something." (His analgesia was successful).

The subjects used their own supplementary images in several ways, chiefly in cutting off the arm so that it could not feel or finding themselves (in fantasy) remote from the stressful event. Examples of detaching the arm were given by several of those interviewed:

"My arm was not part of me anymore. . . . I daydreamed, concentrated on my trip to Europe."

This subject imagined her entire arm was numb and that she didn't feel any cold or distress. . . . She also imagined that it was not even her own arm.

Arm was thought severed, no longer part of her. For extra insurance, she felt that if it were part of her it would be unable to feel.

These comments show how some subjects gained distance through fantasy:

"I used the image of being occupied doing something like hunting an animal or making an arrowhead. On the ice water side, at the left, my arm was in a cloud and I didn't want to look in." (He said he was a little bothered by the fact that there was something he didn't know, and, although absorbed in the hunting, he had a few fleeting thoughts that he should look into the cloud, but he decided not to.)

"I placed myself in a forest where a deer was walking. I constantly built on images until I found one that was working." (She indicated that she had to be active in her imagining, because if the images had been passive, "if they involved just being there," she would go back into the reality of the arm hurting.)

"By not being in the room. I went to a tropical island, walked on the beach, and swam with both arms."

"I reduced the pain by using different images. I became involved in the image. I was on a hillside, watching a sunset with friends, singing, talking, laughing, doing something together. In the beginning I focused on the setting, such as the colors and smells, then I focused on the activities."

"I pictured myself as Alice-in-Wonderland, in a tunnel; I examined things in the tunnel. I had two arms to search the tunnel. I kept my mind occupied doing that." (She indicated that she sometimes slipped back into feeling a little pain and had to give herself more suggestions. "I repeated the suggestions of the hypnotist to myself.")

Although these methods proved successful in reducing pain for the subjects quoted, not all of the highly hypnotizable succeeded in reducing pain.

"I tried different images to distance me from my arm. Some involved cutting off the arm. The images seemed real, but the arm retained its full sensitivity."

A male student who was highly hypnotizable fully expected to be able to reduce pain. He tried a number of techniques, but none succeeded. In his case there was a history of indulgence when he experienced pain as a child. He learned that it was rewarding to complain of pain, and the history of reinforcement for expressing pain conceivably made it harder for him to reduce the experimental pain despite his expectation of success.

These are some highlights from the interviews. There were a few highly idiosyncratic responses, one of which is worth describing because it shows how a few such cases can distort correlations obtained from small samples. One young woman, because of the manner in which she entered hypnosis, required no suggestions of analgesia to reduce pain; hence she would distort the usual finding that hypnosis without suggested analgesia typically does not reduce pain.

When this student goes into hypnosis her arms gradually shrink into her shoulders until they are nonexistent. Distortions of body image are frequently reported in hypnosis, but hers was extreme. This distortion has nothing to do specifically with suggestions for pain reduction; for her it happens regularly in hypnosis. This affects pain reduction, for she feels *no pain* during normal hypnosis and of course none subsequently when there are specific directions for pain reduction. "In hypnosis my physical body begins to shrink, especially my upper extremities. My arms begin to pull into my body. Nothing happens to my legs until later. . . ." (Why during hypnosis alone was there no pain in the ice water on the first day?) "Because my upper extremities had already shrunk. You should have stuck my legs in the ice water because they were still very much there." As she goes into very deep hypnosis, her legs move into her body, and finally her head sinks in so that "I finally feel like a torso."

Two conclusions are pertinent from these reports on pain reduction methods by the highly hypnotic responsive:

1. Regardless of the method used, the subject has nearly always taken some initiative and worked to attain success.

2. The method very commonly makes use of active imagery, producing responses incompatible with the pain experience. Both arms may be used in the fantasied experience, hence negating the passive helplessness of the arm

in the ice water. A favorite fantasy, at a distance, is being in the midst of nature, in the woods, at the beach, or on a tropical isle.

Because the responses are so much under the direction of the subject, consciousness seems "normal," and in that sense responses may appear to be compliant ones on the part of imaginative subjects. However, this interpretation is partial and misleading. The reports of the subjects, briefly summarized, show that they do indeed manipulate their imagery purposefully; the reports fail to make clear that, once the setting for the imagery is adopted, it takes on a self-generating nonvoluntary quality as the subjects become immersed in the experience. The hypnotic state, as background, may serve as a facilitater, enhancing the reality of the experience beyond the fantasies of nonhypnotic experience. As a consequence of this sequence of events, the fantasy becomes so all absorbing as to compete with the stressful condition and exclude it from consciousness.

Pain Reduction in Daily Living

Those who favor a role interpretation of hypnosis commonly emphasize the compliant behavior of the subject in trying to come up to the expectations of the hypnotist. Such behavior is clearly present, as indicated by the evident efforts of the subjects to reduce pain; however, it is an insufficient explanation of the success in pain reduction for a number of reasons. Many compliant subjects are unsuccessful. In addition, much evidence indicates that subjects use similar techniques to reduce pain *for themselves*, either prior to any experience of hypnosis or after they have learned pain reduction in the laboratory. Were it in any sense unsuccessful, there would be no reason to fool themselves. The following illustrations are of pain reduction in daily living, prior to experiences in hypnosis; thus any inference to posthypnotic suggestion is invalid. The experiences also testify to the fact that highly responsive subjects can engage in behavior similar to hypnotic behavior prior to any formal induction of hypnosis, before establishing an interpersonal relationship with a hypnotist.

One subject used her capacity for imagery and imagination during long workouts in competitive swimming. For a while she swam 3½–4 hours per day. During the backstroke she would look at the sky, see the clouds, place herself on a cloud, and see herself swimming past a cloud. She did not feel normal fatigue and pain. . . . "When I'm hot, I think of being in a place that's cool. If I keep up the image, I get cool."

Another subject used comparable techniques in his distance swimming. For five years he had been competing in 3000 and 5000 yard swims. "In workouts of 5000 to 10,000 yards, I used to sing. I'd get a song in my mind and it would be there for the rest of the practice. I'd pace my whole stroke to it. That's fine for distance swimming." He gave another illustration. "While biking up Old La Honda Road, my legs are killing me and I tell myself they don't hurt as much as they do and I can make it to the top. Then I get into a rhythm, a constant beat or rhythm. It's easier to pedal to a constant beat or rhythm."

A student had cut her knee seriously the year before, the repair requiring 38 stitches. Because of an allergy to novocain, she controlled the pain subjectively, by blocking everything from her mind, concentrating on breathing, and picturing her head filled with something like foam rubber which would block sensation. This successful experience had been later used in hypnosis.

As a final illustration, one subject gave the following report: A few weeks before, the lotus position, during Zen meditation, had become painful for his back and legs, "Instead of doing meditation, images floated through my mind and I ended up by closing my eyes and going into hypnosis. Sitting for 50 minutes seemed like 15 minutes."

The experience of this final subject had been influenced by his experience of hypnosis, but what the others reported had occurred prior to acquaintance with hypnosis. The experiences are indeed hypnotic in character; once the student has been hypnotized, he recognizes the overlap. Because the usual practice of hypnosis is known to take place in a setting of relaxation, the illustrations from active sports might also have seemed far from hypnosis. As previously noted, hypnosis can in fact be produced by an active-alert induction as well as by a relaxed-passive one. Once the subject has experienced pain reduction in formal hypnosis, he is better prepared to identify places where the pain-reducing skill can be used. We have had many reports of the successful use of self-hypnosis by our experienced subjects after they became acquainted with hypnosis, for example, in painful ski accidents and while dancing in a play with a broken bone in a foot (with the doctor's permission.)

Hypnotic Deafness

Because pain has a distress component in addition to its sensory component, it seemed desirable to study a purer sensory experience by methods similar to those used in the study of pain reduction. For this purpose we turned to the problem of hypnotic deafness, using 1000 Hz tones presented binaurally through headphones at a range of intensities above threshold in steps of 10–70 db. The pain of ice water mounts continuously with the time that the hand and forearm are in the water; thus the arrangement may predispose to a report of uniform increase in pain over time. The tones were presented in random sequence, so that, if a uniform increase in magnitude of the heard sound resulted with increase in physical intensity, it could not be assigned to the order of presentation of the tones. As it turned out, the magnitude estimates for increasing loudness fitted the same type of power function as the magnitude estimates for pain over time, providing an indirect validation of the appropriateness of the pain reports.

For an unselected population of students success in reducing hearing through suggested deafness corresponded to measured hypnotizability; this can be expressed as a correlation of $r = .56$, a value about the same as that found for pain reduction. The relative successes expressed in terms of the percents of subjects who reduced hearing by given amounts are shown in Figure 18. It proved somewhat more difficult to reduce hearing than to reduce pain. For the more highly responsive subjects, only half as many could reduce hearing one-third or more, as compared with the proportion who could reduce pain by that amount, as shown previously in Figure 17, p. 172. None of the lows reduced their hearing by as much as one-third.

These results are based on a preliminary analysis of the data. A curious finding was that, among those who could not reduce hearing at all, there were a large number for whom the same tones were reported as louder under

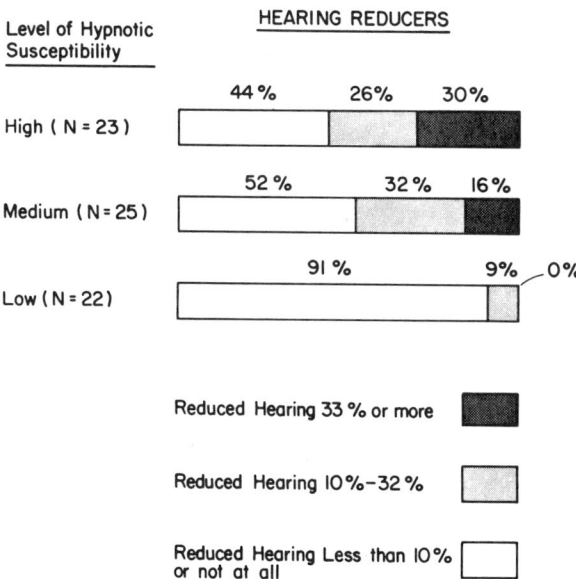

Figure 18 Reduction of hearing through hypnotically suggested deafness as related to susceptibility to hypnosis. The subjects were 70 students whose prior experience of hypnosis was limited to a standard test of hypnotic responsiveness following standardized procedures. The data have been adjusted to represent the unselected population from which the subjects were drawn. Unpublished data, Stanford Laboratory.

the conditions of suggested deafness. This finding was not confined to the lows, although 74% of lows reported the tones as louder than normal when it was suggested that they would not hear them. Two possibilities will have to be explored. One is that the general quiescence of the hypnotic relaxation procedures enhances the attention to sounds, even for the nonhypnotizable, so that the level of hearing from which the sounds have to be reduced has been enhanced above normal. A second possibility is that there may be some undetected artifact that accounts for the finding. It cannot be attributed to a general negativism to the instructions, because the effect is too widespread relative to other signs of occasional negativism. If correction proves to be necessary, it will change the absolute values but not the relative success in hearing reduction as related to hypnotic susceptibility.

The generally greater difficulty in the reduction of hearing over the reduction of pain is coherent with available evidence about the persistence of hearing when other senses are deadened by chemical anesthetics. The familiar experience of a mother's being awakened by her child's cry in the night is a corresponding example of the persistence of hearing. The retention of words spoken within general anesthesia also shows how resistant is the sense of hearing to being abolished.

Following the completion of the hypnotic deafness study reported in Figure 18, a number of highly responsive subjects who had participated in the pain experiment were invited to take part in a corresponding deafness experiment. Later a new group of subjects were tested on both analgesia and deafness; thus more could be found out about similarities and differences in the way the experiences were managed. These subjects were carefully interviewed to find out how they used or supplemented the hypnotist's deafness suggestions in the production of the overt hearing loss.

Because of the frequent spontaneous use of imagery in the pain studies, imagery was now directly suggested in the deafness studies. The reports in the later interviews should be interpreted with these suggestions in mind. The suggestions for reduced hearing were given in taped form. This is what the subject was told:

> As you know, you can normally experience partial deafness by placing your hands over your ears very tightly. I'd like you to find some image that will assist you here to experience the deafness when I count in a little while. Some people have used images of a stereo being turned down or something covering or plugging their ears or being far away from tones—there are so many images to assist you. Find the image that works best for you.
>
> When a little later I count to ten, your hearing will become poorer and poorer, so that you may not even hear me get to ten. Then your hearing will be completely gone. Your hearing will remain absent until I restore it by touching my finger to your forehead. As you know, deaf people can easily talk. So even

though you are experiencing deafness, you will still be able to give your loudness reports verbally. You will say "zero" for hearing nothing, and say other numbers if an occasional tone breaks through your hearing loss. Assign numbers to the loudnesses, just as you were instructed to do, when I lift and replace my finger on your hand.

I am now going to place my finger on your hand, ready to signal the possible presence of tones. Now I am going to count to ten and as I do so the sound of my voice will fade along with other sounds, and by the time I get to ten, you will be deaf and unable to hear tones. (Counts from one to ten).

The method of designating the tone interval by lifting the experimenter's finger and then replacing it was devised so that the subject, with his eyes closed, even though deaf, would know when to signal that he heard nothing, and also, if any false responses were being made, he would report hearing a tone in an interval during which no tone was presented.

The subjects accepted or supplemented the hypnotist's suggestions in three ways: first, by some form of plugging or muffling the ears; second, by producing a competing sound to make it more difficult to hear the presented tone; third, by gaining distance from the sound through fantasy, either by removing the sound or themselves. The three devices are so frequently combined that examples from individual subjects will often reflect more than one method. Some subjects plugged of muffled their ears as suggested.

The image one used to produce deafness included a pillow over her head and earplugs in her ears while in a room far away from the sounds. (She reported that she successfully blocks out sound while reading at home.)

"I pictured myself getting further away from it. Also I put corks in my ears which was successful in muffling the lower tones."

Another tried plugging her ears, being under water, or being on the other side of a large room. (This subject was only slightly successful).

"I tried to think of a sound proof box in my mind and that didn't work for me. So I did it by putting my mind somewhere else, as I had in pain. I'd think of what I'd done during the day."

Other subjects used competing sounds to block the tone.

"I found the best way was to listen to the San Francisco Symphony. I was there with a good friend, totally absorbed, and hearing nothing but the music."

"I realized I had to have an image with a lot of noise. I transferred myself to the beach where there was the noise of the waves."

Another subject also used the sound of the beach and the waves. In addition she walked away from the tones.

"I was at the beach, listening to the waves crash. It worked moderately well. I heard 'fuzzy tones.'"

With still others, the main emphasis was on gaining distance from the tones.

> "All the sounds moved out the door that was way at the end of a corridor. Once the door was shut, I couldn't hear anything."
> On a moving sidewalk, moving further and further away from the sounds.
> "I reduced hearing tones by putting myself in a different scene so I was no longer aware of being in the room and sitting in the chair with headphones on. I dissociated myself from that experience. I had difficulty at times when I had to respond to the experimenter to tell him a number value for the tones. That would bring me back a little from the image."

These reports of supplementary images were not universal. A highly successful male subject found that all he could say was "I just let things happen."

The report of one subject unsuccessful in reducing tones despite her high hypnotic responsiveness illustrates the idiosyncratic experiences that occur.

> "Initially I pictured myself as a deaf person walking down Market Street. I couldn't hear the busses or cars that I expected to hear on Market Street, but I heard all the tones."

Next she fantasied that she was listening to a man with a jack hammer next to her. "I got a headache from listening to the man with the jack hammer. The noise was so bad and I felt the vibration." She continued to hear the tones. The headache lasted throughout the hypnosis until the experimenter suggested that she relax up in some clouds.

Headaches, she said, were very rare occurrences for her. Whether the headaches were produced, as she thought, by the noise and vibration of the fantasied jack hammer or as a consequence of conflict over the failure to produce deafness is uncertain and unanswerable from the information available.

Because most of those interviewed in this series had experienced reduction in both pain and hearing, there was some possibility that a successful first experience might have made the second easier. Of eight subjects whose direct answers are available to questions about the two experiences, their replies were as follows:

> Three of them thought the earlier experience had indeed been helpful by establishing confidence, and providing methods that worked, although one of these qualified the assertion by remarking: "It helped only a little bit."
> Three others found the later experience too different for the earlier one to be helpful. One stated pointedly: "Hearing was harder, for you don't have as much control over your ears as you do over your limbs. It's harder to isolate your ears."
> Of the remaining two, one was not sure whether the earlier experience helped any, and the other had succeeded so poorly both times that a comparison was not useful.

The results for both pain and hearing show that for these very difficult performances the successful subject must use considerable effort, initiative, and ingenuity to achieve success. In less strenuous settings, the hypnotic dissociations are much easier and less effortful. Subjects have told us that they like to enjoy hypnosis, and some of them resent being asked to participate in experiments of this kind in which tasks place unpleasant strains on them. They are willing to go along for the sake of science or for the possible benefits that may accrue for helping patients clinically. Experiments on deep hypnosis, more similar to meditative practices, make fewer demands on the subject; thus those who are only moderately hypnotizable may achieve many of the experiences corresponding to those of the more highly hypnotizable (Feldman, 1975). The subject under strain, however, brings into sharper focus how the highly responsive subject achieves the required dissociative experience.

THE HYPNOTIZED PERSON AS A SOURCE OF INFORMATION ABOUT HYPNOSIS

Encouraging the desire of psychologists to make psychology an objective science like other sciences was a useful contribution of behaviorism, but at the height of behaviorism the aim led to a neglect of a major source of information: what went on from the point of view of the experiencing person. Today we are better able to combine objective observations, inferences from them as to underlying processes, and the person's own observations to achieve a less restricted view of psychological reality while retaining the advantages of reproducibility of observations and clarity of communication that we associate with the scientific method.

In this chapter reliance is placed on reports by highly hypnotizable persons of what happens within hypnosis. A more objective and quantitative approach led to their identification as a small upper fraction of the total population. We now know a great deal about the distribution of hypnotizability and how hypnotic responsiveness correlates with special abilities such as reducing pain and hearing by suggestion. The information has been reviewed chiefly to place the highly hypnotizable in proper perspective and to show how they achieve the required dissociations.

Our subjects know that something happens to their orientation to external reality when they become involved in hypnosis, and they have no difficulty in assigning a numerical value to their depth of involvement. They know that what they experience as depth fluctuates up and down in a single hypnotic session. Their reports of these experiences, including the ones at depths beyond those usually studied in the laboratory, make some of the conceptual controversies over the hypnotic condition appear rather sterile.

There are indeed many matters that remain at issue and call for careful exploration. For example, the problem of hypnotic talent versus hypnotic state is a very real one, for many of these highly responsive subjects are so talented in hypnotic performance that they gain what appears to be essentially hypnotic control through the exercise of imagination in circumstances of life in the real world where they are unconcerned about a definition of hypnosis: in riding a bicycle uphill, in distance swimming, in surgery without anesthetics. Have they then engaged in self-hypnosis? This is a question to be pondered and studied, not to be decided a priori. However the answer comes out, these performances were not undertaken either to please the hypnotist or to fulfill the expectations of a hypnotist in order not to embarrass him.

The relationships among evoked imagery, imaginative involvements, and hypnosis appear to place these cognitive products on a continuum. Images can be evoked voluntarily and purposefully by these subjects, who come to hypnosis with rich experiences of both imagery and imaginative involvements. Once the imagery has been evoked, it takes on an autonomous quality when the imagery leads to involvements, as though the person is engaging in and enjoying a set of experiences in the real world of colors, sounds, smells, and sociability. There are many indications that being involved in hypnosis enhances the realism of the experiences for those people who are already attuned to them. Because the involvement is so thorough, other concurrent experiences are blocked from consciousness; perhaps they are still registered in some dissociated manner.

The highly hypnotizable person is capable of reality distortion; hence it might be argued that he is an unreliable observer. However, he knows very well about his own reality distortions, he has ways of maintaining an integrated hold on reality, and he gives a very plausible account of what happens within hypnosis. His account agrees with the inferences that an objective outsider might make to explain the observed conduct.

The highly hypnotizable normal subject should not be confused with the hysterical person who is using reality distortions to solve persistent personal problems, or with the psychotic person whose delusional or hallucinatory experiences are not subject to ready reversal. The typical high subject in our experiments has a "strong ego" by any measure, a firm hold on reality when he wishes, and adds a flexibility of adjustment in which the *temporary* setting aside of his reality orientation plays a large part.

NOTES

The Hypnotizable Person

A fuller account of the measurement of hypnosis is given in the appendix. An earlier discussion, including some conjectures about the origin of bimodality in the distribution of hypnotizability, may be found in Hilgard (1965). The earliest discussion of the bimodality problem was by Eysenck and Furneaux (1945). Results of interviews that led to the importance of imaginative involvements can be found in J. R. Hilgard (1965, 1970, 1974).

The Hypnotic State

There are conceptual problems defining hypnosis as an altered state, and these have been a source of controversy (e.g., Barber, 1969; Bowers, 1976; Sarbin and Coe, 1972; Sheehan and Perry, 1976). However, from the point of view both of the subject experiencing hypnosis and the experimenter observing his behavior, the indications are of alterations that, at a phenomenal level, are most conveniently described as changes in total condition, or state, just as drunkenness or sleep are described as altered states. There is little point in introducing circumlocutions to avoid the use of the word "state."

That hypnosis is probably not a single state is clear enough from the transformations that take place when a conventionally hypnotized subject is alerted or when an active-alert state is produced directly by the induction procedure. For discussions, see Gibbons (1976), Ludwig (1966), Vingoe (1973), in addition to the references cited in the text.

The quotation from Heraclitus on depth is borrowed from Hillman (1975, p. xi).

Tart's single subject has had to carry the major burden as a description of deep hypnosis (Tart, 1970, 1972), and it is to be hoped that more details will become available from others he has studied. Comparable data can be found in an unpublished dissertation by Sherman (1971) and a more recent one by Feldman (1975). Additional informal studies have been performed in the Stanford Laboratory, but have not been reported.

How the Subject Responds to Suggestions: Hypnotic Analgesia and Deafness

The selection of these two kinds of suggestion was made because many details were available from our investigations on them and because they were the areas most completely explored in reference to covert or hidden experiences, to be described in the next chapters.

The pain studies are conveniently summarized in the book by Hilgard and Hilgard (1975).

The deafness studies have not yet been reported; the one on which Figure 18 is based is from Macdonald, Crawford, and Hilgard (1977).

The Hypnotized Person as a Source of Information About Hypnosis

Cautions in interpreting verbal responses are needed, because even a subject who wishes to report honestly may distort reality. However, distinction must be made between honest reporting and experienced distortion; an honest report of an optical illusion, for example, tells us about the subject's true experience, even if he sees the lines as unequal when in reality they are of the same length. Objective behavior, such as a stiffened arm, can be just as readily "faked" as words; merely the fact that something can be observed or recorded by instruments does not guarantee that inferences from it will be correct. Scientific caution applies as much to electrical responses of the skin as to verbal reports. With this warning of the need for scientific caution regarding the interpretation of all observations, the current relaxation within psychology of strictures against reporting private experiences is a gain for the completeness of our knowledge of man.

CHAPTER

DIVIDED CONSCIOUSNESS
IN HYPNOSIS:
THE "HIDDEN OBSERVER"

Divided consciousness is familiar in ordinary waking life; the division permits fantasy to continue even while the person is performing the obligations of the work life or satisfying the proprieties of social interactions and communications. Because he is able to pay sufficient attention to the obligations and proprieties, this fantasizing may go largely unnoticed. In hypnosis the fantasied world may become more prominent, and, at least in some instances, the realities may be denied. The question arises whether the denied realities are completely obliterated, or whether instead they are concealed behind an amnesia-like mask that is possible within hypnosis. We found in some demonstrations and experiments within our laboratory that two kinds of information processing may go on at once within hypnosis; some aspects are available to the hypnotic consciousness within hypnosis as ordinarily studied; other aspects are available only when special techniques have elicited the concealed information. When these techniques are used, the additional information is reported as though it had been observed in the usual manner. Because the observing part was hitherto not in awareness, we have come to use the metaphor of a "hidden observer" to characterize this cognitive system. The theoretical questions it raises are discussed in Chapter 11. Now we turn to its discovery and manifestations.

THE HIDDEN OBSERVER REVEALED IN A CLASS DEMONSTRATION

The instructor was conducting a classroom demonstration of hypnotic deafness. The subject of the demonstration was a blind student, experienced in hypnosis, who had volunteered to serve; his blindness was not related to the demonstration, except that any visual cues were eliminated. After the induction of hypnosis, he was given the suggestion that, at the count of three, he would become completely deaf to all sounds. His hearing would be restored to normal when the instructor's hand was placed on his right shoulder. To be both blind and deaf would have been a frightening experience for the subject had he not known that his deafness was quite temporary. Loud sounds were then made close to the subject's head by banging together some large wooden blocks. There was no sign of any reaction; none was expected because the subject, in a previous demonstration, had shown a lack of responsiveness to the shots of a starter's pistol. He was also completely unresponsive to any questions asked of him while he was hypnotically deaf.

One student in the class questioned whether "some part" of the subject might be aware of what was going on. After all, there was nothing wrong with his ears. The instructor agreed to test this by a method related to interrogation practices used by clinical hypnotists. He addressed the hypnotically deaf subject in a quiet voice:

> As you know, there are parts of our nervous system that carry on activities that occur out of awareness, of which control of the circulation of the blood, or the digestive processes, are the most familiar. However, there may be intellectual processes also of which we are unaware, such as those that find expression in night dreams. Although you are hypnotically deaf, perhaps there is some part of you that is hearing my voice and processing the information. If there is, I should like the index finger of your right hand to rise as a sign that this is the case.

To the surprise of the instructor, as well as the class, the finger rose! The subject immediately said:

> Please restore my hearing so you can tell me what you did. I felt my finger rise in a way that was not a spontaneous twitch, so you must have done something to make it rise, and I want to know what you did.

The instructor placed his hand on the subject's right shoulder to restore his hearing, and the following conversation took place.

Can you hear my voice now?
Yes, I hear you. Now tell me what you did.
What do you remember?
I remember your telling me that I would be deaf at the count of three, and could have my hearing restored when you placed your hand on my shoulder. Then everything was quiet for a while. It was a little boring just sitting here, so I busied myself with a statistical problem I have been working on. I was still doing that when I suddenly felt my finger lift; that is what I want you to explain to me.

The subject was assured that he would soon be informed about everything that had transpired. At this point an important innovation was introduced. In the laboratory we had been doing some experiments on automatic writing, as described in Chapter 7. We had found that material not in the subject's awareness could be recovered through the writing of the hand of which the subject was unaware. It seemed worth testing with this highly hypnotizable subject whether, by analogy, "automatic talking" might yield results similar to automatic writing. Hence, with the subject hypnotized again but able to hear, the instructor spoke as follows:

When I place my hand on your arm like this (he demonstrated) I can be in touch with that part of you that listened to me before and made your finger rise—that part that could hear and knew what was going on when you were hypnotically deaf. When I question that part, it will be able to answer me and tell me what it knows about what happened. But this hypnotized part of you, to whom I am now talking, will not know what you are saying—or even that you are talking—until, out of hypnosis, I shall say, "Now you can remember everything." All right, now I am placing my hand on your arm.

The following conversation ensued: "Do you remember what happened when you were hypnotized and what the hypnotized part of you reported?" "Yes." (This very literal response is characteristic of this subject when hypnotized. If a question can be answered "yes" or "no," it commonly gets no more extensive answer without further probing.)

On further questioning he repeated much of the earlier conversation, including his surprise at the finger's lifting.

Does the part to whom I am now talking know more about what went on?
Yes.
Tell me what went on.
After you counted to make me deaf you made noises with some blocks behind my head. Members of the class asked me questions to which I did not respond. Then one of them asked if I might not really be hearing, and you told me to raise my finger if I did. This part of me responded by raising my finger, so it's all clear now.

The instructor then lifted his hand from the arm.

Please tell me what has happened in the last few minutes.
You said something about placing your hand on my arm, and some part of me would talk to you. Did I talk?

The subject was aroused from hypnosis and told that he would remember everything. He then recalled all that had happened and had been said.

This unplanned demonstration clearly indicated that a hypnotized subject who is not aware of a source of stimulation (in this case auditory) may nevertheless be registering the information coming from the stimuli. Further, he may be understanding it; thus, under appropriate circumstances, what was unknown to the hypnotized part of him can be uncovered and talked about. For convenience of reference, we speak of the concealed information as available to a "hidden observer."

It should be noted that the "hidden observer" is a metaphor for something occurring at an intellectual level but not available to the consciousness of the hypnotized person. It does not mean that there is a secondary personality with a life of its own—a kind of homunculus lurking in the shadows of the conscious person. The "hidden observer" is merely a convenient label for the information source tapped through experiments with automatic writing and automatic talking.

THE HIDDEN OBSERVER IN THE HYPNOTIC REDUCTION OF PAIN

For some time we had been studying the reduction of pain in our laboratory, using two types of induced pain: placing the hand and forearm in circulating ice water (cold pressor pain) and fastening a tourniquet to the upper arm, followed by exercise of the hand now deprived of blood (ischemic pain). An introduction to these experiments is given in Chapter 8.

Despite some ten years experience of successfully reduced pain, we had never had a single report of the memory of pain returning spontaneously after the experience of no pain. Still, the possible applications of the foregoing observations seemed too important to leave unexamined, so we determined to find if there were some covert pain experiences not revealed in the overt reports.

Because the automatic writing technique was already available to us, we decided to use it as an alternative to the ordinary verbal report of the pain. The usual scale we had been using assigned 0 for no pain and 1–10 for pain of increasing intensity, with 10 a pain so severe that the subject would prefer to remove the hand from the ice water; however, the subject was told to keep the hand in the water until asked to remove it and to count beyond 10 as the pain mounted. The level of 10 and above was usually reached in less than a minute in the waking condition. Hence the adaptation of the experiment was to have one hand in the ice water, with the subject reporting the pain on the numerical scale in the usual way; the other hand was to reply with a number on the same scale, but in writing, with what the hand was writing out of awareness (subconscious).

The first subject on whom we tried this was a young woman experienced in hypnosis; she had no difficulty reducing the ice water pain completely in one arm while keeping the other arm out of awareness for purposes of automatic writing.

She was hypnotized and instructed to feel nothing in the water; she verbally reported "0" in reply to all successive requests for reports at 5-second intervals. She had been instructed under hypnosis to use the same numerical reporting scale with her hand out of awareness; she would of course not know what her hand was writing. While she was overtly reporting "0," the hand out of awareness was simultaneously writing scale values for increasing pain—2, 5, 7, 8, 9. The "hidden observer" was reporting essentially normal pain while the hypnotized part of her was feeling no pain at all!

Automatic writing is a cumbersome technique for questioning a hypnotized subject; therefore, beginning with this same subject, we applied the automatic talking method, using a refinement of the instructions given in the deafness demonstration. With this method, the same pilot subject told us that, while her hypnotized part felt no pain, the hidden part had felt pain of about the same sensory intensity as that produced by the cold water without hypnosis. However, the covert pain bothered her much less at this hidden level within analgesia than overt pain bothered her in the normal waking state.

We extended this kind of experiment to samples of subjects who showed many variations on the common theme; some of the subjects who experienced pain reduction under hypnosis were able to recover an experience of covert pain differing from their overt experience, and some were not. For this latter group, it is important to find out if the covert experience is more deeply buried in some manner that other techniques might uncover or if the experience of pain is actually obliterated.

As an example of the findings, results for the eight most successful subjects in a group of 20 selected as high scorers on tests of hypnotic susceptibility are reproduced in Figure 19. All experienced a vivid distinction between overt and covert pain in hypnotic analgesia. In this arrangement, we returned to a condition similar to automatic writing, referred to in the figure as automatic key pressing. Instead of reporting the magnitude of the pain by writing with a pencil, the subject pressed small keys arranged somewhat like a small calculator, one key for tens and the other for digits. This gave not only a clearer report, but permitted recording on tape against time; thus, by also

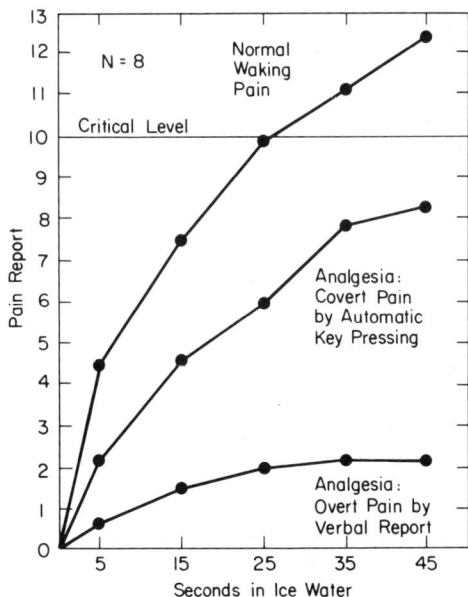

Figure 19   Overt and covert pain as reduced by hypnotic suggestion. Means are plotted for the eight most successful subjects out of 20 highly hypnotizable subjects who participated in the study of ice water pain (cold pressor response). The highest curve shows the normal waking pain in the ice water, the lowest the hypnotically reduced overt pain as ordinarily reported in hypnosis. The middle curve (covert pain) was reported in this instance through a key-pressing device that was the equivalent of automatic writing, reporting the experience of the "hidden observer." Data from Hilgard, Morgan, and Macdonald (1975); reproduced from Hilgard and Hilgard (1975).

recording the voice report of overt pain we could determine the synchrony of the concealed and open reports of pain. As seen in Figure 19, while the pain was mounting scarcely at all at the overt verbal reporting level, it was mounting much more rapidly at the covert level, although it averaged below the normal waking pain. The two reporting systems—overt and covert—operated essentially simultaneously, or, in current information-processing language, in parallel. When at the end of the session the subject, still hypnotized, was questioned by the automatic talking method, the report of maximum covert pain agreed with that reported on the keys; the same information was being tapped by the two methods.

The separation between overt and covert experiences of pain appears to be maintained by an amnesia-like barrier, because the concealed experience, like other hypnotic amnesias, is recoverable. However, this difference must be noted: *the covert experience, unlike the experiences of posthypnotic amnesia, has never been consciously present.* The covert information from the experience somehow registered and was processed, but it was masked by the amnesia-like process before it ever became conscious.

Because two levels of pain reduction were shown in the data of Figure 19, there may be two components to the process by which pain is reduced through suggestion. The lesser reduction, to the level of the overt pain, might possibly occur as a consequence of analgesia suggestions given without hypnosis. Then the further reduction to the overt level of pain reported by responsive hypnotized subjects might be a component added by the hypnosis. We assign the second portion to hypnosis because this part is recoverable, much like other experiences in hypnosis hidden by amnesia-like processes.

It was possible to test this hypothesis by an investigation in which, in balanced order, subjects reduced their pain to waking suggestions and, on another occasion, to suggestions given following induction of hypnosis. The first conjecture to be tested is that, following waking suggestion, the overt pain will be greater than the overt pain felt in hypnotic analgesia. The second conjecture is that the overt pain following waking suggestion will be approximately equal to that reported covertly in hypnotic analgesia. The results with 20 subjects, half of whom had hypnotic analgesia first and half of whom had waking analgesia first, supported the predictions. In hypnotic analgesia the pain was reduced from a mean of 14.2 on the reporting scale to 4.2; the residual pain was 30% of normal. In waking analgesia, the reduction was from 14.2 to 8.5, to 60% of normal. The first part of the prediction was confirmed by these results in that the hypnotic residual pain was half that of the pain reduced by waking suggestion. How did the second part of the prediction fare? The covert pain, as tested by the hidden observer method, rose to 7.3, a value representing 51% of normal, not significantly different from the 60% in waking analgesia.

The first component of the two-component inferred process is the partial reduction of pain by waking suggestion and the equivalent remaining reduction when the overt hypnotic analgesia has been reported as covertly felt pain. It may be assumed that this reduction is caused by such processes as relaxation and inattentiveness to the pain, processes available to the nonhypnotized person and relatively independent of the special abilities of the hypnotized one. An added inference, with this interpretation in mind, is that there should be no covert component to the overt pain reduced by waking suggestion, because nothing additional was registered as pain. To test this possibility, the hypnotizable subjects who had reduced pain by waking suggestion were hypnotized after this experience, and the hidden observer technique was used to explore covert pain. The pain reported at the covert level was exactly the same as that reported overtly, agreeing with the assumptions regarding this first component of the pain reduction.

It was possible to obtain additional evidence bearing on the two-component theory by studying the results for a group of nonhypnotizable subjects in response to waking suggestions of pain reduction, compared to actual pain reduction when they simulated hypnosis. Additional hypnotizable subjects served as a comparison group; this investigation was in part a replication, and in part an extension, of the one just cited. The first prediction was that nonhypnotizable subjects should be able to reduce their pains through waking suggestion to approximately the same level as hypnotizable subjects in that condition. The second prediction was that the nonhypnotizable subjects, simulating hypnosis, would not be able to reduce their actually felt pain below the waking suggestion level. This required a subsequent "honest report" interview; otherwise, as simulators, they had typically reported less pain than the truly hypnotizable. Exaggerated reports in response to suggestions are characteristic of simulators.

The hypnotizable subjects repeated findings similar to those already reported. For the low hypnotizables, behaving normally in waking pain reduction and simulating hypnosis in hypnotic analgesia, the honestly reported results came out as predicted, with waking and hypnotic analgesia (honesty reports) essentially alike (Figure 20). The covert responses for the hypnotizable subjects are not shown because only six of 12 gave such reports; for those

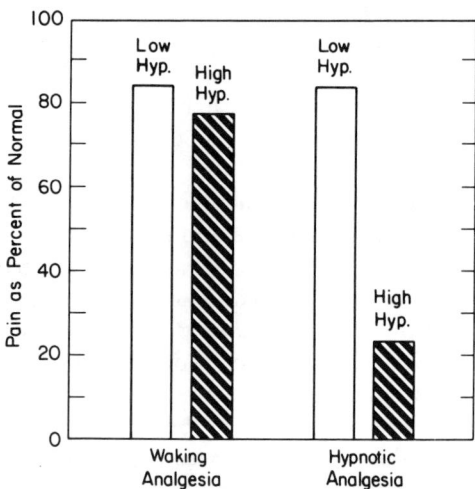

Figure 20 Differential between waking analgesia and hypnotic analgesia: High hypnotizable subjects and less hypnotizable subjects. Both groups responded nonhypnotically to suggestions of analgesia in the waking condition. Honest reports of low subjects simulating hypnosis in the "hypnotic" condition; honest reports of high subjects responding as they normally do in hypnosis. (N=12 in each group.) Unpublished data, Stanford Laboratory.

giving covert reports, the earlier findings were confirmed. The supplementary study therefore provided further evidence in support of the two-component theory.

The observation made by the first pilot subject that, at the covert level, the pain remained while the suffering was reduced was true for many others who reported covert sensory pain in the ice water experiments. The division between sensory pain and suffering was further investigated, this time using ischemic pain. It was found that *both* pain and suffering were reduced by hypnotic analgesia at the overt level, and both were represented at higher values at the covert level (Knox, Morgan, and Hilgard, 1974). However, there were indications of individual differences, shown in a subsequent experiment with three exceptionally high subjects.

The three subjects were all able to reduce overtly reported pain and suffering to essentially zero through hypnotic suggestion, although one reported slight distress, without pain, toward the end of the stressful period. Covert reports were obtained at the end of the session, with the subject remaining hypnotized. It was found for two of them that covert pain was reported at nearly normal levels, whereas no covert suffering was reported; the third subject reported both covert pain and covert suffering at normal levels. To clarify these somewhat complex findings, the maximum pains felt under the three conditions (normal, overt within hypnotic analgesia, and covert within hypnotic analgesia) are presented in Table 11. For two of the three subjects, a differential between pain and distress was reported, with covert pain present, but covert distress absent; the third subject did not agree. That at least some subjects show this difference indicates a possible division between the systems for experiencing pain and distress, for which neurophysiological evidence exists (Melzack and Casey, 1968).

What is it like to the subject when he discovers that there is a part of him that experiences pain or distress at a level of which he is unaware within hypnotically suggested analgesia? Matters of this kind are difficult to put into words, and the reports by subjects vary greatly. Consider two typical illustrations. One report is of a feeling of annoyance that some intruding part is looking on behind a curtain and, in superior fashion, is amused at the person for his self-deception. A second is a reported sense of satisfaction that there is a kind of guardian protecting the body in homeostatic fashion against a failure to use information coming to it through sensory channels. Because those reports bear importantly on the nature of concealed information processing, the next chapter is devoted to a further discussion of them.

Returning to the question of a division of consciousness, as contrasted with two different depths or levels of consciousness, the evidence from the subjects' remarks clearly favors the idea of a vertical division (split consciousness) rather than a horizontal division, in which the material would come from

Table 11
OVERT AND COVERT PAIN AND DISTRESS
IN THREE SELECTED HIGH HYPNOTIZABLES
(Data from Goldstein and Hilgard, 1975)

	Pain rating			Distress rating		
	Normal waking	Analgesia		Normal waking	Analgesia	
		Overt	Covert		Overt	Covert
Subject 1	12	0	13	12	0	0
Subject 2	12	0	15[a]	4	0	0
Subject 3	8	0	8	8	2.5	8

[a]The tourniquet was kept in place longer under analgesia than in waking, and the covert pain continued to mount, although overt pain was absent.

more primitive depths (cf. Figure 9, p. 81). There is no regression in the subject's language; the hidden observer uses the same conceptual language to describe the covert experience as the hypnotized part does to describe the overt experience, including an estimation of the magnitude of the pain on the arbitrary numerical scale. The implications of this are considered in Chapter 11.

THE HIDDEN OBSERVER IN HYPNOTIC DEAFNESS

The first evidence for the hidden observer came in a classroom demonstration of hypnotic deafness that was not concerned with pain at all. We have recently returned to a more thorough study of hypnotic deafness over a sample including all levels of hypnotic susceptibility to explore additional evidence on the frequency of a hidden observer. To demonstrate the hidden observer, at least two conditions must be met: the subject must be able to reduce his hearing substantially as a result of the hypnotic suggestions of deafness, and he must have a special ability that permits the successful use of the method that leads to the covert report. These special abilities appear to be of the kinds involved in posthypnotic amnesia and automatic writing.

The deafness studies have not yet been completed, but from the data gathered thus far it appears that the conditions for demonstrating satisfactory hidden observers, that is, covert experiences of hearing following substantially reduced hearing at the overt level, are about the same as for pain. For those who have participated in both pain and hearing experiments, there is a high correspondence between those who do and those do not respond in this way.

A finding not yet satisfactorily explained is that among the highly responsive hypnotic subjects, that is, those who can reduce both pain and hearing substantially when appropriate suggestions are given, only half have access to covert pain or hearing by the hidden observer technique.

THE HIDDEN OBSERVER IN CREATIVE ACTIVITY

The intimacy between imagination and creativity on one hand and imagination and hypnosis on the other leads to the inviting possibility that hypnotic ability as a talent, or the hypnotic state as a condition, may favor creative activity. The results thus far, although promising, have not been startling (Chapter 5).

Sudden inspirations have long been suspected of revealing some sort of unconscious or subconscious rumination or consolidation that at the moment of illumination yields a creative product. The product, whether the solution to a mathematical problem or the resolution of a writer's plot, is something the mathematician or the author was not previously able to achieve. Hadamard (1945) gathered the evidence from mathematicians, Ghiselin (1955) from composers and writers, as well as from scientists, and, Tooker and Hofheins (1976) from novelists. All tell much the same story of a period of puzzlement, of something worked on but unresolved, and then a sudden solution either complete or setting the direction for completion.

The distinction that Freud made between primary process thinking and secondary process thinking is sometimes thought to be one of his most germinal formulations. The tendency has been to believe that creativity is more likely to be found in the spontaneity of primary process thinking than in the realistic and logical secondary process. The distinction can be overworked, however, for what emerges in the sudden solutions of problems, or the sudden creation of poetry, may be products that are highly constrained by the demands of secondary process. That is, the mathematical solution is orderly and logical; the poetic lines that emerge are in the proper language of the author and may appear in a meter that is as formal as the constraints of analysis of variance. Hence unconscious cerebration may duplicate conscious cerebration, with an appropriate interplay between primary and secondary process. The appearance of logical solutions does not deny a hidden process according to which they are elaborated. As Poincaré has said: "Most striking at first is the appearance of sudden illumination, a manifestation of long unconscious prior work. The role of this unconscious work in mathematical work appears incontestable."

Of poetic inspiration, A. E. Housman has written: ". . . there would flow into my mind, with sudden and unaccountable emotion, sometimes a line or two of verse, sometimes a whole stanza at once, accompanied, not preceded, by a vague notion of the poem which they were destined to become a part of." There is some primary process flavor here, but a line or two of verse, or a whole stanza, is not without rich secondary process components.

Writers of fiction commonly assert that their characters "take over" and live lives of their own once they have been created. According to Kay Boyle: "And that's when I think you're doing well, when the characters come to life. They take the story somewhere else from where you had planned." The self-fulfillment of a story may have other than unconscious roots, however. Wallace Stegner says: "By the time I've got a first draft, I've written everything fifteen times and read it twenty-five times, just trying to learn from my own words where I'm going."

Whether creative artists and writers, because they are imaginative, are also hypnotizable has not been established, but the possibility exists, and perhaps those who report products far advanced when they emerge in consciousness have within them ongoing cognitive activities similar to those attributed here to a hidden observer.

An Informal Experiment in Creative Story Telling

The subject of this informal experiment was a highly hypnotizable student whose story telling was of a high order whether he was hypnotized or not. Although I report a story told under hypnosis, he was quite capable of telling stories of essentially the same vividness when not hypnotized. He came to our attention because, with someone else, under hypnosis he had told a story of early nineteenth century England with such clarity and verisimilitude that he convinced those who heard him—himself as well—that it must have been a case of regression to a prior experience (see p. 51). Only careful depth interviewing proved that he had forgotten memories sufficient to supply the details he had recounted so that the reincarnation concept was not necessary.

I gave him, under hypnosis, the following assignment:

> Just transport yourself to the scene I am about to describe. This is a place where you and some friends are exploring a newly discovered cave. You have already found the cave so you've come back to it with all the necessary equipment and you're prepared to explore it. Just describe what the scene is around you now.

The story took 17 minutes for him to tell; he reported his hypnotic depth as at 20 where 8–10 was sufficient for him to follow the usual suggestions in hypnosis of analgesia, hallucinations, amnesia and the rest. I quote a few passages and summarize the rest.

Well, this cave we discovered is in Mexico, in the southern part of Mexico. The climate in this area is very lush. It's not tropical because the altitude is too high, but it's at a latitude that if it were at lower altitude it would be a tropical rain forest. But the combination of this latitude and altitude makes it a very lush green mountain area that doesn't ever get too hot. It keeps cool, around in the 70's or so, and it's really an ideal place for living as far as weather is concerned. It is still, however, rather moist and most afternoons for an hour or two it rains.

The cave that several friends of mine and I are about to explore, we stumbled upon just a week ago when we were having a day off and taking a picnic. We just came to this spot that had been a favorite spot of one of my friends, we saw this huge rock, just a mammoth rock, several of them, sort of juxtaposed upon each other and covered with all sorts of vegetation. We climbed up and had our lunch. As we climbed down we realized that there was sort of a little tunnel that was formed by the series of rocks not quite touching each other. We climbed down about 15 feet which was as far as the light filtered into it, and we were afraid to go any further. We had no means of artificial light so we couldn't see. I yelled, however, down in the cavern and the echoing of my voice made us believe that this would be quite a large cavern.

So we've come back. . . .

He proceeded to tell in great detail how they used ropes to ease themselves into the cavern, flashlights to guide them, what they saw, stalactites, stalagmites, a reflecting lake—fanciful shapes and exciting colors.

One of the friends found another opening, and they crawled through on hands and knees to discover a veritable Shangri-La.

To our amazement we found ourselves in a beautiful small valley with vines growing down the sides and hills going sharply up in all directions, and in the back of the valley a waterfall falling down, cascading over rocks, forming a little river that went down along the base of the valley, formed one pool and trickled onward underneath the rocks. Flowers of every variety grew in abundance in this valley, so that one saw just as much yellows and reds and blues and all other types of colors as one saw the green vegetation. Again there was no sign of mankind having been there, although we were sure that we could not have been the only people to have ever enjoyed the beauty of this sight. Some of the flowers we see are huge flowers like none I have ever seen before. The blossoms would be as large as a basketball, thick with pollen, beautiful bright colors.

They remained for the afternoon, swam in the pool, lay in the sun, and found their way back deciding to keep their discovery to themselves in order to come back and enjoy it.

As I mentioned, I had him tell other stories while not hypnotized, such as the experiences of a coal miner in England during the early period of the industrial revolution, experiences with Indians on the western plains with a pioneer family, and the life of a stone cutter in medieval Italy. He did each of these so vividly that my concern became the difference between telling a story under hypnosis and in the waking state. I use his words:

> In hypnosis, once I create the pattern, I don't have to take any more initiative; the story just unfolds. In fact once I start talking I know the main outlines of what is happening.
>
> For instance, I knew ahead of time that there would be another room outside of the cavern, and I knew I would go outside but I didn't know what it would look like until I walked through and was describing it.
>
> In the waking state it seems more fabricated. I don't *see* things that I describe in waking in the way I actually *see* them in hypnosis. I really saw everything today that I described.

Inquiry by the hidden observer technique revealed that there was a part of him doing the planning, more like a stage director providing the promptings for the hypnotized part, the actor.

The hidden part knew, for example, that the cavern was to have a beautiful room and that there would be a garden beyond. The hypnotized part did not know their *qualities* until *seeing* them.

As he put it, "The two parts worked together to form a story." The hidden part also planned (and monitored) the length of the story.

The planning aspect in the waking state appears to hold a much larger part of the story telling. Here we find an additional complexity, for we have little difference in the overt experiences while creating in hypnosis and creating in the waking state, but we may have a concealed helper when the story is being created in hypnosis. Jesamyn West believes that much that she writes comes out of her stored memories, even though she does not model her characters after real people. "The bits and pieces you remember should fall down into your unconscious and become compost. . . .So, for me, the thing to do in writing is to ask myself questions, not to tell myself answers." Does she perhaps have a hidden observer to organize the material for her?

EARLIER EVIDENCES OF A HIDDEN OBSERVER

Something brought to light as readily as covert pain felt in hypnotic analgesia, covert hearing in hypnotic deafness, or the other evidences of a hidden observer, represent events that most likely have been noticed in the past. Investigators have too long been interested in hidden aspects of the mind not to have stumbled across almost everything that we rediscover.

Durand de Gros, in 1868, indicated his belief that some subego might suffer when surgery was performed with hypnotic analgesia, even though the conscious ego was ignorant of the suffering. Early in this century, Myers (1903) wrote: "A man's nervous system is quite as active and vigorous as ever (when hypnotic suggestion has rendered him incapable of pain)—quite as capable of transmitting and feeling pain—although capable of also inhibiting it altogether." He showed that lack of pain under chemical anesthesia is also no assurance that pain is not felt, for he gave several instances of memories recovered following general anesthesia under chloroform and nitrous oxide. In one such case, the memory of what had happened was recovered in a dream.

Automatic writing, popular in the late nineteenth century as previously noted (Chapter 7), led to several observations on pain in hypnotically anesthetic arms. One such observation was reported by William James, whose account was given in the *Proceedings of the American Society for Psychical Research* (1889). His subject, one Smith, was a student at the Massachusetts Institute of Technology. Smith had prior experience in automatic writing and was apparently able to prepare himself for the experiment without any formal induction of hypnosis. He sat with his right hand—the writing hand—on the planchette and his face "averted and buried in the hollow of his left arm," which was lying on the table. After the writing hand had scrawled illegibly for ten minutes, James pricked the back of it 15–20 times; there was no response to indicate feeling. As a control, James pricked the normally sensitive left hand twice, and the subject asked: "What did you do that for?" James replied that he wanted to find out whether Smith was going to sleep. Later, as the experiment continued, the anesthetic hand wrote: "Don't you prick me any more." When shown the automatic writing after the session, Smith laughed and said that he had been conscious of only two pinpricks, those on the left hand. He said of his right hand: "It's working those two pinpricks for all they are worth." In a session two days later, James had Smith write with his left hand. When questioned about the prior session, the hand wrote that he had been pricked "nineteen times on the other hand." James was uncertain whether the number was correct, but it was near enough. He summarized the situation as follows: "We have the consciousness of a subject split into two parts, one of which expresses itself through the mouth, the other through the hand, whilst both are in communication through the ear."

James reported the experiment again in his *Principles of Psychology* (1890), along with some related experiments of Binet (1889–1890). For example, using compass points to measure the two-point threshold, under hypnotic anesthesia Binet showed that the subject might be completely insensitive, yet through automatic writing normal sensitivity could be demonstrated. This account by James is reported to have had a profound influence on the thinking of the physicist Niels Bohr, influencing him in reaching the generalization known as the principle of complementarity. In fact, James had even used the word in a context similar to his.

James wrote:

> It must be admitted, therefore, that in *certain persons,* at least, *the total possible consciousness may be split into parts which coexist but mutually ignore each other,* and share the objects of knowledge between them. More remarkable still, they are *complementary.* Give an object to one of the consciousnesses, and by that fact you remove it from the other or others. Barring a certain common fund of information, like the command of language, etc., what the upper self knows the under self is ignorant of, and *vice versa.* (James, 1890, I, p. 206).

The physicist and philosopher of science, Holton (1970), in an essay on the roots of complementarity as advanced by Niels Bohr, gives considerable attention to the possible influence of James on Bohr's thought, because Bohr himself acknowledged it. Just before his death in 1962, Bohr was interviewed by Thomas S. Kuhn, another philosopher of science, and Aage Petersen, who had been Bohr's research assistant. To Petersen's question whether he was influenced by philosophers, he had little to say until he mentioned his friendship with Rubin, who had been a fellow student and had introduced him to the work of William James. Rubin, it may be recalled, was the discoverer of the figure-ground relationship, which is, in a sense, another illustration of complementary ways of perceiving the same object. The coat of arms that Bohr selected when he was awarded the Danish Order of the Elephant in 1947 has a figure-ground perceptual figure in it—the symbol for Ying and Yang. Bohr went on to say that he at first read some paragraphs from "The Stream of Thoughts," and James was wonderful. Later he read more, but there is some uncertainty whether it was in 1905 or a little later; in any case, he said it was before 1912. He offered to go into the matter further, but that night he died.

The nonphysicist is not likely to be familiar with Bohr's views on how general he thought the principle of complementarity to be. The principle, stated very briefly, is that knowledge derived in one way and with some one set of instruments may deny the possibility of finding out something else about the event, although there are other, equally valid ways, of finding out something else if the investigator is willing to forego knowledge of the first kind. The concept is related to Heisenberg's uncertainty principle; Heisenberg had been one of Bohr's associates. Although the ideas were proposed within physics, Bohr felt that they were universally applicable. If the sequence is correct, he may have derived some of his ideas from James.

Other accounts of hidden reports have appeared from time to time, of which two will suffice. Estabrooks (1957) reported an experiment with a friend who was reading *Oil for the Lamps of China* while his right hand, screened from view by passing it through a cloth curtain, was engaged in automatic writing. The hand was not in awareness because of hypnotic procedures; it was also anesthetic. However, when Estabrooks pricked the hand with a needle, it wrote a stream of profanity "that would have made a top sergeant blush with shame." This went on for five minutes and included an attack on the hypnotist for having pricked him. The subject continued his reading calmly, "without the slightest idea that his good right arm was fighting a private war."

The second of these more recent cases was reported later by Kaplan (1960). He gave a deeply hypnotized subject the suggestions that his left arm was analgesic and insensitive and that his right arm would write automatically; the subject would not be aware of what he was writing. When the experimenter pricked the left (anesthetic) arm several times with a hypodermic needle, the other hand wrote: "Ouch, damn it, you're hurting me." After a few minutes had passed, the subject, oblivious to what had transpired, asked Kaplan when he was going to begin the experiment. Kaplan interpreted the result to mean that, although the subject was not conscious of his pain, it was being felt at some level and experienced as discomfort.

Our own observations along these lines are clearly not alone.

NOTES

The problems of divided consciousness in ordinary waking experience are beginning to receive attention from the point of view of scientific psychology, as in the studies of day dreaming and make-believe (Singer, 1966, 1973) and literary fantasy (Helson, 1973). The "stream of consciousness" writers have caught the essence of the experience.

The Hidden Observer in the Classroom Demonstration

When a group of inquiring people work together in a laboratory, interacting daily, it is difficult to recall who first originated the emerging ideas. The possibility of automatic talking as an alternative to automatic writing was originally suggested by Hugh Macdonald and James Stevenson, to whom I am pleased to assign the credit. Related methods have been used by clinicians to search for hidden material. One of their methods is to use lifted fingers as alternatives to speech in reply to questions directed to "the unconscious." This method is, of course, a form of communication, with the suggestion that it is a form differing from ordinary speech (Cheek and LeCron, 1968, p. 85-88). It was such a finger sign that I used in the reported demonstration of something heard in hypnotic deafness.

The Hidden Observer in Pain

The chief published reports on our studies of the hidden observer when pain has been reduced in the laboratory are those of Knox, Morgan, and Hilgard (1974) and Hilgard, Morgan, and Macdonald (1975), reviewed with some additional data in Hilgard and Hilgard (1975).

We have used simulators as controls, following Orne's (1972) procedures, to see what happens when the nonhypnotizable subject tries to respond *as if* he has a hidden observer. Although he does indeed come up with an attempted hidden observer at least as often as the truly hypnotized, there is little difficulty in distinguishing between the faked and the true reports (Hilgard, Hilgard, Macdonald, Morgan, and Johnson, 1977). In making this distinction reliance has been placed upon "honesty" interrogation, the importance of which was brought to attention by Bowers (1967).

The Two-Component Theory of Pain Reduction

Two components of pain reduction have also been recognized by McGlashan, Evans, and Orne (1969), with the component available to both lows and highs identified by them as a placebo effect, and the second component limited to the more highly hypnotizable. Although I am not prepared to limit the first component entirely to a placebo effect, the implications of their interpretation and mine are similar.

The results as reported on pages 191–193 appear to contradict those of two earlier studies, each involving ice-water pain, in which the conclusion was reached that pain reduction by suggested analgesia is independent of the effects of hypnotic induction, hence available to the hypnotized and nonhypnotized alike. However, in the first of these, waking-imagination instructions substituted for hypnosis (Barber and Hahn, 1962), and it is known that, for highly hypnotizable subjects, some will drift into hypnosis following such instructions (Hilgard and Tart, 1966). In the second study, the waking condition called for 25 minutes of self-relaxation as an alternative to hypnotic induction (Evans and Paul, 1970). Such a condition readily leads to self-hypnosis in those who are highly hypnotizable. In neither of these studies were there sufficient later interrogations to determine what the subjects had actually experienced. These interpretations bear on our findings that high hypnotizables reduce pain more by hypnotic analgesia than by waking analgesia.

The fact that Evans and Paul found the same correlation (.48) between pain reduction and measured hypnotizability for their "waking" and hypnotic condition is also explicable if their "waking" condition was, in fact, hypnotic. The correlation is of the same order as that reported by Hilgard (1967) between pain reduction and hypnotizability with hypnotic analgesia instructions. According to this interpretation, the fact that in waking analgesia we found that lows and highs reduce their pain essentially alike does not contradict the earlier studies when they are properly interpreted.

The Hidden Observer in Other Hypnotic Demonstrations

The deafness experiments referred to have not yet been published, but reports are in preparation (Macdonald, Crawford, and Hilgard, 1977; J. R. Hilgard and others, 1977).

A number of investigations of geometrical illusions employing hypnotically produced hallucinations have resulted in paradoxical findings. The investigations of Graham (1969), Miller, Hennessy, and Leibowitz (1973), Perry and Chisholm (1973), Sarbin and Andersen (1963), Sutcliffe (1961), and Underwood (1960) are representative of these. Ignoring the many contradictory findings that remain to be clarified, a common result is as follows. Subjects capable of forming subjectively convincing positive or negative visual hallucinations may be given the suggestion in hypnosis that a background of radiating lines presented on a screen is not there, that the screen is blank—a negative hallucination. Such lines, when present, can create illusory differences in the perceived lengths of equal lines superimposed across the radiating lines at different distances from the point at which the background lines converge. The hypnotized subject often reports that the equal lines appear of different lengths, as though the illusion persists despite the "invisibility" of the lines responsible for it. In an unpublished study from the Stanford laboratory, Gettinger (1974) found results of this kind; however, when he used the hidden observer technique, some of the subjects were able to report a covert perception of the physical stimuli as they were actually presented. The overt results correspond to those of source amnesia, in which material present at a covert level may affect overt, conscious performance.

The paradox that physiological indicators of response persist even when the subject is hypnotically analgesic or deaf is resolved if covert responses, concealed by amnesia, are recognized to be present. For example, Halliday and Mason (1964) found that evoked potentials remained normal in both hypnotic deafness and hypnotic analgesia; these results do not deny the reality of the overt deafness or analgesia.

When Pattie earlier pushed his subjects to report what had happened when they gave unusual perceptual performances in hypnosis, he was led to interpret their results, in part at least, as confabulation to please the hypnotist. The first of these studies was on uniocular blindness, tested by having the subject plot her blindspot with both eyes open; after much probing she was found to have practiced plotting the blindspot at home (Pattie, 1935). His later studies produced doubts about anesthesia of the skin, because an illusion persisted that required skin sensitivity (Pattie, 1937), and about unilateral deafness, because he was able to show that the deaf ear was still performing some normal hearing functions (Pattie, 1950). If one accepts the reality of hysterical sensory disturbances, in which intactness of the sensory mechanisms can be demonstrated, hypnotic distortions may be similar, and the confabulations of the uniocularly blind subject need not be used in explanation of the persistence of function in the other cases. The possibility remains of two kinds of observation, one overt and one covert.

A warning is in order against generalizing too far from the evidence at present available on covert observation. Its reality can scarcely be doubted, but its limitations and explanation are uncertain. As in cases of multiple personality that appear to be generated by the hypnotist's suggestions, extreme caution is needed lest probing by the hypnotist create a "hidden observer" out of the ordinary divisions of consciousness in waking life.

The Hidden Observer in Creative Activity

The quotations in the text are from the sources indicated. Poincaré's is cited by Hadamard, 1945, p. 14; Housman's is from Ghiselin (1955, p. 91); the others are from Tooker and Hofheins (1976): Boyle, p. 19; Stegner, p. 174; West, p. 185.

The permission of the student story teller to reproduce his story told under hypnosis is gratefully acknowledged, although he remains anonymous.

CHAPTER 10

HOW THE HYPNOTIZED PERSON PERCEIVES AND INTERPRETS THE HIDDEN OBSERVER

The results of the hidden observer method bear directly on the kinds of dissociation that can be interpreted as a form of parallel information processing—feeling and not feeling pain, hearing and not hearing tones. The quantitative evidence is presented in the preceding chapter, with only a few hints at subjective reactions. The report of the hypnotized person, following these puzzling experiences, is too valuable a source of information not to be explored more fully. In what follows, comments are presented from interviews with highly responsive subjects. Most of the subjects had experienced, at different times, the reduction of both pain and hearing, followed by the hidden observer technique for uncovering covert responses to the noxious stimulation and covert responses to the auditory stimuli. The metaphor of a hidden observer was used in discussions with them and is used in this chapter to refer to the report of covert pain or hearing substantially greater than that reported overtly in hypnotic analgesia and deafness as usually studied. The hidden observer technique refers to gaining access to the covert material primarily through a special interrogation while the hypnotist's hand has been placed on the subject's shoulder, according to a prior announced plan that, while the hand is there, the subject will be in touch with a hidden part of himself that knows more than the hypnotized part about what is going on.

As proposed earlier, these hidden experiences may represent the more profound kind of dissociation limited to highly hypnotizable persons—those in the upper mode of the bimodal distribution. Not all highly responsive persons report these experiences, and it may be that the upper mode as judged by test scores includes some who are extremely suggestible, according to the criteria of more direct responses to suggestion, without being capable of the deeper involvements and dissociations discussed here.

PRESENCE OR ABSENCE OF A HIDDEN OBSERVER

In considering the reports concerning a hidden observer, the first point to be noted is that successful pain reduction or hearing reduction following hypnotic induction and suggestions for analgesia or deafness are no guarantee of an experience of covert response reportable by the hidden observer method. Second, the method is obviously inappropriate unless reduction in response has occurred at the overt level; otherwise there would be no recovery to be reported at the covert level. These subjects, however, were selected so that all 18 reduced overt pain through hypnotic suggestions sufficiently to allow room for a covert recovery.

It might be conjectured that the presence of covert pain, even among those able to reduce pain substantially, might be conditional on extreme pain reduction. As it turned out, exactly half of this group of 18 gave indications of covert pain greater than overt pain (hence of a hidden observer), whereas the other half did not. Is there evidence that they differed in their overt pain reduction? Those with a hidden observer had reduced their overt pain to a mean of 21% of normal, whereas those without a hidden observer had reduced their pain to 27%, a nonsignificant difference. At least one of those without a hidden observer had experienced no pain whatever in hypnotic analgesia.

The findings for deafness were no different. Assuming a hearing loss of one-third at the overt level, to have sufficient reduction to allow for a satisfactory hearing recovery at the covert level, only ten of the deafness subjects qualified for the comparison on the presence or absence of a hidden observer. Again, half showed a hidden observer through their reports of covert hearing, and half did not. With this small sample, the difference in mean retained hearing at the overt level of 7% for those with a hidden observer and 33% for those without is not statistically significant. One of the subjects without a hidden observer had complete hearing loss within hypnotically suggested deafness. Some explanation for the absence of covert reports must be found elsewhere than in the capacity to reduce pain and hearing within hypnosis.

It is possible that some subjects found the idea of a hidden observer so implausible that they would resist searching for or reporting a covert experience. Responses to a specific inquiry are available from seven subjects who had reported a hidden observer to determine whether the report was conditional on initial acceptance of the idea. In advance of the experience, two of them had been genuinely skeptical of the idea, and one was confused by it. Despite these negative or uncertain expectations, all subsequently experienced a hidden observer.

Here are the comments of these three:

> I thought the hidden observer was corny, because I thought it impossible. I told the hypnotist so at the time.

> I was skeptical. I didn't see how I could alter who I was . . . I was skeptical that I could really be objective about the experience I was going through while I was in the midst of imagining.

> I was somewhat confused because I thought there could be a difference, but I didn't think there really would be a difference.

The other four thought the idea plausible:

> I felt that the part of consciousness that is in control is a small part of our awareness. The rest of the mind-body unit is much larger and we can tap in on it.

> I accepted the idea. No reason, except why not? It wouldn't hurt me.

> Because things have happened before in hypnosis which were unexpected.

> Due to a class I have had, I believed that a part of you is in control but that isn't all of you.

These four all had hidden observers. Two without hidden observers were also divided on plausibility:

> A plausible idea, but nothing happened to me. (Excellent pain reducer; no covert report.)

> It sounded fishy, occult, foreign, almost eerie. It would not be possible in something as sophisticated as the mind. (This subject was very successful in reducing both pain and hearing through hypnosis, but reported no covert experience of pain or hearing.)

Although the initial attitude is not controlling in all instances, in some cases it appears to influence the acceptability of the idea of a hidden part of the cognitive system and hence a readiness to make the necessary search. One reason for this connection is that some of the subjects had experiences prior to hypnosis that made a divided consciousness plausible to them. Several of the subjects reported experiences in which they acted on information that reached them when they were not aware of it, or information to which they responded when they were not aware of responding:

Mother would call me; I'd answer but I wasn't aware I was answering.

When I'm totally involved in a walk, and Mom wants me home in 30 minutes, I'll stop 5 minutes before. I am totally involved, yet there's a clock inside, telling me to surface to complete reality. I'm not aware of it until that moment.

Your name is called, you don't realize it. Later when you're all through with what's absorbing you, you answer. They say, "We called you a long time ago." . . . Your mind isn't ready to act on it, it's too involved in something else. (Later) An objective side has been set aside. It would normally take in all information around you. (She explained that the great involvement in the subjective experience meant that the objective information, though "taken in," was kept but not acted on until later.)

When reading a book, a comment is made to me by two other people. I'm not aware of it at the time because I'm absorbed in my book. But if something happens later on, we're talking, and a similar comment is made, that will trigger the memory of that and I'll say, "Oh yes, I heard you."

Yesterday, when reading *God is an Englishman,* a friend who lives next door was talking with my roommate in her room. The walls are thin in the trailer we live in. I didn't know what they were talking about. Later, about six o'clock, I asked Mary, "When are you and Evelyn going out?" . . . Suddenly I wondered: How did I know that? . . . I could not remember having heard it.

It comes as no surprise that each of these subjects was favorably disposed to the idea of a hidden observer and reported covert experiences within hypnosis.

Although attitudes toward covert experiences occasionally will be reflected in the presence or absence of a hidden observer, these attitudes are insufficient explanations of the phenomena; first, because subjects successful at the overt level and with favorable expectations do not report a hidden observer, and second, the favorable attitudes have, in some instances, been created by spontaneous experiences that have already given an indication of the reality of something like a covert experience that is recoverable.

In searching for other reasons why, in responsive and successful subjects, the hidden observer might be absent, two chief possibilities emerged. One was that there was an alternation between the reality distortions of hypnosis and the "clear thinking part" which did not qualify as a hidden observer because it was available at all times. The other was the possibility that the hypnotic involvement was so profound as to exclude any realistic observing part.

The first interpretation was presented by the comments of a subject very successful in reducing both pain and hearing.

> The clear thinking part of me was saying: "Hey, you're in pain" but I had so much allegiance to my hypnotic state that I could deny it.... When the clear thinking observer intervened it brought me away from my hypnotic suggestion; it experienced reality. It was available the entire time. If I lost my depth, or if there was an alteration (in the pain, for example), the clear thinking part intruded to explain the reality.

This subject may represent those who are high scorers on hypnotic tests but lack the special capacities required for more massive dissociations.

The second interpretation was implied by a subject who gave many evidences of altered experiences within hypnosis, some suggesting divided consciousness, but none clearly showing access to a covert experience.

> He had thought the idea of a hidden observer plausible because of an earlier experience in hypnosis. In one of the tests a light appears at one end of a metal box, but the suggestion is that the subject will see two lights, one at each end. "I thought I saw two lights but some part of me didn't agree and said: 'No, there's only one light there.' Actually this dawned on me gradually and I felt some tension. The two lights were different. I saw two lights but there was a reality-oriented, critical side that said one." This experience was the nearest he came to an awareness of a hidden part—an inconsistency in his experience while hypnotized.
>
> He had used hypnotic-like experiences frequently, as in jogging around the hills. "On a very dry, hot day, the hills are dry. I thought of a cool spring in the middle of a desert in Israel, like an oasis. With this image my body was more under my control, my breathing was more even, my mouth was not as dry, and I didn't feel the distress. Then I focused on the people I was with in the experience; I was having fun with the people at the spring. Next I thought my body was getting lighter, the wind was carrying me because I was light. I ran very fast for 20 minutes with no feeling of fatigue. I was not aware I was running, how my body felt, if my muscles hurt, because I concentrated so heavily on the image." (Were you aware of any part of you observing the realities of your condition?) "There was no hidden observer; it didn't intrude in the least, not a bit. I felt only that I was powerful. I was only aware I was running really fast. I don't know how I could do it as long as I did." He insisted that his images were so powerful as not to permit any intruding thoughts.
>
> "In hypnosis I had no hidden observer. In the process of searching for one, I was more critical and started to analyze the experiences I had. I didn't come to any different conclusions: my images had blocked all pain and distress. I wasn't as successful in hearing, although the tones became muffled and distant; no ambiguity, no hidden observer."

These two explanations for the absence of a hidden observer are both plausible: first, lacking in some dissociative ability, the separated part remains available to consciousness, either simultaneously or in alternation much as it does for most subjects in the easier hypnotic tests; second, the dissociation is so complete that the methods used have not succeeded in uncovering the hidden part. The studies have not been carried far enough to be definitive regarding these explanations and their relative frequencies.

CHARACTERIZATIONS OF THE HIDDEN OBSERVER

Perhaps through the choice of metaphor, the hidden observer has tended to connote either some sort of persisting secondary personality or a mysterious part of the mind lurking in the shadows. Because of the covert reports of experiences of which the subject had not been aware, a reader may think of untapped depths of experience, possibilities of consciousness expansion, unrealized human potential, and other rather mystical ideas that are welcomed by many in our contemporary culture.

The evidence from the reports of our subjects is quite otherwise. They report discovering genuinely covert experiences, but these turn out to be objective, matter-of-fact, scientific, accurate observations of contemporary events. There is little evidence of any upsurge from the deeper recesses of the mind. If anything, the "primary process" experiences are confined to the overt experiences of hypnosis in which images of hallucinatory intensity are prominent and there are many reality distortions. The covert experiences, by contrast, are reality bound.

We were prepared to find it otherwise, but from the very beginning were impressed by the mature language used in describing the overt experiences and by the "secondary process" conceptual structure of the comments, including the use of the arbitrary magnitude scales they had been taught to employ in describing pain and hearing.

Let the subjects speak for themselves:

> The hidden part doesn't deal with pain. It looks at what is, and doesn't judge it. It is not a hypnotized part of the self. It knows all parts.

> The hidden observer is watching, mature, logical, has more information.

> The hidden observer seemed like my real self when I'm out of hypnosis, only more objective. When I'm in hypnosis, I'm imagining, letting myself pretend, but somewhere the hidden observer knows what's really going on. I think this is part of the same process as the tendency in hypnosis to stand back and say: Look what's happening to you. You're slowly going under hypnosis.

> The hidden observer was an extra, all-knowing part of me. I was not at all aware of it when I blotted out the hearing. It was not there until it was told to be there.

The hidden part knows the hypnotized part, but the hypnotized part does not know the hidden one.

It's strange, because I didn't knowingly feel the pain reported, and (in automatic writing) I didn't knowingly know I was writing. . . . Maybe the tones register in your memory and skip going through the conscious part of your brain. (He thought the hidden observer had a scanning function limited to events distorted by hypnosis, as in analgesia and deafness. He was asked whether he thought the two processes alternated or went side by side.) It's parallel processing. One is overriding the other. There are no interrupted breaks.

The hidden observer is analytical, unemotional, business-like. The part of me that was hypnotized was off on a tropical island talking with the birds, and was the romantic part. This part on the island was in control during hypnosis, and felt threatened by the hidden observer. It seemed like reality, the real world. (She was one of the few who used the analogy of a divided personality.) I felt like I had two personalities. They're related. They're both "Me." They add up to the person here. They balance. I'm not a pure romantic nor a pure analytical. I'm about 50/50. . . . In the experiment they got separated. "Laurie" is "She," the romantic, sensory, feeling person in hypnosis, while "Lauretta," the "I" when speaking for the hidden part, was analytical and unemotional.

Because of the reflectiveness evidenced in her remarks, Rachel's characterizations of the splits in her cognitive apparatuses set the stage for the interpretation of divisions of cognitive controls to be explained in the next chapter. Rachel described her split selves thus:

The hidden observer is a portion of Me. There's Me 1, Me 2, and Me 3. Me 1 is hypnotized, Me 2 is hypnotized and observing, and Me 3 is when I'm awake. . . . The hidden observer is cognizant of everything that's going on; it's a little more narrow in its field of vision than Me 3, like being awake in a dream and fully aware of your action. . . . The hidden observer sees more, he questions more, he's aware of what's going on all of the time but getting in touch is totally unnecessary. The first time (ice water pain) I thought maybe it was an artifact of the situation, but after the second time, with hearing, I don't think that's the case. He's like a guardian angel that guards you from doing anything that will mess you up. . . . The hidden observer is looking through the tunnel, and sees everything in the tunnel. . . . It's focused, doesn't pay attention to extraneous things. It's aware that the tones are coming through, aware that I was saying "zero," that the Me 1 was also busy floating. Me 2 is watching all of this. Unless someone tells me to get in touch with the hidden observer I'm not in contact. It's just there.

Summarizing this insightful characterization, we note that Rachel has described three cognitive functions or systems as three fractions of the "Me":

Me 3, the awake Me, of which the hidden observer is a restricted fraction, until called forth.

Me 2, the observing part in the midst of hypnosis, described as hypnotized because subject to the distortions of perception that hypnosis has permitted or produced, watching Me 1.

Me 1, the hypnotized part, busy floating, and overtly reporting no pain.

This is as clear a statement of the phenomenology of the experiences within the analgesia and deafness experiments as any of the subjects has given.

CAUTIONS AGAINST OVERGENERALIZING

Dissociative experience, in some respects a concealed part of the "normal me" (as in Rachel's Me 3), is of great theoretical importance and will be referred to again as a basis for distinguishing between dissociation and repression. The experiments conducted with the hidden observer technique have thus far explored only a limited range of experiences, and they should not be generalized to cover the whole range of experiences, especially those with deep emotional commitment, and where highly charged motivational conflicts may be involved. The results in the reported experiments are genuine: the surprise of the subjects who discover that they have covert experiences differing from their overt ones attests to that. The use of simulators shows that the circumstances are such as to invite particular kinds of report, but the differences between the quality of the experiences as reported by the reals and the simulators also support the genuineness of the distinctions between covert and overt for the highly hypnotizable.

That the covert experience appears to be highly rational and reality oriented may be in part a consequence of the options that are open. That is, the overt analgesia and deafness following hypnotic suggestion are distortions of reality; if there is a concealed part that "knows more," the high probability is that it will report either pain or hearing. Such a realistic report of concealed information processing suffices to show that under appropriate circumstances there can be a dissociated fraction representing "secondary process" instead of "primary process." This must not be allowed to exclude the possibility, however, that in some other arrangement the dissociated part concealed from awareness may be laden with affect and will then show derivatives from the deeper unconscious. Similar cautions were stated earlier (Chapter 2) regarding generalizations from multiple personality.

CONFLICT AND INTEGRATION

The bland, objective, purely cognitive interpretations of the hidden observer do not do justice to the full range of experiences associated with it, including both positive and negative affect.

The majority report in the interviews was that the hidden observer contributed to a feeling of unity and integration and hence was associated with positive affect. That is, the hidden part, continuous with the reality orientation of the normal environmental interaction, made the hypnotic distortions more acceptable.

> With the hidden observer present, I'm one being. I don't separate mind and body.
>
> The hidden observer is looking at the hypnotized state of my hypnotized self; there's an awareness that my hypnotized self and my hidden observer are like two different parts of my real self. Both are an integrated me.

There were others who disliked the experience of a hidden observer. One was offended by it throughout. She used the word "betrayed" to signify what it meant to her. She was one of those who, in advance, thought the idea of a hidden observer not at all plausible because "you don't think of yourself as having all these parts." She expressed her surprise at the revelation of the hidden observer, and her betrayal, thus:

> I was surprised. The hidden part wasn't surprised because it was aware of its own existence as well as the existence of the hypnotized part. The hypnotized part was surprised because it's usually in the foreground [during hypnosis], and now was shocked to be pushed into the background. It isn't used to that; it felt kind of betrayed.

In common with one or two others who reported negative affect connected with the covert experience she reported an amused quality in the hidden observer. "He seems more mature than the rest of me. More logical, and amused by the me that couldn't hear because of course you can hear." She explained that she used the masculine pronoun for the hidden observer because she thinks of males as more logical, females as more intuitive.

When automatic writing went on for one subject without amnesia for what was happening, she felt very conflicted, but in a later session, when there was amnesia for the divided part, the conflict was no longer experienced.

> How can I be thinking and verbalizing something, yet be doing precisely the opposite with my hand? . . . Part of my mind was observing both of these things going on, and was curious about them. I felt I had set up a conflict in observing this. . . . It's like a hierarchy.

Asked to explain, she indicated that the observing part, corresponding to what would ordinarily have been a hidden observer, was not hidden, was instead at the top of her hierarchy, observing everything with curiosity. Next was the verbal part, and at the bottom of the hierarchy was the compulsive automatic writing. This divided and conflictual experience upset her. Later, in the pain experiment, the hidden observer remained covert until revealed by the special techniques, and she was less troubled. Amnesia is important for driving the disturbing conflictual part out of awareness. Relating the dissociation to repression helps to explain the nature of the division that occurs.

Another subject had been disturbed by finding in the pain experiment that her mind was divided into two parts. A year later she returned for the hearing experiment and felt differently about it.

> It was neat to have a hidden observer because it was integrated. My whole mind was flowing in one direction rather than in separate parts.

CONCLUDING REMARKS

The interview comments in this chapter represent the best evidence we have been able to obtain on the experience of the subject who has had a hidden observer uncovered or who has failed to discover one even though the subject is highly hypnotizable and able to experience substantial losses of pain and hearing. The evidence supports the interpretation that hypnotic responses represent two stages of dissociation: a more superficial kind represented by the usual responses to suggestion, which practically all subjects share to some degree, and the more profound dissociation that rests on an amnesic-like process that permits some information to be processed below the level of awareness. The identification of these two components means that the highly hypnotic responsive subject must have the abilities associated with the second component, which may be lacking in the subject who is less responsive but still capable of earning moderately high scores on a scale of hypnotizability. Despite the bimodalities in the distribution of scores, there need not be two sharply defined "types" of subject, for the two components may be shared in different amounts by any one subject. Most efforts to improve hypnotizability of those initially low fail to produce improvement beyond a few points in the lower range of scores. This result indicates that the first component permits limited gains through training; the second component, if present, allows a more widespread improvement in hypnotic responsiveness.

For those subjects who demonstrated recoverable information by the hidden observer technique, what they have told us bears importantly on how the more profound dissociations are to be interpreted. With this background, and that of the earlier discussion, we are prepared to turn to theoretical considerations, with the aims of explaining hypnotic dissociations and placing dissociation in a larger context.

NOTES

This chapter, relying as it does on data from interviews, could not have been written without the collaboration of Josephine R. Hilgard, who did all the interviewing from which the quotations are selected.

The 18 subjects who were interviewed were the residual ones who had been successful in either the analgesia or the deafness experiments; they were brought back to experience whichever of these they had not previously participated in. The data have not yet been fully reported (J. R. Hilgard and others, in preparation).

Presence or Absence of a Hidden Observer

In the ischemic study by Knox, Morgan, and Hilgard (1974), subjects had been very carefully selected for their ability not only to reduce pain but to have a concealed experience such as the hidden observer technique reveals; hence the fact that seven of the eight subjects manifested a hidden observer is not an indication that the presence of a hidden observer can be predicted in advance by selecting high subjects on the basis of test scores. In the cold pressor (ice water pain) study by Hilgard, Morgan, and Macdonald (1975), of 20 high subjects selected without regard to the special capacity for revealing covert resonses, only eight of the 20 gave clear evidence of a hidden observer. The deafness experiments to which references have been made both here and in Chapter 9 have not yet been published (Macdonald, Crawford, and Hilgard, 1977). The high correspondence between those with hidden observers in pain and deafness indicates that there is some dissociative ability in common between the two experiences. Hence no sharp distinctions have been made in the reported comments between pain and hearing, except as the subject has pointed out differences.

Characterizations of the Hidden Observer

It appears somewhat paradoxical that the most profound of the dissociations that we have studied, involving the covert experiences brought to light by the hidden observer technique, should turn out to be very objective, realistic, and matter-of-fact. What then becomes of the characterization of hypnosis as a regressed state?

The conception of hypnosis as a regressed state was stated most firmly by Gill and Brenman (1959), employing the concept of an adaptive regression, or "regression in the service of the ego." Their evidence came primarily from hypnosis with patients in a psychoanalytic setting, and the manifestations they considered were those that have here been assigned to overt response within hypnosis.

Because the covert experience as described has turned out to be objective and realistic, it can be described as representing the "secondary process" mode of cognitive activity. What then of the overt experience? At the overt level, appropriate realistic experience in hypnosis is distorted, changed by hallucination, or perhaps denied through negative hallucination or amnesia. These aspects may be attributed to an illogical process that exhibits some of the cognitive features of primary process. We have not found it necessary to employ the concept of regression to describe the minor dissociations leading to responsiveness to suggestions, or exhibited in the responses themselves, and hence have not made use of primary process conceptually because of its imbeddedness in an alternative explanation of cognitive functioning. However, others in addition to Gill and Brenman have found primary process manifestations in hypnosis (Gruenewald, Fromm, and Oberlander, 1972). They found some facilitation of access to primary process ideation in hypnosis, but they did not find it tenable to equate hypnosis with adaptive regression. For an earlier discussion of primary process in relation to hypnosis, see Hilgard (1962a).

Conflict and Integration

Because our experimentation has been conducted with samples of university students participating out of curiosity or a willingness to serve science, we do not find many of the expressions of extreme affect common in clinical practice. This has the advantage of permitting us to distinguish between what belongs to hypnosis itself and what may belong to the therapeutic interaction in the clinical setting. It is not surprising, for example, that transference phenomena are much less prevalent in the laboratory (J. R. Hilgard, 1971) than in studies done primarily with patients (Gill and Brenman, 1959). At the same time, because of somewhat lesser affective involvement with the hypnotist, our data suffer some restrictions.

CHAPTER 11

A NEODISSOCIATION INTERPRETATION OF DIVIDED CONSCIOUSNESS

It is important for a modern form of dissociation theory to explain the nature of the executive control and the monitoring systems that permit information processing and behavior management to proceed without conscious representation. The clinical and experimental material to be comprehended has been presented in the preceding chapters. Especially pertinent is the fact that information once concealed has ultimately been retrieved in the individual consciousness. That is not all, however, because the roles played by the executive and monitoring functions can illuminate the manner in which divisions of control operate.

EXECUTIVE AND MONITORING FUNCTIONS IN THE NONHYPNOTIC CONDITION

For many years psychologists paid little attention to central control functions, avoiding the problems of a central "will" behind acts that they felt were better understood as "habits." They introduced some ancillary functions such as "sets" or "determining tendencies" to account for sustaining one direction of activity against competing alternatives, but these were somewhat local and temporary. Of two extreme interpretations about how decisions lead to action, one interpretation may accept a powerful central control system, replacing the concept of a strong will, whereas the other may deny central control altogether, substituting instead a hierarchy of possible thoughts and actions determined by the competitive strengths of the activated subsystems, whether habits or cognitive structures. These subsystems would then fight according to their strengths for control of the final common path leading to action. Because psychologists had evaded the problems of a planning and initiating self, they tended to adopt the second of these alternatives. To the extent that man was thought to be controlled by external stimuli, and the habits conditioned to them, it was felt that his actions represented a compromise behavior adapted to the totality of forces upon him. However, now that planning and control functions are gaining recognition, the entire matter of central processes requires reexamination.

A central regulating mechanism characterized by both temporary and enduring aspects, limited in what it does and can do, may be accepted as a starting point. Many subsystems of habits, attitudes, prejudices, interests, and specialized abilities are available, although at any one time they may be latent; these are actuated according to the demands of the situation and the plans of the central system. This central regulatory mechanism is responsible for the facilitations and inhibitions that are required to actuate the subsystems selectively. A hierarchy of subsystems is implied, although it is a shifting hierarchy under the management of the control mechanisms. Once a subsystem has been activated it continues with a measure of autonomy; the conscious representation of the control system may recede, leading to some degree of automatization. William James noted, as others had before him, and others since, that as habit takes over, it diminishes the conscious representation of what goes on:

> A strictly voluntary act has to be guided by idea, perception, and volition, throughout its whole course. In an habitual action, mere sensation is a sufficient guide, and the upper regions of brain and mind are set comparatively free (James, 1890, I, 115–116).

The automatization of habit, setting the rest of the mind free, allows such dual actions as carrying on a conversation while engaged in habitual activity.

An earlier attempt to convey the idea of multiple subsystems under central control is presented in Figure 21, designed to indicate the availability of substructures in hierarchical arrangement; only three are shown. Their positions in the chart suggest their hierarchical order; once activated, each has its

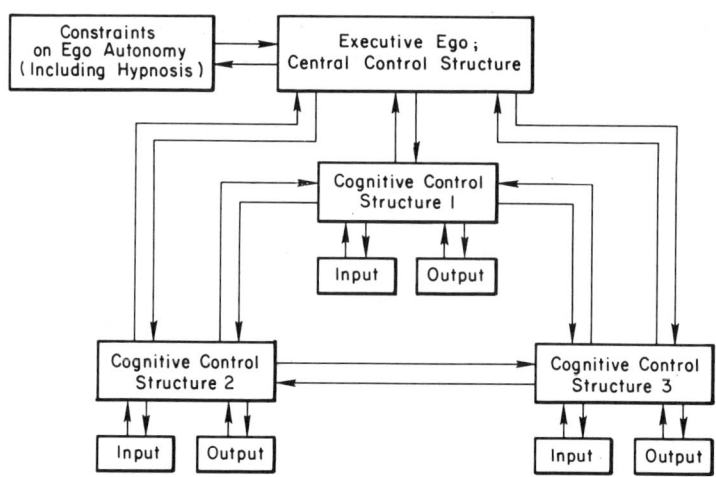

Figure 21 Subordinate cognitive control systems, in a hierarchical order subject to change, under a dominant executive ego or central control structure. From Hilgard, 1973b, p. 405.

own input and output, thus indicating a relative autonomy. At the top is an executive ego or central control structure with the planning, monitoring, and managing functions required for using the subsystems appropriately. The autonomy of the subsystems is restrained by the feedback relations among the systems, as well as by the central mechanism. The Executive Ego has no absolute authority, as indicated by the box representing constraints on it. These are the familiar constraints against a purely voluntary control of action and are determined by the individual history and situational influences; the constraints become particularly clear when hypnotic influences are imposed. Suggestions from the hypnotist may influence the executive functions themselves and change the hierarchical arrangement of the subsystems.

Other psychologists, whether or not they have included a central control system, have found it desirable to recognize organized subordinate cognitive structures. Once such a substructure becomes active it has a certain degree of autonomy; a simple illustration is that of a bilingual person deciding to talk in one of his two languages, after which the appropriate language forms are used automatically and the other language is inhibited. Brief mention of the positions that several others have taken, without elaboration, shows that an analysis along these general lines is closely allied to other developments within general psychology. Seven of these positions follow; in only two of them does the planning function find expression.

1. The term *cognitive structure* was made familiar by Edward Tolman (1932, 1938) and taken over by Kurt Lewin (1935). Such a structure may be

pervasive but it is not all-embracing, and there are problems of communication between structures.

2. One of Clark Hull's central concepts was that of *habit-family hierarchy*, in which a number of habits (each of which may be considered a small substructure) permit the organism to achieve its goals in a given situation, and these small substructures are organized in a preferential or hierarchical system, so that if one is blocked the next is activated (Hull, 1934).

3. Donald Hebb's conception of *cell assemblies* serves to provide a physiological substratum for cognitive structures (Hebb, 1949), and in a talk before the Canadian Psychological Association in 1974 he noted a possible coordination between his proposals and the existence of the "hidden observer" as I have described it (Hebb, 1975).

4. Sarbin's *roles* can also be considered to be cognitive substructures (e.g., Sarbin and Coe, 1972).

5. The *cognitive networks*, prominent in the model proposed by Blum, Geiwitz, and Stewart (1967), serve comparable functions.

6. The *images* and *plans* of Miller, Galanter, and Pribram (1960) represent their levels of analysis that would provide for control of thought and action; these, too, may be considered to be substructures, with some hierarchy implied.

7. The *subordinate ego-structures* of Gill and Brenman (1959), with a dominant ego, represent an interpretation similar to mine, at least within hypnosis. In a larger setting the various ego-apparatuses of Hartmann (1958), especially those in his *conflict-free ego sphere*, are readily assimilated.

Even though a central planner is lacking in several of the foregoing proposals, the idea is a congenial one and is familiar in everyday experience. Even a simple matter such as making an appointment for luncheon next week is negotiated with those involved, written down, and then acted on at a later time. This planfulness controls the possible behavior on that future date quite effectively. The many competing thoughts that occur the morning of the luncheon do not appear to be as determinative of what is going to happen in the midday as the plans that were made by some responsible part of the cognitive apparatus during the prior week. Appointments of this kind are kept with a very high probability—perhaps as high as 90% of the time—so that the planning function must be taken seriously. The event may be trivial, but its implications are not.

The support for a special executive function has come into the open from an unlikely source—the computer. Heuristic computer programs commonly have an executive program that monitors the computer's attempts to solve problems (Newell and Simon, 1972). If one direction goes on too long without reaching a solution, the executive calls a halt and a new direction is taken.

This close analogy makes the idea of control a plausible one (Neisser, 1967). From another direction, control processes have been noted as important in such processes as rehearsing to hold information in short-term memory (Atkinson and Shiffrin, 1971), and since then more attention has been given to problems of control as part of the "working memory" (e.g., Bower, 1975).

Central control systems and activated subsystems are complex, and only those features are considered that bear on the problems which are of specific concern here, particularly the changes brought about through hypnotic procedures. To be as clear as possible, executive functions are treated separately from monitoring functions, although the two functions are always intertwined and their interactions are important. The activated subsystems are considered, both in their degree of autonomy and the nature of the control exercised over them.

Executive Functions

Central executive functions are responsible for planning in relation to goals, initiating action commensurate with these plans, and sustaining action against obstacles and distractions. Long- and short-range plans are enmeshed in complex networks. For example, a youth planning a career in medicine knows the broad outlines of what will be necessary for premedical education, medical school, internship and residency training, becoming licensed, and setting up practice. This is not as simply sequential as it sounds, yet it provides an overarching plan that bears on many of the intermediate steps in planning. Within any one step, such as gaining admission to a medical school, there are many detailed choices to be made and acts to be performed, including such prosaic decisions as how many applications to submit, and writing for the forms. Ancillary choices, perhaps summer employment to help pay the costs, all become related to the general plan. As soon as any one subordinate program is selected to fit into the larger plan, the program has to be initiated and sustained—down to such details as studying for the examination in a course that is a premedical prerequisite. Of course the youth is not only a prospective physician, and long-range plans will be colored by other aspects of life planning, such as those for marriage and a family. These matter-of-fact aspects of executive planning and action are noted here to dispel the thought that by acknowledging central executive functions something mysterious or alien is being introduced into the psychological understanding of a person. These functions are not alien, although they have suffered from neglect in scientific psychology.

Monitoring Functions

The monitor must be constantly alert. It has a scanning function that includes alertness to all that is taking place, a recognition of the familiar, and a readiness for the unexpected. The monitoring function must be vigilant for threats to safety; it picks up signs from the environment and from the body; a toothache is unplanned, but it is monitored. In addition to this general scanning, the monitor is selective in what is attended to. Selectivity is the mark of attentive focusing. When the restriction is to a larger area, related to more long-range goals, it is likely to be described as an *interest* or *preoccupation* that makes the person read one article rather than another in the newspaper, or watch one TV program selected from several. Psychologists tend to use the word *attention* in experimental settings for selectivity regarding more specific sources of information, such as attention to color rather than to words in a colored-word conflict, or to the message to one ear rather than to the other when two messages are being received. A selective "set" may be generated, as when listening for the starter's gun to start a foot race. Here we already have a hint of the interaction between executive and monitoring functions, because the executive has determined the action to be initiated, whereas the monitor watches for the signals. In addition to scanning and selection, the monitoring function includes a *critical* or *judgmental* role, based on feedback from initiated and sustained action as what is done is compared with intended goals and performances. Not all action is initiated according to plan, and not all performances, whether at the level of thought or action, are successful according to their intended outcomes. The monitor, as critic, brings this information to bear, whether in connection with long-range plans or immediate actions. It may reflect the voice of conscience if long-range plans are being interrupted by secondary interests or inappropriate behavior; it may alert the typist to spelling errors in the immediately activated short-range task.

Interaction Between Executive and Monitoring Functions

It is artificial to separate executive and monitoring functions sharply because all initiated action is monitored. When the relationships are harmonious, the interplay between executive and monitor seems entirely natural and sensible, as in any "trial-and-error" setting. If one course of action does not work, another may be tried. Whether the second course works better is determined by monitoring; the executive acts on this information. If a harmonious relationship were always found, little more than academic interest would be served by separating the functions. Often, however, the two functions are not well balanced, and this is demonstrated particularly well in hypnosis. In some cases outside hypnosis, an alert monitoring function will be helpless in modifying executive action through feedback. In obsessive-compulsive behavior, for example, when executive control is weak, the monitoring function may be well aware of the behavior and critical of it, yet unable to alter it by way of the information available. On other occasions, the monitor in its critical role may become persuasive and modify executive functioning. If, for example, the person is subjected to temptation toward antisocial behavior, the monitor may throw its weight against yielding and be successful. Internal conflicts of this sort are familiar enough; it is appropriate to describe some of them as conflicts between the monitoring and executive functions.

These familiar illustrations are intended to show that executive control and monitoring are part of a general system that can be recognized in our ordinary lives. There are always interrelations between more immediate and more long-range goals, and consequently the need for feedback occurs all along the way. When specific activity is initiated by the central mechanisms, the activated subsystem achieves some degree of independence from the central control systems; at least the conscious representation of these systems appears to retreat as the person becomes absorbed in what he is doing. This calls for further discussion.

Subsystems of Activity: Latent and Actuated

A person's life is made up of an almost infinite number of activities, from trivial responses to stimuli (brushing a fly off the face), to those consuming more time, still with definable beginnings and endings (writing a letter, playing a game of golf, listening to a symphony), and on to activities that are enduring over many years and complexly interacting with each other (raising a family, doing the housework, saving for retirement).

Psychologists have found it difficult to decide on the best level of analysis, and the search for a satisfactory unit of behavior or experience still goes on. There is widespread agreement that the sensation and the reflex were too reductive as units. The hope that the unit of information—the "bit"—might serve proved disappointing, too, as the "bit" proved too reductive and "chunks" of information had to be added to describe how information is actually handled (Miller, 1956). The TOTE unit (Test-Operate-Test-Exit) was later proposed as a more meaningful unit than the reflex, in part to permit information concepts to be used, as implied by the repeated "testing" within the unit of behavior (Miller, Galanter, and Pribram, 1960). Habits and cognitive structures, discussed earlier in the chapter, are other consequences of attempts to "package" experience and behavior to permit consideration of one topic at a time in the midst of complexity.

For the purposes of the present discussion, the identifiable activities in which a person can engage are referred to as *subsystems* to distinguish them from the larger control and monitoring functions according to which they are regulated. These subsystems are the visible or reportable happenings when a person is engaged in any definable activity—reading a book, operating a machine, scratching his head, solving a problem.

Because these subsystems are so numerous, yet only a few are visibly going on at a time, it is possible to distinguish between those that are active and those that are inactive. Those that are not operative, but available, are referred to as *latent*, whereas those that are active in the present are described as *actuated*. A latent subsystem can become actuated in many ways, as a consequence of the impact of the physical or social environment, by bodily changes such as those influencing organic motivational systems, or by self-initiation through the cognitive activities of reflection and planning.

Hypnotic suggestion is one of the ways of actuating a specific set of subsystems, and it is particularly useful because it permits the manipulation of the hierarchies according to which subsystems are controlled. The subsystems actuated in hypnosis—the behaviors and experiences represented by the usual hypnotic "items" or "tests" of ideomotor action, hallucinations, age regression, amnesia, and the rest—are sufficiently limited to be studied repeatedly and in detail, providing data to serve as a basis for theoretical interpretation. Hypnotic fantasies may include an extensive range of activities, but such fantasies are typically under control and limited to the hypnotic period, hence they serve to illuminate the roles of simultaneous cognitive activities.

The Actuated Subsystem in Relation to Central Controls

The acceptability of central controls, in the form of executive and monitoring functions, does not mean that all behavior and experience has to be referred to them. We need not return to a new form of the older self-psychology that always found a self in every act of introspection. What happens is that once an activity is under way it becomes relatively self-sustaining. Woodworth (1918) recognized this in his principle that any activity once aroused may generate its own "drive," and Allport (1937) later indicated that motives may lose connection with their origins and become "functionally autonomous" in sustaining behavior.

It is readily observed that a person absorbed in a skilled task may be little conscious of himself; the task and its completion are self-monitored once the activity has been initiated. The subsystem's own monitoring and control systems operate through habit as mediated by feedback; these activity-related controls permit the high degree of autonomy with which the skilled act is performed. Of course the individual absorbed in his work may now and then step back to admire his work, at which time the monitoring function is active both as observer and as critic. Observation, as such, ties the monitor to perceptual operations; criticizing the work according to standards of value ties the monitor to esthetic appreciation, rationality, and conceptions of right and wrong. Hence the monitor, as part of the central control system, is a member of the family of controls that includes conscience and superego. The conceptual problem of distinguishing a general monitoring function from a specific one arises because, as noted, the activated subsystem has its own internal executive and monitoring subsystems. The typist must attend to the copy and observe the proprioceptive feedbacks from the keys as well as occasional visual feedback from the typed material. These controls belong to the typing subsystem itself and are a matter of the interplay between the typist and the typewriter. The superordinate control systems in which the behavior of typing from copy is imbedded include such larger contexts as the self-image of the typist and the interactions with the superior who assigns the work and will judge the product. If we have difficulties in distinguishing the appropriate levels of analysis of participant and control functions in familiar experience, we might expect these difficulties to be compounded when dealing with hypnosis. Fortunately, however, some of the changes within hypnosis exhibit the control mechanisms in such dramatic form as to make the task clearer rather than more confusing.

HOW THE HYPNOTIC INTERACTION READIES THE SUBJECT FOR DISSOCIATIVE EXPERIENCES

To examine in greater detail the modifications that take place in hypnosis as they bear on dissociation, the hypnotic process can be divided into the initial contract, the induction, and the experiences that are subsequently produced.

The Hypnotic Contract

It is generally recognized that a person's cooperation is required if he is to experience hypnosis; that is, he need not become hypnotized if he does not wish to. There may be occasional exceptions to the generalization, as when one person watching another being hypnotized inadvertently becomes hypnotized himself without having agreed or planned to participate, but such instances are atypical. One way to interpret this is that there is an initial contract between the subject and the hypnotist according to which the subject agrees to conform to the conditions and expectations appropriate to hypnosis (Hodge, 1976). The contract does not guarantee that the subject will experience hypnosis, for many are unable to achieve a hypnotic condition even if they cooperate fully.

The importance of the initial commitment was demonstrated in one of the very early investigations completed in our laboratory (Weitzenhoffer, Gough, and Landes, 1959). The study was designed to determine whether fixating attention on a small target object would suffice to produce hypnosis in the susceptible. The method goes back to Braid, the nineteenth century coiner of the word hypnosis, and has been known as the Braid effect.

We were not yet established as a hypnosis laboratory; thus subjects came to the laboratory without expecting to be hypnotized. Instead, they were told that they were being invited for an experiment on the effects of sustaining voluntary attention. Their instructions were to fixate a small object (thumbtack) and to keep their eyes open without blinking for as long as possible. After attention had been sustained for some time, they were given a few tests of suggestion of the kind given in hypnotic susceptibility scales. The eye fixation led to no evidence of increased response to subsequent suggestions. Subjects in another group, treated like those of the first group except for an initial suggestion that eye fixation would induce hypnosis, responded as if hypnotized; the amount of hypnotic response was indistinguishable from that following a usual induction procedure. The experiment showed that a formal induction procedure, beyond eye fixation, was unnecessary provided expectation of hypnosis was present.

The requirement of an initial agreement to cooperate is not unique to hypnosis and does not reflect on the genuineness of the subsequent hypnotic experience. Initial cooperation is also needed, for example, in a memory experiment if recall is desired that goes beyond what would be found in uninstructed incidental memory; nobody says that this makes the memorial performance questionable.

The Hypnotic Induction and the Established Hypnotic State

The hypnotic induction of a cooperative subject provides a training ground for the hypnotic experience similar to the initial experiences often given to subjects in other experiments. Initial trials are commonly given in reaction-time experiments, in investigations of perceptual discriminations, in verbal memorizing—whenever the context of the experience is unfamiliar and some initial acquaintance seems desirable.

The postural sway test with which the Stanford Hypnotic Susceptibility Scale, Form A (SHSS-A), begins illustrates such an initial experience. The subject is informed that this will help him discover what involuntary response to suggestion is like. While standing with feet together, arms at his sides, and eyes closed, he is told that he will feel himself falling backwards, to be caught by the hypnotist if he loses his balance, so that he will not hurt himself. The presence of a fall under these circumstances correlates only $r = .38$ with the remaining tests of hypnotic responsiveness, but it is included in the scale as contributing something to the estimate of hypnotizability.

The next item in the scale, eye closure, carries out the same idea, except that an element of conflict is added. The subject is told to keep his eyes open and to stare at the target while the hypnotist repeats suggestions that the eyes are closing involuntarily, by themselves. The involuntary eye closure correlates $r = .57$ with the total score. This type of suggestion has sometimes been interpreted as a "double-bind," because contradictory instructions are given: Keep the eyes open, but let them close (Haley, 1958). Haley has proposed that the problem can be resolved through dissociation if the voluntary act for which the subject feels responsible (keeping his eyes open) is counteracted by an involuntary act for which he does not feel responsible (closing the eyes as a consequence of the hypnotist's repeated suggestions.)

Subjects who are able to participate comfortably in meeting the expectations of the hypnotic interaction find experiences like these convincing; many fail despite their desire to experience hypnosis.

Looked at in other ways, we find that hypnotic procedures are designed to produce a readiness for dissociative experiences by disrupting the ordinary continuities of memories and by distorting or concealing reality orientation through the power that words exert by direct suggestion, through selective attention and inattention, and through stimulating the imagination appropriately.

The stress on muscular relaxation, familiar in hypnotic induction, assists in disorientation, because one of the ways in which we keep oriented is to know where our hands and feet are. By moving his feet about, a person ordinarily sees that they do not go to sleep; he carries his hands frequently to his face and adjusts his clothing repeatedly. By knowing where the parts of his body are and adjusting them from time to time, everything is kept on the alert. In the relaxation suggested by the hypnotist, these ties to continuity are disrupted by the relaxation emphasis through trying *not* to have any sensory feedback from the body. A loss of the experience of the body is commonly reported in deep hypnosis. Even such suggestions as having the arms float freely through the air produce some sense of detachment, carried further in fantasy when hypnosis is deepened by imagined floating on a cloud.

The metaphor of sleep, continued today even though everyone knows that hypnosis is not sleep, serves the same purpose, because sleep is expected to disrupt memories. The term somnambulist, as noted earlier, originally meant that the hypnotized subject resembled the sleepwalker because he could not remember what he had done in hypnosis.

Excessive activity can also serve the purpose of breaking ordinary memorial processes, and it is not surprising that the distance runner, as he becomes unaware of the pain in his legs, also fails to be conscious of the legs that he sees running beneath him. It has been pointed out that these processes can be paralleled in alert hypnosis.

The lack of appropriately aroused memories makes the hypnotically responsive person less critical. To be critical requires comparing a present observation with familiar ones to judge its veridicality. If the memory context recedes, criticism also recedes. Hence imagination more readily becomes hallucination, and what is observed now may be drastically altered from what was observed a few minutes ago. The broken watch item in one of our scales may be cited. Here the hypnotized subject is told that when he opens his eyes he will see a broken watch, with the long minute hand operating, but the shorter hour hand missing. When some subjects open their eyes, the working watch is seen as a broken one, but the meaning of that fact is ignored because of a failure of memory; when asked to tell the time the subject tells it as if the two hands were overlapped, reading the time as if the hour hand were beneath the minute hand. He has not lost all memory, for he has interpreted the present in terms of an instruction from the past and retains information from the past about how to read time. However, the critical controls that memory ordinarily provides are missing as he is influenced solely by the present set of stimuli as he perceives them. The dissociations implied by this illustration are subtle ones.

The alterations of consciousness produced in deep hypnosis, where specific suggestions need not be responded to, appear to fall into the same general pattern of memory disruption. By emphasis on quiescence and on ceasing to think, the consecutive processes of memory are disrupted, the body is not experienced or the body-image distorted, there is a feeling of selflessness, and the mystical experiences that may result appear to reveal knowledge that is not communicable. Lack of communication is to be expected if memory has been interfered with. These illustrations show how memory interference has helped produce the dissociations found in hypnosis.

In summary, the altered background for receiving suggestions, the state of hypnosis, is one of felt changes from normal in that the usual orientation to reality has been disturbed, and familiar reality testing does not go on. Memory is interfered with, so that, even if all memory is not lost, its critical role in specific instances is weakened. Under such circumstances, response to the stimulation provided by the hypnotist takes precedence over planned or self-initiated action, and the voice of the hypnotist becomes unusually persuasive.

A subject can bring himself to a similar condition or state through autohypnosis, preserving a verbal system that can take the same role as an external hypnotist. It is a sign of readiness to fractionate the central executive and monitoring system when a person decides to divide himself into the two roles of hypnotist and hypnotized. The matter evidently includes more than an enhancement of responsiveness to suggestions.

MODIFICATION OF CONTROLS IN HYPNOSIS

The actuated subsystems in hypnosis, that is, the typical behaviors shown when the subject responds to the hypnotist's suggestions, have been modified in relation to the control systems as they normally operate. The movement response itself, represented by the complex balance of muscular movement and proprioceptive feedbacks, may be essentially unchanged from normal when it occurs in hypnosis; what characterizes it as hypnotic is the change in voluntariness from the point of view of the subject. The less it is felt to be under the subject's control the more it has been dissociated from the normal executive functions, regardless of how it is represented in consciousness as a movement. Once memory has been distorted, as when a movement has been made as a consequence of a posthypnotic suggestion for which the subject is amnesic, the dissociation of the act from its normal controls is more evident. This follows because to the subject the central control of what he does is obscure, referred by him neither to himself nor to the hypnotist, hence assigned a spurious reason through rationalization. A modification of the quality of consciousness in hypnosis and a modification of the controls over thought and action may be distinguished. The emphasis here is on the modification of controls rather than on an alteration in the quality of consciousness. The modification of controls can be described as dissociative if the usual controls are inoperative, and are replaced by new ones. This emphasis need not deny that alterations of the quality of consciousness often occur; however, they are not essential to the interpretation of hypnotic behavior as dissociated.

Executive Functions in Hypnosis

The central executive functions in hypnosis are typically thought to be divided between the hypnotist and the hypnotized person. The latter retains a considerable portion of the executive functions from his normal state; he can answer questions about his past and his plans; he can accept or refuse invitations to move about, or to participate in specific kinds of activities. At the same time he turns over some of his executive functions to the hypnotist, so that, within the hypnotic contract, he will do what the hypnotist suggests, experience what the hypnotist suggests, and lose control of his movements if this is indicated. The retained and relinquished fractions will depend upon circumstances, including the degree of hypnotic responsiveness or talent that the subject brings to hypnosis, and the depth of involvement in hypnosis as a function of what transpires between him and the hypnotist.

A striking illustration of what is meant by the division of the executive system into two parts is provided by what occurs in self-hypnosis. The central executive function now divides itself into two parts, representing the role of hypnotist and hypnotized. Although this appears essentially irrational, it is no more irrational than heterohypnosis, in which dissociated controls are the very essence of what happens. In fact, heterohypnosis is primarily "aided self-hypnosis" when a hypnotist is present; the person accepts the hypnotist as an aid to hypnotizing himself. It has often been supposed that self-hypnosis must be a kind of response to post-hypnotic suggestion of a person who has "internalized" the hypnotist. That is, once a person has been hypnotized, the hypnotist can tell him: "You can hypnotize yourself by counting to 10." In that way, the hypnotist has really implanted the suggestion, even though the subject engages in self-hypnosis. This is not quite correct, for with the barest of instructions a subject can proceed to hypnotize himself and yield the usual responses to suggestion, *even if he has never had the experience of being hypnotized by another* (Ruch, 1975). Surprising as this may seem, a hypnotizable subject may suggest to himself that his arm will become stiff until he gives himself a release signal, and he will be unable to bend it, no matter how hard he tries, until he releases the suggestion, say, by counting to five. The arm does indeed become stiff, he exerts all possible effort to bend it without success, then starts to count, and at the count of five the arm relaxes and he can again bend it. It is as though he has created a small version of the Frankenstein monster, his own creation that then defies him by its autonomous behavior. This is the essence of the split of the executive function in hypnosis, a retained normal part that has permitted the hypnotized part to become active, with the hypnotized part then, in its own sphere, having considerable strength in conflict with the residual normal executive.

As a first step in hypnosis, the central executive function becomes sufficiently divided so that the usual initiative of the executive is lost. Its planning side is inhibited, and it does not independently undertake new lines of thought or action. The hypnotized person, asked to behave normally while remaining hypnotized, finds the effort at initiative distasteful and commonly withdraws to a comfortable chair if given the opportunity. We have observed this in informal demonstrations in our laboratory. One subject, asked to show an interest in a box of small objects at the other end of the room, replied: "I don't want to, but I'll do it if you insist." Interesting and convincing observations along these lines have been reported by Gill and Brenman (1959, p. 36–37). For example, after asking a subject how he knew he was hypnotized, if he said, "I feel relaxed," he was told that he would no longer feel relaxed, but would remain in hypnosis. Taking away one after another of his subjective signs of being hypnotized, while remaining hypnotized, the final reply turned out, for several subjects, to be "I know I am in hypnosis because *I know* that I will do what you tell me." This still defines hypnosis by suggestion but includes *readiness to respond* to suggestions as part of the background associated with being in the state.

Once initiative has been relinquished, the hypnotized person is prepared to respond to suggestions, as though the initiative resides either with the hypnotist, or, in self-hypnosis, with the nonhypnotized fraction.

The type of cooperation that the hypnotized person exercises in hypnosis adds features that modify the common misconception of the subject as a passive pawn manipulated by the hypnotist. Even though the subject has turned over a large measure of his executive function to the hypnotist, he remains essentially the hypnotist's assistant in producing the phenomena. This state of affairs appears transitional between heterohypnosis and self-hypnosis. Many subjects report repeating the hypnotist's suggestions to themselves, occasionally modifying the wording to make the suggestions more acceptable. If the hypnotist requests that they select an appropriate fantasy to implement a suggestion, they cooperate by doing so; in fact, they may choose an appropriate fantasy to help out the suggestion even if not asked to do so. Spanos and his associates have shown in a series of experiments that the involuntariness of a suggestion that the arm is becoming stiff is associated with the extent to which the subject has aroused appropriate fantasies. These may include picturing the arm in a splint, or as made of wood or iron, so that it cannot bend. Spanos has named them "goal-directed fantasies" because they have the purpose of making the suggestion more convincing. They may be invoked even when the hypnotist's suggestion has made no reference to fantasy, having suggested directly: "Your arm is now becoming stiff" (Spanos, Rivers, and Ross, 1977). The subject, cooperating with the hypnotist, is exercising some initiative *within* hypnosis. It can be argued that, except for relinquishing control over the subsystems that are specifically dissociated from central control by suggestion, and the readiness for relinquishing control, the central executive functions have not been much modified in hypnosis. In superficial hypnosis, these mild dissociations can occur through waking suggestion, with little alteration of the general state of consciousness. When varied suggestions to a talented hypnotic subject have cumulative effects, as in suggestions of relaxation and detachment from the environment, the more general features of the hypnotic state begin to appear. A more massive dissociation, so far as the executive is concerned, may be the consequence of the summing up of many specific subsystems for which control has been relinquished. Such an interpretation permits hypnosis as a state to be a relative matter, the specific dissociations being identifiable, but the general state being a matter of how many specific dissociations are operative and how pervasive they are. Only when they are sufficiently pervasive is it appropriate to speak of a change of state.

Monitoring Functions in Hypnosis

The divisions in executive functions bear importantly upon the divided roles within the monitoring functions in hypnosis. Having accepted the hypnotic contract, the executive "issues an order" to the monitor to reduce the amount of critical scanning, to relinquish, as Shor (1970) has put it, the usual "reality orientation." The monitor may then report what occurs ("The arm is now stiff") without questioning the cause of its stiffness.

In the usual waking condition, the monitoring functions proceed in a satisfactorily integrated manner as they perceive and take account of the information that becomes available from the external world and from the body. The distortion of reality in hypnosis depends on the degree of hypnotic involvement, and much normal monitoring is retained in hypnosis. A subject who is hypnotically analgesic, or deaf, or amnesic for a list of words previously memorized, is still able to use his other senses normally and has available his usual memories. Even the behaviors that have been produced within hypnosis by way of suggestion can be described in a normal matter-of-fact manner: "My hands are rising as if by themselves," "I see a red and a white box on the table." The characteristic distortion that can be used to indicate a partial fractionation of the monitoring function is its uncritical acceptance of distorted reality as though it were undistorted, without making the usual reality tests. That is, a normal person may be subject to reality distortion, as in a size-weight illusion whereby a pound of lead feels heavier than a pound of cotton, but he is likely to be suspicious of his judgment, and to test the weights on a balance. The hypnotized person, told that one of two objects of equal weight is heavier than the other, reports that that is the way they feel, but he is unconcerned to test the reality in some other way, unless asked to do so. Examples of hypnotic distortion include the hallucinations, both positive and negative, and age regression. The exact relation between the monitoring and the activated subsystem is not readily defined, for to the extent that the experience belongs to the subsystem in which the subject is deeply involved, the monitor may be reporting accurately. That is, the person may be reported as phenomenally a child again, on the playground of the third grade in school. All available information is not used by the activated subsystem, and the monitor does not offer a correction; hence imagination may be confused with external reality. As noted earlier (p. 99), the lack of normal criticism was called "trance logic" by Orne (1959), who used as his illustration the hallucination of a double of a person actually present and perceived. The hypnotic subject accepts this doubling without concern, even though at first a little puzzled as shown by his looking back and forth between them in behavior known as a "double-take." Correspondingly, in one of the items on the Stanford Profile Scales, the hypnotized subject hallucinates a second light at the other end of a box on which a real light is present. This is not logically contradictory, as in the case of the doubled person, but it has some similar characteristics. For example, in both illustrations the subject tends to act as if the hallucinated experience is like the actual perceptual one, even when, upon questioning, he may often detect differences between them. The point is that he is typically unconcerned about exercising critical discrimination until his monitoring functions are again mobilized by the hypnotist.

Another way in which the fractionation of the monitoring function from the activated subsystem is shown is in the detachment of the observing part from what is happening. The monitor may express surprise that an arm cannot be bent or amusement over some fantasied reality, such as floating on a cloud. The monitoring system knows what is going on from the point of view of the hypnotized person, but some information is concealed from it. The executive system, in collaboration with the hypnotist, succeeds in giving rise to the actuated experiences. How this has been done may be concealed from the monitor or lost by the fractionation of memory. For example, if an arm is made stiff by suggestion and the subject is unable to bend it even when he tries, the monitor reports just that: "You said my arm would be stiff and I couldn't bend it; I have tried to bend it and I can't do it." The monitor may go further: "I fantasied having my arm in a splint and I think that helped me to understand how stiff it was." What is lacking to the monitor is the information that some part of the person, in response to the hypnotist's suggestions and his own supplements, contracted both antagonistic muscle groups, one voluntarily, the other involuntarily, when he attempted to bend the arm, so that it remained stiff, as the arm does when you "make a muscle." This would appear to have more to do with a fractionation of the executive than of the monitor, although the possibility of this resolution is not ordinarily noted by the uncritical monitor. Somewhat the same can be said about the concealments present in negative hallucinations and amnesia: the monitor can report the absence of the appropriate perceptions and the memories without being a party to how they came about.

Except for some information denied it and the lack of criticism shown by the failure to insist on reality tests, very much of the normal monitoring function is retained in hypnosis at the ordinary levels of involvement. Less of the usual monitor is retained when the hypnotic involvement is greater, as in deep hypnosis, or when the subject becomes more deeply engrossed in an activated system that has been aroused. In such cases, the reality-oriented part of the monitor may fade out of the picture, and the unified experience seems to the subject the total reality. In these deeply involved experiences, the reports become similar to those described by existentialists, in which the observer and observed merge into one. In the lighter stages of hypnotic involvement, by contrast, the central monitor may be described as an observer standing in the wings while the hypnotic events are taking place in the center of the stage. As one subject put it:

> Part of me knew I was being hypnotized; it was watching. It was like a person inside of me, looking out through my eyes but not being able to control what was

happening. I thought I was still in control because I didn't do some of the suggested things. But review of the ammonia convinced me. He had made me smell it twice, and the first time there was nothing. I asked him: "Was that a trick?" When he assured me that I had smelled the same bottle twice, but hadn't smelled ammonia the first time, I knew I was hypnotized. . . . The part that was watching always thought that *it* was in control, and that I wasn't being hypnotized, and yet I was.

This capacity for detachment from the participative events themselves has led to a distinction between the monitor and the events. At times the separation is much less than at other times. Usually there is a representation of a Central Monitor commenting in the detached manner of a sideline observer, reporting what is going on as the person is involved in the hypnotically experienced events. Some essential information appears to be denied the monitor, however; the subsystems do their own monitoring and uncritically accept the many reality distortions; the monitor merely describes what the subsystem experiences, perhaps separating itself only enough to be surprised, pleased, or disappointed, but without reality testing of its own. This is very like the person reporting the manifest content of his dream, unaware of its latent content or how the dream was formed.

The Hidden Observer as a Fraction of the Monitoring Function

The covert experiences in hypnotic analgesia and hypnotic deafness, as studied by the hidden observer techniques, yield additional evidence on the fractionation of the monitoring function, because some fraction of it exists behind an amnesic-like barrier. This is the part of the monitor that has been called the hidden observer and becomes accessible only through automatic writing or automatic talking.

The temptation is strong to see the hidden part as a persistent system that must have been there all along. More extremely, the hidden part may be viewed as an upsurge from a deep unconscious. Many practicing hypnotists, for example, believe that they can "talk to the unconscious" by way of the finger-signalling technique. Under the conditions of our experiments, the characterization of the hidden observer that emerges from the interviews with our subjects denies these interpretations. A summary statement of what our subjects say would read more like this: *"The hidden observer is in all respects like the normal observing part as found in waking. It is objective and well oriented to reality."*

Although the interviews on which this conclusion is based are quoted extensively in Chapter 10, some further statements from a reflective and well-organized subject, whom we may call Louella, will serve as a reminder of some of the attitudes encountered. She was the one who had felt somewhat betrayed by the emergence of the hidden observer, because the hypnotized part, usually in the foreground, had been shocked to be in the background when the hidden part emerged (page 212).

In a further inquiry about what she meant by betrayal, she indicated that the hidden part was supposed to stay hidden: "There's an unspoken agreement that the hidden observer is supposed to stay hidden and not come out. He broke his promise, he's not abiding by the rules. He's betraying his agreement. He's gone back on his word. He's stealing something from the hypnotized part. He's stealing by taking his power." Despite this resentment of the hidden observer, she thought of the hidden observer as more mature than the rest of her, and he had more information than the hypnotized part; in fact, the hidden observer brought back all the information. "The hidden part has all the information. . . . He knows that sounds are coming into my ear and I must be hearing, that it's only due to suggestion that I'm not."

From considerations already stated, that part of the monitoring function revealed as the hidden observer can be further characterized as follows: (1) It is split off from the normal monitor and differs from it only in that it is concealed behind an amnesic-like barrier. (2) The fractionation occurred at the same time that the pain and hearing were denied conscious expression. (3) The hidden part, after it has been reintegrated with the normal monitoring function, persists only as a memory for an incident connected with the hypnotic experience; it has no independent existence as a part of the personality or its control systems, although it can of course be created again under appropriate circumstances.

The role of the monitoring function in the several stages of the experiments indicates three divisions that occur within it.

1. There is the normal role of the monitor in waking, with its usual scanning, critical testing, and reporting of reality as it is usually perceived.

2. Within hypnosis, the reality distortions reported suggest that a fraction of the monitor is involved in the ongoing experiences, is uncritical of them, and gives an overt account as though the distorted or fantasied experiences were part of the real world. A substantial part of the normal monitor is retained in the areas of behavior and experience not specifically involved in the hypnosis; it is only the hypnotic fraction that is dissociated from the normal whole.

3. The third fraction is the one concealed behind an amnesic-like barrier that can be broken by the special methods exposing the hidden observer. This turns out to be a part of the normal monitor and like it in its reality orientation.

When the report from the hidden observer is made public and all amnesia removed, the way is open for a reintegration of the subject's experiences. It may be recalled that it is common in multiple personality for one of the hidden personalities to be more normal than the manifested one (Chapter 2, page 40). This fact parallels the relationship of the hidden observer to the hypnotic monitor. It is the hidden part that knows all: both what the hypnotized part reported overtly and what information was available covertly. Here the parallel ends, because the hidden observer is a temporary construction in hypnosis, whereas multiple personalities persist through time.

The similarities and differences between the hidden observer and a multiple personality were well brought out by another experience of the subject Louella, in which the hidden observer technique had not been involved. After discussing the hidden observer, she reflected on her attitude toward age regression in an earlier hypnotic session, and through these reflections elaborated on why she felt "betrayed" by the hidden observer. In age regression, her 9-year-old self emerged as separate from her grown hypnotized self and was "sent back into its slot" when the hypnotist terminated the suggestion.

> This little 9-year-old is a little person who belongs to me, most of the time in the background as a memory or recollection and as an influence on my opinions but not an active decision-maker because it's so immature. When it had a chance to come to the foreground the rest of me was stuck in the background. It switched places with me, had me acting entirely as me at 9, with what belonged to the other me as recollections and influences instead of the active part. . . . It's your body; somebody who is part of me, but seems like a wholly different person, does not have the right to take over. It's already had its turn at 9. That's why the other part of me felt the same kind of shock of betrayal.

Her regression to age 9 appeared to be an analog of multiple personality, the 9-year-old part of herself carrying on in an autonomous manner when she emerged in hypnosis. In fact, this experience caused the subject to worry lest she might have many different people inside her. "When I'm conscious they merge as one."

That this 9-year-old was not really a persisting multiple personality was clear from the normal role this well-adjusted subject defined for her. When the 9-year-old was "back in her slot" she was *only a set of 9-year-old memories.* Because there are things to be learned from the experiences lived through, even immature ones, Louella felt that "these memories had a right to influence my opinions, but had no right to become an active decision maker." The distortion produced by hypnosis had produced the hallucination of the 9-year-old as a real person, taking over autonomously, and in that way threatening the more mature college student. In multiple personality, if the concealed part is a persisting system that goes beyond a memory, it is very different from this temporary personality created in hypnosis. In some sense, however, this created personality, even though temporary, is transitional to a multiple personality. It would be a mistake, however, to see it as a "latent" multiple personality, revealed by hypnotic age regression. It exists normally only as a set of memories; through hypnotic suggestion corresponding memories can produce a similar "personality" at any age.

PARALLEL OR INTERMITTENT INFORMATION PROCESSING?

Most puzzling, particularly in the experiments on analgesia and deafness, was the evidence that the *overt* experience, as commonly reported by the hypnotized subject, differed from the *covert* experience reported when special techniques were used. Because this is crucial evidence of a distinct dissociation between two information-processing systems, it has great theoretical importance for cognitive psychology generally. The picture that has been presented is one of parallel processing, of two experiences going on simultaneously; of one the subject is aware, of the other he is unaware. The data and the interview reports from the subjects are in sufficient agreement to permit the experiences to be classified as dissociated from each other.

At a more microscopic or analytical level, however, a second possibility exists, that there may be some alternation of the experiences. Instead of continuously experienced pain or hearing at the covert level, there may be an occasional experience of pain or hearing followed by a rapid reestablishment of the amnesia for it, giving the impression that the covert experience is continuous when the amnesia is lifted. Figure 22 illustrates the two possibilities.

The diagrams in Figure 22 represent the alternative interpretations of the analgesia and deafness experiments, using pain as an illustration. Because a succession of probes is shown, alternating between those searching the overt and covert levels, the investigation on ischemic pain (Knox, Morgan, and Hilgard, 1974) is best represented. In that study at the end of each two minutes the subject reported his overt experience in hypnotic analgesia, and then, with the hypnotist's hand on his shoulder according to the hidden observer technique, he reported his covert experience. The typical overt report was of little or no pain and the covert report of pain near to that of normally felt pain in the nonhypnotic condition.

The parallel processing interpretation (upper diagram) is that both the overt and covert experience are continuous, hence simultaneous and in parallel. They are separated by an amnesic barrier; thus the typical questioning of the subject in hypnosis, shown as Probes 1, 3, and 5, reveals only the overt experience of no pain. The hidden observer questionings, Probes 2 and 4,

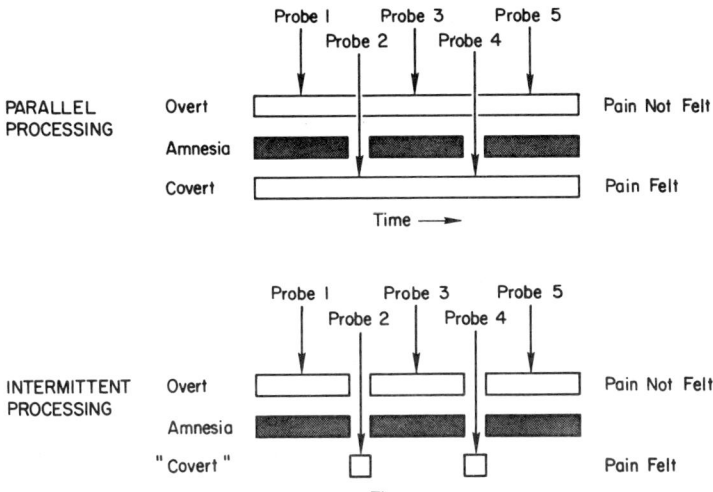

Figure 22 Two interpretations of the relationship between overt and covert pain. For explanation, see text.

temporarily break the amnesic barrier and yield replies of the pain at that moment; the pain is inferred to have been continuous.

The intermittent or serial interpretation (lower diagram) is that the pain is not actually felt at the time of the "no pain" reports to Probes 1, 3, and 5; that is, there is no covert pain. The hidden observer inquiry, Probes 2 and 4, redirects attention to the noxious stimulation that has been ignored all along, and the pain is felt and reported. According to this interpretation, overt experiences are the only ones in consciousness, and they succeed each other at intervals; what has been called "covert" is pain that occurs only intermittently at the time that it is sampled; it has not been experienced at any level in the meantime. That is why "covert" is written in quotation marks in the lower diagram. To be sure, amnesia for something previously conscious is familiar in hypnosis and readily produced in highly hypnotizable subjects.

If all the available information consisted only of pain reports at the time of the successive probes, there would be no way of choosing between these two interpretations; they would fit the facts equally well. Before turning to other evidence bearing on a choice between the interpretations, the point can be made that the classification of the two behaviors as dissociated applies to both interpretations. This is true because the amnesic component common to both convinces the subject that the two reports represent a pair of ongoing experiences.

However, the deeper nature of the dissociation will be differently interpreted depending on whether parallel or intermittent processing is accepted as characterizing the dissociated experience.

The evidence that favors the parallel processing interpretation over the intermittent one can be summarized as follows:

1. Plausibility for intermittent processing as a competing alternative comes primarily from probes that are injected while the stimulation is going on. This is true of both the automatic talking arrangement used in the ischemic pain experiment and the automatic key pressing in the ice water experiments. However, if the information is requested after the experiment has been completed, as in most pain experiments and the hearing experiments, when only the *memory* can be tapped, the information must have been stored while the analgesia or deafness persisted. The fact that the maximum pain as remembered agreed with that reported during the stimulation makes it probable that continuous information-processing was also tapped by the probes during stimulation. Hence the postexperimental inquiry through the hidden observer technique supports parallel processing.

2. Patterned series of stimuli that could not have been recovered by intermittent probing are recovered from memory by the hidden observer methods. For example, moderately painful electrical stimuli through electrodes at different positions on the forearm, at different intensities, and in different orders, can be accurately reported afterwards, even though the subject felt nothing at all while they were occurring. This is a convincing illustration of a kind of information processing requiring some degree of attention during its storage, hence of a concealed cognitive system operating in parallel to the overt anesthesia.

3. Subjective reports have never been those of "sampled" or "intermittent" experiences of stimulation, as the hidden experiences have been reviewed after all amnesia has been eliminated. By contrast, at a conscious, overt level, reports of the occasional intrusion of the pain (or tones) are not infrequent (Chapter 10). These reports show that the subject is quite capable of reporting occasional or intermittent intrusions when they occur; because these reports are not given when the covert experience is accounted for, the continuity of the concealed experience is supported. One observation that came about incidentally in the midst of one of the experiments attests further to the continuity of the covert experience. This subject remaining hypnotized had just had the tourniquet removed following the release of hypnotic analgesia in a repetition of an ischemic pain session. When asked whether the arm was comfortable, he replied that it was comfortable enough, but that there was some throbbing in the arm, gradually decreasing. With the hypnotist's hand on his shoulder for the hidden report, he described the concealed pain he had experienced in analgesia. With the hand removed and the subject amnesic for the covert experience, he reported that there had been a "step decrease" in the throbbing of his arm. While the hidden observer inquiry was going on, the overtly responding part was unaware of the throb-

bing. The hypnotist placed his hand on the shoulder again, and the subject reported that the throbbing had decreased continuously and that the previous report of a sudden change was a mistake. The hypnotist lifted his arm from the shoulder, and the subject repeated: "That's funny, there's been another step decrease in the throbbing." The interruption of the normal throbbing according to the overt report, while the hidden part was being questioned, indicates the role of amnesia in keeping the two parts separate; the important bearing on the continuity of the covert experience, however, is that the concealed part was always aware of the gradual decline in the throbbing.

These observations that support parallel processing appear to require fewer assumptions than the arguments in favor of an alternation of experiences at the overt level.

The simultaneous experiences are not completely independent, as our experiments on conflicting tasks and automatic writing have shown (Chapter 7). Holding a task subconscious does not reduce the interference between it and a conscious task; on the contrary, the interference may increase. As previously pointed out, such interferences pose empirical problems for study, but they are not decisive with respect to the concept of dissociation.

If parallel processing is accepted in this demonstration, it opens up the possibility of parallel processing in other cases of simultaneous task performances, including dichotic listening, and bears on the possibilities of subliminal perception. The possibility does not lie outside the known facts of neurophysiology:

> The organization of the brain implies parallel processing; there are many different routes for information to pass from input to output structures in the brain (Thompson, 1976, p. 224).

CONCLUDING REMARKS

The roles of central control processes, here characterized as executive and monitoring functions, recently have received increasing recognition by both experimental and social psychologists. Consciousness is accepted somewhat haltingly after the many years that it suffered under the taboos of behaviorism, and it is still somewhat more congenial to talk about information-processing and decision-making, with mathematical formulations of the transitions taking place, than to examine the internal characteristics of the central agencies that may be inferred. The changes in conceptualization are coming in many fields, including attention, memory, psycholinguistics, problem solving and creativity; they have resulted from influences derived from the wider culture and from the science of psychology itself.

These issues intrude themselves necessarily within an account of hypnotic phenomena because of the dramatic changes that take place in the hypnotic interaction, and the equally dramatic restoration of function when the interaction is terminated. The concept of dissociation is appropriate in dealing with the modifications of control in the familiar behaviors and experiences of hypnosis. The evidence brought out by the hidden observer technique yields another facet that bears upon the intellectual activity that may go on in parallel with altered cognition at the overt level.

The fractionation of the monitoring function is particularly impressive, with its three major divisions: (1) the preserved normal observing function, (2) a fraction of this normal function concealed beneath an amnesic barrier, and (3) a distorted, uncritical fraction, which as a consequence of suggestion, accepts distorted reality as though it were undistorted.

The caution against overgeneralization in Chapter 10 (p. 211) deserves repetition. The experiments on which these conclusions are based are of limited scope. The directions in which they point are clear; new findings will not destroy the facts as they have been observed, but they may assign them a more restricted place in the totality. Human psychology is too unfinished a science for any restricted demonstration to describe human consciousness in all its richness.

The parallel processing that appears to occur in these experiments contributes to the understanding of a problem baffling in other areas, such as attention and memory. Although some of these demonstrations can be made only with the help of those in the general population who are highly responsive to hypnosis, they are just as "normal" as virtuosos in other areas of skill and creative activity, and the lessons learned from them are essential to a deeper understanding of human psychology.

NOTES

Because this is an interpretive chapter much of the evidence on which the conclusions are based has already been reported in the earlier chapters and is not repeated here.

Executive and Monitoring Functions in the Nonhypnotic Condition

The executive and monitoring functions imply consciousness in that voluntary planning and decision making, as executive functions, are viewed as conscious, along with the observing and critical functions of the monitor. A growing interest in consciousness in the post behaviorist era is reflected in the titles of numerous books covering many topics other than those dealt with here. Some examples are the books of Globus, Maxwell, and Savodnik (1976), Ornstein (1972) (1973), Schwarz and Shapiro (1976), and Tart (1969) (1975).

How the Hypnotic Interaction Readies the Subject for Dissociative Experiences

Nearly everyone who wishes to account for hypnotic phenomena tries his hand at what goes on in the hypnotic induction and what characterizes the hypnotic state. For a representative account of what happens within a variety of hypnotic induction procedures, see London (1967). A psychodynamic account, based on their own observations, is given by Gill and Brenman (1959).

Alternative paradigms of the hypnotic interaction have been compared and contrasted by Sheehan and Perry (1976). There has been no attempt here to mediate the controversies, many of which lie at a conceptual level and have little direct bearing on what is perceived to occur in the hypnotic situation. In other words, there is more agreement on empirical matters than the controversial literature implies.

Modification of Central Controls in Hypnosis

The only other discussion of the last several decades that deals with the separation of superordinate control functions from actuated ones as here described is that of Gill and Brenman (1959), whose theory is embedded in psychoanalytic ego psychology. The background lies in Hartmann (1939) as interpreted by Rapaport (e.g., Rapaport, 1958). The emphasis in the present discussion is rather different, largely because of the evidence that came to light through the study of covert pain and covert hearing in hypnotic analgesia and hypnotic deafness.

Parallel or Intermittent Information Processing?

The issue of parallel versus intermittent or serial processing recurs frequently in the attention and information-processing literature. An introduction to the problems can be found in Neisser (1967).

CHAPTER 12

NEODISSOCIATION IN A WIDER CONTEXT

Whatever we have learned about dissociation has applications to the broader field of psychology, of which the investigations of hypnosis represent a specialized part. Our nervous systems are not organized to deal, like an encyclopedia, with one topic isolated from another; whatever the subsystem activated, repercussions are found throughout the brain. The neurons do not respond differently when one topic is being studied rather than another, and when one theorist assigns a label that differs from that assigned by another. If this orientation is taken for granted, and the evidences for dissociative processes accepted, then we are prepared to find signs of dissociation in experimental investigations unrelated to hypnosis and in clinical practices not guided by dissociation theory.

NONHYPNOTIC EXPERIMENTAL APPROACHES TO DISSOCIATION

Hypnosis is an unusually fruitful method by which to bring out the two kinds of dissociation, one the change of control systems that takes place in compulsions, inhibitions, and separations primarily at a performance level, the other related to the deeper dissociations whereby some parallel processing goes on outside of consciousness. The first of these kinds is exhibited in the variety of things that people do in response to hypnotic suggestions as these are usually studied; the second kind emerges in the investigations using the hidden observer technique. As repeatedly pointed out, however, the phenomena exhibited within hypnosis in dramatic and controlled form are seldom unique to it, so that, once attention is directed toward dissociations, many of them can be observed outside hypnosis. A few of those to which earlier attention has been called are reviewed briefly now that a context has been proposed for all that has been presented.

Divided Attention

The study of *divided attention* is relevant to these issues. One theoretical issue is whether when one of two channels of information is suppressed the information by way of the suppressed channel is filtered out before registration or perhaps processed but the information not perceived. At least one of the theories, that of the Deutsches, hypothesizes the very kinds of processes that our experiments on neodissociation have revealed: some information is incorporated within a cognitive system but does not reach the conscious level until special procedures are used to bring it to subsequent awareness. No theory has yet won the day; as noted earlier, Norman (1976) has given his support to a theory very like that of the Deutsches (Chapter 7). The relevant work of Blum and his associates has not yet found its way into this literature (for example, Blum and Porter, 1973).

The Recovery of Unavailable Memories

Studies that bear on *recoverable memories*, whatever the source of the amnesia, are pertinent to dissociation theory. The studies of directed forgetting are relevant also, especially if more attention is given to the recovery of the voluntarily forgotten material (Chapter 4). A possible direction of research is that in which hypnosis is used as a method for manipulating the context in which presented material is learned and remembered (Blum, 1967).

Subliminal Perception

The area of *subliminal perception* is given tangential support by the evidence for parallel processing; if something can be registered and concealed by an amnesia-like process before it becomes conscious, a nonconscious variety of perception is implied. The expression subliminal perception is misleading because the relevant events of which the subject is not consciously aware need not lie below some physiologically defined threshold. The mystery of registering the "subliminal" is removed if it is assumed that in appropriate experiments, such as those in backward masking or metacontrast, material can be presented above a threshold of *registration* but below a threshold of *conscious perception*. The subjects who heard none of the tones when hypnotically deaf were by this definition engaged in an experiment on subliminal perception. If they heard nothing at all, and could not guess beyond chance, the tones could be classified as "subliminal" for them, even if the tones were of ample intensity to register in their nervous systems, and to be subsequently recoverable as heard. There is no a priori reason why there should not be other experiences of this kind, outside of hypnosis.

Subliminal perception has been largely discredited on the basis of criticisms of the experiments yielding positive results. Dixon (1971), in a careful review, shows that subliminal perception has been a kind of "taboo topic." He attempted to rescue it from oblivion. My own excursion into the field was based on the recovery of residues from pictures perceived at short intervals in a tachistoscope, using methods of word association and drawings following the exposures. Some originally unnoticed details appeared to be recovered later (Hilgard, 1962b), and a dissertation in the Stanford laboratory gave related results (Giddan, 1967). The prior mention of backward masking and metacontrast arises from another dissertation from the laboratory (Landes, 1967), in which it was shown that masking might vary with the congruity or incongruity between the masked and masking stimulus and, therefore, operate to some extent in terms of meanings. The study had been suggested by an earlier one by Smith and Henriksson (1956). There are still possibilities to be explored in the study of subliminal perception as redefined.

State-Dependent Learning

If information acquired in one state, as under the influence of a drug, is forgotten in the nondrugged state, but recalled again in the drug state, that is an experimental illustration of a reversible amnesia. This arrangement is of course the paradigm of *state-dependent learning*. The literature has been reviewed by Overton, who is also one of the leading investigators in the field (Overton, 1972, 1973). An alternative method of studying the differential effects of the drugs has been used, especially with animal subjects. For example, a rat can be taught to turn right in a T-maze under the influence of a drug and to the left in the normal nondrugged state. According to Overton (1973) drug discrimination can be established more rapidly than most sensory discriminations, and it is doubtful that the discriminations involve the sensory consequences of the drug action. Instead, he believes that the differential responding may be based "on the dissociative barrier which impairs a transfer of training between the drug and no-drug conditions." The concept of dissociation employed by Overton is consonant with neodissociation theory; that is, two types of behavior may be isolated from each other because of differentially available information.

A number of experiments with human subjects indicate the possibilities. Several anesthetics are "dissociative" in that they permit the patient to be analgesic but conscious, and perhaps to remain amnesic for the operation after the experiment is over. Ketamine is such an anesthetic in common clinical use; patients are not unconscious, their cardiac functions and respiration are not depressed, and they can reply to the surgeon's questions. They may have some delirium, possibly as an accompaniment of the memory disorder; after the drug wears off the patient is amnesic for what has happened. Unfortunately there are few studies in which there has been any serious effort made to see if the memories are recoverable. The study of the amnesic effects of thiopental in which our laboratory participated gave somewhat tantalizing results, because there were some statistically significant results on recovery from the amnesia by hypnotic methods, but the recoveries, except in some pilot cases, were not dramatic (p. 71). There have been reports of the recall of remarks by the surgeon in ordinary general chemoanesthesia, when later tested by hypnotic methods, as mentioned earlier (p. 71). In these experiments the action of the drugs was the primary consideration; hypnosis was used merely as a method of inquiry to determine whether the amnesia produced was recoverable. It makes a difference whether the absent memories have simply not made their way into the permanent memory store or whether they are present and in some sense dissociated and unavailable to recall by ordinary methods.

Sleep and Sleeplike States

The *dissociations within sleep* provide another source of information. For example, as previously mentioned (Chapter 5) the studies on sleep-walking and sleep-talking (somniloquy) illustrate states in which considerable control may be manifested, including interactions with the geographical and social environment, yet forgotten when the person has returned to normal sleep. The dreams recalled from the night are not usually connected with these episodes.

The excitement created by electrophysiological studies of sleep and dreaming have deflected interest away from the content of the *night dream* as an illustration of involuntary activity. REM indicators and hypnosis open up many possibilities of obtaining dream samples under experimental conditions (Hilgard and Nowlis, 1972).

Excessive daytime sleepiness also has dissociative aspects. In a study of 190 patients with this complaint, 65% were diagnosed as narcoleptic and 22% as suffering from a sleep-induced apnea syndrome (inability to breath) (Guilleminault and others, 1975). One evidence of an altered state of consciousness included automatic behavior for which such a patient was amnesic. A patient may experience a temporary "blackout" in which he drives a car satisfactorily for some miles and presently finds himself registering at a hotel forgetting how he got there, or why he is there. Others do bizarre things, such as placing the dinner dishes in the clothes dryer instead of the dishwasher, or running an inappropriate program at great expense on a computer, doing all the necessary rewinding, talking appropriately to the assistants, but not remembering the episode at all. Patients with this problem are numerous within the sample studied, and when they have the problem it occurs almost daily, with a duration between a few seconds and several hours. The nature of the disturbance is being investigated experimentally in the Stanford sleep laboratory.

Pain and Distress

In the earlier discussion of *pain and distress*, the differential effects of hypnosis on the two reporting systems was noted (Chapter 9). The double system of pain afferents, described as sensory-discriminative and motivational-emotional by Melzack and Casey (1968) provides a convenient illustration of alternatives within the nervous system that might presumably be useful in the study of dissociative processes. The two components have an anatomical basis in separate pathways in the spinal cord and higher regions, with differing central connections. The integration of the systems has been explored in the gate control theory of Melzack and Wall (1965). The possibilities of dissociation can be shown in either of two ways. In one approach the stimulation of the large and small fiber systems simultaneously closes the gate and reduces felt pain. This is the interpretation given to the control of deep pain by superficial stimulation (Wall and Sweet, 1967). The other aspect holds that in the relief of intractable pain, stimulation of parts of the thalamus may reduce the distress component, while leaving the sensory component intact (Mark, Erwin, and Yakovlev, 1963). Because morphine often has comparable effects and can be shown to affect the same areas of the thalamus, it is an interesting conjecture that hypnosis in reducing covert distress while not reducing covert pain may be acting in a manner parallel to morphine.

The dissociation of the pain and suffering systems that shows in the hypnosis experiments may have a basis in the separate conduction systems. What would be a possible mechanism by which this might come about? If hypnotic analgesia were to modify the central neural activity occurring in the medial portions of the thalamus that are related to the suffering system but not to the sensory pain system, the separate effects could be explained. The implications have been discussed earlier (Chapter 9).

Pain and suffering represent a special case, illustrative of divided controls with some anatomical representation. In many other varieties of hypnotic dissociation any anatomical representation is unclear, but the pain illustration suggests that appropriate multiple paths may be found in the nervous system.

Divisions in the Nervous System

One would like to know the physiology behind dissociated states, but the physiology of consciousness is elusive in any case. The distinctive paths proposed for the two aspects of pain cannot be generalized to all experiences. One interesting lead that has come to prominence in recent years concerns the differential function of the two hemispheres, which, at least in the split-brain studies, represents a massive dissociation of two brains in one head (Chapter 5). As these studies are carried over into the study of normal laterality of function, it is quite possible that additional aspects related to dissociation will emerge. For example, as noted earlier (p. 111), it has been shown that in well-lateralized right-handed males, a preference for right hemisphere function is associated with hypnotizability. The distinction has to be made between specialization of function and preference, for those who consistently do "right-hemisphere tasks" with evidence that they are using the right hemisphere, and "left hemisphere tasks" with evidence that they are using the left hemisphere, do not by these signs indicate hypnotizability. Given both kinds of tasks, the hypnotizable right-hander tends to use his right hemisphere more frequently than the nonhypnotizable right-hander, that is, he shows a preference for using that hemisphere. This is both puzzling and challenging. There may be intermediaries to provide the explanation, such as a preference for the use of visual imagery when presented with a problem.

It is easy to carry these analogies too far, because the essence of the normal brain lies in its integration rather than in its separation into halves. Furthermore, the layering of the brain is in higher-lower dimension as well as in a right-left dimension.

An interesting speculation about the possible relevance of the higher-lower dimension was given by Zeeman (1976) in discussing anorexia nervosa in the context of catastrophe theory. Anorexia nervosa is an illness most common among adolescent girls and young women whose initial dieting has turned into extreme fasting, leading to severe malnutrition and the risk of death. Often, after about two years of self-starvation, the anorexic finds herself alternately fasting and secretly gorging food.

Zeeman represents the state of alternation between fasting and gorging as bimodal behavior, a rapid ("catastrophic") jumping between two abnormal extremes. The physiological model that he proposes is that the fasting phase represents a pathological domination of the cortex over the limbic system lower in the brain, whereas the gorging state represents the abnormal dominance of the limbic system over the cortex. The disturbed balance is here a higher-lower one, not a right-left one.

Because the limbic system is responsible for impulse behavior such as sex and aggression in addition to food-related compulsion, it is tempting to speculate that problems of the unconscious may be related to an imbalance between cortex and limbic system, whereas dissociations may be related to the right-left hemisphere distinction. This bit of analogical thinking is speculative, yet it points out that divisions of consciousness are not to be explained by hemispheric differences alone.

Sometimes commitment to a particular way of viewing psychological phenomena is instrumental in calling attention to neglected aspects. The several topics that are briefly cited show how, once one looks for dissociations, they are more prevalent than might at first be suspected.

CLINICAL SIGNIFICANCE OF DISSOCIATION

In the discussion that follows distinctions are made between an approach to therapy based primarily on dissociation and an approach based primarily on the concept of repression, as these interpretations were earlier distinguished (Figure 9, Chapter 4). The intent is only to show the relevance of these distinctions to clinical practice, not to give a general theory of therapy. Therefore, many other developments in therapy and methods of behavior change, such as therapies based on conditioning principles, biofeedback, and the developments within social learning theory, are not included in this discussion. The limited focus is based in part on the failure of the therapies based on learning theories to address themselves to any extent to the problems of consciousness. This may now be changing; the recent emphases on cognitive processes have led some of the theorists to focus attention on self-reinforcements and other aspects of self-control. When Bandura (1977) discusses the "representational guidance of behavior" he appears to bring conscious processes into social learning theory. Therapies, other than those dealing with dissociation and repression, are omitted from discussion without implying evaluative judgments about their efficacies.

Access to the Unconsciousness versus Access to a Dissociated Consciousness

The unconscious posited in psychodynamic interpretations has some features that are accessible through inference and interpretation without direct access to them. As Jung says of the deep unconscious: "It is *really* unconscious" (Evans, 1964, p. 62). The deep unconscious of Freud, although it differs from Jung's collective unconscious, also is often accessible only by way of its derivatives. According to Freud, dream interpretation—the royal road to the unconscious—is a most important way to learn about the unconscious. The manifest dream, what is remembered on awakening, is conscious; it is produced, however, by unconscious dream work. The dream's latent content can be inferred and the transformations attributed to the dream work can then be understood, as aided by free association. The communication with the unconscious, by these processes, is an indirect one. For Jung, a patient may have a mandala dream, with four people filling the four corners of a quaternary arrangement. The dream, a derivative from the deep unconscious of the archetypes, has to be interpreted; it does not picture the unconscious directly.

By contrast, in automatic writing or hypnosis, when a dissociated part of consciousness has been uncovered, the amnesic barrier is broken, and it is possible to converse *directly with the dissociated consciousness*. The same direct discourse takes place with a multiple personality, once it has emerged. This is an important difference between a psychodynamic unconscious as described previously and the dissociation interpretation of divided consciousness. Morton Prince was correct in speaking of the dissociated consciousness as a coconsciousness, for it is a genuine consciousness corresponding to the familiar one. When a multiple personality surfaces and is engaged in conversation, or a hidden observer is uncovered in the laboratory, the dissociated parts talk normally, without either the distortions of primary process thinking or archaic symbols. In fact, the reverse of the relationship between the normal consciousness and the primitive unconscious sometimes appears to be the case in both multiple personality and in hypnosis. In the clinical setting the concealed part sometimes turns out to be healthier than the openly presented part, and the hidden part in the laboratory may report reality experiences closer to the nonhypnotized person than to the experiences of the same person when hypnotized.

Access to dissociated thoughts or ideas implies that they are like normal ones except that they are not available because of the amnesic barrier. Were this the whole story, an operationally defined distinction between a deeply repressed thought and a dissociated one could rest on the possibility of reversing the amnesia in dissociation. If veridical memories not previously available became conscious, we could, accordingly, define the prior state of these memories as dissociated; if they never became directly available, but gave evidence of their presence only by inference from their derivatives, they would be assigned as repressed to the deep unconscious.

The definition of dissociation is somewhat more difficult when the alterations that indicate a split in the consciousness or personality are in the control processes, rather than in the memories. The characteristic processes in hypnosis are the alterations in sensory function, as in analgesia and deafness, or in motor functions, as in suggested paralysis of movement. The same criterion of restoration of function, employed with amnesia, is useful in showing that the alterations of sensory or motor functions have psychological or functional causation, but as an indication of dissociation the parallel is incomplete. To establish the parallel with memory and thought functions, it would be necessary to show that, at some level, the original ability is not only present, but functioning out of awareness. This has been demonstrated for the sensory functions but not as clearly for the motor ones. The parallelism would be supported if it were shown that the dissociated part of the person was voluntarily refusing to try to bend a stiff arm, or was deliberately contracting antagonistic muscles to prevent contraction, while concealing these executive acts from the conscious part in hypnosis. Although not experimentally demonstrated, the analogy appears to be sound that there may be a dissociation of controls over movement parallel to the controls over sensation. The distorted monitoring functions in hypnosis cannot report how the concealed controls have produced the changes in function. The monitoring part knows that the hypnotist said the arm was becoming stiff, he knows that as a hypnotized subject he was cooperative, and he knows that the arm became stiff; what he does not know is what went on behind the scenes.

In clinical settings it may be expected that some dissociative phenomena and some repressive phenomena will be found together and sharp distinctions between dissociative and repressive interpretations may be inappropriate. The residual differences in access to dissociations and to deeper aspects of the psychodynamic unconscious have implications both at a conceptual level and at the level of clinical practice.

Compatibility Between Dissociative and Psychodynamic Concepts

The two conceptions are compatible and can be integrated. As earlier noted (Chapter 4), there is a difference between the usual interpretation of repression and amnesia, but they also have aspects in common. A repressive concept—denial—was used earlier to help explain the setting up of the amnesic barrier between overt and covert experiences in hypnosis. Correspondingly, an interference between available memories *within* a psychoanalytic hour shows momentary forgetting to have much in common with amnesia. According to the symptom-context method, Luborsky (1970) showed that a patient while discussing a specific symptom might suddenly be overwhelmed by thoughts from a larger context. He might say "I just forgot what I was going to say. . . . Oh, yes. . . ." The momentary forgetting was then restored, in the manner according to which a superficial amnesia might be lifted. Study of these lapses in 25 cases showed that the threatening thought that intruded tended to be sexual or aggressive, or a concern over control or loss of control.

Both Freud and Jung made use of explanations that can be stated in dissociative terms, more frequently early in their careers. The distortions that Freud described in his *Psychopathology of Everyday Life* (1901) can be thought of as rather minor dissociations, not necessarily motivated by deeper unconscious impulses. Such events as forgetting the keys to the office when you prefer to stay at home, or slipping in an unintended negative that tells the truth, when you were trying to falsify to be polite, are minor dissociations of familiar experience, with the interpretations often obvious to the person who is exhibiting them. Jung's "complex indicators" found in the word association tests early used by him in detecting the thief among a group of hospital nurses provide a superficial illustration of processes out of central control. The guilty nurse tried to conceal evidence of her guilt, but the automatic processes of word association overcame her voluntary concealment, and, as in lie-detection tests, "let the cat out of the bag." A superficial suppression of this kind has some aspects in common with a superficial repression. Amnesia is absent in suppression, present in repression. The amnesia, too, can be broken by word association tests, as shown by Williamsen, Johnson, and Eriksen (1965), and noted earlier (Chapter 4).

In a descriptive sense, the concept of dissociation appears a number of times in the Gill and Brenman (1959) psychoanalytic interpretation of hypnosis. Their first mention is in the separation between voluntary and involuntary control, when the hypnotist says, "Now you will notice that, *without your doing anything about it,* your hand will move up toward your face" (p. 8). They discuss abstracted states or dissociations as common in the course of daily living among the Balinese (p. 297), who also show dissociations between words and actions (p. 309). They give a short theoretical interpretation of dissociation (p. 187–188). Regardless of the interpretation, psychoanalytically oriented investigators may recognize the appropriateness of dissociation as descriptive of much that happens in hypnosis and may feel it of sufficient importance to offer a subordinate theoretical explanation of some of its conditions.

The focus on dissociation as compatible with psychoanalysis leads to a distinction that may be made between two kinds of repressed experiences. The first kind of repression overlaps with amnesia as it is studied in hypnosis. It can be explained as repression because of the motivation for forgetting, but it can be defined as amnesia because it is a repressed *memory* that can be recovered as a veridical memory. If an actual historical incident—possibly some traumatic experience of childhood—has been forgotten, it may often be again brought to memory through free association. If a repressed memory can have the repression lifted, so that the actual remembered event is retrieved in consciousness, such a recovery corresponds to the reversal of amnesia. In principle, hypnotic procedures should also be able to revive such memories. According to the definition of dissociation as unavailable information subject to recovery, this kind of repression classifies as a dissociation. Such a classification allows the dissociation to be a consequence of repression, a position that McDougall (1938) espoused.

The second kind of repression does not classify as dissociation in the sense that dissociation is used here, and justifies retaining a distinction between repression and dissociation. In this kind of repression, the contents that are concealed have to be *inferred;* they are not recovered directly but are known only through their derivatives. This second kind of repression, if one follows psychoanalytic thinking, includes conflictual material arising in the earliest stages of development, when affect and ideation are not clearly distinguished, and when impulses are inadequately translated into verbal symbols. The repressed material may include later material deeply repressed because of its associations with trauma and guilt. Whatever the origins of the deeply repressed material, it is not directly recovered in free association, in dreams, or in the hallucinations of the troubled mind. The "return of the repressed," mentioned earlier as one manner of characterizing some schizophrenic hallucinations, is commonly manifested by highly symbolic utterances or profane and derogatory statements expressing affect rather than the return of the actual content of repressed memories. The derivatives of the unconscious, expressed in a variety of ways, are subject to understanding through interpretation, but the experience, in order to be interpretable, does not require the recovery of actual memories. This second kind of repression, in which derivatives of the unconscious are emphasized, preserves the distinction between dissociation and repression.

The Clinical Implications of the Distinctions

Because hypnotic therapies and dynamic psychotherapies can be used either separately or together, in those instances in which the hypnotic method is to be recommended the question arises, Where do its advantages lie?

To answer this question it is important to recognize that clinical problems arise in various ways, and the appropriate method of treatment is related to the conditions of origin of the symptoms. Where the initiation of symptoms has a sudden cause, as in the case of war neuroses or traumatic neuroses, the rapidity with which the cause can be discovered through hypnosis may make it a particularly efficient method of treatment. Many clinical cases present themselves with significant aspects that are not deeply repressed and have not developed into elaborate derivative symptoms based on unconscious processes, or, even though their origin is in the remote past, because of changes in the life situation they may no longer serve the purposes that initiated them in the first place. The advantage of hypnosis in such cases is the readiness with which hypnotic procedures through "uncovering techniques" can help gain access to thoughts and memories not otherwise available and can modify control processes in the ways that have been described.

An important strategy available to the hypnotherapist is the teaching of self-hypnosis to the patient. Through the use of that method the patient can learn to gain self-control and independence from the therapist. This practice counteracts the stereotype of the passive-dependent hypnotic subject; hypnosis, instead of "weakening the will," by the use of self-hypnosis enlarges areas of self-control and "strengthens the resolve" to modify behavior in desirable directions. This strategy differs from that of psychoanalytic therapists who expect the development of transference and the dependency that is inherent in it. The interpretation of transference can be a therapeutic aid, as the transference is gradually resolved. By contrast, through the early teaching of self-hypnosis, transference problems may be minimized. When a long-continued relationship is formed in hypnotherapy, the familiar problems of transference arise; that is one of the reasons for the hypnotherapist to be trained in a broader approach.

Symptom-treatment, with which hypnosis when used alone is likely to be identified, as distinct from a causal or insightful treatment, with which the psychodynamic therapies are identified, has both advantages and disadvantages. Experienced clinicians, using hypnosis in connection with symptom removal, go to great lengths to give emotional support to the patient, and they discourage single-encounter cures. Using hypnosis in an ancillary role to lessen or remove symptoms, while attending to the psychodynamic context in which the symptoms arose and in which they are maintained, appears to be a reasonable compromise (Frankel, 1976). A fear has long been expressed that if a symptom fulfills a need for the patient, and that symptom is treated, another symptom will take its place. Although grounded in a few cases, this problem has been exaggerated. The attendant gain in personal strength when the symptom is surmounted may itself have favorable therapeutic value. Symptom cure may be permanent and the appearance of substitute symptoms not prevalent, particularly when the disorder has been relatively peripheral to the total personality (Brenman and Gill, 1947).

A case that came to the attention of Josephine Hilgard is illustrative. A man presented himself for treatment at the hospital because he could no longer use his right leg properly in walking. The foot would buckle under him, and he walked uncertainly, more or less dragging the right foot. Neurological examination indicated that the difficulty was functional rather than organic. Under hypnosis he was readily regressed to the occasion when the symptom first appeared, in which he had quarreled with his boss and suppressed the desire to kick him. As he relived the situation within hypnosis, the expression of feeling and the accompanying insight were enough to restore the use of his foot. Note that in hypnosis the attention was in fact on the symptom. Because both it and the incident responsible for it were recent and the memory was not deeply repressed, the hypnotic method was successful. Further psychodynamic aspects were subsequently recovered, relating his problems with his boss to earlier problems with his father, but it was not necessary to have achieved this deeper understanding to relieve the presenting symptoms. From a psychotherapeutic standpoint it was desirable to discuss the broader context so that the patient could learn more about himself from the incident. This he did in the course of three subsequent sessions.

Why did the hypnosis succeed in bringing everything to the surface, as though the incident with the boss was only mildly repressed? The answer appears to lie in the relaxation of the monitoring function, so that, without a sense of guilt, the patient could recount the interplay with the boss and his desire to kick him. A difficulty in harmonizing the different interpretations is partly a linguistic one, because instead of talking about a relaxed monitor one might say that the defense had been weakened. If the statements are equivalent, that means only that the facts are being understood similarly. It is not necessarily the case that the removal of the symptom, to be effective in the total therapy, must await insight; the opposite order may be the case. Attention to the symptom may open the door to the insight.

> Our clinical experience has not supported the traditional view that "insight" first occurs, followed by improvement in the presenting symptoms. In both psychotherapy and hypnotherapy patients have repeatedly shown an initial improvement in their presenting symptoms; *then* they have begun to see the origin of the symptoms in the unresolved psychological conflicts (Crasilneck and Hall, 1975, p. 65).

Skilled hypnotherapists combine psychodynamic principles with hypnotic techniques, sometimes in the framework of psychoanalysis, as indicated by the term "hypnoanalysis" in this context (Fromm, 1965; Wolberg, 1967). The hypnotherapist needs training in psychodynamics if he is to achieve a general understanding of his patient and of the patient's problems in their larger context.

The conclusion that appears justified is that hypnosis at times stands on its own as a therapy, at other times provides useful adjuncts to other therapies, supplementary but not competitive. The basis for these supplements rests largely in the aspects of dissociated experiences and controls that may be neglected unless the therapist is familiar with hypnosis.

THE GOALS OF NEODISSOCIATION THEORY

As this discussion comes to a close, it is well to review the purposes for which it was undertaken and to reflect upon how well these purposes have been fulfilled.

The first goal was to call attention to the numerous instances of dissociation, clinical and experimental, that emerge when they are looked for. Many of these have nothing directly to do with hypnosis but belong to a general understanding of human consciousness and cognitive functioning. Such observations gave rise to the older dissociation theories; when the theories went out of favor the evidence was overlooked. The material in Chapters 2 to 7 brings this evidence back into view.

A second purpose was to show how laboratory studies using hypnosis provide not only dramatic instances of the variety of dissociations but a method of studying them with some precision. Experimental hypnosis is still in its infancy, so that what is presented is an invitation for further study.

A third purpose was to propose possibilities that would relate neodissociation theory to recent trends within psychology. The three basic areas that appeared most promising were (1) memory and its distortions, particularly in recoverable amnesia; (2) attention and its divisions, with the possibilities inherent in parallel processing; and (3) central control mechanisms, in which a superordinate control system was conceived as having two aspects (for the limited purposes of this model), a central monitoring function and a central executive function. The hierarchical nature of cognitive structures and their modification through superordinate control mechanisms represent problems that an advanced psychology must solve. Neuropsychological explanations should be sought, but there is a division of labor here, and those working at the level of behavior and experience need not wait for neuropsychological explanations to become firmer.

A fourth purpose is to contribute to the advance of psychology as a science. Psychological methods are now sufficiently robust that psychologists need not be afraid of their subject matter, especially when it includes hidden aspects of consciousness. The nonpsychologist will realize that experimental psychologists are broader in outlook than they once were.

NOTES

Nonhypnotic Approaches to Dissociation

The topics in this chapter represent primarily summarizations of material in earlier chapters, where the pertinent references may be found. Each topic is represented by a large experimental literature.

Subliminal perception is newly introduced, as a possible implication of parallel processing. For a discussion, in historical context, see Dixon (1971). See also Mayman (1973). Visual masking offers unexplored possibilities, circumventing a too-literal interpretation of "subliminal." Most of the studies have used nonsense figures or geometrical ones with a paucity of meaning, therefore missing important aspects of the cognitive search for meanings when stimulus material is confusing. For reviews of the conventional studies, see Kahneman (1968) and Lefton (1973). An interesting demonstration of how interfering material can be ignored when it is rich in contextual meaning has been given by Neisser and Becklen (1975). Two active games were simultaneously displayed visually, overlapping on a screen, one a hand-slapping game, the other one with three players throwing a ball to each other. When selectively attending to either game, the second interfered scarcely at all. Performance deteriorated when both games had to be monitored at once.

The discussion of anorexia nervosa in connection with levels of neural integration is based on a report by Zeeman (1976), supplemented by material in a privately published original draft of the article kindly furnished by Professor Zeeman.

Clinical Significance of Dissociation

Because the primary distinction made is that between the neodissociation interpretation and a psychodynamic one, the two points of greatest importance may be restated. First, the access to a dissociated structure (such as a multiple personality or a hidden observer) is direct, whereas access to a deep unconscious is often by inference. Second, the two approaches are compatible and supplementary, as they bear upon therapy. Hart (1927) early recognized these differences and overlaps.

Hypnosis in the context of therapies not considered here may be found in the books by Dengrove (1976), Kroger and Fezler (1976), and Wickramasekera (1976).

The Goals of Neodissociation Theory

It is hoped that the prevalence of dissociative experiences has been sufficiently attested that they should be again taken seriously in general psychology.

There have been some changes in the conceptions and terminology since the author's earlier discussions of dissociation and the neodissociation interpretation (e.g., Hilgard, 1973a, 1973b, 1976). The present version is the one that he feels he can best support today. The theory is necessarily incomplete as it stands because of the many unknowns remaining to be explored.

APPENDIX

THE MEASUREMENT OF HYPNOTIC RESPONSIVENESS

Because so much reliance is placed in the preceding chapters on hypnotic phenomena and the differences in hypnotic responsiveness from one person to another, it is useful to provide further information about detailed hypnotic practices for those who lack direct familiarity with them. This acquaintance is important not only as an introduction to methods of estimating hypnotizability, but also to give some appreciation of the manner in which a typical hypnotic induction influences the expectations of the person regarding the experience. Most scales used to assess hypnotizability begin with a standard induction procedure and continue with a number of specific suggestions which are then scored. The more of these suggestions that are "passed," the higher the score.

EXAMPLES OF STANDARD INDUCTION PROCEDURES

A practicing hypnotist can use a great variety of procedures to lead the patient or subject into a hypnotic condition. These may be quite informal, and they become greatly abbreviated once the person has become accustomed to entering hypnosis. In an initial testing situation, however, the procedures are more routinized to assure that all have been treated alike. A measurement setting is designed to obtain comparative results, not to arrange the most ideal procedure for any one individual. In what follows, two standard inductions, selected from published hypnotic susceptibility scales, serve as representatives of other methods.

An Eye-Closure-Relaxation Induction. Eye closure as an initial procedure in hypnotic induction goes back to the practice of James Braid in the early nineteenth century. Relaxation suggestions, accompanied by references to sleep, are associated with this method. The specimen induction to follow is slightly abbreviated from the standard induction of the Stanford Hypnotic Susceptibility Scale, Form B (SHSS-B, Weitzenhoffer and Hilgard, 1959). This is included to show the kind of language used, illustrating the somewhat monotonous degree of repetitiveness in such inductions. Its presentation is not intended as an instruction on how to hypnotize someone.

A small bright object (button, metal thumb tack) is placed in such a way that a seated subject must turn his eyes upward to look at it. It may be placed on the ceiling, at least six feet from the eyes of the subject.

The hypnotist begins:

Do you see the small button (tack, etc.) above and in front of you? (*If necessary, point to it.*) Good. That is what I shall call the target.

Now please seat yourself comfortably by placing a hand on each arm of the chair. You may just look straight ahead. I am about to help you to relax, and meanwhile I shall give you some instructions that will help you gradually enter a state of hypnosis. Now turn your eyes upward and look at the target. You may tilt your head a little so that you won't strain your eyes too much.

Please look steadily at the target and while staring at it keep listening to my words. You can become hypnotized if you are willing to do what I tell you to, and if you concentrate on the target and on what I say. You have already shown your willingness by coming today, and so I am assuming that your presence here means that you want to experience all that you can. You can be hypnotized only if you want to be. There would be no point in participating if you resisted being hypnotized. Just do your best to concentrate on the target, to pay close attention to my words, and let happen whatever you feel is going to take place. Just let yourself go. Pay close attention to what I tell you to think about; if your mind wanders bring your thoughts back to the target and my words, and you can easily experience more of what it is like to be hypnotized.

The relaxation in hypnosis is very much like the first stages of falling asleep, but you will not really be asleep in the ordinary sense because you will continue to hear my voice and will be able to direct your thoughts to the topics I suggest. . . . What I want from you is merely your willingness to go along and let happen whatever is about to happen. Nothing will be done to embarrass you. Most people find this a very interesting experience.

Now take it easy and just let yourself relax. Keep looking at the target as steadily as you can, thinking only of it and my words. If your eyes drift away, don't let that bother you . . . just focus again on the target. Pay attention to how the target changes, how the shadows play around it, how it is sometimes fuzzy, sometimes clear. Whatever you see is all right. Just give way to whatever comes into your mind, but keep staring at the target a little longer. After a while, however, you will have stared long enough, and your eyes will feel very tired, and you will wish strongly that they were closed. Then they will close, as if by themselves. When this happens, just let it happen.

Staring at the target so long has made your eyes very tired. Your eyes hurt and your eyelids feel very heavy. Soon you will no longer be able to keep your eyes open. You will have stood the discomfort long enough; your eyes are tired from staring, and your eyelids will feel too tired to remain open. Your eyes are becoming moist from the strain. You are becoming more drowsy and sleepy. The strain in your eyes is getting greater and greater. It would be a relief just to let your eyes close and to relax completely, to relax completely. You will soon have strained enough; the strain will be so great that you will welcome your eyes closing of themselves, of themselves.

The hypnotist watches the subject's eyes, and he discontinues suggestions of eye closure when the eyes have closed. If they have not closed after about seven minutes of suggestions similar to those above, he tells the subject that it is not necessary to strain his eyes any further, but just to close them. Once the eyes have closed, either spontaneously or following the specific instruction to close them, the induction continues a little longer. It ends by a slow count from one to 20, with interspersed suggestions of relaxation and sleep, concluding as follows:

> Eleven—twelve—thirteen—fourteen—fifteen—although deep asleep you can hear me clearly. You will always hear me clearly. You will always hear me distinctly no matter how deeply asleep you feel you are. Sixteen—seventeen—eighteen—deep asleep, fast asleep. Nothing will disturb you. You are going to experience many things I will tell you to experience. . . . Nineteen—twenty. Deep asleep! You will not wake up until I tell you to. You will wish to sleep comfortably and to have the experiences I describe to you.

The remaining suggestions, used to test hypnotic responsiveness, then follow.

A Hand Levitation Induction Without the Sleep Metaphor. The hand levitation method was introduced by Milton Erickson a number of years ago. It has the convenience of providing an indication to the hypnotist of the progress of the

hypnosis as the subject's hand approaches his face. The account presented here is a slight condensation of the induction used in the revised Stanford Profile Scales of Hypnotic Susceptibility, Form I (Weitzenhoffer and Hilgard, 1967).
The hypnotist says:

Please place your hands on your lap, well separated, palms down. I want you first of all to look at your right hand (left hand, *whichever is dominant*) and notice the various sensations that you may have in it. I would like you to keep watching your hand and to be interested in seeing what sort of experiences you may have. There are many sensations in your body that you normally do not notice because you are not paying attention to them; but when you concentrate as you are now doing, on some part of your body, such as your right (left) hand, you then become aware of many different things which were there all along. Perhaps right now, or even earlier, you became aware of the presence of your lap against your hand, and you noticed the texture of the cloth under your hand. And as you continue to pay close attention to your hand and the sensations in it, perhaps you begin to experience a sort of tingling, or perhaps feel a warmth in your hand.

Perhaps you will not have these feelings but will have others about which you do not know and I do not know. I will be interested in finding out what sort of sensations you may have in your hand and you can be interested, too, in finding out. . . . Most people sooner or later experience a feeling of lightness in their hand . . . as if it were a feather ready to float away . . . I wonder if you have this sensation . . . that your hand is getting lighter and lighter . . . more and more light . . . and perhaps you have noticed a sort of feeling of tenseness . . . very soon your hand *is* going to move . . . it is going to rise.

The pressure between your hand and your lap is decreasing . . . getting less and less. Your hand is rising, lifting, lifting up in the air. . . . That's right, it is lifting up . . . up. . . . I am going to count to twenty and this will help your hand to rise.

One . . . your hand is lifting up . . . more and more up. . . . Two . . . rising even more . . . Three . . . still higher . . . lifting, lifting, lifting. . . . While your hand rises and continues to rise you continue to go deeper and deeper into the hypnotic state . . . Four . . . Five. . . . You may wonder just where your hand is going . . . and I do not know, and you do not know exactly where it will end . . . but your hand is really moving toward your face . . . up toward your face, as if your face were a magnet attracting your hand . . . and perhaps it feels just like that . . . a force pulling your hand up toward your face . . . Six . . . You can be interested in finding out just what part of your face it will touch. . . . I am interested . . . and you too wonder where it will touch . . . Seven . . . Eight . . . still going up . . . and you keep going deeper into hypnosis, and by the time I reach twenty you will be very much hypnotized . . . deeply hypnotized . . . Nine . . . Ten . . . You're half way there. . . . By the time I reach twenty you will be deeply hypnotized . . . perhaps your hand will have reached your face by then, and perhaps not. . . . It really is not important, but it would be interesting to know whether your hand will touch your face when I reach twenty . . . Eleven . . . Twelve. . . .

Your eyes are very heavy and closing . . . closing . . . getting so heavy. . . . Your eyes will most likely be closed by the time your hand reaches your face . . . Thirteen . . . deeper . . . and your hand is getting closer to your face . . . Fourteen . . . closer and closer. . . . When your hand touches your face you will be deeply hypnotized . . . Sixteen . . . Seventeen . . . deeper and deeper. . . . I wonder just what part of your face your hand will touch. . . . Perhaps the chin . . . or the forehead . . . or the cheek. . . . You do not know and I do not know, but we can wait and find out. . . . It will be interesting to see if your hand will reach your face when I get to twenty . . . Eighteen . . . closer and closer . . . Nineteen . . . Twenty . . . and now you are deeply hypnotized.

And now your hand can come slowly back to your lap.

You will remain deeply hypnotized until I tell you otherwise. You will be able to speak, open your eyes, and move while remaining deeply hypnotized, if I should ask you to do this. Whatever you do or experience, you will remain hypnotized.

By contrast with the previous eye-closure induction, nothing whatever has been said about sleep; the nearest to it is the suggestion that the eyes are heavy and closing. For the rest, all references are to becoming hypnotized, allowing the condition to be defined by the experience of the subject.

SUGGESTIONS DESIGNED TO TEST HYPNOTIC RESPONSIVENESS

The simpler suggestibility or susceptibility scales depend heavily on motor items, that is, movements that are made either as a consequence of direct suggestions that they will occur, such as the hands moving together or apart, or that they cannot be produced voluntarily when the subject is asked to try, as when he is asked to raise an immobilized arm or to bend an arm stiffened by suggestion. The other suggestions classify primarily as cognitive ones. They include distortions of memory, as in posthypnotic amnesia; distortions of perception, as in positive and negative hallucinations; and calling for imaginative productions, as in dreams and reliving past experiences in age regression. The various Stanford Scales can serve as illustrations, because they overlap with other existing scales, and, in the Profile Scales, cover a wider range than most of the other standardized scales.* The original Stanford Hypnotic Susceptibility Scales, Forms A and B, are alternate forms of essen-

---

*Modern scales have derived primarily from Friedlander and Sarbin (1938). Two others, in addition to the Stanford ones, are closely related to these: London (1962) and Shor and Orne (1962). A suggestibility scale designed primarily for use without a prior induction is that of Barber (1969), although all of the scales, with very slight modification, can be used with or without an induction. A comparison of Barber's scale with the Stanford Form A can be found in Ruch, Morgan, and Hilgard (1974). Spiegel (1974) has produced a scale of somewhat different kind, designed to serve purposes of psychodiagnostics along with measuring hypnotic responsiveness.

tially the same items, ordinarily substituting the right hand for the left hand in the two forms (Weitzenhoffer and Hilgard, 1959). The Harvard Group Scale of Hypnotic Susceptibility is an adaptation of the Stanford Form A for group administration; the items are similar, although not identical (Shor and Orne, 1962). Motor items are heavily represented in both of these scales. The later Form C of the Stanford Scales was similarly constructed and repeated some of the same items, but gave more emphasis to cognitive items (Weitzenhoffer and Hilgard, 1962). The item lists from Form A and Form C are given in Table 12. A further difference between the scales lies in the arrangement by item difficulty. In Form A the order by difficulty is essentially random, whereas in Form C the difficulty increases throughout the scale. This permits an earlier termination of the testing for those subjects who are unable to succeed with the easier early items. Both scales are internally consistent, in the sense that each item correlates with the total scale minus that item. In the Form A standardization sample of 124 students, these correlations varied from a low of .38 for postural sway (tested by waking suggestion) to .83 for arm rigidity, the average correlation being .65. The comparable results for Form C with a standardization sample numbering 203 was a correlation between the individual item and the whole minus that item from a low of .49 for moving hands apart to a high of .87 for the negative visual hallucination, with an average of .71. These are unusually high correlations for single items with total test scores and indicate, in factorial language, a very high common factor running through the tests. This also means that, for practical purposes, if one is simply interested in a classification of subjects into high and low groups, one or two items will suffice.

There is a common general factor in hypnotizability, but it does not follow that because there is a common general factor special abilities have no place. For example, the items in Form C that correspond to those in Form A, when summed, were found to correlate .72 with total Form A scores obtained in another testing, whereas the new cognitive items of Form C correlated somewhat lower, as expected; there was a correlation with Form A scores of .62.

The Stanford Profile Scales of Hypnotic Susceptibility, Forms I and II, were designed to cover a wider range of hypnotic abilities, both as a means of exploring the distribution of these abilities in a large population and as a practical means for selecting subjects for further experimentation on the basis of their special abilities. After preliminary explorations, the items were ultimately gathered into six subscales, described briefly in Table 13. The subscales were validated by intercorrelating all the item scores, factor analyzing, and rotating to a hypothetical model that permitted an oblique relationship between factors. The details need not concern us here; an exposition can be found in Hilgard (1965, p. 264–270), with some revised data in Weitzenhoffer and Hilgard (1967).

Table 12
ITEMS IN STANFORD HYPNOTIC SUSCEPTIBILITY SCALES, FORMS A AND C

Form A		Form C	
Item name	Nature of suggestion	Item name	Nature of suggestion
1. Postural sway	Waking suggestion of falling backwards	1. Hand lowering[a]	Cf. Form A, Item 3
2. Eye closure	Eye closure induction	2. Moving hands apart[a]	Cf. Form A, Item 7
3. Hand lowering	Suggested heaviness of outstretched arm, forcing it down	3. Mosquito hallucination[a]	Cf. Form A, Item 9
4. Arm immobilization	Arm too heavy to lift voluntarily	4. Taste hallucination	Hallucination of sweet taste followed by sour
5. Finger lock	Unable to open interlocked fingers	5. Arm rigidity[a]	Cf. Form A, Item 6
6. Arm rigidity	Unable to bend arm stiffened by suggestion	6. Dream	Dream within hypnosis about hypnosis
7. Moving hands together	Suggested attraction of outstretched hands and arms	7. Age regression	Regression to fifth grade and second grade, with specimens of handwriting at each age
8. Verbal inhibition	Unable to speak own name	8. Arm immobilization[a]	Cf. Form A, Item 4
9. Fly hallucination	Annoying fly to be shooed away	9. Anosmia to ammonia	Inability to smell household ammonia
10. Eye catalepsy	Unable to open closed eyes	10. Hallucinated voice	Answers questions raised by hallucinated voice
11. Posthypnotic suggestion	Moving from one chair to another at posthypnotic signal	11. Negative visual hallucination	Sees only 2 of 3 small colored boxes
12. Posthypnotic amnesia	Inability to recall previously suggested items until release signal is given	12. Posthypnotic amnesia[a]	Cf. Form A, Item 12

[a]Note that the six marked items are equivalent to items in Form A. The new items of Form C are all of cognitive form.

Table 13

TEST ITEM CONTENT OF THE STANFORD PROFILE SCALES
OF HYPNOTIC SUSCEPTIBILITY,
FORMS I AND II

Adopted name and initials of subscale	Functions intended to be tested	Item content of tests in subscale
AG: Agnosia and cognitive distortion	Distortion of meaning and value, rather than of sense perception	I:7 Agnosia I: house I:8 Arithmetic impairment II:7 Agnosia II: scissors II:8 Personality alteration (reduced intelligence)
HP: Hallucinations: positive	The experiencing of sensory and perceptual phenomena in the absense of appropriate stimuli	I:2 Music hallucination I:5 Hallucinated light II:1 Heat hallucination II:3 Hallucinated ammonia
HN: Hallucinations: negative	Lack of awareness of stimulation that would normally be perceived	I:1 Hand analgesia to shock I:3 Anosmia to ammonia II:2 Selective deafness II:5 Missing watch hand (visual)
DR: Dreams and regressions	Memory revival and fantasy production, including fantasied "reliving" of events in the past	I:4 Recall of meal I:6 Dream I: general II:4 Regression to birthday II:6 Dream II: about hypnosis
AM: Amnesia and posthypnotic compulsions	Behavior suggested during hypnosis but carried out after arousal from hypnosis, usually with forgetting of the instructions	Amnesia: rescored from Form A I:9 Posthypnotic verbal compulsion II:9 Posthypnotic automatic writing
MC: Loss of motor control	Motor responses carried out automatically as a result of direct suggestion; loss of volitional control over movement as a result of suggestion	Motor pool (a) from Form A: 1. Postural sway 2. Eye closure 4. Arm immobilization 5. Finger lock Motor pool (b) from Form A: 6. Arm rigidity 7. Hands moving together 8. Verbal inhibition 10. Eye catalepsy

It was of interest to find how consistent individuals would be over all the subscales and the extent to which they might show predominant abilities in one or another of these subscales. If a nondeviating profile is defined as one in which no single subscale score departs as much as one standard deviation from the mean of the other scores, 38% of the standardization sample showed profiles of this kind, in which the same general level of hypnotizability was reflected in all the scales, whether that level was low, medium, or high. For the rest of the subjects, one or more scales deviated as much as one standard deviation from the mean of the remaining scales; thus in some cases a subject would be well below average on all subscales except one, and that might be almost any of the scales, such as hallucination, motor control items, or amnesia. Correspondingly, the subject might be well above average on all others but be unable to respond to one subscale, such as dreams and regressions. These facts are to be noted as allowing the possibility of unique configurations of cognitive controls within hypnosis, in addition to whatever it is that produces the strong common ability.

STABILITY OF MEASURED HYPNOTIC RESPONSIVENESS

The general stability of measured hypnotic responsiveness is shown by the high reliabilities in retesting, commonly in the .80s and .90s over a period of weeks. Students who had been tested with Form A while undergraduates were retested in their home communities ten years later, when their lives had changed very greatly. The resulting correlation was .60, showing a substantial persistence of measured hypnotizability over time (Morgan, Johnson, and Hilgard, 1974). The possibility of some inherited biological basis for the hypnotic talent cannot be ruled out. A study of twins and their families showed a higher correlation between monozygotic twins (identical twins) than between like-sexed dizygotic twins (fraternal twins) and a low correlation with parental hypnotizability. As in other twin studies with human subjects, the genetic implications are confounded by the environmental influences on twins who look alike, as monozygotic twins do, but the possibility of some inborn differences, perhaps in the capacity for imagination, cannot be denied (Morgan, 1973). The studies of hemispheric laterality also suggest a possible biological underpinning, but laterality preferences, like handedness, may be subject to environmental influences.

These results do not mean that hypnotizability is immutable. Most studies show slight gains with various kinds of training and modeling procedures (Diamond, 1974), but the final scores usually correlate with the initial ones; thus the gains capitalize on what was there at the time of initial testing. There is little evidence that a fully cooperative subject who is unable to respond to hypnosis to begin with can become a highly hypnotizable person by any of the training methods now available. The studies continue, and it is to be hoped that methods may be found for providing greater success in the improvement of hypnotizability beyond the successes reported thus far and in that way making the benefits of hypnosis available to more people.

Many of those who use hypnosis in clinical practice believe that the relationship of a patient to the physician, and the motivation for help can yield a higher proportion of people who are hypnotizable than is usually found in laboratory studies. Hypnotherapists commonly assert that the capacity for hypnosis improves with training and practice, so that a substantial proportion of patients can be deeply hypnotized. Such claims have not been well supported by firm evidence, but the observations deserve consideration. Careful studies are urgently needed.

REFERENCES
AND INDEX
TO AUTHORS
OF WORKS CITED

The numbers in boldface following each reference give the pages on which the paper or book is cited. Citations in the chapters and notes are made by author and date of publication.

Aas, A. (1963) Hypnotizability as a function of nonhypnotic experiences. *Journal of Abnormal and Social Psychology, 66,* 142–150. **106**

Aas, A., Hilgard, E. R., and Weitzenhoffer, A. M. (1963) An attempt at experimental modification of hypnotizability through repeated individualized hypnotic experience. *Scandinavian Journal of Psychology, 4,* 81–89. **48**

Agnew, H. W., Jr., *see* Williams, Agnew, and Webb (1964).

Albert, D. J., *see* Mah and Albert (1973); Mah and Albert (1975).

Allison, R. B. (1974) A guide to parents: How to raise your daughter to have multiple personalities. *Family Therapy, 1,* 83–88. **41**

Allison, R. B. (1975) A new treatment approach for multiple personalities. *American Journal of Clinical Hypnosis, 17,* 15–32. **41**

Allport, G. W. (1937) *Personality: A psychological interpretation.* New York: Holt. **223**

Andersen, M. L., *see* Sarbin and Andersen (1963).

Anderson, J. R., and Bower, G. H. (1973) *Human associative memory.* Washington, D. C.: V. H. Winston.

Anderson, K., *see* Von Wright, Anderson, and Stenman (1975).

Appignanesi, A., *see* Perry, Wilder, and Appignanesi (1973).

Arkin, A. M., Hastey, J. M., and Reiser, M. F. (1966) Post-hypnotically stimulated sleep-talking. *Journal of Nervous and Mental Disease, 142,* 293–309. **94, 96**

Arkin, A. M., Toth, M. F., Baker, J., and Hastey, J. M. (1970) The frequency of sleep talking in the laboratory among chronic sleep talkers and good dream recallers. *Journal of Nervous and Mental Disease, 151,* 369–374. **95**

Aserinsky, E., and Kleitman, N. (1953) Regularly occurring periods of eye motility, and concom-

267

itant phenomena, during sleep. *Science, 118,* 273–274. **91**

Atkinson, G., *see* Tellegen and Atkinson (1974).

Atkinson, R. C., and Shiffrin, R. M. (1971) The control of short-term memory. *Scientific American, 224,* 82–90. **86, 220**

Attard, L., and Holden, W. J. (1976) Hypnotic susceptibility and the reproduction of earlier patterns of cognitive development: A study of individual differences. Paper presented at 11th annual conference, Australian Psychological Society, August 22–27. **61**

Azam, E. E. (1887) *Hypnotisme, double conscience et altération de la personnalité.* Préface de J. M. Charcot. Paris: Baillière. **27**

Bacon, J., *see* Roberts, Schuler, Bacon, Zimmerman, and Patterson (1975).

Baddeley, A. D. (1975) Theories of amnesia. In A. Kennedy and A. Wilkes (Eds.). *Studies in long term memory.* New York: Wiley. **84**

Baddeley, A. D. (1976) *The psychology of memory.* New York: Basic Books. **83**

Bain, A. (1859) *The emotions and the will.* New York: D. Appleton. **129**

Bakan, P. (1969) Hypnotizability, laterality of eye movements, and functional brain asymmetry. *Perceptual and Motor Skills, 28,* 927–932. **110, 111**

Baker, J., *see* Arkin, Toth, Baker and Hastey (1970).

Bandura, A. (1977) *Social learning theory.* Englewood Cliffs, N.J.: Prentice-Hall. **248**

Banyai, E. I., and Hilgard, E. R. (1976) A comparison of active-alert hypnotic induction with traditional relaxation induction. *Journal of Abnormal Psychology, 85,* 218–224. **127, 166**

Barber, T. X. (1961) Antisocial and criminal acts induced by hypnosis: A review of experimental and clinical findings. *Archives of General Psychiatry, 5,* 301–312. **129**

Barber, T. X. (1969) *Hypnosis: A scientific approach.* New York: Van Nostrand Reinhold. **41, 58, 183, 261**

Barber, T. X. (1972) Suggested ("hypnotic") behavior: The trance paradigm versus an alternative paradigm. In E. Fromm and R. E. Shor (Eds.) *Hypnosis: Research developments and perspectives.* Chicago: Aldine-Atherton, 115–182. **59**

Barber, T. X., and Calverley, D. S. (1966) Effects on recall of hypnotic induction, motivational suggestions, and suggested regression: A methodological and experimental analysis. *Journal of Abnormal Psychology, 71,* 169–180. **60**

Barber, T. X., and Hahn, K. W., Jr. (1962) Physiological and subjective responses to pain-producing stimulation under hypnotically suggested and waking-imagined "analgesia." *Journal of Abnormal and Social Psychology, 65,* 222–228. **202**

Barber, T. X., and others (Eds.) (1971) *Biofeedback and self-control, 1970; An Aldine Annual.* Chicago: Aldine-Atherton. **129**

Barber, T. X., *see also* Johnson, Maher, and Barber (1972).

Barron, F., *see* Walsh and Barron (1963).

Barry, H., Jr., MacKinnon, D. W., and Murray, H. A., Jr. (1931) Studies in personality: A. Hypnotizability as a personality trait and its typological relations. *Human Biology, 3,* 1–36. **9, 153**

Beck, L. F. (1936) Hypnotic identification of an amnesia victim. *British Journal of Medical Psychology, 16,* 36–42. **68**

Becklen, R., *see* Neisser and Becklen (1975).

Bem, D. J. (1972) Self-perception theory. *Advances in experimental social psychology.* New York: Academic Press, *6,* 1–62. **3**

Bendfeldt, *see* Ludwig, Brandsma, Wilbur, Bendfeldt, and Jameson (1972).

Bennett, D. R., *see* Greene and Bennett (1974).

Benson, D. F., *see* Gilbert and Benson (1972).

Berk, A. M., *see* Miller, Ott, Berk, and Springer (1974).

Bernheim, H. (1888) *Hypnosis and suggestion in psychotherapy* (Reissued with an introduction by

E. R. Hilgard). New Hyde Park, N.Y.: University Books, 1963. **12, 163**

Bernstein, M. (1956) *The search for Bridey Murphy.* New York: Doubleday. **49**

Berreman, J. V., and Hilgard, E. R. (1936) The effects of personal heterosuggestion and two forms of autosuggestion upon postural movement. *Journal of Social Psychology, 7,* 289–300. **x**

Betts, G. H. (1909) The distribution and functions of mental imagery. *Teachers College Contributions to Education,* No. 26. **101**

Billiard, M., *see* Guilleminault and others (1975).

Binet, A. (1889–1890) *On double consciousness.* (Reprinted as new edition, 1896). Chicago: Open Court Publishing Co. **4, 12**

Bini, L., *see* Cerletti and Bini (1938).

Bjork, R. A. (1970) Positive forgetting: The noninterference of items intentionally forgotten. *Journal of Verbal Learning and Verbal Behavior, 9,* 255–268. **65**

Blum, G. S. (1961) *A model of the mind.* New York: Wiley. **154**

Blum, G. S. (1967) Experimental observations on the contextual nature of hypnosis. *International Journal of Clinical and Experimental Hypnosis, 15,* 160–171. **243**

Blum, G. S., Geiwitz, P. J., and Stewart, C. G. (1967) Cognitive arousal: The evolution of a model. *Journal of Personality and Social Psychology, 5,* 138–151. **154, 219**

Blum, G. S., and Porter, M. L. (1972) The capacity for rapid shifts in level of mental concentration. *Quarterly Journal of Experimental Psychology, 24,* 431–438. **148**

Blum, G. S., and Porter, M. L. (1973) The capacity for selective concentration on color versus form of consonants. *Cognitive Psychology, 5,* 47–70. **148, 151, 152, 154, 243**

Bogen, J. E., *see* Gazzaniga, Bogen, and Sperry (1962).

Bourguignon, E. (1968) World distribution and patterns of possession states. In R. Prince (Ed.) *Trance and possession states.* Montreal: R. M. Bucke Memorial Society. **20, 21**

Bower, G. H. (1972) Mental imagery and associative learning. In L. W. Gregg (Ed.) *Cognition in learning and memory.* New York: Wiley. **66**

Bower, G. H. (1975) Cognitive psychology: An introduction. In W. K. Estes (Ed.) *Handbook of learning and cognitive processes.* Vol. 1. Hillsdale, N.J.: Lawrence Erlbaum. **80, 86, 220**

Bower, G. H., Clark, M. C., Winzenz, D., and Lesgold, A. (1969) Hierarchical retrieval schemes in recall of categorized word tests. *Journal of Verbal Learning and Verbal Behavior, 8,* 323–343. **67**

Bower, G. H., *see also* Anderson and Bower (1973); Hilgard and Bower (1975).

Bowers, K. S. (1967) The effect of demands for honesty upon reports of visual and auditory hallucinations. *International Journal of Clinical and Experimental Hypnosis, 15,* 31–36. **202**

Bowers, K. S. (1971) Sex and susceptibility as moderator variables in the relationship of creativity and hypnotic susceptibility. *Journal of Abnormal Psychology, 78,* 93–100. **108, 109**

Bowers, K. S. (1976) *Hypnosis for the seriously curious.* Monterey, Calif.: Brooks/Cole Publishing Co. **183**

Bowers, K. S., and Bowers, P. G. (1972) Hypnosis and creativity: A theoretical and empirical rapprochement. In E. Fromm and R. E. Shor (Eds.) *Hypnosis: Research developments and perspectives.* Chicago: Aldine-Atherton. **107, 114**

Bowers, K. S., and Brenneman, H. A. (1976) Listen here! Posthypnotic responsiveness to attended and unattended auditory information. Paper presented at Annual Meeting of the Society for Clinical and Experimental Hypnosis, Philadelphia, June 30. **150**

Bowers, K. S., and van der Meulen, S. J. (1970) Effect of hypnotic susceptibility on creativity test performance. *Journal of Personality and Social Psychology, 14,* 247–256. **108**

Bowers, M. K., and Brecher, S. (1955) The emergence of multiple personalities in the course of hypnotic investigation. *Journal of Clinical and Experimental Hypnosis, 3,* 188–199. **42**

Bowers, M. K., Brecher-Marer, S., Newton, B. W., Piotrowski, Z., Spyer, T. C., Taylor, W. S., and Watkins, J. G. (1971) Therapy of multiple personality. *International Journal of Clinical and Experimental Hypnosis, 19,* 57–65. **42**

Bowers, P. G. (1967) Effect of hypnosis and suggestions of reduced defensiveness on creativity test performance. *Journal of Personality, 35,* 311–322. **108**
Bowers, P. G., *see also* Bowers and Bowers (1972).
Bowersbuch, M. K., *see* Gidro-Frank and Bowersbuch (1948).
Brandsma, J. M., and Ludwig, A. M. (1974) A case of multiple personality: Diagnosis and therapy. *International Journal of Clinical and Experimental Hypnosis, 22,* 216–233. **32**
Brandsma, J. M., *see also* Ludwig, Brandsma, Wilbur, Bendfeldt, and Jameson (1972).
Brecher, S., *see* Bowers and Brecher (1955).
Brecher-Marer, S., *see* Bowers, Brecher-Marer, Newton, Piotrowski, Spyer, Taylor, and Watkins (1971).
Brenman, M., and Gill, M. M. (1947) *Hypnotherapy: A survey of the literature.* New York: International Universities Press. **253**
Brenman, M., *see also* Gill and Brenman (1959).
Brenneman, H. A., *see* Bowers and Brenneman (1976).
Breuer, J., and Freud, S. (1895) *Studies in hysteria.* In *Standard Edition,* Vol. 2. London: Hogarth Press, 1955. **80**
Broadbent, D. E. (1958) *Perception and communication.* London: Pergamon Press. **148, 153**
Bromfield, E., *see* Schwartz, Davidson, Maer, and Bromfield (1973).
Brown, R. W., and McNeill, D. The "tip-of-the-tongue" phenomenon. *Journal of Verbal Learning and Verbal Behavior, 5,* 325–337. **79**
Bruce, D., and Papay, J. J. (1970) Primacy effect in single-trial free recall. *Journal of Verbal Learning and Verbal Behavior, 9,* 473–486. **65**
Bunker, J. P., *see* Osborn, Bunker, Cooper, Frank, and Hilgard (1967).
Burnett, C. T. (1925) Splitting the mind. *Psychological Monographs, 34,* No. 2. **8, 153**
Bykov, K. M. (1957) *The cerebral cortex and the internal organs.* (Translated by W. H. Gantt.) New York: Chemical Publishing. **124**
Calverley, D. S., *see* Barber and Calverley (1966).
Casey, K. L., *see* Melzack and Casey (1968).
Cass, W. A. (1942) An experimental investigation of the dissociation hypothesis, utilizing a post-hypnotic technique. Unpublished master's thesis, University of Oregon. **140**
Cerletti, U., and Bini, L. (1938) L'Electroshock. *Archivio generali di Neurologia e Psiciatrica e Psicoanalisi, 19,* 266. **72**
Cheek, D. B. (1959) Unconscious perception of meaningful sounds during surgical anesthesia as revealed in hypnosis. *American Journal of Clinical Hypnosis, 1,* 101–113. **85**
Cheek, D. B. (1964) Surgical memory and careless conversation. *American Journal of Clinical Hypnosis, 6,* 237–240. **85**
Cheek, D. B. (1966) The meaning of continued hearing sense under general chemoanesthesia: A progress report and report of a case. *American Journal of Clinical Hypnosis, 8,* 275–280. **85**
Cheek, D. B., and Le Cron, L. M. (1968) *Clinical hypnotherapy.* New York: Grune and Stratton. **137, 201**
Cherry, E. C. (1953) Some experiments on the recognition of speech, with one and two ears. *Journal of the Acoustical Society of America, 25,* 975–979. **154**
Cherry, E. C., and Taylor, W. K. (1954) Some further experiments upon the recognition of speech with one and two ears. *Journal of the Acoustical Society of America, 26,* 554–559. **154**
Chertok, L., Michaux, D., and Droin, M. C. (1977) Dynamics of hypnotic analgesia: Some new data. *Journal of Nervous and Mental Disease, 164,* 88–96. **85**
Chevreul, M. (1933) Lettre à M.Ampère sur une classe particulière de mouvements musculaires. *Revue des Deux Mondes,* 2nd series, *2,* 258–266. **153**
Chevreul, M. (1854) *De la Baguette divinatoire, du pendule dit explorateur et des tables tournantes, au point de vue de l'histoire, de la critique et de la méthode expérimentale.* Paris: Mallet-Bachelier. **153**

Chisholm, W., *see* Perry and Chisholm (1973).
Chong, T. M. (1975) *The truth about hypnosis.* Singapore: Choong's Clinic. **19, 40**
Christopher, M. (1975) *Mediums, mystics, and the occult.* New York: Crowell, **133, 153**
Churchill, B. A., *see* Spanos, McPeake, and Churchill (1976).
Clark, M. C., *see* Bower, Clark, Winzenz, and Lesgold (1969).
Cleckley, H., *see* Thigpen and Cleckley (1957).
Clemes, S. R. (1964) Repression and hypnotic amnesia. *Journal of Abnormal and Social Psychology, 69,* 62–69. **82**
Clyde, D. J. (1947) Hypnotherapy and phobias. Unpublished master's thesis, Pennsylvania State College. **59**
Coe, W. C. (1977) The problem of relevance versus ethics in researching hypnosis and antisocial conduct. *Annals of the New York Academy of Sciences, 296,* 90–104. **129**
Coe, W. C., *see also* Sarbin and Coe (1972).
Cooper, L. M. (1966) Spontaneous and suggested source amnesia. *International Journal of Clinical and Experimental Hypnosis, 14,* 180–193. **74**
Cooper, L. M. (1972) Hypnotic amnesia. In E. Fromm and R. E. Shor (Eds.) *Hypnosis: Research developments and perspectives.* Chicago: Aldine-Atherton. **75, 85**
Cooper, L. M., and Moore R. K. (1967) Individual recall of serially presented motor tasks. Group presentations. Unpublished manuscript, Brigham Young University. **75**
Cooper, L. M., *see also* Hilgard and Cooper (1965); Osborn, Bunker, Cooper, Frank, and Hilgard (1967).
Corkin, S., *see* Milner, Corkin, and Teuber (1968).
Corteen R. S., and Wood, B. (1972) Autonomic responses to shock-associated words in an unattended channel. *Journal of Experimental Psychology, 94,* 308–313. **148, 154**
Cory, C. E. (1920) A divided self. *Journal of Abnormal Psychology, 14,* 281–291. **26**
Crasilneck, H. B., and Hall, J. A. (1975) *Clinical hypnosis: Principles and applications.* New York: Grune and Stratton. **40, 254**
Crawford, H. J., Macdonald, H., and Hilgard, E. R. (1979) Hypnotic deafness: A psychophysical study of responses to tone intensity as modified by hypnosis. *American Journal of Psychology, 92,* 193–214.
Crookes, W. (1874) *Researches in the phenomena of spiritualism.* London: Burn and Oates. **132**
Crutchfield, L., *see* Knox, Crutchfield, and Hilgard (1975).
Cutler, B., and Reed, J. (1975) Multiple personality. A single case study with a 15 year follow-up. *Psychological Medicine, 5,* 18–26. **41**
Dashiell, J. F. (1928) *Fundamentals of objective psychology.* Boston: Houghton Mifflin. **66**
Davidson, R. J., *see* Schwartz, Davidson, Maer, and Bromfield (1973).
Day, M. E. (1964) An eye movement phenomenon relating to attention, thought, and anxiety. *Perceptual and Motor Skills, 19,* 443–446. **110**
Deikman, A. J. (1971) Bimodal consciousness. *Archives of General Psychiatry, 25,* 481–489. **13, 15**
Dement, W. C. (1967) Discussion. In S. S. Kety, E. V. Evarts, and H. L. Williams (Eds.) *Sleep and altered states of consciousness.* Baltimore, Md.: Williams and Wilkins. **92**
Dement, W. C. (1972) *Some must watch while some must sleep.* Stanford, Calif.: Stanford Alumni Association. **91, 111**
Dement, W. C., and Kleitman, N. (1957) The relation of eye movements during sleep to dream activity: An objective method for the study of dreaming. *Journal of Experimental Psychology, 53,* 339–346. **91**
Dement, W. C., and Wolpert, E. (1958) The relation of eye movements, bodily motility, and external stimuli to dream content. *Journal of Experimental Psychology, 53,* 543–553. **91**
Dement, W. C., *see also* Guilleminault and others (1975).
Dengrove, E. (Ed.) (1976) *Hypnosis and behavior therapy.* Springfield, Ill.: Thomas. **256**
De Rochas, A. (1911) *Les vies successives. Documents pour l'etude de cette question.* Paris: Charconac. **48**

Dessoir, M. (1890) *Das Doppel-Ich* (2nd enlarged ed., 1896). Leipzig: Ernst Günthers Verlag. **4**
Deutsch, D., *see* Deutsch and Deutsch (1963).
Deutsch, J. A. (1973) *The physiological basis of memory.* New York: Academic Press. **85**
Deutsch, J. A., and Deutsch, D. (1963) Attention: Some theoretical considerations. *Psychological Review, 70,* 80–90. **148**
De Vietti, T. L., and Hopfer, T. M. (1974) Complete amnesia induced by ECS and complete recovery following reinstatement treatment. *Physiology and Behavior, 12,* 599–602. **73**
Diamond, M. J. (1974) The modification of hypnotizability: A review. *Psychological Bulletin, 81,* 180–198. **265**
Diamond, M. J., and Taft, R. (1975) The role played by ego permissiveness and imagery in hypnotic responsivity. *International Journal of Clinical and Experimental Hypnosis, 23,* 130–138. **113**
Di Cara, L. V., and Miller, N. E. (1968) Instrumental learning of vasomotor responses by rats: Learning to respond differentially in the two ears. *Science, 159,* 1485–1486. **125**
Diamond, S. J., and Beaumont, J. G. (Eds.) (1974) *Hemisphere function in the human brain.* New York: Halsted Press. **114**
Dixon, N. F. (1971) *Subliminal perception: The nature of a controversy.* London: McGraw-Hill. **244, 256**
Dorcus, R. M. (1960) Recall under hypnosis of amnestic events. *International Journal of Clinical and Experimental Hypnosis, 7,* 57–61. **45**
Droin, M. C., *see* Chertok, Michaux, and Droin (1977).
Dubovsky, S., *see* Trustman, Dubovsky, and Titley (1977).
Dumas, R. (1976) Operant control of EEG alpha and hypnotizability. Unpublished Ph.D. dissertation. Stanford University. **126**
Duncan, C. P. (1949) The retroactive effect of electroshock on learning. *Journal of Comparative and Physiological Psychology, 42,* 32–44. **72**
Duncan, N., and Hunt, E. (1972) Reduction of ECS-produced retrograde amnesia by post-trial induction of strychnine. *Physiology and Behavior, 9,* 295–300. **73**
Durand de Gros, J. P. (1868) *Polyzoïsme ou pluralité animale chez l'homme.* Paris: Imprimerie Hennuyer. **198**
Earle, B. V., and Theye, F. W. (1968) Automatic writing as a psychiatric problem. *Psychiatric Quarterly, Supplement, 42,* 218–222. **153**
Ebbinghaus, H. (1885) *Memory.* (English translation, New York: Teachers College, 1913; paper edition, New York: Dover, 1964). **63**
Editorial (1974) Anguish unremembered? *Lancet 1 (864),* 968–969. (18 May). **71**
Ellenberger, H. F. (1970) *The discovery of the unconscious.* New York: Basic Books. **14, 15, 25, 40, 41, 44, 152**
Epstein, W. (1972) Mechanisms of directed forgetting. In G. H. Bower (Ed.) *The psychology of learning and motivation: Advances in research and theory.* Vol. 6. New York: Academic Press. **65**
Erickson, M. H. (1937) Development of apparent unconsciousness during hypnotic reliving of a traumatic experience. *Archives of Neurology and Psychiatry, 38,* 1282–1288. **60**
Erickson, M. H. (1952) Deep hypnosis and its induction. In L. M. LeCron (Ed.) *Experimental hypnosis.* New York: Macmillan. **170**
Erickson, M. H., and Kubie, L. S. (1941) The successful treatment of a case of acute hysterical depression by a return under hypnosis to a critical phase of childhood. *Psychoanalytic Quarterly, 10,* 592–609. **60**
Erickson, M. H., and Rossi, E. L. (1974) Varieties of hypnotic amnesia. *American Journ ̄Clinical Hypnosis, 16,* 225–239. **85**
Eriksen, C. W., *see* Williamsen, Johnson, and Eriksen (1965).
Erikson, E. H. (1954) The dream specimen of psychoanalysis. *Journal of the A₁ ₀choanalytic Association, 2,* 5–56. **111**

Ervin, F. R., *see* Mark, Ervin, and Yakovlev (1963).
Estabrooks, G. H. (1957) *Hypnotism.* New York: Dutton. **200**
Evans, F. J., Gustafson, L. A., O'Connell, D. M., Orne, M. T., and Shor, R. E. (1970) Verbally induced behavioral responses during sleep. *Journal of Nervous and Mental Disease, 150,* 171–187. **94**
Evans, F. J., and Kihlstrom, J. F. (1973) Posthypnotic amnesia as disrupted retrieval. *Journal of Abnormal Psychology, 82,* 317–323. **76**
Evans, F. J., and Thorn, W. A. F. (1966) Two types of hypnotic amnesia: Recall amnesia and source amnesia. *International Journal of Clinical and Experimental Hypnosis, 14,* 162–179. **74**
Evans, F. J., *see also* Kihlstrom and Evans (1976).
Evans, M. B., and Paul, G. L. (1970) Effects of hypnotically suggested analgesia on physiological and subjective responses to cold stress. *Journal of Consulting and Clinical Psychology, 35,* 362–371. **202**
Evans, R. I. (1964) *Conversations with Carl Jung.* New York: Van Nostrand Reinhold. **249**
Eysenck, H. J., and Furneaux, W. D. (1945) Primary and secondary suggestibility: An experimental and statistical study. *Journal of Experimental Psychology, 35,* 485–503. **183**
Fast, I. (1974) Multiple identities in borderline personality organization. *British Journal of Medical Psychology, 47, 291–300.* **41**
Feldman, B. E. (1975) A phenomenological and clinical inquiry into deep hypnosis. Unpublished Ph.D. dissertation, University of California, Berkeley. **181, 183**
Féré, C. (1887) *Sensation et mouvement.* Paris: Alcan. **129**
Fezler, W. D., *see* Kroger and Fezler (1976).
Figge, H. H. (1973) Development and stabilization of secondary personalities within the framework of possession cults (German). *Confinia Psychiatrica, 16,* 18–37. **40**
Fink, M., Kety, S., McGaugh, J., and Williams, T. A. (Eds.) (1974) *Psychobiology of convulsive therapy.* Washington, D. C.: V. H. Winston. **84**
Finke, R. A., and Macdonald, H. (1977) Two personality measures relating hypnotic susceptibility to absorption. *International Journal of Clinical and Experimental Hypnosis* (in press). **113**
Fishman, S., *see* Spiegel, Shor, and Fishman (1945).
Flexner, J. B., and Flexner, L. B. (1975) Puromycin's suppression of memory in mice as affected by caffeine. *Pharmacology and Biochemistry of Behavior, 3,* 13–17. **73**
Flexner, L. B., *see* Flexner and Flexner (1975).
Flinn, F. H., Wineland, P., and Peterson, L. J. (1975) Duration of amnesia during sedation with diazepam and pentazocine. *Journal of Oral Surgery, 33,* 23–26. **71**
Flournoy, T. (1890) *From India to the Planet Mars. A study of a case of somnambulism with glossolalia.* New York: Harper. **25**
Ford, L. F., and Yeager, C. L. (1948) Changes in the electroencephalogram in subjects under hypnosis. *Diseases of the Nervous System, 9,* 190–192. **54**
Foulkes, D., *see* Monroe, Rechtschaffen, Foulkes, and Jensen (1965).
Frank, G. S., *see* Osborn, Bunker, Cooper, Frank, and Hilgard (1967).
Frankel, F. H. (1976) *Hypnosis: Trance as a coping mechanism.* New York: Plenum Medical Book Co. **36, 40, 253**
Frankel, F. H., and Orne, M. T. (1976) Hypnotizability and phobic behavior. *Archives of General Psychiatry, 33,* 1259–1261. **129**
Franz, S. I. (1933) *Persons one and three.* New York: McGraw-Hill. **27**
Frazier, S. H., and others (Eds.) (1975) *A psychiatric glossary* (4th ed.). Washington, D. C.: American Psychiatric Association. **118**
French, T. M., and Fromm, E. (1964) *Dream interpretation: A new approach.* New York: Basic Books. **89, 90, 111**
Freud, A. (1936) *The ego and the mechanisms of defense.* New York: International Universities Press,

1946. **122**
Freud, S. (1898) The psychical mechanism of forgetfulness. In *Standard Edition*, Vol. 3, 289–322. London: Hogarth Press, 1962. **84**
Freud, S. (1900) *The interpretation of dreams.* In *Standard Edition*, Vols. 4 and 5. London: Hogarth Press, 1953. **111**
Freud, S. (1901) *Psychopathology of everyday life.* In *Standard Edition*, Vol. 6. London: Hogarth Press, 1960. **84, 251**
Freud, S., see also Breuer and Freud (1895).
Friedlander, J. W., and Sarbin, T. R. (1938) The depth of hypnosis, *Journal of Abnormal and Social Psychology, 33,* 453–475. **261**
Fromm, E. (1965) Hypnoanalysis: Theory and two case excerpts. *Psychotherapy: Theory, Research, and Practice, 2,* 127–133. **61, 254**
Fromm, E. (1970) Age regression with unexpected reappearance of a repressed childhood language. *International Journal of Clinical and Experimental Hypnosis, 18,* 79–88. **48**
Fromm, E., see also French and Fromm (1964); Gruenewald, Fromm, and Oberlander (1972).
Furneaux, W. D., see Eysenck and Furneaux (1945).
Furst, B. (1958) *Stop forgetting: How to develop your memory and put it to practical use.* Garden City, N.Y.: Doubleday. **84**
Galanter, E., see Miller, Galanter, and Pribram (1960).
Galin, D., and Ornstein, R. (1972) Lateral specialization of cognitive mode: An EEG study. *Psychophysiology, 9,* 412–418. **110**
Galton, F. (1883) *Inquiries into human faculty and its development.* London: Macmillan. **101, 107**
Gardner, M. (1957) *Fads and fallacies in the name of science.* New York: Dover. **50**
Garrett, J. B., see Walker, Garrett, and Wallace (1976).
Gazzaniga, M. S. (1970) *The bisected brain.* New York: Appleton-Century-Crofts. **114**
Gazzaniga, M. S., Bogen, J. E., and Sperry, R. W. (1962) Some functional effects of sectioning cerebral commissures in man. *Proceedings of the National Academy of Sciences, 48,* 1765. **109**
Gebhard, J. W. (1961) Hypnotic age-regression. *American Journal of Clinical Hypnosis, 3,* 139–168. **59**
Geiwitz, P. J., see Blum, Geiwitz, and Stewart (1967).
Gettinger, D. (1974) Levels of awareness in hypnosis: A preliminary study. Unpublished senior honors thesis, Stanford University. **203**
Gezahegn, Y., see Giel, Gezahegn, and van Luijk (1968).
Gheorghiu, V. (1969) Some peculiarities of posthypnotic source amnesia of information. In L. Chertok (Ed.) *Psychophysiological mechanisms of hypnosis.* New York: Springer Verlag, 112–122. **74**
Ghiselin, B. (1955) *The creative process: A symposium.* New York: Mentor Books. (Originally published, Berkeley, Calif.: University of California Press, 1952). **195, 203**
Gibbons, D. E. (1976) Hypnotic vs. hyperempiric induction procedures—experimental comparison. *Perceptual and Motor Skills, 42,* 834. **183**
Gibson, W. B., see Young and Gibson (1966).
Giddan, N. S. (1967) Recovery through images of briefly flashed stimuli. *Journal of Personality, 35,* 1–19. **244**
Gidro-Frank, L., and Bowersbuch, M. K. (1948) A study of the plantar response in hypnotic age regression. *Journal of Nervous and Mental Disease, 107,* 443–458. **54**
Giel, R., Gezahegn, Y., and van Luijk, J. N. (1968) Faith-healing and spirit-possession in Ghion, Ethiopia. *Social Science and Medicine, 2,* 63–79. **40**
Gilbert, J. J., and Benson, D. F. (1972) Transient global amnesia: Report of two cases with definite etiologies. *Journal of Nervous and Mental Disease, 154,* 461–464. **84**
Gill, M. M., and Brenman, M. (1959) *Hypnosis and related states: Psychoanalytic studies in regression.*

REFERENCES AND INDEX 275

New York: International Universities Press. **43, 107, 128, 214, 215, 219, 229, 241, 251**
Gill, M. M., *see also* Brenman and Gill (1947).
Globus, G. G., Maxwell, G., and Savodnik, I. (Eds.) (1976) *Consciousness and the brain.* New York: Plenum Press. **15, 240**
Gmelin, E. (1791) *Materialen für die anthropologie,* I. Tübingen: Cotta. (From Ellenberger, 1970). **26**
Gold, P. E., and King, R. A. (1974) Retrograde amnesia: Storage failure versus retrieval failure. *Psychological Review, 81,* 465–469. **85**
Goldstein, A., and Hilgard, E. R. (1975) Lack of influence of the morphine antagonist naloxone on hypnotic analgesia. *Proceedings of the National Academy of Sciences, 72,* 2041–2043. **194**
Goodwin, D. W. (1971) Two species of alcoholic blackout. *American Journal of Psychiatry, 127,* 1665–1670. **71**
Gordon, R. (1949) An investigation into some of the factors that favor the formation of stereotyped images. *British Journal of Psychology, 39,* 156–167. **101**
Gordon, R. (1950) An experiment correlating the nature of imagery with performance on a test of reversal of perspective. *British Journal of Psychology, 41,* 63–67. **101**
Gough, P. B., *see* Weitzenhoffer, Gough, and Landes (1959).
Graham, K. R. (1969) Brightness contrast by hypnotic hallucination. *International Journal of Clinical and Experimental Hypnosis, 17,* 62–73. **202**
Graham, K. R., and Patton, A. (1968) Retroactive inhibition, hypnosis, and hypnotic amnesia. *International Journal of Clinical and Experimental Hypnosis, 16,* 68–74. **85**
Greene, H. H., and Bennett, D. R. (1974) Transient global amnesia with a previously unreported EEG abnormality. *Brain Research, 81,* 133–144. **84**
Gruenewald, D. (1971) Hypnotic techniques without hypnosis in the treatment of dual personality. A case report. *Journal of Nervous and Mental Disease, 153,* 41–46. **41**
Gruenewald, D., Fromm, E., and Oberlander, M. I. (1972) Hypnosis and adaptive regression: An ego-psychological inquiry. In E. Fromm and R. E. Shor (Eds.) *Hypnosis: Research Developments and Perspectives.* Chicago: Aldine-Atherton. **86, 215**
Gründer, H. (1920) *Is the ouija board a harmless toy?* Chicago: Loyola University Press. **153**
Guilford, J. P. (1959) *Personality.* New York: McGraw-Hill. **108**
Guilleminault, C., Billiard, M., Montplaisir, J., and Dement, W. C. (1975) Altered states of consciousness in disorders of daytime sleepiness. *Journal of the Neurological Sciences, 26,* 377–393. **246**
Gur, R. C., and Gur, R. E. (1974) Handedness, sex, and eyedness as moderating variables in the relation between hypnotic susceptibility and functional brain asymmetry. *Journal of Abnormal Psychology, 83,* 635–643. **111**
Gur, R. C., and Hilgard, E. R. (1975) Visual imagery and the discrimination of differences between altered pictures simultaneously and successively presented. *British Journal of Psychology, 66,* 341–345. **113**
Gur, R. C., and Reyher, J. (1976) Enhancement of imagery via free-imagery and hypnosis. *American Journal of Clinical Hypnosis, 18,* 237–249. **109**
Gur, R. C., *see* McKenley and Gur (1975).
Gur, R. E. (1975) Conjugate lateral eye-movements as an index of hemispheric activation. *Journal of Personality and Social Psychology, 31,* 751–757. **110**
Gur, R. E., *see also* Gur and Gur (1974).
Gustafson, L. A., *see* Evans, Gustafson, O'Connell, Orne, and Shor (1970).
Hadamard, J. (1945) *The psychology of invention in the mathematical field.* Princeton: Princeton University Press. **195, 203**
Haley, J. (1958) An interactional explanation of hypnosis. *American Journal of Clinical Hypnosis, 1,* 41–57. **226**
Hall, C. S. (1953) *The meaning of dreams.* New York: Harper. **111**

Hall, C. S., and Van de Castle, R. L. (1966) *The content analysis of dreams.* New York: Appleton-Century-Crofts. **93, 111**
Hall, J. A., *see* Crasilneck and Hall (1975).
Halliday, A. M., and Mason, A. A. (1964) The effect of hypnotic anesthesia on cortical responses. *Journal of Neurology, Neurosurgery, and Psychiatry, 27,* 300–312. **203**
Hammer, A. G., *see* Nace, Orne, and Hammer (1974).
Hansel, C. E. M. (1966) *ESP: A scientific evaluation.* New York: Scribner's. **153**
Hart, B. (1929) *Psychopathology* (2nd edition). Cambridge: Cambridge University Press. **16, 256**
Harriman, P. L. (1942) The experimental production of some phenomena related to multiple personality. *Journal of Abnormal and Social Psychology, 37,* 244–255. **138, 153**
Hartmann, E. v. (1869) *Philosophie des Unbewussten.* Berlin: Duncker **4**
Hartmann, H. (1939) *Ego psychology and the problem of adaptation.* New York: International Universities Press, 1958. **86, 219, 241**
Hastey, J. M., *see* Arkin, Hastey, and Reiser (1966); Arkin, Toth, Baker, and Hastey (1970).
Hebb, D. O. (1949) *The organization of behavior.* New York: Wiley. **219**
Hebb, D. O. (1975) Science and the world of imagination. *Canadian Psychological Review, 16,* 4–11. **219**
Heise, M. R., *see* Wagner and Heise (1974).
Helson, R. (1973) The heroic, the comic, and the tender: Patterns of literary fantasy and their authors. *Journal of Personality, 41,* 163–184. **201**
Hennessy, R. T., *see* Miller, Hennessy, and Leibowitz (1973).
Henriksson, M., *see* Smith and Henriksson (1956).
Herz, M. J., *see* McGaugh and Herz (1972).
Hilgard, E. R. (1931) Conditioned eyelid reactions to a light simulus based on the reflex wink to sound. *Psychological Monographs, 41,* No. 184. **x**
Hilgard, E. R. (1938) An algebraic analysis of conditioned discrimination in man. *Psychological Review, 45,* 472–496. **x, 125**
Hilgard, E. R. (1949) Human motives and the concept of the self. *American Psychologist, 4,* 374–382. **x**
Hilgard, E. R. (1962a) Impulsive vs. realistic thinking: An examination of the distinction between primary and secondary processes in thought. *Psychological Bulletin, 59,* 477–488. **86, 215**
Hilgard, E. R. (1962b) What becomes of the input from the stimulus? In C. W. Eriksen (Ed.) *Behavior and awareness: A symposium of research and interpretation.* Durham, N.C.: Duke University Press. **244**
Hilgard, E. R. (1963) Ability to resist suggestions within the hypnotic state: Responsiveness to conflicting communications. *Psychological Reports, 12,* 3–13. **119, 121**
Hilgard, E. R. (1965) *Hypnotic susceptibility.* New York: Harcourt Brace Jovanovich. **52, 53, 93, 119, 129, 164, 183, 262**
Hilgard, E. R. (1967) A quantitative study of pain and its reduction through hypnotic suggestion. *Proceedings of the National Academy of Sciences, 57,* 1581–1586. **202**
Hilgard, E. R. (1971) Hypnosis and childlikeness. In J. P. Hill (Ed.) *Minnesota Symposia on Child Psychology,* Vol. 5. **106**
Hilgard, E. R. (1972) A critique of Johnson, Maher, and Barber's "Artifact in the 'essence of hypnosis': An evaluation of trance logic," with a recomputation of their findings. *Journal of Abnormal Psychology, 79,* 221–233. **112**
Hilgard, E. R. (1973a) Dissociation revisited. In M. Henle, J. Jaynes, and J. Sullivan (Eds.) *Historical conceptions of psychology.* New York: Springer Publishing Co. **14, 256**
Hilgard, E. R. (1973b) A neodissociation interpretation of pain reduction in hypnosis. *Psychological Review, 80,* 396–411. **14, 218, 256**
Hilgard, E. R. (1973c) The domain of hypnosis, with some comments on alternative paradigms.

American Psychologist, 28, 972–982. **41**
Hilgard, E. R. (1974) Toward a neodissociation theory: Multiple cognitive controls in human functioning. *Perspectives in Biology and Medicine, 17,* 301–316. **14**
Hilgard, E. R. (1976) Neodissociation theory of multiple cognitive control systems. In G. E. Schwartz and D. Shapiro (Eds.) *Consciousness and self-regulation: Advances in research, Vol. 1.* New York: Plenum Press. **14, 81, 256**
Hilgard, E. R., and Bower, G. H. (1975) *Theories of learning* (4th ed.) Englewood Cliffs, N.J.: Prentice-Hall, **64, 66, 83, 85**
Hilgard, E. R., and Cooper, L. M. (1965) Spontaneous and suggested posthypnotic amnesia. *International Journal of Clinical and Experimental Hypnosis, 13,* 261–273. **74**
Hilgard, E. R., and Hilgard, J. R. (1975) *Hypnosis in the relief of pain* (Revised edition, 1983) Los Altos, Calif.: William Kaufmann, Inc. **184, 190, 201**
Hilgard, E. R., Hilgard, J. R., Macdonald, H., Morgan, A. H., and Johnson, L. S. (1978) The reality of hypnotic analgesia: A comparison of highly hypnotizables with simulators. *Journal of Abnormal Psychology, 87,* 239–246. **202**
Hilgard, E. R., Lauer, L. W., and Morgan, A. H. (1963) *Manual for Stanford Profile Scales of Hypnotic Susceptibility.* Palo Alto, Calif.: Consulting Psychologists Press. **140**
Hilgard, E. R., and Marquis, D. G. (1940) *Conditioning and learning.* New York: Appleton-Century-Crofts. **118, 128**
Hilgard, E. R., and Morgan, A. H. (1976) Heart rate and blood pressure in the study of laboratory pain in man under normal conditions and as influenced by hypnosis. *Acta Neurobiologiae Experimentalis, 35,* 741–759. **172**
Hilgard, E. R., Morgan, A. H., and Macdonald, H. (1975) Pain and dissociation in the cold pressor test: A study of hypnotic analgesia with "hidden reports" through automatic keypressing and automatic talking. *Journal of Abnormal Psychology, 84,* 280–289. **190, 201, 214**
Hilgard, E. R., and Nowlis, D. P. (1972) The contents of hypnotic dreams and night dreams: An exercise in method. In E. Fromm and R. E. Shor (Eds.) *Hypnosis: Research Developments and Perspectives.* Chicago: Aldine-Atherton. **93, 245**
Hilgard, E. R., and Tart, C. T. (1966) Responsiveness to suggestions following waking and imagination instructions and following induction of hypnosis. *Journal of Abnormal Psychology, 71,* 196–208. **93, 202**
Hilgard, E. R., Weitzenhoffer, A. M., Landes, J., and Moore, R. K. (1961) The distribution of susceptibility to hypnosis in a student population: A study using the Stanford Hypnotic Susceptibility Scale. *Psychological Monographs, 75,* (Whole number 512). **157**
Hilgard, E. R., *see also* Aas, Hilgard, and Weitzenhoffer (1963); Banyai and Hilgard (1976); Berreman and Hilgard (1936); Goldstein and Hilgard (1975); Gur and Hilgard (1975); Hilgard, Macdonald, and Crawford (1977); Knox, Crutchfield, and Hilgard (1975); Knox, Morgan, and Hilgard (1974); Liebert, Rubin, and Hilgard (1965); Macdonald, Crawford, and Hilgard (1977); Morgan, Johnson, and Hilgard (1974); Osborn, Bunker, Cooper, Frank, and Hilgard (1967); Ruch, Morgan, and Hilgard (1974); Slotnick, Liebert, and Hilgard (1965); Weitzenhoffer and Hilgard (1959); Weitzenhoffer and Hilgard (1962); Weitzenhoffer and Hilgard (1963); Weitzenhoffer and Hilgard (1967).
Hilgard, J. R. (1965) Personality and hypnotizability: Inferences from case studies. In E. R. Hilgard, *Hypnotic susceptibility.* New York: Harcourt Brace Jovanovich. **104, 160, 183**
Hilgard, J. R. (1970) *Personality and hypnosis: A study of imaginative involvement* (Second edition, 1979) Chicago: University of Chicago Press. **102–106, 113, 160, 183**
Hilgard, J. R. (1971) How the subject perceives the hypnotist: A study of the hypnotist-subject relationship. Frieda Fromm-Reichmann Lecture, Stanford Medical School (Unpublished). **215**
Hilgard, J. R. (1974) Imaginative involvement: Some characteristics of the highly hypnotizable

and the non-hypnotizable. *International Journal of Clinical and Experimental Hypnosis, 22,* 138–156. **104, 160, 161, 183**

Hilgard, J. R., Hilgard, E. R., Macdonald, H., and Crawford, H. J. (1977) The hidden observer in hypnotic analgesia and hypnotic deafness: A study in dissociation (unpublished). **202, 214**

Hilgard, J. R., *see also* Hilgard and Hilgard (1975); Hilgard, Hilgard, Macdonald, Morgan, and Johnson (1977).

Hillman, J. (1975) *Re-visioning psychology.* New York: Harper and Row. **183**

Hodge, J. R. (1976) The contractual aspects of hypnosis. *International Journal of Clinical and Experimental Hypnosis, 24,* 391–399. **224**

Hofheins, R., *see* Tooker and Hofheins (1976).

Holden, W. J., *see* Attard and Holden (1976).

Hollister, L. E., *see* Sjoberg and Hollister (1965).

Holt, R. R. (1963) *Manual for the scoring of primary process manipulations in Rorschach responses* (9th ed.). New York: Research Center for Mental Health, New York University. **108**

Holt, R. R. (1964) Imagery: The return of the ostracized. *American Psychologist, 19,* 254–264. **111**

Holt, R. R., *see also* Pine and Holt (1960).

Holton, G. (1970) The roots of complementarity. *Daedalus,* fall, 1015–1055. **200**

Homme, L. E. (1965) Control of coverants: The operants of the mind. *Psychological Record, 15,* 501–511. **3**

Hopfer, T. M., *see* De Vietti and Hopfer (1974).

Horowitz, S. L. (1970) Strategies within hypnosis for reducing phobic behavior. *Journal of Abnormal Psychology, 75,* 104–112. **45**

Hudgins, C. V. (1933) Conditioning and the voluntary control of the pupillary light reflex. *Journal of General Psychology, 8,* 3–51. **124**

Hull, C. L. (1933) *Hypnosis and suggestibility.* New York: Appleton-Century. (Paper edition, with Foreword by E. R. Hilgard. New York: Appleton-Century-Crofts, 1968). **8–10, 16, 122, 130, 153**

Hull, C. L. (1934) The concept of the habit-family hierarchy and maze learning. *Psychological Review, 41,* 33–54. **219**

Hull, C. L. (1962) Psychology of the scientist: IV. Passages from the "idea books" of Clark L. Hull. *Perceptual and Motor Skills, 15,* 807–882. **153**

Hunt, E., *see* Duncan and Hunt (1972).

Huppert, F. A., *see* Piercy and Huppert (1972).

Irion, A. I., *see* McGeoch and Irion (1952).

Jacobson, A., and Kales, A. (1967) Somnambulism: All-night EEG and related studies. In S. S. Kety, E. V. Evarts, and H. L. Williams (Eds.) *Sleep and altered states of consciousness.* Baltimore, Md.: Williams and Wilkins. **95**

James, W. (1889) Automatic writing. *Proceedings of the American Society for Psychical Research, 1,* 548–564. **199**

James, W. (1890) *Principles of psychology.* 2 vols. New York: Holt. **5, 22, 116, 122, 199, 200, 217**

Jameson, D. H., *see* Ludwig, Brandsma, Wilbur, Bendfeldt, and Jameson (1972).

Janet, P. (1889) *L'Automatisme psychologique.* Paris: Felix Alcan. **4, 12, 29, 30, 44, 153**

Janet, P. (1907) *The major symptoms of hysteria.* New York: Macmillan. **5, 6**

Jaynes, J. (1977) *The origin of consciousness in the breakdown of the bicameral mind.* Boston: Houghton Mifflin. **15**

Jeans, R. F., *see* Osgood, Luria, Jeans, and Smith (1976).

Jensen, J., *see* Monroe, Rechtschaffen, Foulkes, and Jensen (1965).

Johnson, D. L., *see* Morgan, Johnson, and Hilgard (1974).

Johnson, H. T., *see* Williamsen, Johnson, and Eriksen (1965).

Johnson, L. S., *see* Hilgard, Hilgard, Macdonald, Morgan, and Johnson (1977).
Johnson, R. F. Q. (1972) Trance logic revisited: A reply to Hilgard's critique. *Journal of Abnormal Psychology, 79*, 234–238. **112**
Johnson, R. F. Q., Maher, B. A., and Barber, T. X. (1972) Artifact in the "essence of hypnosis;" an evaluation of trance logic. *Journal of Abnormal Psychology, 79*, 212–220. **112**
Jones, E. E., and other (1972) *Attribution: Perceiving the causes of behavior.* Morristown, N.J.: General Learning Press. **3**
Jones, J., *see* Sutcliffe and Jones (1962).
Jones, M.K. (1974) Imagery as a mnemonic aid after left temporal lobectomy: Contrast between material-specific and generalized memory disorders. *Neuropsychologia, 12*, 21–30. **85**
Kahneman, D. (1968) Method, findings, and theory in studies of visual masking. *Psychological Bulletin, 70*, 404–423. **256**
Kahneman, D. (1973) *Attention and effort.* Englewood Cliffs, N.J.: Prentice-Hall. **153**
Kales, A., *see* Jacobson and Kales (1967).
Kamiya, J. (1969) Operant control of the EEG alpha rhythm and some of its reported effects on consciousness. In C. T. Tart (Ed.) *Altered states of consciousness.* New York: Wiley. **125**
Kanfer, F. H., and Marston, A. R. (1963) Conditioning of self-reinforcing responses. An analogue to self-confidence training. *Psychological Reports, 13*, 63–70. **14**
Kaplan, E. A. (1960) Hypnosis and pain. *Archives of General Psychiatry, 2*, 567–568. **201**
Kelsey, D. E. R. (1953) Phantasies of birth and prenatal experiences recovered from patients undergoing hypnoanalysis. *Journal of Mental Science, 99*, 216–223. **50**
Kety, S., *see* Fink, Kety, McGaugh, and Williams (1974).
Kiev, A. (1969) Primitive religious rites and behavior: Clinical considerations. *International Psychiatric Clinics, 5*, 119–131. **40**
Kihlstrom, J. F. (1972) Order of recall in posthypnotic amnesia and in waking memory. Paper presented at the 43rd annual meeting of the Eastern Psychological Association, Boston, April. **76**
Kihlstrom, J. F. (1975) *The effects of organization and motivation on recall during posthypnotic amnesia.* Unpublished Ph.D. dissertation, University of Pennsylvania. **76, 85**
Kihlstrom, J. F. (1977) Models of posthypnotic amnesia. *Annals of the New York Academy of Sciences, 296*, 90–104. **76, 85**
Kihlstrom, J. F., and Evans, F. J. (1976) Recovery of memory after posthypnotic amnesia. *Journal of Abnormal Psychology, 85*, 558–563. **76, 85**
Kihlstrom, J. F., *see also* Evans and Kihlstrom (1973).
King, R. A., *see* Gold and King (1974).
Kinsbourne, M. (1972) Eye and head turning indicates cerebral lateralization. *Science, 176*, 539–541. **110**
Kinsbourne, M., and Smith, W. L. (Eds.) (1974) *Hemispheric disconnection and cerebral function.* Springfield, Ill.: Thomas. **114**
Kirshner, L. A. (1973) Dissociative reaction: An historical review and clinical study. *Acta Psychiatrica Scandinavia, 49*, 698–711. **40**
Kleitman, N., see Aserinsky and Kleitman (1953); Dement and Kleitman (1957).
Kline, M. V. (1951) Hypnosis and age progression: A case report. *Journal of Genetic Psychology, 78*, 195–206. **50**
Kline, M. V. (1952) A note on primate-like behavior induced through hypnosis. *Journal of Genetic Psychology, 81*, 125–131. **50**
Kline, M. V. (1953) Hypnotic retrogression: A neuropsychological theory of age regression and progression. *Journal of Clinical and Experimental Hypnosis, 1*, 21–28. **50**
Kline, M. V. (Ed.) (1956) *A scientific report on the search for Bridey Murphy.* New York: Julian Press. **49**

Kline, M. V. (1960) Hypnotic age regression and psychotherapy: Clinical and theoretical observations. *International Journal of Clinical and Experimental Hypnosis, 8,* 17–35. 61

Klüver, H. (1966) *Mescal, and mechanisms of hallucinations.* Chicago: University of Chicago Press (Originally published 1928, 1942). 112

Knox, V. J., Crutchfield, L., and Hilgard, E. R. (1975) The nature of task interference in hypnotic dissociation: An investigation of hypnotic behavior. *International Journal of Clinical and Experimental Hypnosis, 23,* 305–323. 146

Knox, V. J., Morgan, A. H., and Hilgard, E. R. (1974) Pain and suffering in ischemia: The paradox of hypnotically suggested anesthesia as contradicted by reports from the "hidden observer." *Archives of General Psychiatry, 30,* 840–847. **193, 201, 214, 236**

Kohlenberg, R. J. (1973) Behavioristic approach to multiple personality: A case study. *Behavior Therapy, 4,* 137–140. 41

Krippner, S., *see* Ullman, Krippner, and Vaughan (1973).

Kris, E. (1934) *Psychoanalytic explorations in art.* New York: International Universities Press. 107

Kroger, W. S., and Fezler, W. D. (1976) *Hypnosis and behavior modification: Imagery conditioning.* Philadelphia: Lippincott. 256

Kubie, L. S. (1958) *Neurotic distortion of the creative process.* Lawrence: University of Kansas Press. 113

Kubie, L. S., *see also* Erickson and Kubie (1941).

Kupfer, H. I. (1945) Psychic concomitants in wartime injuries. *Psychosomatic Medicine, 7,* 15–21. 54

Lam, D., *see* Morgan and Lam (1969)

Lambert, G. W. (1971) Studies in the automatic writing of Mrs. Verall: X. Concluding reflections. *Journal of the Society for Psychical Research,* 217–222. 133

Lancaster, E. (1958) *The final face of Eve.* New York: McGraw-Hill. 41

Landes, J. (1967) The influence of visual backward masking on the perception of congruent and incongruent meaningful stimulus pictures. Unpublished Ph.D. dissertation, Stanford University. 244

Landes, J., *see also* Hilgard, Weitzenhoffer, Landes, and Moore (1961); Weitzenhoffer, Gough, and Landes (1959).

Lauer, L. W., *see* Hilgard, Lauer, and Morgan (1963).

Leavitt, H. C. (1947) A case of hypnotically produced secondary and tertiary personalities. *Psychoanalytic Review, 34,* 274–295. 42

Le Cron, L. M., *see* Cheek and Le Cron (1968).

Lee-Teng, E. (1965) Trance-susceptibility, induction susceptibility, and acquiescence as factors in hypnotic performances. *Journal of Abnormal Psychology, 70,* 383–389. 106

Lefton, L. A. (1973) Metacontrast: A review. *Perception and Psychophysics, 13 (supplement),* 161–171. 256

Leibowitz, H. W., *see* Miller, Hennessy, and Leibowitz (1973).

Leone, M. P., *see* Zaretsky and Leone (1974).

Lesgold, A., *see* Bower, Clark, Winzenz, and Lesgold (1969).

Levinson, B. W. (1967) States of awareness during general anesthesia. In J. Lassner (Ed.) *Hypnosis and psychosomatic medicine.* New York: Springer Verlag. 71

Levitt, E. E. (1977) Research strategies in evaluating the coercive power of hypnosis. *Annals of the New York Academy of Sciences, 296,* 86–89. 129

Lewin K. (1935) *A dynamic theory of personality* (Translated by D. K. Adams and K. E. Zener). New York: McGraw-Hill. 218

Liebert, R. M., Rubin, N., and Hilgard, E. R. (1965) The effects of active and passive hypnosis on attention, acquisition, and retention during paired associate learning. *Journal of Personality, 33,* 605–612. 166

Liebert, R. M., *see also* Slotnick, Liebert, and Hilgard (1965).

REFERENCES AND INDEX 281

Lindner, R. M. (1944) *Rebel without a cause: The hypnoanalysis of a criminal psychopath*. New York: Grune and Stratton. **153**
Litvag, I. (1972) *Singer in the shadows: The strange case of Patience Worth*. New York: Macmillan. **136**
London, P. (1962) *The Children's Hypnotic Susceptibility Scale*. Palo Alto, Calif.: Consulting Psychologists Press. **261**
London, P. (1967) The induction of hypnosis. In J. E. Gordon (Ed.) *Handbook of clinical and experimental hypnosis*. New York: Macmillan, 44–79. **241**
Luborsky, L. (1970) New directions in research on neurotic and psychosomatic symptoms. *American Scientist*, 58, 661–668. **250**
Ludwig, A. M. (1966) Altered states of consciousness. *Archives of General Psychiatry*, 26, 225–234. **183**
Ludwig, A. M., Brandsma, J. M., Wilbur, C. B., Bendfeldt, F., and Jameson, D. H. (1972) The objective study of a multiple personality, or, are four heads better than one? *Archives of General Psychiatry*, 26, 298–310. **32, 33, 34**
Ludwig, A. M., and Lyle, W. H. (1964) Tension induction and the hyperalert trance. *Journal of Abnormal and Social Psychology*, 69, 70–76. **166**
Ludwig, A. M., *see also* Brandsma and Ludwig (1974).
Luria, A. R. (1968) *The mind of a mnemonist*. New York: Basic Books. **66**
Luria, Z., *see* Osgood and Luria (1954); Osgood, Luria, Jeans, and Smith (1976).
Lyle, W. H., *see* Ludwig and Lyle (1964).
Lynch, S., and Yarnell, P. R. (1973) Retrograde amnesia: Delayed forgetting after concussion. *American Journal of Psychology*, 86, 643–645. **69**
Lynch, S. *see also* Yarnell and Lynch (1973).
Macdonald, H., Crawford, H. J., and Hilgard, E. R. (1977) Hypnotic deafness: A study of individual differences in responsiveness to hypnotic suggestions (unpublished); *see* Crawford, Macdonald, and Hilgard (1979). **184, 202, 214**
Macdonald, H., *see also* Finke and Macdonald (1977); Hilgard, Hilgard, Macdonald, and Crawford (1977); Hilgard, Hilgard, Macdonald, Morgan, and Johnson (1977); Hilgard, Morgan, and Macdonald (1975).
MacKinnon, D. W., *see* Barry, MacKinnon, and Murray (1931).
Madigan, S. A., *see* Tulving and Madigan (1970).
Maer, F., *see* Schwartz, Davidson, Maer, and Bromfield (1973).
Mah, C. J., and Albert, D. J. (1973) Electroconvulsive shock-induced retrograde amnesia: An analysis of the variation in the length of the amnesia gradient. *Behavioral Biology*, 9, 517–540. **85**
Mah, C. J., and Albert, D. J. (1975) Reversal of ECS-induced amnesia by post-ECS injections of amphetamine. *Pharmacology, Biochemistry, and Behavior*, 3, 1–5. **73**
Maher, B. A., *see* Johnson, Maher, and Barber (1972).
Mark, V. H., Ervin, F. R., and Yakovlev, P. I. (1963) Stereotactic thalamotomy. *Archives of Neurology*, 8, 528–538. **246**
Marks, D. F. (1973) Visual imagery differences in the recall of pictures. *British Journal of Psychology*, 64, 17–24. **103**
Marquis, D. G., *see* Hilgard and Marquis (1940).
Marshall, G. D., *see* Maslach, Marshall, and Zimbardo (1972).
Marston, A. R., *see* Kanfer and Marston (1963).
Martin, L. J. (1907) *Zur Begründung und anwendung der suggestions-methode in der normal-psychologie*. Leipzig. **138**
Martin, L. J. (1917) An experimental study of the subconscious. In J. E. Coover, *Experiments in psychical research*. Stanford, Calif.: Stanford University Press. **138**
Martin, M. F., *see* Taylor and Martin (1944).

Maslach, C., Marshall, G. D., and Zimbardo, P. G. (1972) Hypnotic control of peripheral skin temperature: A case report. *Psychophysiology, 9,* 600–605. **126**

Maslow, A. H. (1954) *Motivation and personality.* New York: Harper and Row. (2nd edition, 1970) **14**

Mason, A. A., *see* Halliday and Mason (1964).

Mathieson, G., *see* Penfield and Mathieson (1974).

Maxwell, G., *see* Globus, Maxwell, and Savodnik (1976).

May, R. (1975) *The courage to create.* New York: Norton. **107, 113**

Mayman, M. (Ed.) (1973) Psychoanalytic research: Three approaches to the experimental study of subliminal processes. *Psychological Issues, 8,* Monograph 30. **256**

McCleave, J. C. (1968) Advantage of repetition in achieving the maximally effective suggestion in a motor task. Unpublished master's thesis, Stanford University. **123**

McConkey, K., *see* Sheehan, Obstoj, and McConkey (1976).

McDonald, R. D., and Smith, J. R. (1975) Trance logic in tranceable and simulating subjects. *International Journal of Clinical and Experimental Hypnosis, 23,* 80–89. **112**

McDougall, W. (1938) The relation between dissociation and repression. *British Journal of Medical Psychology, 17,* 141–157. **16, 252**

McGaugh, J. L., and Herz, M. J. (1972) *Memory consolidation.* San Francisco: Albion. **85**

McGaugh, J. L., *see also* Fink, Kety, McGaugh, and Williams (1974).

McGeoch, J. A., and Irion, A. I. (1952) *The psychology of human learning.* (2nd edition). New York: Longmans, Green. **63**

McGlashan, G. A., Evans, F. J., and Orne, M. T. (1969) The nature of hypnotic analgesia and the placebo response to experimental pain. *Psychosomatic Medicine. 31,* 227–246. **202**

McKellar, P., and Tonn, H. F. (1967) Negative hallucination, dissociation, and the five stamps experiment. *British Journal of Social Psychiatry, 1,* 260-270 **98**

McKenley, P., and Gur, R. C. (1975) Imagery, absorption, meditation, and drug use as correlates of hypnotic susceptibility. Paper presented at annual meeting of Society for Clinical and Experimental Hypnosis, Chicago, October 10. **104**

McNeill, D., *see* Brown and McNeill (1966).

McPeake, J. K., *see* Spanos and McPeake (1975); Spanos, McPeake, and Churchill (1976).

Melzack, R., and Casey, K. L. (1968) Sensory, motivational, and central control determinants of pain: A new conceptual model. In D. Kenshalo (Ed.) *The skin senses.* Springfield, Ill.: Thomas. **193, 246**

Melzack, R., and Wall, P. D. (1965) Pain mechanisms: A new theory. *Science, 150,* 971–979. **246**

Menzies, R. (1937) Conditioned vasomotor responses in human subjects. *Journal of Psychology, 4,* 75–120. **124**

Messerschmidt, R. (1927–1928) A quantitative investigation of the alleged independent operation of conscious and subconscious processes. *Journal of Abnormal and Social Psychology, 22,* 325–340. **7, 9, 139**

Michaux, D., *see* Chertok, Michaux, and Droin (1977).

Miller, G. A. (1956) The magical number seven, plus or minus two: Some limits on our capacity for processing information. *Psychological Review, 63,* 81–97. **222**

Miller, G. A., Galanter, E., and Pribram, K. H. (1960) *Plans and the structure of behavior.* New York: Holt, Rinehart and Winston. **3, 116, 122, 127, 219, 222**

Miller, N. E., *see* Di Cara and Miller (1968).

Miller, R. J., Hennessy, R. T., and Leibowitz, H. W. (1973) The effect of hypnotic ablation of the background on the magnitude of the Ponzo perspective illusion. *International Journal of Clinical and Experimental Hypnosis, 21,* 180–191. **202**

Miller, R. R., Ott, C. A., Berk, A. M., and Springer, A. D. (1974) Appetitive memory restoration after electroconvulsive shock in the rat. *Journal of Comparative and Physiological Psychology, 87,* 717–723. **73**

Miller, R. R., and Springer, A. D. (1973) Amnesia, consolidation, and retrieval. *Psychological Review, 80,* 69–79. **85**

Miller, R. R., and Springer, A. D. (1974) Implication of recovery from experimental amnesia. *Psychological Review, 81,* 470–473. **85**

Milner, B. (1966) Amnesia following operation on the temporal lobes. In C. W. M. Whitty and O. L. Zangwill (Eds.) *Amnesia.* New York: Appleton-Century-Crofts; London: Butterworths. **70**

Milner, B., Corkin, S., and Teuber, H-L. (1968) Further analysis of the hippocampal amnesic syndrome: 14-year follow-up study of H. M. *Neuropsychologia, 6,* 215–234. **69**

Milner, B., *see also* Scoville and Milner (1957).

Mischel, W. (1973) Toward a cognitive social learning reconceptualization of personality. *Psychological Review, 80,* 252–283. **3**

Mitchell, T. W. (1925) Divisions of the self and co-consciousness. In C. M. Campbell, and others (Eds.) *Problems of personality: Studies presented to Dr. Morton Prince.* New York: Harcourt, Brace. **27**

Monroe, L. J., Rechtschaffen, A., Foulkes, D., and Jensen, J. (1965) The discriminability of REM and NREM reports. *Journal of Personality and Social Psychology, 2,* 456–460. **111**

Montplaisir, J., *see* Guilleminault and others (1975).

Moore, H. T. (1914) The genetic aspect of consonance and dissonance. *Psychological Review, Monographs Supplements,* Vol. 17. **114**

Moore, R. K., *see* Cooper and Moore, (1967); Hilgard, Weitzenhoffer, Landes, and Moore (1961).

Moray, N. (1969a) *Listening and attention.* Baltimore: Penguin Books. **153**

Moray, N. (1969b) *Attention: Selective processes in vision and hearing.* London: Hutchinson Educational Ltd. **153**

Morgan, A. H. (1973) The heritability of hypnotic susceptibility in twins. *Journal of Abnormal Psychology, 82,* 55–61. **265**

Morgan, A. H., Johnson, D. L., and Hilgard, E. R. (1974) The stability of hypnotic susceptibility: A longitudinal study. *International Journal of Clinical and Experimental Hypnosis, 22,* 249–257. **265**

Morgan, A. H., and Lam, D. (1969) The relationship of the Betts Vividness of Imagery Questionnaire and hypnotic susceptibility. Stanford, Calif.: Hawthorne House Memorandum #103. **113**

Morgan, A. H., *see also* Hilgard, Hilgard, Macdonald, Morgan, and Johnson (1977); Hilgard, Lauer, and Morgan (1963); Hilgard and Morgan (1976); Hilgard, Morgan, and Macdonald (1975); Knox, Morgan, and Hilgard (1974); Ruch, Morgan, and Hilgard (1974).

Moss, C. S. (1967) *The hypnotic investigation of dreams.* New York: Wiley. **111**

Mostert, J. W. (1975) States of awareness during general anesthesia. *Perspectives in Biology and Medicine,* Autumn, 68–76. **85**

Mühl, A. M. (1930) *Automatic writing.* Dresden and Leipzig: Theodor Steinkopff. **137, 153**

Mühl, A. M. (1952) Automatic writing and hypnosis. In Le Cron, L. M. (Ed.) *Experimental hypnosis.* New York: Macmillan. **153**

Munthe, A. (1929) *The story of San Michele.* New York: Dutton. **152**

Murray, H. A., Jr., *see* Barry, MacKinnon, and Murray (1931).

Myers, F. W. H. (1887) Automatic writing III. *Proceedings of the Society for Psychical Research, 4,* 209–261. **135**

Myers, F. W. H. (1903) *Human personality and its survival of bodily death.* 2 vols. London: Longmans, Green. (Reprinted, with introduction by Gardner Murphy, 1954). **136, 152, 198**

Myers, F. W. H. (1961) *Human personality and its survival of bodily death.* Abridged by Susy Smith, with Foreword by Aldous Huxley. New Hyde Park, N.Y.: University Books. **152**

Nace, E. P., Orne, M. T., and Hammer, A. G. (1974) Posthypnotic amnesia as an active psychic

process: The reversibility of amnesia. *Archives of General Psychiatry, 31,* 257–260. **76, 85**
Neisser, U. (1967) *Cognitive psychology.* New York: Appleton-Century-Crofts. **13, 15, 220, 241**
Neisser, U. (1976) *Cognition and reality.* San Francisco: W. H. Freeman. **107**
Neisser, U., and Becklen, R. (1975) Selective looking: Attending to visually-specified events. *Cognitive Psychology, 7,* 480–494. **256**
Newell, A., and Simon, H. A. (1972) *Human problem solving.* Englewood Cliffs, N.J.: Prentice-Hall. **219**
Newman, R., *see* Rubenstein and Newman (1954).
Newton, B. W., *see* Bowers, Brecher-Marer, Newton, Piotrowski, Spyer, Taylor, and Watkins (1971).
Norman, D. A. (1968) Toward a theory of memory and attention. *Psychological Review, 75,* 522–536. **148**
Norman, D. A. (Ed.) (1970) *Models of memory.* New York: Academic Press. **83**
Norman, D. A. (1976) *Memory and attention: An introduction to human information processing.* (2nd edition). New York: Wiley. **148, 149, 153, 243**
Nowlis, D. P., *see* Hilgard and Nowlis (1972).
Oberlander, M. I., *see* Gruenwald, Fromm, and Oberlander (1972).
Obstoj, I., *see* Sheehan, Obstoj, and McConkey (1976).
O'Connell, D. N., Shor, R. E., and Orne, M. T. (1970) Hypnotic age regression: An empirical and methodological analysis. *Journal of Abnormal Psychology Monographs, 76* (3, Pt. 2). **56**
O'Connell, D. N., *see* Evans, Gustafson, O'Connell, Orne, and Shor (1970).
Orne, E. C., *see* Shore and Orne (1962).
Orne, M. T. (1951) The mechanisms of hypnotic age regression: An experimental study. *Journal of Abnormal and Social Psychology, 46,* 213–225. **55**
Orne, M. T. (1959) The nature of hypnosis: Artifact and essence. *Journal of Abnormal and Social Psychology, 58,* 277–299. **56, 112, 126, 144, 165, 231**
Orne, M. T. (1962) Hypnotically induced hallucinations. In L. J. West (Ed.) *Hallucinations.* New York: Grune and Stratton. **99**
Orne, M. T. (1965) Social control in the psychological experiment: Antisocial behavior and hypnosis. *Journal of Personality and Social Psychology, 1,* 189–200. **129**
Orne, M. T. (1966) On the mechanism of posthypnotic amnesia. *International Journal of Clinical and Experimental Hypnosis, 14,* 121–134. **85**
Orne, M. T. (1972) On the simulating subject as a quasi-control group in hypnosis research: What, why and how. In E. Fromm and R. E. Shor (Eds.) *Hypnosis: Research developments and perspectives.* Chicago: Aldine-Atherton. **144, 202**
Orne, M. T., and Scheibe, K. E. (1964) The contribution of nondeprivation factors in the production of sensory deprivation effects: The psychology of the "panic button". *Journal of Abnormal and Social Psychology, 68,* 3–12. **112**
Orne, M. T., *see also* Evans, Gustafson, O'Connell, Orne, and Shor (1970); Frankel and Orne (1976); McGlashan, Evans, and Orne (1969); Nace, Orne, and Hammer (1974); O'Connell, Shor, and Orne (1970); Shor and Orne (1962).
Ornstein, R. E. (1972) *The psychology of consciousness.* San Francisco: Freeman; Second edition, New York: Harcourt Brace Jovanovich, 1977. **15, 240**
Ornstein, R. E. (Ed.) (1973) *The nature of human consciousness.* New York: Viking (Paper, San Francisco: Freeman). **15, 240**
Ornstein, R. E. *see also* Galin and Ornstein (1972).
Osborn, A. G., Bunker, J. P., Cooper, L. M., Frank, G. S., and Hilgard, E. R. (1967) Effects of thiopental sedation on learning and memory. *Science, 157,* 574–776. **71**
Osgood, C. E., and Luria, Z. (1954) A blind analysis of a case of multiple personality using the semantic differential. *Journal of Abnormal and Social Psychology, 49,* 579–591. **41**

Osgood, C. E., Luria, Z., Jeans, R. F., and Smith, S. W. (1976) The three faces of Evelyn: A case report. *Journal of Abnormal Psychology, 85,* 247-286. **37, 41**

Osgood, C. E., Suci, G. J., and Tannenbaum, P. H. (1957) *The measurement of meaning.* Urbana,: Univ. of Illinois Press. **41**

Ott, C. A., *see* Miller, Ott, Berk, and Springer (1974).

Overton, D. A. (1972) State-dependent learning produced by alcohol and its relevance to alcoholism. In B. Kissin and H. Begleiter (Eds.) *The biology of alcoholism.* Vol. 2. New York: Plenum Press. **244**

Overton, D. A. (1973) State-dependent learning produced by addictive drugs. In S. Fisher and A. M. Freedman (Eds.) *Opiate addiction: Origins and treatment.* Washington, D.C.: Winston. **244**

Paivio, A. (1971) *Imagery and verbal processes.* New York: Holt, Rinehart and Winston. **66**

Papay, J. J., *see* Bruce and Papay (1970).

Patten, B. M. (1971) Transient global amnesia syndrome. *Journal of the American Medical Association, 217,* 690-691. **84**

Patterson, R., *see* Roberts, Schuler, Bacon, Zimmerman, and Patterson (1975).

Pattie, F. A. (1935) A report of attempts to produce uniocular blindness by hypnotic suggestion. *British Journal of Medical Psychology, 15,* 230-241. **203**

Pattie, F. A. (1937) The genuineness of hypnotically produced anesthesia of the skin. *American Journal of Psychology, 49,* 435-443. **203**

Pattie, F. A. (1950) The genuineness of unilateral deafness produced by hypnosis. *American Journal of Psychology, 63,* 84-86. **203**

Patton, A., *see* Graham and Patton (1968).

Paul, G. L., *see* Evans and Paul (1970).

Penfield, W., and Mathieson, G. (1974) Memory: Autopsy findings and comments on the role of hippocampus in experiential recall. *Archives of Neurology, 31,* 145-154. **69**

Perry, C. W. (1964) Content analysis of dream reports. In. J. P. Sutcliffe (Ed.) *The relation of imagery and fantasy to hypnosis.* (Progress report on N.I.M.H. Project M-3950). Sydney, Australia: University of Sydney. **94**

Perry, C. (1973) Imagery, fantasy, and hypnotic susceptibility: A multidimensional approach. *Journal of Personality and Social Psychology, 26,* 208-216. **113**

Perry, C., and Chisholm, W. (1973) Hypnotic age regression and the Ponzo and Poggendorff illusions. *International Journal of Clinical and Experimental Hypnosis, 21,* 192-204. **202**

Perry, C., Wilder, S. and Appignanesi, A. (1973) Hypnotic susceptibility and performance on a battery of creativity measures. *American Journal of Clinical Hypnosis, 15,* 170-180. **109**

Perry, C. W., *see also* Sutcliffe, Perry, and Sheehan (1970); Sheehan and Perry (1976).

Peterson, L. J., *see* Flinn, Wineland, and Peterson (1975).

Piercy, M. and Huppert, F. A. (1972) Efficient recognition of pictures in organic amnesia. *Nature, 240,* 564. **85**

Pine, F., and Holt, R. R. (1960) Creativity and primary process: A study of adaptive regression. *Journal of Abnormal and Social Psychology, 61,* 370-379. **108**

Piotrowski, Z., *see* Bowers, Brecher-Marer, Newton, Piotrowski, Spyer, Taylor, and Watkins (1971).

Porter, M. L., *see* Blum and Porter (1972); Blum and Porter (1973).

Pribram, K. H., *see* Miller, Galanter, and Pribram (1960).

Prince, M. (1890) Some of the revelations of hypnotism: Post-hypnotic suggestion, automatic writing, and double personality. *Boston Medical and Surgical Journal, 122,* May 8, 463-467; 475-476; May 22, 493-495. **25**

Prince, M. (1906) *The dissociation of a personality.* New York and London: Longmans Green. **6, 30, 31**

Prince, M. (1909) Experiments to determine co-conscious (subconscious) ideation. *Journal of*

Abnormal Psychology, 3, 33–42. **7, 12**
Prince, M. (1914) *The unconscious.* New York: Macmillan. **136**
Prince, M. (1929) *Clinical and experimental studies in personality.* Cambridge, Mass.: Sci-Art. **7**
Prince, M. (1939) *Clinical and experimental studies in personality.* Revised and enlarged, with introduction and notes by A. A. Roback. Cambridge, Mass.: Sci-Art. **15**
Prince, M. (1975) *Psychotherapy and multiple personality: Selected essays.* Edited with an introductory essay by Nathan G. Hale, Jr. Cambridge, Mass.: Harvard University Press. **15, 25**
Prince, R. (Ed.) (1968) *Trance and possession states.* Montreal: R. M. Bucke Memorial Society. **40**
Puységur, A. M. J. Chastenet de (1784) *Mémoires pour servir à l'histoire et à l'établissment du magnétisme animal.* (No publisher; cited by Ellenberger, 1970.) **73**
Quartermain, D., and Botwinick, C. Y. (1975) Role of the biogenic amines in the reversal of cycloheximide induced amnesia. *Journal of Comparative and Physiological Psychology, 88,* 386–401. **73**
Rapaport, D. (1958) The theory of ego autonomy: A generalization. *Bulletin of the Menninger Clinic, 22,* 13–35. **241**
Ready, W. B. (1956) Bridey Murphy: An Irishman's view. *Fantasy and Science Fiction,* August. **49**
Rechtschaffen, A., *see* Monroe, Rechtschaffen, Foulkes, and Jensen (1965).
Reed, J., *see* Cutter and Reed (1975).
Reiff, R., and Scheerer, M. (1959) *Memory and hypnotic age regression: Developmental aspects of cognitive function explored through hypnosis.* New York: International Universities Press. **55, 59**
Reiser, M. F., *see* Arkin, Hastey, and Reiser (1966).
Reyher, J., *see* Gur and Reyher (1976).
Rivers, S., *see* Spanos, Rivers, and Ross (1977).
Roberts, A. H., Schuler, J., Bacon, J., Zimmerman, R., and Patterson, R. (1976) Individual differences and autonomic control: Absorption, hypnotic susceptibility, and the unilateral control of skin temperature. *Journal of Abnormal Psychology, 84,* 272–279. **126**
Rosenberg, M. J. (1959) A disconfirmation of the descriptions of hypnosis as a dissociated state. *International Journal of Clinical and Experimental Hypnosis, 7,* 187–204. **10**
Ross, S., *see* Spanos, Rivers, and Ross (1977).
Rossi, E. L., *see* Erickson and Rossi (1974).
Rotter, J. B. (1966) Generalized expectancies for internal versus external control of reinforcement. *Psychological Monographs, 80,* Whole No. 609. **3**
Rubenstein, R., and Newman, R. (1954) The living out of "future" experiences under hypnosis. *Science, 119,* 472–473. **50**
Rubin, N., *see* Liebert, Rubin, and Hilgard (1965).
Ruch, J. C. (1975) Self-hypnosis: The result of heterohypnosis or vice versa? *International Journal of Clinical and Experimental Hypnosis, 23,* 282–304. **229**
Ruch, J. C., Morgan, A. H., and Hilgard, E. R. (1974) Measuring hypnotic responsiveness: A comparison of the Barber Suggestibility Scale and the Stanford Hypnotic Susceptibility Scale, Form A. *International Journal of Clinical and Experimental Hypnosis, 22,* 365–376. **261**
Sacerdote, P. (1967) *Induced dreams.* New York: Vantage Press. **112**
Saito, T. (1969) The influence upon memory of posthypnotic suggestions of amnesia and facilitation. *Psychologia: An International Journal of Psychology in the Orient, 12,* 67–73. **76**
Salisbury, R. F. (1968) Possession in the New Guinea highlands. *International Journal of Social Psychiatry, 14,* 113–118. **40**
Samarin, W. J. (1972) *Tongues of men and angels.* New York: Macmillan. **40**
Sanders, B., *see* Schubot and Sanders (1966).
Sarbin, T. R., and Andersen, M. L. (1963) Base-rate expectancies and perceptual alterations in hypnosis. *British Journal of Social and Clinical Psychology, 2,* 112–121. **202**
Sarbin, T. R., and Coe, W. C. (1972) *Hypnosis: A social psychological analysis of influence communication.*

New York: Holt, Rinehart and Winston. 41, **183, 219**
Sarbin, T. R., *see also* Friedlander and Sarbin (1938).
Sargent, E. (1869) *Planchette; or, the despair of science.* Boston: Roberts Brothers. **133, 134**
Schachtel, E. G. (1959) *Metamorphosis: On the development of affect, perception, attention, and memory.* New York: Basic Books. **113**
Scheerer, M., *see* Reiff and Scheerer (1959); Snyder and Scheerer (1961).
Scheibe, K. E., *see* Orne and Scheibe (1964).
Schreiber, F. R. (1973) *Sybil.* Chicago: Regnery. **31**
Schubot, E., and Sanders, B. (1966) The validity of hypnotic age regression in the recall of past events. Stanford, California: *Hawthorne House Research Memorandum,* #50. **60**
Schuler, J., *see* Roberts, Schuler, Bacon, Zimmerman, and Patterson (1975).
Schwartz, G. E., Davidson, R. J., Maer, F., and Bromfield, E. (1973) *Patterns of hemispheric dominance in musical, emotional, verbal, and spatial tasks.* Paper presented at meeting of Society for Psychophysiological Research, October. **110**
Schwartz, G. E., and Shapiro, D. (Eds.) (1976) *Consciousness and self-regulation. Advances in research.* Vol. I. New York: Plenum Press. **15, 240**
Scoville, W. B., and Milner, B. (1957) Loss of recent memory after bilateral hippocampal lesions. *Journal of Neurology, Neurosurgery, and Psychiatry, 20,* 11–21. **69**
Sears, R. R. (1936) Functional abnormalities of memory with special reference to amnesia. *Psychological Bulletin, 33,* 229–274. **11, 15**
Shapiro, D., *see* Schwartz and Shapiro (1976).
Sheehan, P. W. (1967a) A shortened form of Betts' Questionnaire Upon Mental Imagery. *Journal of Clinical Psychology, 23,* 386–389. **101, 113**
Sheehan, P. W. (1967b) Reliability of a short test of imagery. *Perceptual and Motor Skills, 25,* 744. **101, 113**
Sheehan, P. W. (1972a) Hypnosis and the manifestations of "imagination". In E. Fromm and R. E. Shor, *Hypnosis: Research develoments and perspectives.* Chicago: Aldine-Atherton. **113**
Sheehan, P. W. (Ed.) (1972b) *The function and nature of imagery.* New York: Academic Press. **111**
Sheehan, P. W., Obstoj, I., and McConkey, K. (1976) Trance logic and cue structure as supplied by the hypnotist. *Journal of Abnormal Psychology, 85,* 459–472. **112**
Sheehan, P. W., and Perry, C. W. (1976) *Methodologies of hypnosis: A critical appraisal of contemporary paradigms of hypnosis.* Hillsdale, N.J.: Lawrence Erlbaum. **183, 241**
Sheehan, P. W., *see also* Sutcliffe, Perry, and Sheehan (1970).
Sherman, S. E. (1971) Very deep hypnosis: An experimental and electroencephalographic investigation. Unpublished Ph. D. dissertation Stanford University. **183**
Shevach, B. J., *see* White and Shevach (1942).
Shiffrin, R. M., *see* Atkinson and Shiffrin (1971).
Shor, J., *see* Spiegel, Shor, and Fishman (1945).
Shor, R. E. (1960) The frequency of naturally occurring "hypnotic-like" experiences in the normal college population. *International Journal of Clinical and Experimental Hypnosis, 8,* 151–163. **106**
Shor, R. E. (1970) The three-factor theory of hypnosis as applied to the book-reading fantasy and the concept of suggestion. *International Journal of Clinical and Experimental Hypnosis, 18,* 89–98. **105, 231**
Shor, R. E., and Orne, E. C. (1962) *Harvard Group Scale of Hypnotic Susceptibility.* Palo Alto, Calif.: Consulting Psychologists Press. **261, 262**
Shor, R. E., *see also* Evans, Gustafson, O'Connell, Orne, and Shor (1970); O'Connell, Shor, and Orne (1970).
Sidis, B. (1898) *The psychology of suggestion.* New York: Appleton-Century. **12, 15**
Sidis, B. (Ed.) (1902) *Psychopathological researches: Study in Mental dissociation.* New York: Stechert. **15**

Siegel, R. K., and West, L. J. (Eds.) (1975) *Hallucinations: Behavior, experience, and theory.* New York: Wiley. **112**
Simon, H. A., *see* Newell and Simon (1972).
Singer, J. L. (1966) *Daydreaming: An introduction to the experimental study of inner experience.* New York: Random House. **201**
Singer, J. L. (1973) *The child's world of make-believe.* New York: Academic Press. **201**
Sjoberg, B. M., Jr., and Hollister, L. E. (1965) The effects of psychotomimetic drugs on primary suggestibility. *Psychopharmacologia, 8,* 251–262. **97**
Skinner, B. F. (1934) Has Gertrude Stein a secret? *Atlantic Monthly, 153,* 50–57. **15**
Slotnick, R. S., Liebert, R. M., and Hilgard, E. R. (1965) The enhancement of muscular performance in hypnosis through exhortation and involving instructions. *Journal of Personality, 33,* 37–45. **127, 166**
Smith, G., and Henriksson, M. (1956) Studies in the development of a percept within various contexts of perceived reality. *Acta Psychologica, 12,* 263–281. **244**
Smith, R., Jr., *see* McDonald and Smith (1975).
Smith, S. W., *see* Osgood, Luria, Jeans, and Smith (1976).
Smith, W. L., *see* Kinsbourne and Smith (1974).
Snyder, R., and Scheerer, M. (1961) Interrelationships between personality, skeleto-muscular, and perceptual functioning. In W. Ittleson and S. B. Kutash (Eds.) *Perceptual changes in psychopathology.* New Brunswick, N.J.: Rutgers University Press, 166–210. **11**
Spanos, N. P., Barber, T. X., and Lang, G. (1974) Cognition and self-control: Cognitive control of painful sensory input. In H. London and R. E. Nisbett (Eds.) *Thought and feeling.* Chicago: Aldine, 141–158. **172**
Spanos, N. P., and McPeake, J. D. (1975) Involvement in everyday imaginative activities, attitudes toward hypnosis, and hypnotic suggestibility. *Journal of Personality and Social Psychology, 31,* 594–598. **113**
Spanos, N. P., McPeake, J. D., and Churchill, B. A. (1976) Relationships between imaginative ability variables and the Barber Suggestibility Scale. *American Journal of Clinical Hypnosis, 19,* 39–46. **113**
Spanos, N. P., Rivers, S., and Ross, S. (1977) Experienced involuntariness in response to hypnotic suggestion. *Annals of the New York Academy of Sciences, 296,* 208–221. **230**
Sperry, R. W., *see* Gazzaniga, Bogen, and Sperry (1962).
Spiegel, H. (1974) *Manual for Hypnotic Induction Profile.* New York: Soni Medica. **261**
Spiegel, H., Shor, J., and Fishman, S. (1945) An ablation technique for the study of personality development. *Psychosomatic Medicine, 7,* 273–278. **60**
Springer, A. D., *see* Miller and Springer (1973); Miller and Springer (1974); Miller, Ott, Berk, and Springer (1974).
Spyer, T. C., *see* Bowers, Brecher-Marer, Newton, Piotrowski, Spyer, Taylor, and Watkins (1971).
Squire, L. R. (1974) Amnesia for remote events following electroconvulsive therapy. *Behavioral Biology, 12,* 119–125. **84**
Stenman, U., *see* Von Wright, Anderson, and Stenman (1975).
Stevenson, J. H. (1972) The effect of hypnotic and posthypnotic dissociation on the performance of interfering tasks. Doctoral dissertation, Stanford University. *Dissertation Abstracts International, 33,* 8-B, 3998. **144**
Stevenson, J. H. (1976) The effect of posthypnotic dissociation on the performance of interfering tasks. *Journal of Abnormal Psychology, 85,* 398–407. **144, 146**
Stevenson, R. L. (1886) *The strange case of Dr. Jekyll and Mr. Hyde.* London: Longmans. **18**
Stewart, C. G. *see* Blum, Geiwitz, and Stewart (1967).
Suci, G. J., *see* Osgood, Suci, and Tannenbaum (1957).

Sutcliffe, J. P. (1961) "Credulous" and "skeptical" views of hypnotic phenomena: Experiments on esthesia, hallucination, and delusion. *Journal of Abnormal and Social Psychology, 46,* 678–682. **202**

Sutcliffe, J. P., and Jones, J. (1962) Personal identity, multiple personality, and hypnosis. *International Journal of Clinical and Experimental Hypnosis, 10,* 231–269. **41, 42**

Sutcliffe, J. P., Perry, C. W., and Sheehan, P. W. (1970) The relation of some aspects of imagery and fantasy to hypnotizability. *Journal of Abnormal Psychology, 76,* 279–287. **102, 113**

Swanson, G. E. (1978) Travels through inner space: Family structure and openness to absorbing experiences. *American Journal of Sociology, 83,* 890–919. **113**

Sweet, W. H., *see* Wall and Sweet (1967)

Taft, R., *see* Diamond and Taft (1975).

Talland, G. (1965) *Deranged memory.* New York: Academic Press. **84**

Tamerin, J. S. and others (1971) Alcohol and memory: Amnesia and short-term memory function during experimentally induced intoxication. *American Journal of Psychiatry, 127,* 1659–1664. **70**

Tannenbaum, P. H., *see* Osgood, Suci, and Tannenbaum (1957).

Tart, C. T. (1965a) The hypnotic dream: Methodological problems and a review of the literature. *Psychological Bulletin, 63,* 87–99. **94**

Tart, C. T. (1965b) Toward the experimental control of dreaming: A review of the literature. *Psychological Bulletin, 64,* 81–91. **94**

Tart, C. T. (1966) Types of hypnotic dreams and their relation to hypnotic depth. *Journal of Abnormal Psychology, 71,* 377–382. **93**

Tart, C. T. (Ed.) (1969) *Altered states of consciousness.* New York: Wiley. **15, 240**

Tart, C. T. (1970) Self-report scales of hypnotic depth. *International Journal of Clinical and Experimental Hypnosis, 18,* 105–125. **168, 183**

Tart, C. T. (1972) Measuring the depth of an altered state of consciousness, with particular reference to self-report scales of hypnotic depth. In E. Fromm and R. E. Shor (Eds.) *Hypnosis: Research developments and perspectives.* Chicago: Aldine-Atherton. **168, 169, 183**

Tart, C. T. (1975) *States of consciousness.* New York: Dutton. **15, 240**

Tart, C. T., *see also* Hilgard and Tart (1966).

Taylor, S. E. L. (Ed.) (1932) *Fox-Taylor automatic writing, 1869–1892. Unabridged record.* Minneapolis, Minn.: Tribune-Great West Printing Co. **133**

Taylor, W. S., and Martin, M. F. (1944) Multiple personality. *Journal of Abnormal and Social Psychology, 39,* 281–300. **25, 41**

Taylor, W. S., *see also* Bowers, Brecher-Marer, Newton, Piotrowski, Spyer, Taylor, and Watkins (1971).

Tellegen, A., and Atkinson, G. (1974) Openness to absorbing and self-altering experiences ("absorption"), a trait related to hypnotic susceptibility. *Journal of Abnormal Psychology, 83,* 268–277. **106**

Teuber, H-L., *see* Milner, Corkin, and Teuber (1968).

Theye, F. W., *see* Earle and Theye (1968).

Thigpen, C. H., and Cleckley, H. (1957) *The three faces of Eve.* New York: McGraw-Hill. **18, 41**

't Hoen, P. (1977) Effects of hypnotizability and visualizing ability on imagery-mediated learning. *International Journal of Clinical and Experimental Hypnosis, 83,* 890–919. **104**

Thompson, R. F. (1976) The search for the engram. *American Psychologist, 31,* 209–227. **239**

Thorn, W. A. F. (1960) *A study of the correlates of dissociation as measured by amnesia.* Unpublished B.S. (Hons.) thesis, Department of psychology, University of Sydney. **74**

Thorn, W. A. F. *see also* Evans and Thorn (1966).

Thorndike, E. L. (1913) Ideomotor action. *Psychological Review, 20,* 91–106. **129**

Titley, R., *see* Trustman, Dubovsky, and Titley (1977).

Tolman, E. C. (1932) *Purposive behavior in animals and men.* New York: Appleton-Century. (Reprinted, University of California Press, 1949) 218

Tolman, E. C. (1938) The determiners of behavior at a choice point. *Psychological Review, 45,* 1–41. 218

Tonn, H. F., *see* McKellar and Tonn (1967).

Tooker, D., and Hofheins, R. (1976) *Fiction! Interviews with Northern California novelists.* New York and Los Altos, Calif.: Harcourt Brace Jovanovich/William Kaufmann. 195, 203

Toth, M. F., *see* Arkin, Toth, Baker, and Hastey (1970).

Treisman, A. M. (1969) Strategies and models of selective attention. *Psychological Review, 76,* 282–299. 148

Troffer, S. (1965) *Hypnotic age regression and cognitive functioning.* Unpublished doctoral dissertation, Stanford University. 57

Trustman, R., Dubovsky, S., and Titley, R. (1977) Auditory perception during general anesthesia—myth or fact? *International Journal of Clinical and Experimental Hypnosis, 25,* 88–105. 85

Tulving, E. (1972) Episodic and semantic memory. In E. Tulving and W. Donaldson (Eds.) *Organization of memory.* New York: Academic Press. 57

Tulving, E., and Madigan, S. A. (1970) Memory and verbal learning. *Annual Review of Psychology, 21,* 437–484. 63

Ullman, M., Krippner, S., and Vaughan, A. (1973) *Dream telepathy.* New York: Macmillan. 112

Underwood, H. W. (1960) The validity of hypnotically induced hallucinations. *Journal of Abnormal and Social Psychology, 61,* 39–46. 202

Van de Castle, R. L., *see* Hall and Van de Castle (1966).

Van der Meulen, S. J., *see* Bowers and Van der Meulen (1970).

Van Luijk, J. N., *see* Giel, Gerzahegn, and Van Luijk (1968).

Vaughan, A., *see* Ullman, Krippner, and Vaughan (1973).

Veith, I. (1965) *Hysteria: The history of a disease.* Chicago: University of Chicago Press. 128

Vingoe, F. J. (1973) Comparison of the Harvard Group Scale of Hypnotic Susceptibility, Form A, and the Group Alert Scale in a university population. *International Journal of Clinical and Experimental Hypnosis, 21,* 169–178. 183

Von Wright, J. M., Anderson, K., and Stenman, U. (1975) Generalization of conditioned GSRs in dichotic listening. In P. M. A. Rabbitt and S. Dornic (Eds.) *Attention and performance.* V New York: Academic Press. 154

Wagner, E. E., and Heise, M. R. (1974) A comparison of Rorschach records of three multiple personalities. *Journal of Personality Assessment, 38,* 308–331. 41

Walker, N. S., Garrett, J. B., and Wallace, B. (1976) Restoration of eidetic imagery via hypnotic age regression. *Journal of Abnormal Psychology, 85,* 335–337. 61

Wall, P. D., and Sweet, W. H. (1967) Temporary abolition of pain in man. *Science, 155,* 108–109. 246

Wall, P. D., *see also* Melzack and Wall (1965).

Wallace, B., *see* Walker, Garrett, and Wallace (1976).

Warrington, E. K. (1971) Neurological disorders of memory. *British Medical Bulletin, 27,* 243–247. 84

Watkins, J. G., *see* Bowers, Brecher-Marer, Newton, Piotrowski, Spyer, Taylor, and Watkins (1971).

Webb, W. B., *see* Williams, Agnew, and Webb (1964).

Weitzenhoffer, A. M. (1953) *Hypnotism: An objective study of suggestibility.* New York: Wiley (paper edition, 1963). 54, 59, 130

Weitzenhoffer, A. M., Gough, P. B., and Landes, J. (1959) A study of the Braid effect: Hypnosis by visual fixation. *Journal of Psychology, 47,* 67–80. 225

Weitzenhoffer, A. M., and Hilgard, E. R. (1959) *Stanford Hypnotic Susceptibility Scale, Forms A and*

B. Palo Alto, Calif.: Consulting Psychologists Press. **258, 262**

Weitzenhoffer, A. M., and Hilgard, E. R. (1962) *Stanford Hypnotic Susceptibility Scale, Form C.* Palo Alto, Calif.: Consulting Psychologists Press. **51**

Weitzenhoffer, A. M., and Hilgard, E. R. (1963) *Stanford Profile Scales of Hypnotic Susceptibility. Forms I and II.* Palo Alto, Calif.: Consulting Psychologists Press. **140**

Weitzenhoffer, A. M., and Hilgard, E. R. (1967) *Revised Stanford Profile Scales of Hypnotic Susceptibility, Forms I and II.* (With revised standardization data.) Palo Alto, Calif.: Consulting Psychologists Press. **140, 260, 262**

Weitzenhoffer, A. M., *see also* Aas, Hilgard, and Weitzenhoffer (1963); Hilgard, Weitzenhoffer, Landes, and Moore (1961).

Wells, W. R. (1940) Ability to resist artificially induced dissociation. *Journal of Abnormal and Social Psychology, 35,* 261–272. **119**

Welsh, G. S., and Barron, F. (1963) *Barron-Welsh Art Scale.* Palo Alto, Calif.: Consulting Psychologists Press. **108**

West, L. J. (Ed.) (1962) *Hallucinations.* New York: Grune and Stratton. **112**

West, L. J., *see also* Siegel and West (1975).

White, R. W., and Shevach, B. J. (1942) Hypnosis and the concept of dissociation. *Journal of Abnormal Psychology, 37,* 309–328. **11, 16**

Whitty, C. W. M., and Zangwill, O. L. (Eds.) (1966) *Amnesia.* New York: Appleton-Century-Crofts; London: Butterworths. **84**

Whyte, L. L. (1960) *The unconscious before Freud.* New York: Basic Books. **5**

Wickramesekera, I. (1976) *Biofeedback, behavior therapy, and hypnosis.* Chicago: Nelson-Hall. **256**

Wilbur, C. B., *see* Ludwig, Brandsma, Wilbur, Bendfeldt, and Jameson (1972).

Wilder, S., *see* Perry, Wilder, and Appignanesi (1973).

Williams, R. L., Agnew, H. W., Jr., and Webb, W. B. (1964) Sleep patterns in young adults: An EEG study. *EEG Clinical Neurophysiology, 17,* 376–381. **92**

Williams, T. A., *see* Fink, Kety, McGaugh, and Williams 1974).

Williamsen, J. A., Johnson, H. J., and Eriksen, C. W. (1965) Some characteristics of posthypnotic amnesia. *Journal of Abnormal Psychology, 70,* 123–131. **82, 251**

Wineland, P., *see* Flinn, Wineland, and Peterson (1975).

Winzenz, D., *see* Bower, Clark, Winzenz, and Lesgold (1969).

Wolberg, L. R. (1945) *Hypnoanalysis.* New York: Grune and Stratton. **153, 254**

Wolpert, E., *see* Dement and Wolpert (1958).

Woodworth, R. S. (1918) *Dynamic psychology.* New York: Columbia University Press. **223**

Yarnell, P. R., and Lynch, S. (1973) The "ding": Amnestic states in football trauma. *Neurology, 23,* 196–197. **69**

Yarnell, P. R., *see also* Lynch and Yarnell (1973).

Yeager, C. L., *see* Ford and Yeager (1948).

Young, M. N., and Gibson, W. B. (1966) *How to develop an exceptional memory.* Hollywood: Wilshire Press. **84**

Young, P. C. (1927) Is *rapport* an essential characteristic of hypnosis? *Journal of Abnormal and Social Psychology, 22,* 130–139. **119**

Zangwill, O. L., *see* Whitty and Zangwill (1966).

Zaretsky, I. I., and Leone, M. P. (Eds.) (1974) *Religious movements in contemporary America.* Princeton, N.J.: Princeton University Press. **40**

Zeeman, E. C. (1976) Catastrophe theory. *Scientific American, 234,* 65–83. **247, 256**

Zikmund, V. (1972) Physiological correlates of visual imagery. In P. W. Sheehan (Ed.) *The function and nature of imagery.* New York: Academic Press. **98**

Zimbardo, P. G., *see* Maslach, Marshall, and Zimbardo (1972).

Zimmerman, R., *see* Roberts, Schuler, Bacon, Zimmerman, and Patterson (1975).

ADDENDUM

The interpretation was advanced in the first edition (Chapters 1–12) that the concept of dissociation is useful in the understanding of divided consciousness as found in ordinary waking experience as well as in hypnosis and in such manifestations as multiple personality. This is compatible with the developing interest in cognitive psychology and with the return of consciousness to psychology (Hilgard, 1980). Some recent support for the neodissociation theory is provided by additional studies of the "hidden observer" phenomenon, by concealed but recoverable memories in chemical anesthesia, by alternative interpretations of hypnotic analgesia, and by further studies of multiple personalities.

THE HIDDEN OBSERVER PHENOMENON

The "hidden observer" was introduced as a metaphor to describe a memory structure based on material that the person had registered and stored in memory without being aware that the material had been experienced and processed. With some highly hypnotizable persons, the presence of such memories could be detected by the recovery through the use of appropriate methods such as automatic writing or a technique described as automatic talking (Chapters 9 and 10).

The Limited Occurrence of Hidden Observers in Experimental Studies

The results of the early experiments had led to three empirical generalizations: First, that such recovery of concealed memories was limited to highly hypnotizable persons; second, that not all highly hypnotizable persons had access to such hidden memories; and third, that once the memories were restored, they appeared to be very matter-of-fact and realistic, without showing any upsurge of material from some deep unconscious. In the years since publication, these generalizations, particularly the second one, have stimulated further investigations to explain the phenomena exhibited.

Subsequent experiments confirmed the limited presence of the hidden observer phenomenon. In our study of hypnotic deafness, it was found that some 25 percent of highly hypnotizable subjects recovered the fact that some part had heard the tones at normal level, despite the partial or complete hypnotic deafness (Crawford, Macdonald, and Hilgard, 1979). The methods of selecting the highly hypnotizables to participate meant that about 20 percent of a random university sample were designated as highly responsive to hypnosis. The 25 percent of these who showed the hidden observer hence represented about 5 percent of the general student population. Two other investigations of pain reduction and the recovery of pain experienced while little pain was being felt within suggested hypnotic analgesia showed hidden observers in 39 percent and 25 percent of their highly hypnotizable samples (Laurence and Perry, 1981; Piccione, 1981). Thus our original findings of hidden observers in a fraction of highly hypnotizable persons was confirmed.

The phenomenon of the hidden observer was criticized by Spanos and Hewitt (1980) on the grounds that the instructions to the hypnotized subjects produced the effect through a wording that strongly suggested compliance. A study in our laboratory had used the real-simulator design to test the reality of the hidden observer in analgesia (Hilgard and others, 1978). When they used instructions that were similar to ours, they apparently found the hidden observer in all of their highly hypnotizable subjects, but when they used a different form of instructions, the hidden observer was not demonstrated. Laurence and Perry were joined by Kihlstrom to make a careful analysis of the Spanos and Hewitt data (Laurence, Perry, and Kihlstrom, 1983). They doubted the Spanos/Hewitt conclusion that the hidden observer results depended entirely on the cues provided by the experimenter. Spanos (1983) in his reply did not convincingly refute their argument. This does not mean that Spanos and his associates were persuaded to modify their beliefs (Spanos, de Groot, Tiller, Weekes, and Bertrand, 1985).

The phenomena remained sufficiently interesting, however, to justify an experiment meticulously designed by Nogrady, McConkey, Laurence, and Perry (1983), with instructions that were unlikely to give any compliance cues. By using the real simulator design of Orne (1971), in which if such cues are present those simulating hypnosis will respond to them, they were able to show that such cues were not operative. Then to avoid any experimenter bias in interpreting what the subject experienced, the postsession interview was conducted by one of the investigators who was "blind" as to which subjects were genuinely responding as high hypnotizables and which were merely acting as if they were highly hypnotizable. The interviewing was assisted by use of the Experimental Analysis Technique (EAT) of Sheehan, McConkey, and Cross (1978), which the interviewer (McConkey) had helped develop. The technique consists of showing the subject at a later time a videotape of the session, what was done and what was said, both by the hypnotist and by the subject. A structured form was used in which at predetermined points the videotape was stopped and the subjects were encouraged to comment on the observed material that they found meaningful. They could also request that the tape be stopped at other points when they wished to make a comment. The interviewer occasionally asked specific questions, for example, with regard to the hidden observer experience, "Is this an experience you had following the instructions, or is it one that you were having throughout the session?" Another member of the investigative team, unfamiliar with the subjects' hypnotic responsiveness levels or with the ratings made by the first interviewer, rated aspects of the experiment bearing specifically on dissociation and the hidden observer experience. This critically designed experiment confirmed the results of the studies by Hilgard and others (1978) and of Laurence and Perry (1981) by finding a hidden observer response in 5 of 12 highly hypnotizable subjects, in none of 10 high-medium subjects, and in none of 10 low hypnotizables simulating hypnosis.

Correlates of the Hidden Observer

The important question of why some should reveal a hidden observer and others not was illuminated by a finding in the study by Laurence and Perry (1981) and confirmed by Nogrady and others (1983). In the course of hypnosis, one of the suggestions tested was that of age regression in which subjects were to experience themselves again as children of five years of age. With highly hypnotizable subjects, most are successful in having a realistic experience of becoming a young child again. This experience takes two different forms. In one form the subject becomes completely absorbed in the experience of being a child again, while in the second form the subject becomes a child again in a manner that feels convincing, but in addition there is an observer present. This observer has some of the properties of the hidden observer in pain in that it knows all that is going on in the inward experience as well as in the environmental contexts of the experience. Sometimes this is reported in statements that are variants of this one: "I felt sorry for that child who was lost and frightened lest her mother would not find her, because I knew all along that she would return soon." The experience can be considered one of duality—at once a child and an adult. Regression was recorded before there had been an opportunity to test for a hidden observer. It turned out, however, that the presence or absence of the duality experience was almost perfectly correlated with the subsequent experience of a hidden observer, but in a direction opposite to that which would be expected were the subjects simply complying with the hypnotist's demands. Conforming to the hypnotist's suggestions of becoming a child of five again does *not* imply preserving an observing adult part, even if in the pain experience the suggestion *may* imply demonstrating a hidden observer. Yet it was those who reported a dual experience in age regression who also reported a hidden observer. If the duality in age regression does not conform to social compliance, there is no reason to assign the hidden observer to social compliance.

The fact that this duality of experience was also related to the hidden observer experience appears to be coherent with the possibility that the persons who report these events in the experimental setting are more likely to experience simultaneous dissociative experiences in daily life. Indeed, such experiences were reported by some of those with hidden observers who did not therefore find the experience unusual or remarkable. Other highly responsive hypnotic subjects who demonstrate other forms of dissociative experience, such as recoverable posthypnotic amnesia, are unable to demonstrate the hidden observer effect. One possibility is that their amnesic experiences are more profound and hence less permeable to intrusions from the concealed but stored memories.

Care is needed in advancing plausible interpretations as though they do not require experimental justification. In a later study, Perry (1983) reported new data showing that amnesia was *more* profound in those with hidden observers. His findings can be squared with the absence of a hidden observer in other subjects if it is assumed that focused attention by those *without* hidden observers leads to a failure to record and store in memory events not in focus. Those with a hidden observer have available reversible amnesia for such marginal events. According to this interpretation, they can better divide consciousness and store the unattended material, subject to later recall when the amnesia is lifted.

The events are complex, and supplementary experimentation will be required to clarify the individual differences involved.

THE RECOVERY OF INEXPERIENCED SURGICAL PAIN

New observations on the hidden observer phenomenon were obtained in clinical settings in which surgical pain was investigated. Bennett, Davis, and Giannini (1981) initially conducted a carefully controlled study of 47 patients undergoing inguinal hernia repair and gallbladder removal under deep planes of chemical anesthesia in order to study the registration of events during the surgery. They conducted posthypnotic interviews two to five days after the operation was terminated. Before the hypnotic session, the patients recalled nothing of what had happened during surgery. However, when hypnotically regressed to the time of the operation, among those who were highly hypnotizable, by contrast to those who were not, there were more who gave convincing evidence of the registration of their memories of events that had occurred during deep chemical anesthesia. The proportion with "hidden observers" in this setting was higher than in the laboratory experiments, with two-thirds of the highly hypnotizables showing recovered memories and about a fourth of the lows. The methods in the laboratory studies and the surgical studies were, of course, not strictly comparable. This investigation supplements the earlier ones reported in Chapter 4 (p. 71f and 85).

The same investigators conducted an additional study of a nonverbal response suggested while the patient was anesthetized and operated upon, with memory tested days later during convalescence (Bennett, Davis, and Giannini, 1985). In this study 33 patients were recruited from two university training hospitals. They represented 13 requiring repair of an inguinal hernia, 12 removal of a gall bladder, and 8 undergoing orthopedic procedures. The patients had consented to the investigation, in which they expected to wear headphones, to receive at normal listening volume either of two tape sequences: one the actual operating room sounds and voices, the other a prerecorded tape. The tapes were played continuously beginning with the initial incision. The prerecorded tape contained suggestions of rapid postoperative healing interspersed with music and songs. The patients knew that they would be interviewed during convalescence to determine what they remembered, and that their memories might then be assisted by hypnosis.

The procedures in the operating room were the normal ones, and none of the medical personnel were participants in the investigation. Premedication was followed by anesthetization by thiopentone, then nitrous oxide and enflurane or halothane. All patients also received neuromuscular blocking drugs. The effective agents at the time that posthypnotic suggestions were given were nitrous oxide and either enflurane or halothane. The patient and all in contact with the patient were blind as to which tape was being played, so that the double-blind model was followed. The tape for the suggestion condition ended with a 3-minute personal message, not included in the control tape, given about 5 minutes before the anesthesia was reversed. The message suggested that the patient would pull on his or her ear when the convalescent interview occurred to assure the interviewer that the message on the tape had been heard. The results showed, in brief, that in the nonhypnotic portion of the interview a substantially larger portion of the patients in the suggestion condition than in the control condition pulled their ears (Fisher's exact $p = .05$). No suggestion patient recalled having heard the ear-pulling suggestion during this interview, or indeed later when regressed through hypnotic procedures to the operative session. The bearing on dissociation is that a comprehended verbal message may have behavioral consequences even though the memory is not accessible by way of verbal report. To be sure, some of the patients, under hypnosis, were able to identify other aspects of the repeated messages on the tape, such as the titles of some of the pieces of music that had been played. The results reaffirm the desirability of caution in operating-room conversation, despite failures to retrieve verbal reports of what was said during the operation, opposite to the position taken by Dubovsky and Trustman (1976).

ALTERNATIVE INTERPRETATIONS OF HYPNOTIC ANALGESIA

The presence of a hidden observer reporting residual pain among those who are able to relieve pain through hypnosis does not account completely for the effectiveness of hypnosis, for there are many who reduce pain who give no evidence of a hidden observer. Hence the importance of the hidden observer phenomenon rests more largely on its contributions to the understanding of dissociative processes. It is, however, coherent with the common finding that physiological indicators of pain persist even when there is no longer felt pain.

It is not surprising that problems of pain can be met by psychological methods that have little to do with the more profound aspects of hypnosis. For example, counterirritants have long been used to reduce pain, as in mustard plasters or liniments that produce skin pain to relieve muscular or other pains beneath the skin area.

Although it has been shown that the more hypnotizable person can reduce pain by hypnotic methods to a greater extent than the less hypnotizable, this does not mean that the less hypnotizable cannot reduce pain by other psychological methods such as counterirritants, distractions, progressive relaxation, or biofeedback. Because all methods overlap to some extent, it is not always easy to determine the exact processes that are most significant in any one setting.

The difficulties have been well shown in the study of pain relief by hypnotic methods with children and adolescents (J. Hilgard and LeBaron, 1984). The primary method of inducing hypnosis in this study was the exercise of fantasy by the child patients undergoing the painful experiences of bone marrow aspiration in the treatment of cancer. While the children were involved in these fantasies the pain was commonly reduced, as evident in the patient's demeanor and subsequent report about the felt pain. Children are more highly hypnotizable than adults, and the amount of relief found in the investigation was attributed primarily to hypnosis because the degree of improvement correlated with measured hypnotizability. However, in the exercise of imagination and in the elaborating of fantasies children become so readily involved that it is difficult to say exactly when they are hypnotized.

One of the striking findings was that many of the patients being treated by the same methods that were so distressing to others found no need for psychological help because they had found distraction techniques by themselves that served their purposes (J. Hilgard and LeBaron, p. 111–124). Some of them found relief through self-induced pressure, as by clenching their hands or grasping the treatment table, by screaming that produced massive stimulation that circumvented the localized pain of the needle, by involved conversation, or by religious ceremonies such as reciting the 23rd psalm. Many of these distractors simply redirected attention and had little resemblance to hypnosis as usually conceived. In other instances the self-induced fantasies were very close to self-hypnosis. The more deeply involved in fantasy the patient was, the more the condition resembled the induced hypnosis of the other patients who had requested help from the hypnotist.

Distraction can be conceived as dissociative, whether or not it is interpreted as related to hypnosis. It is dissociative because in the competition for alternative demands upon attention weight is given to the alternative more acceptable to the person involved. In established hypnosis there are features that may be interpreted as beyond simple distraction, such as the less effort required to maintain the alternate orientation once hypnotic involvement has been achieved.

Because alternatives exist with some ambiguities always present, the room that remains for the exercise of personal preference sustains some of the disagreements among those engaged in hypnotic research.

EGO STATES AND MULTIPLE PERSONALITIES

Laboratory studies of dissociative phenomena have dealt primarily with evidence based on the recovery of information recently stored in memory but not available to ordinary recall. The "hidden observer" metaphor was intended to imply only a temporary division of consciousness, so that a recent experience was registered—and the information processed—even though the information was never conscious and was not normally available to recall. It was not intended to imply a hidden fraction of the personality persisting through time, but merely an organized cognitive structure of recent information acquired covertly that could be made available only through special procedures (Hilgard, 1984). This conception was challenged by an interpretation that accepted preestablished ego states that had a history of their own and had endured through time.

Watkins and Watkins (1979–1980) reported the results of two studies bearing on the hidden observer phenomenon, one with volunteer highly hypnotizable subjects, the other with patients. They were interested primarily in relating the hidden observer to ego-state theory, as earlier propounded by Federn (1952). They described an ego state as an enduring fraction of the total personality, like a "covert" or incipient multiple personality. The Watkins' methods yielded hidden observers in all of their subjects and patients. The equivalence between hidden observers and ego states was brought out most clearly in five patients who had been intensively treated previously in hypnoanalytic ego-state therapy. The ego states of these patients were well known to the investigators and had names and personal histories. It is understandable that the patients should have assigned the hidden observer to one or more of these acknowledged states. Perhaps less expected was that within the same person some ego states reported while other ego states denied that they had knowledge of the concealed pain (or hearing in the study with students). There are clearly some analogies between the hidden observer phenomenon and the ego-state interpretation, with both representing dissociations. However, the states as studied by the Watkins' had features that did not appear in the more focused laboratory studies in which only a fraction of the highly hypnotizable subjects reported hidden observers. The interpretation of ego states as incipient multiple personalities is an intriguing possibility, suggesting that multiple personalities may be more prevalent than commonly believed.

Multiple Personalities

Alternating and multiple personalities in their various forms are considered in Chapter 2 (p. 24–42). For whatever reasons, the occurrence of reported multiple personalities has accelerated in the last few years. This may perhaps be attributed to the increasing use of hypnosis by psychotherapists, because hypnosis, by contrast with other forms of psychological treatment in their standard forms—psychoanalytic or behavior modification varieties—are less likely to recognize the symptoms of multiple personality or to accept the diagnosis of multiple personalities in preference to diagnoses of hysteria or borderline schizophrenia (Bliss, 1980).

The prevalence of reported cases is clearly on the increase. Greaves (1980) listed 37 cases reported between 1971 and 1980. Of these, 16 were reported from Allison's practice by Allison and Schwarz (1980). Bliss (1980) added 14 cases of his own to those which Greaves included. Putnam and others (1983) referred to 100 cases. Greaves concluded that "contemporary reports raise serious doubts as to whether multiple personality can any longer be regarded as a rare condition, and whether the past paucity of reports arose mainly out of clinical oversight" (Greaves, 1980, p. 594). There seems little doubt that among the many cases there are enough which can be considered genuine as reflections of the reality of this type of extreme personality dissociation. A whole issue of the *International Journal of Clinical and Experimental Hypnosis* was later devoted to evidence and issues related to multiple personality (April 1984, *32*, No. 2).

DISSOCIATION AND COGNITIVE PSYCHOLOGY

Modern cognitive psychology in its familiar information-processing mode devotes a great deal of attention to the storing and retrieval of information, and hence to the problems of memory. Because posthypnotic amnesia is one of the prevalent forms of dissociation studied in hypnosis (Chapter 4, p. 73–83) and is a characteristic distortion of retrieval, its investigation fits well into cognitive psychology. The relationships have been brought out in an edited volume, *Functional Disorders of Memory*, by Kihlstrom and Evans (1979). A further integration between cognitive psychology and aspects of dissociative experience is presented in a well-documented chapter on "Conscious, Subconscious, Unconscious: A Cognitive Perspective" (Kihlstrom, 1984). In it, the relationships diagrammed in Figure 21 (p. 218) are developed in greater detail with due regard to the advances in cognitive psychology. He makes the case that unless the phenomena of dissociation are taken seriously, the currently evolving model of the mind which is designed to help in the understanding of the cognitive system may lead us seriously astray.

The supplementary data and their interpretation indicate the psychological reality of the observations reported in the early chapters. That there is still some imprecision in our understanding of the phenomena provides a challenge to further investigation.

REFERENCES CITED IN ADDENDUM

Allison, R., and Schwartz, T. (1980) *Minds in many pieces*. Wade, N.Y.: Rawson.
Bennett, H. L., Davis, H. S., and Giannini, J. A. (1981) Post-hypnotic suggestions during general anesthesia and subsequent dissociated behavior. Paper presented to the Society for Clinical and Experimental Hypnosis, Annual Convention, Portland, Oregon, October 17.

Bennett, H. L., Davis, H. S., and Giannini, J. A. (1985) Non-verbal response to intraoperative conversation. *British Journal of Anaesthesia, 57,* 174–179.
Bliss, E. L. (1980) Multiple personalities: A report of 14 cases with implications for schizophrenia and hysteria. *Archives of General Psychiatry, 37,* 1388–1397.
Crawford, H. J., Macdonald, H., and Hilgard, E. R. (1979) Hypnotic deafness: A psychophysical study of responses to tone intensity as modified by hypnosis. *American Journal of Psychology, 92,* 193–214.
Dubovsky, S. T., and Trustman, R. (1976) Absence of recall after general anesthesia: Implications for theory and practice. *Anesthesia and Analgesia, 55,* 696–701.
Federn, P. (1952) *Ego psychology and the psychoses.* New York: Basic Books.
Greaves, G. B. (1980) Multiple personality: 165 years after Mary Reynolds. *Journal of Nervous and Mental Disease, 168,* 577–596.
Hilgard, E. R. (1980) Consciousness in contemporary psychology. *Annual Review of Psychology, 31,* 1–26.
Hilgard, E. R. (1984) The hidden observer and multiple personality. *International Journal of Clinical and Experimental Hypnosis, 32,* 248–253.
Hilgard, E. R., Hilgard, J. R., Macdonald, H., Morgan, A. H., and Johnson, L. S. (1978) Covert pain in hypnotic analgesia: Its reality as tested by the real-simulator design. *Journal of Abnormal Psychology, 87,* 239–246.
Hilgard, J. R., and LeBaron, S. (1984) *Hypnotherapy of pain in children with cancer.* Los Altos, CA: William Kaufmann, Inc.
Kihlstrom, J. F. (1984) Conscious, subconscious, unconscious: A cognitive perspective. In K. S. Bowers and D. Meichenbaum (Eds.) *The unconscious: A reappraisal.* New York: Wiley.
Kihlstrom, J. F., and Evans, F. J. (Eds.) (1979) *Functional disorders of memory.* Hillsdale, N.J.: Erlbaum.
Laurence, J.-R., and Perry, C. (1981) The "hidden observer" phenomenon in hypnosis: Some additional findings. *Journal of Abnormal Psychology, 90,* 334–344.
Laurence, J.-R., Perry, C., and Kihlstrom, J. F. (1983) "Hidden observer" phenomenon in hypnosis: An experimental creation? *Journal of Personality and Social Psychology, 44,* 163–169.
Nogrady, H., McConkey, K. M., Laurence, J.-R., and Perry, C. (1983) Dissociation, duality, and demand characteristics in hypnosis. *Journal of Abnormal Psychology, 92,* 223–235.
Orne, M. T. (1971) The simulation of hypnosis: Why, how, and what it means. *International Journal of Clinical and Experimental Hypnosis, 19,* 183–210.
Perry, C. (1983) Dissociative phenomena and hypnosis. Invited address, American Psychological Association, Annual Convention, Anaheim, California, August 29.
Piccione, C. (1981) The paradox of hypnotic analgesia: The hidden observer? Paper presented to the Society for Clinical and Experimental Hypnosis, Annual Convention, Portland, Oregon, October 17.
Putnam, F. W., Post, R., Guroff, J., Silberman, E., and Darban, L. (1983) One hundred cases of multiple personality disorder. Paper presented at the American Psychiatric Association, Annual Meeting, May.
Sheehan, P. W., McConkey, J. M., and Cross, D. (1978) Experiential analysis of hypnosis: Some new observations on hypnotic phenomena. *Journal of Abnormal Psychology, 87,* 570–573.
Spanos, N. P. (1983) The hidden observer as an experimental creation. *Journal of Personality and Social Psychology, 44,* 170–176.

Spanos, N. P., de Groot, H. P., Tiller, D. K., Weekes, J. R., and Bertrand, L. D. (1985) Trance logic duality and hidden observer responding in hypnotic, imagination control, and simulation subjects. *Journal of Abnormal Psychology, 94,* 611–623.

Spanos, N. P., and Hewitt, E. C. (1980) The hidden observer in hypnotic analgesia: Discovery or experimental creation? *Journal of Personality and Social Psychology, 3,* 1201–1214.

Watkins, J. G., and Watkins, H. H. (1979–1980) Ego states and hidden observers. *Journal of Altered States of Consciousness, 5,* 3–18.

INDEX

Ablation theory, of regression, 53–54, 60
Absorption, 106
Active mode, of consciousness, 13
Actuated subsystems, 222–224, 228
Adaptive regression, 86
Age-constancy theory, of regression, 54–57, 60
Age regression, see Regression
Alcoholic blackouts, amnesia from, 70–71
Alert hypnosis, 165–167
Allison, R., 300
Alternating personalities, see Multiple personalities
American Society for Psychical Research, 4
Amnesia:
  bimodality of distribution of, 75
  directed forgetting similar to, 65–66
  and dissociation, 11, 18, 26–30, 62, 250–251, 296
  functional, 67–68
  hypnotic, 73–80
  in laboratory animals, 72–73, 85
  organic, 69–72
  and repression, 80–83, 86
  susceptibility to, 75–76
Amphetamine, 73
Analgesia, hypnotic
  alternative interpretation, 298–299
  hidden observer in, 188–194, 202, 294
  and hypnotizability, 171–175, 294–295
  and information processing, 236–237
  overt and covert pain in, 189–194, 246–247
  reference books for, 184, 201–202
  surgery performed under, 85
  and waking analgesia, 191–192
  without formal hypnosis, 175–176
Anesthesia, 71–72, 85, 245
Animal magnetism, 19
Anna O. case (Breuer), showing hysteria, 81
Anorexia nervosa, 247–248, 256
Ansel Bourne case (James), showing fugue behavior, 22–24
Anterograde amnesia, 70
Artificial somnambulism, 73
Association, doctrine of, 5
Association methods, and concealed memories, 82–83
Attention:
  and automatic writing, 147–151, 153–154
  divided, 1–2, 243
  selection process in, 77, 147–151, 154
Attribution theory, 3
Auditory hallucinations, 96–97
Autohypnosis, see Self-hypnosis
Automatic talking, 188, 190, 201
Automatic writing:
  for dealing directly with dissociated consciousness, 249
  and divided attention, 6, 7, 147–151

305

Automatic writing (*Continued*)
  hidden observer revealed by, 187–189, 199, 212
  and hypnotic amnesia, 79
  in psychotherapy, 136–138
  reference books for, 152–154
  spiritualism as background for, 131–136
Automatisms, 18, 131

Beauchamp case (Prince), as example of dissociation, 6–7, 30–31
Behaviorism, 2, 10–11, 116
Bell tower case (Prince), using automatic writing, 136
Bennett, H.L., 296, 297
Bertrand, L.D., 294
Bicameral mind, 15
Bimodal consciousness, 15
Binet, Alfred, 4
Biofeedback:
  hypnosis paralleling, 125–126
  and voluntary-involuntary controls, 124–125, 129
Birth, regression to, 48–51
Bliss, E.L., 300
Blum, Gerald, 78
Body image, distortions of, 174
Bohr, Niels, 200
Boring, E.G., 132
Brain:
  higher-lower divisions of, 247–248
  role of, in amnesia, 69–70
  split-brain functions, 109–111, 247
Breuer, Josef, 80–81
Bridey Murphy case (Bernstein), showing multiple personalities, 49–50, 59

Cancer patients, regression therapy for, 59
Catastrophe theory, and anorexia nervosa, 247–248
Cell assemblies (Hebb), 219
Central control processes, *see* Control processes
Cerebral hemispheres, functions of, 109–111, 247–248
"Challenge" tests, 119–122, 129
Charles Poultney case (Franz), of multiple personalities, 27–29

Chevreul pendulum, 137, 153
Childhood, difficult, 32, 39–40
Coconsciousness:
  vs. primitive unconscious, 83, 249
  as Prince's term for divided consciousness, 5, 6, 8, 15
Cognitive control systems, *see* Control processes
Cognitive networks (Blum), 219
Cognitive psychology, 13, 15, 293, 301
Cognitive structure (Tolman, Lewin), 218
Cold pressor pain, 188–193
Complementarity principle, 200
Compulsive behavior, 18
Computer, and executive function, 219
Concussion, amnesia from, 69, 84
Conflict-free ego sphere (Hartmann), 219
Conscience, monitoring function including, 224
Consciousness:
  active mode of, 13
  history of interest in, 1–16, 239–240
  in hypnosis, 168, 228
  interference between subconscious and, 139–140, 145–147
  overlapping volition, 117
  receptive mode of, 13
  three states of, 91
  see also Dissociation
Control processes:
  actuated subsystem in relation to, 223–224
  executive and monitoring functions as, 216–222
  hypnosis modifying, 2, 157, 228–236
  in memory theories, 63–64
  psychoanalytic theory of, 241
Conversion reactions, in hysteria, 18, 117–119, 128
Cortex, 248
Coverants, 3
Covert pain, in hypnotic analgesia, 189–191, 193–194, 236–237
Crawford, H.J., 294
Creativity:
  hidden observer in, 195–198, 203
  and imagination, 107–109, 113–114
Cross, D., 295

Darwin, Charles, 3
Davis, H.S., 296, 297
Deafness, hypnotic:
  hidden observer in, 194–195, 202, 294
  and hypnotizability, 176–181
Defense mechanisms, hysterical symptoms as, 117–118
de Groot, H.P., 294
Depth of hypnosis, 167–171, 227
Desagregation, 5
Dessoir, Max, 4
Diazepam, amnesia from, 71
Directed forgetting, 65–66
Disaggregation, *see* Dissociation
Dissociation:
  and amnesia, 18, 26–30, 62, 74–76, 85, 250–251
  automatic writing for study of, 131, 147–152
  brain processes showing, 109–111
  clinical significance of, 248–254, 256
  cognitive psychology and, 301
  criteria of, 18
  dreams as, 87, 89, 92, 95
  fugues as, 22–24
  functional independence of, 9–10
  hallucinations representing, 95
  and hidden observer, 185–203, 204–215, 293–301
  history of, 1–16
  and hypnosis, 155, 224–228, 230
  hysteria and, 81
  imagination experience as, 104, 111
  and information processing, 237
  multiple personalities as, 24–40
  neodissociation interpretation of, 12–14, 216–241, 242–256
  nonhypnotic experimental approaches to, 242–248
  possession states as, 19–22
  and psychodynamic processes, 250–254
  regression and, 45, 47–48, 56–57, 59
  and repression, 80, 83, 250–252
  superficial and profound, 213
  and task interference, 8–12, 139–140, 145–147
  vs. unconscious, 248–250

voluntary-involuntary distinction related to, 115, 121–122, 127–128
  see also Hypnosis
Dissociative hysteria, 118
Distraction, analgesia, 299
Distress, as component of pain, 193, 246–247
Divergent thinking, for creativity, 108, 114
Divided consciousness:
  history of interest in, 1–16
  in hypnosis, 185–203
  neodissociation interpretation of, 216–241
  see also Consciousness: Dissociation
Double-person hallucination, 112
Dream diary method, 93
Dreams:
  as hallucinations of normal, 88–89
  hypnotic influences on, 92–95, 245
  psychoanalytic theory of, 89, 249
  psychophysiology of, 91–92
Dream telepathy, 112
Drugs, hallucinations from, 97
Dubofsky, S.T., 298

Ebbinghaus, H., 63
EEG-alpha, and biofeedback, 125, 126
Ego states:
  hidden observer, 299–300
  multiple personality, 300–301
Electroconvulsive shock (ECS), 72–73, 84
Epileptic seizures, brain surgery for, 69–70
Episodic memory, 65
Evans, F.J., 301
Evelyn case (Osgood), of multiple personality, 37–39
Executive Ego, 218
Executive functions:
  in hypnosis, 228–230
  in interactions with monitoring functions, 221–222
  in nonhypnotic contexts, 216–220
Exorcism, 19, 21
Experience inventories, 106
Experimental Analysis Technique (EAT), 295
Eye-closure-relaxation induction, 258–259
Eye movements, while solving mental problems, 110–111

Federn, P., 300
Fever, hallucinations from, 96
Finger lifting, as alternative to speech, 201, 233
Forgetting:
  directed, 65–66
  ordinary, 75–76, 85
  see also Amnesia
Fox sisters, 3, 132–133, 153
Freud, Sigmund:
  on dream interpretation, 88–89, 249
  and repression, 10, 80–81
  on unconscious, 4
Fugues:
  Ansel Bourne case of, 22–24
  and functional amnesia, 67–68
  reference books for, 40
Functional amnesia, 67–68, 84

Galton, Sir Francis, 101, 107
Gassner, Father J.J., 19
Giannini, J.A., 296, 297
Glossolalia, 20, 40
Glove anesthesia, 117
Goal-directed fantasies (Spanos), 230
Greaves, G.B., 300, 301
Gurney, Edmund, 3

Habit-family hierarchy (Hull), 219
Habits, 217, 219
Hallucinations:
  hidden observer in, 202
  hypnotically produced, 97–100
  in pathological conditions, 96–97
  reference books for, 112
  simulator-real control case for (Orne), 99
Hand levitation induction, 259–261
Handwriting, regressed, 51–53
Harvard Group Scale of Hypnotic Susceptibility, 160, 262
Herbart, J.F., 4
Heterohypnosis, as aided self-hypnosis, 229
Hewitt, E.C., 294
Hidden observer:
  characterizations of, 209–211, 214, 293
  clinical settings, 296–298
  correlates of, 295–296
  in creative activity, 195–198

dissociation, 298–299
early evidence of, 198–201
ego states, 299–300
experimental studies, 293–295
in hypnotic analgesia, 188–194
in hypnotic deafness, 194–195
as a metaphor, 185, 188, 204
and monitoring functions, 233–236
multiple personalities, 300–301
as perceived by hypnotized person, 204–215
presence or absence of, 205–209, 214
relevation of, 186–188
Hierarchical structure:
  for memory retrieval, 67
  of subsystems, 217–218
Hilgard, E.R., 293, 294, 295, 299
Hilgard, J.R., 298, 299
Hippocampus, 69
"Honest report" interview, 192
Hull, Clark L., 138
Humanistic psychology, 2–3, 14
Hypnoanalysis, 254
Hypnosis:
  active form of, 127
  actuated subsystems in, 228
  age regression in, 44–61, 295–296
  and amnesia, 73–80
  automatic writing used in, 140–143, 145–147, 150–151
  and biofeedback, 125–126
  for dealing directly with dissociated consciousness, 249
  depth of, 167–171
  and dissociative experiences, 7–12, 155, 224–228
  and exorcism, 19
  hidden observer in, 185–203, 293–294
  hysterical paralysis and, 117, 119
  and ideomotor control of action, 122–124
  imagination related to, 107–108, 111, 160–162
  influencing dreaming, 92–95
  and information processing, 236–239
  loss of voluntary controls in, 119–122
  modification of controls in, 2, 228–236
  and multiple personality, 29–30, 42
  pain recovery, 296–298

power of words in, 77, 123–124
producing hallucinations, 97–100
and supernormal muscular performance, 126–127, 130
and tract for, 224–225
see also Hypnotic responsiveness; Hypnotic state
Hypnotherapy:
age regression in, 58–59, 61
and psychodynamics, 252–254
Hypnotic age regression, see Regression
Hypnotic amnesia, 73–80, 85–86
Hypnotic analgesia, see Analgesia, hypnotic
Hypnotic contract, 224–225
Hypnotic dream, vs. night dream, 92–94, 111
Hypnotic induction:
examples of, 257–261
as initiating hypnotic experience, 225–227, 241
Hypnotic responsiveness:
and amnesia, 74
bimodality of, 156–158, 183
brain hemisphere preference for, 111, 247
creativity score showing, 108–109
and dreaming, 93
imaginative involvement related to, 104, 160–162
measurement of, 156–159, 183, 257–266
pain reduction and, 202, 298
stability of, 265–266
vividness of imagery and, 101–104
Hypnotic state:
behavior in, 163–165, 227
vs. hypnotic talent, 182
one or more, 165–167, 183
Hypnotic susceptibility, see Hypnotic responsiveness
Hypnotic virtuosos, 155, 158, 159
Hypnotizability, see Hypnotic responsiveness
Hypnotized person:
hidden observer interpreted by, 204–215
as information source about hypnosis, 181–182, 184
Hysteria:
conversion symptoms in, 18, 117–119
splitting of mind in, 81
Hysterical paralysis, 117–119, 128–129

Iatrogenic disease, multiple personalities as, 24–25, 30
Ideomotor action, 122–124, 129
Imagery:
in amnesia, 78
as factor in memory, 66–67, 85, 111
in hypnotic analgesia, 174–175
in hypnotic deafness, 178
in hypnotic state, 163–164
and hypnotizability, 101–104, 113
Images and plans (Miller), as cognitive substructures, 219
Imagination:
and creativity, 107–109
in relation to hallucination, 100–101
in hypnotic state, 163–164
involvement in, 104–106, 113, 160–162
right brain hemisphere for, 109–111
Induction, see Hypnotic induction
Information processing, 204, 236–241, 243
Interference, between conscious and subconscious acts, 8–12, 139–140, 145–147
Intermittent information processing, 236–239, 241
Involuntary processes, voluntary control of, 124–126, 128–130. See also Voluntary-involuntary distinction
Involvement, imaginative, 104–106, 113, 160–162
Irene case (Janet), showing dissociation, 5–6
Ischemic pain, 188, 193, 236

James, William, 3, 5, 152
Janet, Pierre, 4–7
Jonah case (Ludwig), showing multiple personalities, 32–34
Jung, Carl, 249

Katherine case (Arlen), of multiple personalities, 34–36
Kent-Rosanoff word association test, 82
Ketamine, 245
Kihlstrom, J.F., 294, 301
Kohnstamm phenomenon, 11

Language, recovery of childhood, 47–48. See also Words

Laterialization, eye movements related to, 110
Laurence, J.-R., 294, 295
Learning:
  paired-associate, 66
  state-dependent, 244–245
  verbal, 63
LeBaron, S., 298, 299
Left brain hemisphere, 110
Leonie case (Janet), of multiple personalities, 20–30
Limbic system, 248
Locus of control, 3
London Society for Psychical Research, 4
Long-term memory, 63–64
Lower consciousness, 4
LSD, 97
Lucie case (Janet), to support dissociation, 7, 10

Macdonald, H., 294
Marie case (Janet), and hypnotic age regression, 44–45, 54
Martha case (Frankel), of multiple personalities, 36–37
McConkey, J.M., 295
McConkey, K.M., 294
Meditation, 2, 13
Memoria, 57
Memory:
  continuity of, 17
  control processes in, 63–64
  and general anesthesia, 71
  hypnosis disrupting, 226–227
  imagery as a factor in, 66–67
  nature of, 62–65, 83
  recovery of, 243
  and regression, 44–45, 57–59
  see also Amnesia; Memory retrieval
Memory experiments, 63–64, 76
Memory retrieval:
  amnesia disrupting, 76, 85
  depth of processing and, 64
  hierarchical structure for, 67
  and reminder theory, 72–73
Memory theorists, 63
Mescaline, 97, 112
Mesmer, F.A., 19

Messerschmidt, Ramona, 138–140
Mnemonic devices, 66–67, 83–84
Monitoring functions:
  conscience included in, 224
  hidden observer as fraction of, 233–236
  in hypnosis, 230–233
  in interactions with executive functions, 221–222
  in nonhypnotic contexts, 221
  three fractions of, 234, 240
Morphine, 246
Motor skills, memory for, 63
Multiple personalities:
  classifications of, 25–27
  and difficult childhood, 32, 39–40
  as direct discourse with dissociated consciousness, 249
  dual, 7, 30, 34–37
  and hidden observer, 235, 300–301
  and hypnosis, 29–30, 42
  as iatrogenic disease, 24–25, 30
  three or more, 27–34, 37–39, 41
Muscular movement, voluntary and involuntary control of, 115–130
Myers, F.W.H., 3
Mystical experiences, in deep hypnosis, 168, 170

Negative hallucinations, 97–98
Neodissociation, 12–14, 216–241, 242–256, 293
Night dreams:
  versus hypnotic dreams, 92–94
  hypnotic suggestions influencing, 94
Nogrady, H., 294, 295
Noninterference theory:
  and decline of dissociation, 8–12
  in shadowing experiment, 151
Nonverbal memory, 64
NREM sleep, 91, 92, 94

Observing ego, in regression, 46–48, 52
Operant behaviorists, 14
Operants of the mind, 3
Organic amnesia, 69–72, 84
Orne, M.T., 99, 294
Ouija board, 135–136

Overt pain, in hypnotic analgesia, 189–190, 194, 236–237

Pain, surgical, 296–298
Pain reduction, *see* Analgesia, hypnotic
Paired-associate learning, 66
Parallel information processing, 204, 236–239
Paralysis, hysterical, 117–118
Parapsychology, 3
Patience, Worth, and ouija board, 136
Pavlov, J.P., 2
Perry, C., 294, 295, 296
Personality, *see* Multiple personalities
Personality inventories, and hypnotizability, 106
Phobic patients, 129
Piaget, Jean, 54–55, 60
Piccione, C., 294
Planchette, 133–135
Planning function:
 in hypnotic state, 122, 164–165, 229
 in nonhypnotic state, 218–220
 social learning theorists and, 3
Plenary trance (Erickson), 170
Positive forgetting, 65–66
Positive hallucination, 97–98
Possession states, 19–22, 40
Possession trance, 21
Posthypnotic recall amnesia, 74, 301
Postural sway test, 225
Preference, in eye movements, 110–111
Primary personality, as less healthy personality, 27, 40, 83. *See also* Multiple personalities
Primary process thinking:
 in creativity, 108, 195
 in dreams, 88–89
 and regression, 43
 and repression, 83, 86
Primitivation, regression as, 44
Prince, Morton, 5–8
Progression, in age, 50
Psilocybin, 97
Psychoanalysis:
 and dissociation, 10–11, 248–254
 dream theory of, 89, 249
 and repression, 80

Psychotherapy, automatic writing in, 136–138, 153
Purmycin, 73
Putnam, F.W., 301
Puysegur, A.M.J., 73

Reality, and hypnotic state, 165, 182, 231
Receptive mode, of consciousness, 13
Recognition memory, 65
Redintegrative memory, 65
Regression, hypnotic age:
 as an ability, 51–53, 59–60
 behavior characteristic of, 43–48, 59
 to birth or earlier, 48–51, 59
 in clinical settings, 58–59, 61
 hidden observer, 295–296
 theories of, 53–58, 60
Reincarnation, 49–51
Reinforcements, in behaviorism, 2
REM (rapid eye movement) sleep, 91–92, 94
Remembrances, 57
"Reminder effect," 72
Repression:
 and amnesia, 62, 78, 80–83, 86
 and dissociation, 10–11, 248, 250–252
 two kinds of, 251–252
Respiration, as semivoluntary, 124
Retroactive inhibition, and amnesia, 76
Retrograde amnesia, 70, 72
Revivification, regression as, 44, 60
Right brain hemisphere, 109–111
Role-enactment theory, of age regression, 57–58
Roles (Sarbin), 219

Schizophrenia, hallucinations from, 96
Schwarz, T., 300
Secondary personality:
 behavior after identification of, 19
 as most healthy personality, 27, 40, 83
 see also Multiple personalities
Secondary process thinking:
 in creativity, 195–196
 and dreams, 88–89
 vs. primary process, 86, 211
Selective inattention:
 and automatic writing, 147–151, 154
 in hypnotic amnesia, 77

Self-hypnosis:
  division of executive functions in, 227–229
  and hysteria, 81
  for independence from therapist, 253
  for pain reduction, 175–176, 182
  and trance states, 20
Self-reinforcement, 3, 14
Semantic memory, 65
Shadowing experiments, 150
Sheehan, P.W., 295
Short-term memory, 63–64, 70, 220
Sibyl case (Schreiber), of multiple personalities, 31–32
Sidis, Boris, 5
Simulator-real controls:
  in age regression studies, 56
  in amnesia studies, 83
  in hallucination studies, 99
  in hidden observer studies, 202
Simultaneous dual personalities, 25
Skinner, B.F., 2, 3
Sleep:
  dissociations within, 245–246
  eye movements in, 91–92
  as metaphor in hypnosis, 226, 258–259
  see also Dreams
Sleepiness, excessive daytime, 245–246
Sleeptalking, 94–95
Sleepwalking, in relation to dreaming, 95
Social learning theory, 248
Society for Psychical Research, 4
Sodium Pentothal, 71
Somnambulist, 73, 158, 226
Source amnesia, 74, 80
Spanos, N.P., 294
"Speaking in tongues," 20, 40
Spiritualism:
  as background for automatic writing, 131–136, 152–153
  in history of psychology, 3
Split-brain studies, 109–110, 114, 247
Spontaneous amnesia, 74
Stanford Hypnotic Susceptibility Scale, 51, 60–61, 158, 263
Stanford Profile Scales, 52, 140–143, 159, 264
State-dependent learning, 244–245

State, hypnotic, see Hypnotic state
Stein, Gertrude, 15
Strychnine, to reduce ECS amnesia, 73
Subconscious:
  interest in, 4–10, 15
  interference between conscious and, 139–140, 145–147
  see also Dissociation
Subliminal perception, 243–244, 255
Subordinate ego-structures (Gill), 219
Subsystems, multiple:
  actuated, 222–224, 228
  hierarchical arrangement of, 217–220
  latent, 222–223
Successive dual personalities, 25–27
Suffering, as component of pain, 193, 246–247
Suggestibility:
  in hypnotic state, 163
  scales of, 261–262
  see also Hypnotic responsiveness
Superego, monitoring functions including, 224
Symptom-treatment, 253–254

Temporal lobes, 69–70
Tensive perserveration, 11
Thalamus, 246
Thinking, see Primary process thinking; Secondary process thinking
Thiopental, 71
Third personality, 27–30
Tiller, D.K., 294
Tip-of-the-tongue phenomenon, 78–79
Torrance Creativity Test, 109
"Trance logic," 112, 165, 231
Trance states:
  as conceptual problem, 41
  and possession states, 20–21
Transference problems, 253
Transient global amnesia, 68, 84
Traumatic events, regression therapy for, 58–59
Trustman, R., 298
Two-component theory, of hypnotic analgesia, 191–193, 202, 246–247

Unconscious:
  and coconscious, 15, 83, 249
  cortex and limbic system influencing, 248
  Freud and, 4, 5
  vs. dissociated consciousness, 248–250
Unconscious mimicry, 122
Upper consciousness, 4

Valium, 71
Vasomotor responses, and biofeedback, 125
Verbal learning, and memory, 63
Visual hallucinations, 96–97, 100
Visual masking, 244, 256
Volition, 116–117, 216
Voluntary control:
  and hypnosis, 115, 119–122
  of involuntary processes, 124–126, 128–130
  loss of, 117–122
Voluntary-involuntary distinction:
  and dissociation, 14, 127–128, 251
  hypnosis altering, 2, 119–124
  and volition, 116–117
von Hartmann, Eduard, 4

Waking suggested analgesia, 191, 192
Watkins, H.H., 300
Watkins, J.G., 300
Watson, J.B., 2
Weeks, J.R., 294
Will, 116–117, 216
William case (Tart), and hypnotic depth, 168
Wishes, and dreams, 89
Word association tests, 82–83, 251
Words, power of:
  in hypnotic amnesia, 77
  in ideomotor control of action, 123–124, 129
Working forgetting, 86
Working memory, 79–80, 85–86, 220

Zeitgeist, 15, 132